Preface

It is probable that the Bishop of Natal may be held responsible for the contents of a volume written partly by his daughter, and having for its subject the Zulu War; more especially if a general coincidence can be traced between what are known to be his views and those which are expressed in this history. My father's opinions have, naturally, considerable influence over those held or expressed by his family, and I do not imagine that much will be found in these pages from which he will dissent. Nevertheless, it is desirable that my readers should understand from the first that he is in no sense responsible for their contents.

When I left Natal, in September last, the idea of writing upon the subject of the Zulu War had hardly occurred to me; it has developed since to an extent quite beyond my original intentions, and I find that its fulfilment has rather taken my father by surprise. I had no opportunity of consulting him upon the subject, nor has he yet seen a word of what I have written, for on reaching England I found that, to be of any use at all, the book should appear almost at once.

I made, indeed, ample use of the pamphlets which the Bishop of Natal has written on behalf of Langalibalele and Cetshwayo, which have saved me many hours of weary search. Consequently, while the Bishop is in no way responsible for such errors or omissions as may occur in this volume, any merit or usefulness which my portion of the book may contain is due chiefly to his labours.

The general plan of my history was laid out, and the first few chapters were written, during the voyage from Natal, and upon reaching England I obtained the assistance of my friend Lieut.-Colonel Edward Durnford in that portion of the work which deals with the military conduct of the war. While it was desirable that a record of military events should be made by one whose professional knowledge qualified him for the duty, there was an additional reason which made his help appropriate. It may easily be understood from his name that the interest taken by him in his task would be of no ordinary kind. Colonel Durnford has written the military portions of the book, but is not responsible for any expressions of opinion upon matters strictly political.

I am far from feeling that I am the best person to undertake such a work as this, which my father himself would look upon as a serious one, and which he, or even my sister, who has worked with him throughout, would do so much better than I; but they were not at hand, and I have thought it my duty to do what I could, while I could have had no better aid than that given me by Colonel Durnford.

However insufficient the result may prove, we shall at least hope that our work may give some slight assistance to that cause of justice, truth, and mercy, the maintenance of which alone can ensure the true honour of the British name.

Frances Ellen Colenso
January 22nd, 1880

Colenso & Durnford's
Zulu War

Colenso & Durnford's
Zulu War

Frances E. Colenso &
Edward Durnford

LEONAUR

Colenso & Durnford's Zulu War
by Frances E. Colenso & Edward Durnford

Published by Leonaur Ltd

ISBN: 978-1-84677-396-9 (hardcover)
ISBN: 978-1-84677-395-2 (softcover)

http://www.leonaur.com

Publisher's Notes

The views expressed in this book are not necessarily
those of the publisher.

Contents

CHAPTER 1

First Causes

England's collisions with the savage races bordering upon her colonies have in all probability usually been brought about by the exigencies of the moment, by border-troubles, and acts of violence and insolence on the part of the savages, and from the absolute necessity of protecting a small and trembling white population from their assaults.

No such causes as these have led up to the war of 1879. For more than twenty years the Zulus and the colonists of Natal have lived side by side in perfect peace and quietness. The tranquillity of our border had been a matter of pride as compared to the disturbed and uncertain boundaries between Zululand and the Transvaal. The mere fact of the utterly unprotected condition of the frontier farmers on our border, and the entire absence of anything like precaution, evinced by the common practice of building houses of the most combustible description, is a proof that the colonists felt no real alarm concerning the Zulus until the idea was suggested to them by those in authority over them.[1] The only interruption to this tranquil condition of the public mind about the Zulus was in the year 1861, when a scare took place in the colony, for which, as it afterwards proved, there were no grounds whatsoever. A general but unfounded belief was rife that Cetshwayo,[2] the king, or rather at that time

1. "Few things struck me more than the evident haste and temporary character of the defensive measures undertaken by the English part of the population" in the border districts of Natal. (See letter from Sir Bartle Frere to Sir Michael Hicks-Beach, dated March 28th, 1879. P. P. (C. 2318) p. 32.)
2. Spelt thus to give the nearest proper pronunciation of Cetywayo.

prince, ruling Zululand, was about to invade Natal, in order to obtain possession of his young brother Umkungo, a claimant of the Zulu crown, and who had escaped over the border at the time of the great civil war of which we shall presently treat. This young prince had been placed by the Secretary for Native Affairs, Mr. Shepstone at Bishopstowe,[3] for his education in the Native Boys' School there; and it was not until he had been there for years that the fancy arose, suggested and fostered by the border farmers and traders in Zululand, that Cetshwayo intended to take him by force from amongst us, or at all events to make the attempt.

Under the influence of this belief the troops then stationed in Natal were ordered to the frontier, the colonial volunteers were called out, the defence of the principal towns became a matter for consideration; while outlying farmers, and residents in the country, hastened to remove their families to places of comparative safety. Bishopstowe was supposed to be the special object of the expected attack; but the Bishop himself, having occasional opportunities of learning the state of things in Zululand, through his missionary there, could never be brought thoroughly to believe in the gravity of the danger. It is true that, as a matter of precaution, and in deference to the strongly expressed opinion of the Lieut. Governor of the Colony and of Mr. Shepstone, he sent away the threatened boy to some of his own people, in a more remote and safer part of the colony. But he was extremely reluctant to take the further step, strongly urged upon him, of removing his family and people to the adjacent city of Pietermaritzburg, and only consented to do so under protest. During the night following his consent, but before the project had been carried out, he had reason for a few hours to suppose that he had been mistaken in his own judgment. The family at Bishopstowe was knocked up at one o'clock in the morning by a messenger from a passing Dutch farmer, who, on his way into town with his own family, had sent word to the Bishop that Cetshwayo's army had entered the colony, was already between him and Table Mountain that is to say within a distance of nine

---

3. Residence of the Bishop of Natal.

miles and was burning, killing, and destroying all upon the way to Bishopstowe. There seemed to be no doubt of the fact; so, hastily collecting their native villagers,[4] the Colensos left their homes and started for the town, which, they reached, most of them on foot, about daybreak. The consequence of their being accompanied and followed by a considerable party of natives (of both sexes and all ages!) was that the townspeople immediately supposed that the "Zulus had come;" and some of them actually left their houses, and took refuge in the various places of safety such as the fort, the principal churches, and so on previously decided upon by the authorities in case of necessity. In common South African terms they "went into *laager.*"

As the day passed, and still no further tidings arrived of the approach of the Zulus or the destruction of Bishopstowe, the Bishop began to have strong suspicions that, after all, he had been right in his original opinion, and that "the killing, burning, and destroying" had been conjured up by some excited imagination. This opinion was confirmed, if not completely established, in the course of the day, by the reception of a letter from the missionary in Zululand before mentioned, in which he inquired, on the Zulu king's behalf, what fault the latter had committed towards the English, that they should be preparing to invade his country. The missionary added that all was perfectly quiet in Zululand, until the border tribes, seeing the British troops approaching, fled inland in alarm, killing their cattle to prevent their falling into the hands of the invaders, and burying their other possessions where they could not carry them away. In point of fact the "scare" had no foundation whatsoever, and the Zulus were quite as much alarmed by the actual approach of the British troops as the Natalians had been by the imaginary Zulu army. The worst immediate consequence of the mistake was the want, almost amounting to famine, produced amongst the border Zulus by the loss of their cattle. A later and more serious result has been that general impression, which has long obtained credence at

---

4. These people had refused to leave their homes, or desert their Bishop, as long as he and his family remained at Bishopstowe, although both black and white, for miles around, had sought shelter elsewhere.

home in England, that the colonists of Natal have not only been in fear of their lives on account of the Zulus for many years, but have also had good and sufficient reason for their alarm. But for this fixed, though groundless idea, England would hardly have been in such a hurry to send out additional troops for the protection of the colony as she was in the summer of 1878; to her own great loss and to the very considerable injury of the colony itself, not to speak of its unhappy neighbours and heretofore friends the Zulus.

It is certainly true that during the year 1878 the inhabitants of Natal did honestly feel great fear of the Zulus, and of a possible invasion of the colony by them, the alarm in many cases amounting to absolute panic. But this feeling was produced by no warlike menaces from our neighbours, no sinister appearances on our borders. The panic or "scare," as it would popularly be called in Natal, was forced upon the people by the conduct and language of their rulers, by the preparations made for war, troops being sent for from England "for defensive purposes" (as was so repeatedly asserted by both Sir Bartle Frere and Lord Chelmsford, then Lieut.-General the Hon. F. A. Thesiger), and by the perpetual agitation of the local newspaper editors.

It is true indeed that a certain section of the colonists eagerly desired war. To some the presence of the troops was a source of actual fortune, to others the freedom and independence of so large a body of black people, whom they could neither tax nor force to work for them, was, and had long been, odious; the revenue to be derived from a hut-tax levied upon the Zulus, and the cheap labour to be obtained when their power and independence should be broken, formed one of the chief subjects for speculation when the war was first suggested. To others, again, the prospect of war was simply a source of pleasurable excitement, a hunt on a large scale, martial glory to be won, with just spice enough of danger to give zest to the affair; as had been the case in the war just concluded in Kaffraria. Naturally this feeling was commonest amongst the volunteers and their friends. Some of them looked upon the matter in a light which would meet with utter condemnation in any civilised society; but many others, especially the young lads who filled up the ranks of the volunteer corps, were simply dazzled by visions of military distinction, excited by the popular phrases in perpetual use about "fighting for their country, and doing their duty as soldiers," to the extent of losing sight altogether of the question as to whether or no their country really required any defence at all.

Natal cannot honestly claim to be guiltless in bringing about the war with the Zulus, and will hardly deny that in 1878 the prospect was a most popular one amongst her sons. Perhaps Sir Bartle Frere could not so easily have produced a war out of the materials which he had at hand but for the assistance given him by the popular cry in the colony, and the general fear of the Zulus, which called forth England's ready sympathy and assistance. But it must be remembered that the panic was not a genuine one, nor even one like that of 1861, produced by the folly of the people themselves. It was distinctly imposed upon them by those in authority, whose policy was to bring about a collision with the Zulus, and who then made use of the very fears which they had themselves aroused for the furtherance of their own purpose.

The subjugation of the Zulus and the annexation of their country, formed part of a policy which has occupied the minds of certain British statesmen for many years. The ambition of creating a South African Empire, to be another jewel in Victoria's crown, which, if no rival, should at least be a worthy pendant to the great Indian Empire, was a dazzling one, and towards that object all Government action in South Africa has apparently tended since the year 1873. When the idea was first conceived those only know who formed it, but it took practical and visible form in 1873. In that year by crowning the Zulu king we assumed a right to interfere in the internal management of the country, thereby establishing a possible future cause of offence, which, as the Zulus obstinately refused to put themselves in the wrong by any sort of interference with us, was necessary in order to bring about a state of things which should eventually give us a sufficient excuse for taking possession of the country altogether.

The origin of this performance was as follows. In the year 1856 a great revolution took place in Zululand, and a civil war broke out between two claimants to the heirship of the throne (then filled by Umpande), namely, the present king, Cetshwayo, and his brother Umbulazi. Cetshwayo was quite young at the time, and appears to have been put forward by some ambitious warriors, who intended to rule in his name, and did not expect the remarkable power and talent which he afterwards developed.

Umbulazi's party was beaten, he himself being killed in battle, great carnage ensuing, and many fugitives escaping into Natal.

Amidst all the bloodshed and horror which naturally attends such a warfare as this between savages, there stands out the singular, perhaps unprecedented, fact that Cetshwayo, although victorious to the extent of carrying the nation with him, not only never made any attempt upon the old king, his father's, life, but did not even depose him or seize his throne. The old man lived and nominally, at all events reigned for many years, though, owing to his age and obesity, which was so great as to prevent his walking, he seems to have been willing enough to leave the real authority in the hands of his son, while retaining the semblance of it himself. He was treated with all due respect by Cetshwayo and his followers until he died a natural death in the year 1872, when Cetshwayo ascended .the throne which had long been virtually his own, and was proclaimed king of Zululand. This was looked upon as a fitting time for a little display of authority by ourselves, hence the friendly expedition to Zululand of 1873, when we gave Cetshwayo to understand that, however it might appear to him, he held his power from us, and was no true king till we made him such. It was also rightly thought to be an opportunity for suggesting to the Zulu king such reforms in the government of his country as would naturally commend themselves to English ideas. We considered, and with some reason, that capital punishment was an over-frequent occurrence in Zululand, and that, on the other hand, judicial trials before sentence should be the universal rule. It was also desirable, if possible, to decrease the belief in witchcraft, by which so much power was left in the hands of the witch-doctors or priests;[5] and finally it was thought necessary to provide for the safety of the missionaries resident in

---

5. A system not unlike the Inquisition in its evil results.

the land.[6] How far this was a desirable step depends entirely on whether the men themselves were earnest, self-sacrificing, peace-loving teachers of the gospel of Christ, or mere traders for their own benefit, under the cloak of a divine mission, ready to hail a bloody war. "Only the utter destruction of the Zulus can secure future peace in South Africa. . . . we have the approbation of God, our Queen, and our own conscience."[7]

It was frequently asserted at the time in Natal that this coronation ceremony (1st September, 1873) was nothing better than a farce, and the way in which it was carried out seems hardly to have been understood by the king himself. The Natalians were puzzled as to what could be the meaning or intention of what seemed to them a hollow show, and were on the whole rather inclined to put it down to Mr. Shepstone's supposed habit of "petting the natives" and to "Exeter Hall influences," resulting in a ridiculous fuss on their behalf.

From Mr. Shepstone's despatch on the subject of the coronation of Cetshwayo,[9] and from messages brought from the latter to the Government of Natal after his father's death, there appears to have been a strong desire on the part, not only of the people, but of the king himself, that his formal succession to the throne should be unattended by bloodshed and disorder, such as had ushered in the rule of his predecessors for several generations. How greatly the character of the Zulu rule had improved in a comparatively short period may be judged by a comparison of the fact[10] (mentioned by Mr. Shepstone), that during the reigns of Chaka and Dingana (grandfather and great-uncle to Cetshwayo), all the royal wives were put to death either before the birth of their children, or with their infants afterwards, with the behaviour of Cetshwayo, both to his father and to his father's wives.[11] And Mr. Shepstone himself speaks of

---

6. Who, it may be remarked, have always been well treated in Zululand.
7. See letter from a missionary clergyman to Sir Bartle Frere8 dated December 17th, 1878. (P. P. (C. 2316) p. 3.)
8. Portions of this letter are omitted from the Blue-book. It would be interesting to see the letter as originally received.
9. P. P. (C. 1137)
10. p. 5, ibid.
11. One put to death in 1861 was condemned on a charge of high treason.

Cetshwayo on the occasion of this visit in the following manner: "Cetywayo is a man of considerable ability, much force of character, and has a dignified manner; in all my conversations with him," the Secretary for Native Affairs continues, "he was remarkably frank and straightforward, and he ranks in every respect far above any native chief I have ever had to do with." Throughout the despatch, indeed, Mr. Shepstone repeatedly speaks of the king's "frankness" and "sagacity," in direct opposition to the charges of craft and duplicity so recklessly brought against the latter of late.

King Umpande died in October, 1872, having reigned nearly thirty-three years, and on the 26th February, 1873, messengers from Cetshwayo brought the news of his father's death to the Governor of Natal, requesting at the same time that Mr. Shepstone might be sent to install Cetshwayo as his successor,[12] in order that the Zulu nation should be "more one with the government of Natal," and be "covered by the same mantle." The message ended with the request which Cetshwayo never lost an opportunity of making, that we would protect his country from Boer aggressions.[13] "We are also commissioned," say the messengers, "to urge, *what has already been urged so frequently*, that the government of Natal be extended so as to intervene between the Zulus and the territory of the Transvaal Republic."

The mere fact that this proposition was frequently and earnestly pressed upon the Natal Government by the Zulus, is in itself a proof positive that the aggressions were not on their side. They desired to place what they looked upon as an impassable barrier between the two countries, and could therefore have had no wish themselves to encroach.

Further messages passed between Cetshwayo and the Natal Government upon the subject, until it was finally arranged that the coronation should be performed by Mr. Shepstone, in Zululand, and, with a party of volunteers as escort, he crossed the

---

12. As he had previously, in the year 1861, visited Zululand for the purpose of fixing the succession upon the house of Cetshwayo.
13. Since by our desire he refrained from protecting it by force of arms.

16

Tugela on the 8th August, 1873, accompanied by Major Durnford, R.E., Captain Boyes, 75th Regiment, and several other officers and gentlemen.

Mr. Shepstone's long despatch, already quoted from, and in which he describes, with true native minuteness, the most trivial circumstances of the journey, and subsequent proceedings, gives the impression that he looked upon his mission as a service of danger to all concerned. It was, however, carried out without any break in the friendly relations between the Zulus and his party, who returned to Pietermaritzburg "without unpleasant incident" on the 19th September.

The coronation mission was carried out how far successfully entirely depends upon the results expected or desired by those in command. The king himself, while looking upon the fact of his recognition as sovereign of Zululand by the English as important, is quite keen enough to have detected certain elements of absurdity in the proceedings by which they invested him with his dignity. There was perhaps a little good humoured scorn in his reception of the somewhat oddly chosen presents and marks of honour offered him. Without losing that respect for and faith in the English which has always characterised his dealings with them, he felt impatiently that they were rather making a fool of him; especially when they put upon his shoulders a little scarlet mantle formerly a lady's opera-cloak the curtailed dimensions of which made him ridiculous in his own eyes; and upon his head a pasteboard, cloth, and tinsel crown, whose worthlessness he was perfectly capable of comprehending. Mr. Shepstone's despatch represents him as greatly impressed by the ceremony, etc.; but the impression on the minds of many observers was that he put up with much which both seemed and was trifling and ridiculous, for the sake of the solid benefits which he hoped he and his people would derive from a closer connection with the English.

The portion of Mr. Shepstone's despatch, however, which it is important that we should study with attention is that which refers to the "coronation promises" (so called) of Cetshwayo, and treats of the political subjects discussed between king and kingmaker.

Sir Bartle Frere repeatedly speaks of the transaction as "a solemn act by the king, undertaken as the price of British support and recognition;" of Cetshwayo as having "openly violated his coronation promises;" of his "undoubted promises;" while Sir Garnet Wolseley, in his speech to the assembled chiefs and people of the Zulu nation, speaks of the coronation promises as though the want of attention to them had been the chief, if not the only, cause of the king's misfortunes; and the same tone is taken in all late despatches on the subject.

And now let us turn to Mr. Shepstone's own report, prepared at the time, and see whether we gather from it the impression that the conditions of his treaty with Cetshwayo were thought of, or intended by him, to stand as solemn and binding promises, of which the infraction, or delay in carrying out, would render the king and his people liable to punishment at our hands. After giving his reasons for objecting to "formal or written" treaties with savages,[14] Mr. Shepstone himself remarks, "Ours is an elastic arrangement." This is a singularly candid confession, of the truth of which there can be little doubt. Whether such a term *should* be applicable to the treaties made by an English Government is quite another question, to which we will leave the English public to find an answer. We have, however, but to quote from Mr. Shepstone's own despatch to prove the convenient "elasticity" of his propositions, and how greatly they have been magnified of late in seeking a quarrel against the Zulu king. At p. 16 of the report, after enumerating the "arrangements and laws" proposed by him, and heartily approved by the Zulus, Mr. Shepstone remarks:

> Although all this was fully, and even vehemently, assented to, it cannot be expected that the amelioration described will immediately take effect. To have got such principles admitted

---

14. He gives as reasons for his objections: first, that such treaties "involve an admission of equality between the contracting parties," and therefore "encourage presumption" on the part of the inferior, etc.; secondly, that "men who cannot read are apt to forget or distort the words of a treaty." A third reason, which does not seem to have occurred to Mr. Shepstone, lies in the ease with which a savage may be deceived as to the contents of a written document, which facility we shall soon largely illustrate in the matter of Boer treaties with the natives.

and declared to be what a Zulu may plead when oppressed, was but sowing the seed, which will still take many years to grow and mature.

And at p. 17 he says:

I told the king that I well knew the difficulties of his position, and that he could overcome them only by moderation and prudence and justice, but without these they would certainly overcome him.

And again (p. 18, par. 82) he explains that when he left Natal he had looked upon the "charge" which he knew that he would be expected to deliver to Cetshwayo on his installation, as something in the nature of an ordination sermon, or bishop's charge to candidates for confirmation, likely to influence only in so far as the consciences of those addressed might respond, etc.; but that, on entering Zululand, he found that the people thought so much of this part of the duty he had undertaken that he felt himself to have "become clothed with the power of fundamental legislation," and thought it right to take advantage of the opportunity for introducing improvements in the government of the people. "I have already described my success," he continues, "and I attribute it to the sagacity of Cetywayo."

But in all this there is no mention of "solemn promises," to break which would be an insult to the majesty of England, and an excuse for war; nor is there, from beginning to end of the despatch, any token that Mr. Shepstone looked upon them in that light, or had any immediate expectation of proving the usefulness of his "elastic" arrangement.

In describing his interviews and political discussions with the Zulu king, Mr. Shepstone speaks repeatedly in high praise of the ability and behaviour of the former. He says in one place:

Cetywayo received us cordially as before. . . . Major Durnford and my son, with the Natal Native *Indunas*, sat down with me to an interview with Cetywayo and the councillors, that lasted for five hours without intermission. It was of the most interesting and earnest kind, and was conducted with great ability and frankness by Cetywayo. Theoretically, my business

19

was with the councillors who represented the nation; but, had it not been for the straightforward manner in which Cetywayo insisted upon their going direct to the point, it would have been impossible to have got through the serious subjects we were bound to decide in the time we did.

Of the points discussed in this way the most important was that which, a little later, led directly up to the Zulu War namely, the aggressions of the Transvaal Boers and the disputed boundary between them and the Zulus. Mr. Shepstone says:

> The whole of the afternoon was occupied with this subject, about which he occasionally grew very earnest, and declared that he and every Zulu would die rather than submit to them viz. the Boer encroachments. He reproached the Government of Natal for not having taken up the Zulu cause, and for not even having troubled themselves to examine whether their statements were true or not, while they treated them as if without foundation.

In fact, on this, as on every other occasion, the Zulu king lost no opportunity of protesting against the encroachments of the Boers, lest his peaceable conduct towards these latter, maintained in deference to the wishes of the Natal Government, should be brought up against him later as a proof of their rights. Whatever may have been the intentions and opinions of Mr. Shepstone on the subject of the "coronation promises," he left Cetshwayo unfettered in his own opinion, having merely received certain advice as to the government of his people from his respected friends the English, to whose wishes he should certainly give full attention, and whose counsel he would carry out as far as was, in his opinion, wise or feasible. As already stated, the principal item of the English advice related to capital punishment, which we, with some justice, considered a too frequent occurrence in Zululand, especially in cases of supposed witchcraft, this superstition being undoubtedly the bane of the country.

But in judging of the king's acts in this respect, it should be remembered that, to rule a nation without any assistance in the form of gaols or fetters, capital punishment must needs be resorted to rather more frequently than in our own country, where, indeed, it is not so long since we hung a man for stealing a sheep, and for other acts far short of murder. And as to the superstition concerning witches, it can hardly have led to more cruelty and injustice in Zululand than in civilised European countries, where at Treves 7000 victims were burned alive for witchcraft; 500 at Geneva in three months; 1000 in the province of Como; 400, at *once*, at Toulouse; with many other like cases on official record.[15] The practice of smelling out a witch, as it is called, is one to be put a stop to as soon as possible by gradual and gentle means, and Cetshwayo himself had arrived at that conclusion without our assistance, as shown in his conversation with the native printer Magema, whose account of a visit paid to the Zulu king appeared in *Macmillan's Magazine* for March, 1878.

But the custom of a people the law of a land is not to be done away with or altered in an hour; nor could we English reasonably expect such radical changes in the administration of a country to follow our orders as immediately and naturally as we should expect a new ordinance to be received by the natives of Natal living under our own rule. Neither could we justly consider the non-fulfilment of our wishes and commands a sufficient cause for attacking Zululand, although such supposed non-fulfilment was the first, and for a long time the only *casus belli* which could be found against the Zulu king.

The first occasion on which the solemnity of these "coronation promises" was made of importance was in 1875, when Bishop Schreuder undertook to pay Cetshwayo a visit for the purpose of presenting him with a printed and bound copy of Mr.

---

15. See Lecky's *Rationalism in Europe*: 7000 at Treves; 600 by a single Bishop of Bamberg; 800 in one year, in the bishopric of Wurtzburg; 1000 in the province of Como; 400 at *once*, at Toulouse; 500 in three months, at Geneva; 48 at Constance; 80 at the little town of Valary in Saxony; 70 in Sweden; and one *Christian* judge boasted that he himself had been the means of putting to death, in sixteen years, 800 witches! In Scotland, two centuries ago, but after many centuries of Christianity and civilisation, John Brown, the Ayrshire carrier, was shot, and, within a fortnight, an aged widow and a young maid were tied to stakes in the Solway and drowned by the rising tide, for the crime of neglecting Episcopal worship, and going aside into the moor to spend the Sabbath day in prayer and praise.

Shepstone's report upon the coronation in 1873, and impressing him fully with the wishes of the English Government. Even then, judging from Bishop Schreuder's account of his interview, neither king nor councillors were thoroughly satisfied with the result.[16] Cetshwayo, while admiring the exact report given of what took place during Mr. Shepstone's visit, objected that he had reserved his own royal prerogatives and the right of putting criminals to death for certain serious crimes, and pointed out that Mr. Shepstone had neglected to inform the Queen of this fact.

Bishop Schreuder, from his own account, appears to have overruled all objections with a very high hand, and almost forced the "book," with his own interpretation of it, upon the seemingly reluctant king, who, he says, "evidently felt himself out of his depth."

---

16. P. P. (C. 1401) p. 30.

CHAPTER 2

Langalibalele

Meanwhile in Natal mischief was brewing. A certain chief in the north of the colony was supposed to be in a very rebellious frame of mind, and it was rumoured that force of arms would prove necessary in order to bring him to his senses.

This chief was one Langalibalele, who, with his tribe, the Ama-Hlubi, had been driven out of Zululand by Umpande in the year 1848, and had taken refuge in Natal. He was located by the English Government in the country below the Draakensberg Mountains, with the duty imposed upon him of defending Natal against the attacks of the predatory hordes of Bushmen who, in the early days of the colony, made perpetual and destructive raids over the mountains. From this point of view it would seem reasonable that the Hlubi tribe should be permitted the use of firearms, prohibited, except under certain restrictions, to the natives of Natal; inattention to which prohibition was the ground upon which the original suspicions concerning Langalibalele's loyalty were based. The law, however, by which this prohibition and these restrictions were made was one of those enactments which, even when theoretically wise, are often practically impossible, and to which new communities are so prone.

Theoretically no native can possess a gun in Natal which has not been registered before a magistrate. Practically, in every *kraal*, in every part of the colony, there were, and doubtless still are, many unregistered guns, bought by natives, or given to them in lieu of wages by their masters (a common practice at the Diamond Fields), with very vague comprehension or total ignorance on the part of the native that any unlawful act had been committed. This would be more especially natural when the masters who thus furnished their men with the forbidden weapon were themselves in some way connected with the government of the country (Natal), whose sanction would therefore be looked upon by the natives as an equivalent to the permission of Government itself. But in point of fact the law had always been enforced in such an extremely lax way, the evasions of it were so easy and numerous, and so many white men of position and respectability in the colony were party to the infraction of it, that it is no wonder that its reality and importance was but lightly engraved upon the native mind.

The special accusation, however, brought against Langalibalele to prove his rebellious tendencies was that young men of his tribe were in possession of unregistered guns, which, in addition, had not been brought in to the magistrate, when demanded, for registration. The reason for this unwillingness (on the part of the young men) to comply with the above demands, appeared afterwards in the fact that other guns which had been properly produced for registration, had, after considerable delay, been returned to their owners in an injured condition, rendering them unfit for use.

As these guns were the well-earned reward of hard labour, and greatly valued by their possessors, it is little to be wondered at that there should be considerable reluctance on the part of others to risk the same loss. A little forbearance and consideration on the part of those in authority might, however, easily have overcome the difficulty. But in this case, as in others, the mistake was committed of requiring prompt and unquestioning obedience, without sufficient care being taken to protect the rights of those who rendered it. As usual we would not stop to reason or deal justly with the savage. Carelessness of the property of the natives, the overbearing impatience of a magistrate, the want of tact and good-feeling on the part of a commonplace subordinate all these led to an indefinitely uneasy state of things, which soon produced considerable anxiety in the colonial mind. This feeling prevailed during Mr. Shepstone's absence in Zululand, and it was generally understood that the Secretary for Native Affairs' next piece of work after crowning Cetshwayo would be that of "settling Langalibalele."

But beyond the reluctance to produce their guns for registration, there was nothing in the behaviour of the Hlubi tribe to give the colonists cause for apprehension. No lawless acts were committed, no cattle stolen, no farmhouse fired, and the vague fears which existed amongst the white inhabitants as to what might happen were rather the result of the way in which "Government" shook its head over the matter as a serious one, than justified by any real cause for alarm. It was in fact one of those "Government scares" which occasionally were produced from causes or for reasons not apparent on the surface.

On Mr. Shepstone's return from the coronation of Cetshwayo, Government native messengers were sent to Langalibalele, requiring the latter to come down in person to Pietermaritzburg, the capital of Natal, to answer for the conduct of his tribe concerning their guns. The message produced a great and to those who were ignorant of the cause of it a most unreasonable panic in the tribe, in which the chief himself shared considerably. The Ama-Hlubi appeared exceedingly suspicious, even of the designs of the Government messengers, who were made to take off their great-coats, and were searched for concealed weapons before being admitted into the presence of Langalibalele. Such distrust of British good faith was held in itself to be a crime, the insolence of which could not be overlooked. Furthermore it was soon evident that the tribe would not trust their chief, nor he his person, in the hands of the Government, now that he was in disfavour. Without actually refusing to obey the orders he had received and proceed to Pietermaritzburg, Langalibalele sent excuses and apologies, chiefly turning upon his own ill-health, which made travelling difficult to him. This answer was the signal for the military expedition of 1873, which was entered upon without any further attempts to bring about a peaceful settlement of the affair, or to find out the real grounds for the evident fear and distrust of the Hlubi tribe. In October,

1873, the force, partly of regulars, partly colonial, a few Basuto horse, with an entirely unorganised and useless addition of untrained Natal natives, started from Pietermaritzburg, with all the pomp and circumstance of war; and much to the delight of the young colonial blood on the look-out for martial distinction. The tribe, however, far from having the least wish to fight, or intention of opposing the British force, deserted their location as soon as the news reached them that the army had started, and fled with their chief over the Draakensberg Mountains. Our force, commanded by Colonel Milles of the 75th Regiment, and accompanied by the Lieut.-Governor Sir B. C. C. Pine and Mr. Shepstone, reached a place called Meshlyn, situated on the confines of the district to be subdued, on October 31st; but the "enemy" had vanished, and were reported to be making the best of their way out of the colony, without, however, committing ravages of any description on their way, even to the extent of carrying off any of their neighbours' cattle. In fact they were frightened, and simply ran away. Our object now was to arrest the tribe in its flight; and a plan was formed for enclosing it in a network of troops, seizing all the passes over the mountains, and thus reducing it to submission.

Positions were assigned to the different officers in command, and the scheme looked extremely well on paper, and to men who were not acquainted with the district and the exceeding difficulty of travelling through it. Unfortunately, with the same lamentable failure in the Intelligence Department which has characterised the more important proceedings of 1879, very little was known, by those in command, of the country, or of what was going on in it. Mr. Shepstone himself, whose supposed knowledge of the people, their land, and all concerning them was so greatly and naturally relied upon, proved totally ignorant of the distances which lay between one point and another, or of the difficulties to be overcome in reaching them.

In consequence of this singular ignorance a little force was sent out on the evening of November 2nd, under command of Major Durnford, R.E., chief of the staff, with orders to seize and hold a certain pass known as the Bushman's River Pass, over which Langalibalele was expected to escape; the distance having been miscalculated by about two-thirds, and the difficulties of the way immensely underrated.

Major Durnford was himself a new-comer in the colony at that time, and had therefore no personal knowledge of the country; but he was supplied with full, though, as it soon appeared, unreliable information by those under whose command he served, and who were in possession of a plan or diagram of the district which turned out to be altogether incorrect. He did, indeed, reach his assigned post, though four-and-twenty hours after the time by which he expected to be there; while those sent out to take up other positions never reached them at all, owing to the same incorrect information concerning locality.

Major Durnford was in command of a party composed of 2 officers, 6 non-commissioned officers, and 47 rank and file of the Natal and Karkloof Carbineers, 24 mounted Basutos,[1] and a native interpreter. His orders were[2] to seize and hold the Bushman's River Pass, "with a view to preventing the entrance in or out of the colony of any natives until the expedition is ready to cross over." Special orders were also given to him that he was on no account to fire the first shot.

There was one excellent reason, not generally taken into consideration, for this order, in the fact that the three days given by Government to the tribe in which to surrender would not be over until midday on the 3rd of November.

Starting at 8.30 p.m. on the 2nd November, Major Durnford's force only reached its destination at 6.30 a.m. on the 4th, having traversed a most difficult country, broken, pathless, and well-nigh inaccessible. On the line of march many men fell out, utterly unable to keep up; pack-horses with provisions and spare ammunition were lost; and Major Durnford had his left shoulder dislocated, and other severe injuries, by his horse falling with him over a precipice on the 3rd. He pressed on for some hours, but became quite exhausted at the foot of the Giant's Castle Pass, where he lay some time; he was then dragged up with the aid of

---

1. Natives of Basutoland, resident for many years in Natal.
2. See Field Force Order, 1873.

a blanket, reaching the top of the pass at 2 a.m. At 4 a.m. Major Durnford was lifted on his horse, and with his force reduced to 1 officer, 1 non-commissioned officer, 33 troopers, and the Basutos pushed on to the Bushman's River Pass, and occupied it at 6.30 a.m., finding Langalibalele's men already in the pass.

Major Durnford posted his men, and went forward with the interpreter to parley with the chiefs, and induce them to return to their allegiance. This was a service of danger, for the young warriors were very excited. Seeing that the enemy were getting behind rocks, etc., commanding the mouth of the pass, he made every preparation for hostilities, though restricted by the order not to fire the first shot. Finding that, although the natives drew back when he bade them, they pressed on again when his back was turned, and that the volunteers were wavering, he at last reluctantly directed an orderly retreat to higher ground, from whence he could still command the pass. Upon a shot being fired by the natives, the retreat became a stampede, and a heavy fire being opened, three of the Carbineers and one Basuto fell. The horse of the interpreter was killed, and, while Major Durnford was endeavouring to reach the man and lift him on his own horse, the interpreter was killed by his side, and Major Durnford was surrounded and left alone. Dropping the reins, he drew his revolver, and shot his immediate assailants, who had seized his horse's bridle, and, after running the gauntlet of a numerous enemy at close quarters, escaped with one serious wound, an *assegai*-stab in the left arm, whereby it was permanently disabled. He received one or two trifling cuts besides, and his patrol-jacket was pierced in many places. Getting clear of the enemy, Major Durnford rallied a few Carbineers and the Basutos, and covered the retreat. The headquarters camp was reached about 1 a.m. on the 5th. At 11 p.m. on that day, Major Durnford led out a volunteer party of artillery with rockets, 50 men of the 75th Regiment, 7 Carbineers, and 30 Basutos to the rescue of Captain Boyes, 75th Regiment, who had been sent out with a support on the 3rd, and was believed to be in great danger. Major Durnford had received such serious injuries that the doctor endeavoured to dissuade him from further exertion, but as those sent to his support were in danger and he knew the country, he determined to go. He was lifted on his horse, and left amid the cheers of the troops in camp. Having marched all night resting only from 3 to 5 a.m. they met Captain Boyes' party about midday; they had lost their way, and thus did not find the Giant's Castle Pass.

After this, Major Durnford, with a considerable force, occupied Bushman's River Pass, recovered and buried the bodies of his comrades, and held the pass. He afterwards patrolled the disturbed districts. The Lieut.-Governor, Sir B. C. C. Pine, in a despatch dated 13th November, 1873, accepted the responsibility of the orders not to fire the first shot, and said of Major Durnford:

> He behaved, by testimony of all present, in the most gallant manner, using his utmost exertions to rally his little force, till, left *absolutely* alone, he was reluctantly compelled to follow them—wounded.

Colonel Milles, commanding the field force, published the following order:

Camp Meshlyn
7th November, 1873

The Commandant, with deep regret, announces to the field force under his command the loss of three Carbineers, *viz.*: Mr. Erskine, Mr. Potterill, and Mr. Bond, and of one native interpreter, Elijah, who formed part of the small force sent up with Major Durnford, R.E., to secure the passes, and who were killed during the retreat of that party from the passes, which, although they had gallantly seized, they were unable to hold, the orders being for 'the forces not to fire the first shot,' and so having to wait till they were placed at a great disadvantage. The brave conduct of those killed is testified to by all their comrades, and there is consolation alone in the thought that they died nobly fighting for their country. The Commandant must, however, publicly render his thanks to Major Durnford for the way in which he commanded the party, for his courage and coolness, and especially for the noble way in which, after his return from the passes, being almost exhausted, he mustered a volunteer party and marched to the relief of Captain Boyes, who was considered in great danger.

By command,

A. E. Arengo Cross

For Chief of the Staff

Although the main body of the fighting-men of the tribe had left Natal, most of the women and children, the sick and infirm, with a few able-bodied men to watch over them, had taken refuge in holes and caves, of which there are a considerable number in that mountainous part of the colony. The men of the tribe, indeed, were in disgrace with the Government, and thought it best to be out of the way when the British force paid their homes a visit, but it was not for a moment imagined that the soldiers would make war upon women and children. The latter, in any case, could not have taken that tremendous and hurried journey across the great mountains; and, with what soon proved a very mistaken confidence on the part of the people, all who could neither fight nor travel were left in these hiding-places, from which they expected to emerge in safety as soon as the troops, finding no one to oppose them, should have left the district. "The English soldiers will not touch the children,"[3] was the expression used. So far, however, was this idea from being realised, that the remainder of the expedition consisted of a series of attempts, more or less successful, to hunt the unfortunate "children "out of their hiding-places and take them prisoners.

During these proceedings many acts were committed under Government sanction which can only be characterised by the word "atrocities," and which were as useless and unnecessary as they were cruel,[4] Poor frightened creatures were smoked to death or killed by rockets in caves which they dared not leave for fear of a worse fate at the hands of their captors; women and children were killed, men were tortured, and prisoners

---

3. In the Zulu language the word *abantwana* (children) is a general one, including both women and children.

4. It is only fair to Major Durnford to state that during the whole of these proceedings he was away over the mountains, in vain pursuit of an enemy to be fought.

put to death. On one occasion a white commander of native forces is said to have given the significant information to his men that he did not wish to see the faces of any prisoners; and it is reported that a prisoner was made over to the native force to be put to death as the latter chose. The colonial newspapers apologised at the time for some of these acts, on the score that they were the result of the youthful enthusiasm of "Young Natal" fleshing his maiden sword.

These acts were chiefly committed by the irregular (white) troops and native levies, and are a signal proof of how great a crime it is to turn undisciplined or savage troops, over whom no responsible person has any real control, loose upon a defenceless people. The excuse made by those in authority in such cases is always "We did not intend these things to take place, but horrors are always attendant on savage warfare." But such excuses are of small value when, in campaign after campaign, it has been proved that the use of colonial troops under their own officers, and of disorganised masses of armed "friendly natives," is invariably productive of scenes disgraceful to the name of England, without any attempt being made to introduce a better system. Certainly if "horrors" beyond the fair fortune of war are necessarily attendant upon savage warfare, they should not be those inflicted by British troops and their allies upon unarmed or solitary men, women, and children.

So many women were injured in dislodging them from the caves that Major Durnford, on his second return from the mountains, instituted a hospital-tent where they might be attended to; but such humanity was by no means the general rule.

If acts of barbarity were for the most part committed by the irregular troops, there is one instance to the contrary which can never be forgotten in connection with this affair so flagrant a case that the friends of the officer in command, when the story first appeared in the colonial papers, refused to believe in it until it was authenticated beyond a doubt.

A body of troops infantry, irregular cavalry, and undisciplined natives upon one occasion during this expedition were engaged for some hours in trying to dislodge a solitary native from a cave in which he had taken refuge. The force had discovered the hiding place by the assistance of a little boy, whom they captured and induced to betray his friends.

The "rebel" (in this case there was but one) refused to surrender, and for a long while defended himself gallantly against the attacks of the whole force. Shots were fired through the apertures of the cave, rockets (a new and horrible experience to the poor creature) were discharged upon him. At last, after holding out for some hours, the man gave up the struggle, and coming out from his insufficient shelter, begged for mercy at the hands of his numerous foe. He had a good many wounds upon him, but none sufficiently severe to prevent his walking out amongst his captors, and asking them to spare his life. After a short consultation amongst the officers, a decision was arrived at as to the proper treatment of this man, who had proved himself a brave soldier and was now a helpless captive.

By order of the officer commanding, a trooper named Moodie put his pistol to the prisoner's head and blew out his brains. A court-martial sat upon this officer in the course of the following year, and he was acquitted of all blame. The defence was that the man was so seriously injured that it was an act of humanity to put an end to him, and that the officer dared not trust him in the hands of the natives belonging to the English force, who were exasperated by the long defence he had made. But the prisoner was not mortally nor even dangerously wounded. He was able to walk and to speak, and had no wound upon him which need necessarily have caused his death. And as to the savage temper of the native force, there was no reason why the prisoner should be left in their charge at all, as there was a considerable white force present at the time.[5]

---

5. The following account of the above transaction was given by one of those concerned, in a letter to *The Natal Times* of that date: "Twenty of us volunteered yesterday to go up and into a cave about eight miles from here. We found only one native, whom we shot, took a lot of goats (eighty-seven), and any amount of *assegais* and other weapons. We also searched about the country and killed a few niggers, taking fourteen prisoners. One fellow in a cave loaded his rifle with stones, and slightly wounded Wheelwright and Lieutenant Clarke, R.A. We, however, got him out, and Moodie shot him through the brains. Fifteen of ours have just volunteered to go to a cave supposed to contain niggers. We are gradually wiping out the three poor fellows who were shot, and all our men are determined to have some more." (continued on facing page)

The result of the expedition against the Hlubi tribe was so little satisfactory that those in authority felt themselves obliged to look about for something else to do before taking the troops back to Pietermaritzburg. They found what they wanted ready to their hand. Next to Langalibalele's location lay that of the well-to-do and quiet little tribe of Putini. "Government" had as yet found no fault with these people, and, secure in their own innocence, they had made no attempt to get out of the way of the force which had come to destroy their neighbours, but remained at home, herded their cattle, and planted their crops as usual. Unfortunately, however, some marriages had taken place between members of the two tribes, and when that of Langalibalele fled, the wives of several of his men took refuge in their fathers' *kraals* in the next location. No further proof was required of the complicity of Putini with Langalibalele, or of the rebellious condition of the smaller tribe. Consequently it was at once, as the natives term it, "eaten up," falling an easy prey owing to its unsuspecting state. The whole tribe men, women, and children were taken prisoners and carried down to Pietermaritzburg, their cattle and goods were confiscated, and their homes destroyed. Several of the Putini men were killed, but there was very little resistance, as they were wholly taken by surprise. The colony was charmed with this success, and the spoils of the Putini people were generally looked to to pay some of the expenses of the campaign. Whatever may have been the gain to the Government, by orders of which the cattle (the chief wealth of the tribe) were sold, it was not long shared by the individual colonists who purchased the animals. The pasture in that part of the country from which they had come is of a very different description from any to be found in the environs of Pieterma-

---

The Natal Government Gazette, December 9th, 1873, contains the following enactment: "All officers and other persons who have acted under the authority of Sir Benjamin Chillay Campbell Pine, K.C.M.G., as Lieut.-Governor of the colony of Natal, or as Supreme Chief over the native population, or have acted *bona fide* for the purposes and during the time aforesaid, whether such acts were done in any district, county, or division of the colony in which martial law was proclaimed or not, are hereby indemnified in respect of all acts, matters, and things done, in order to suppress the rebellion and prevent the spread thereof; and such acts so done are hereby made and declared to be lawful, and are confirmed.

ritzburg, and, in consequence of the change, the captured cattle died off rapidly almost as soon as they changed hands. But this was not all, for they had time, before they died, to spread amongst the original cattle of their new owners two terrible scourges, in the shape of "lung-sickness" and "red-water" from which the midland districts had long been free. One practical result of the expedition of 1873 seems to be that neither meat, milk, nor butter have ever again been so cheap in the colony as they were before that date, the two latter articles being often unobtainable to this day.

The unhappy prisoners of both tribes were driven down like beasts to Pietermaritzburg, many of the weaker dying from want and exposure on the way. Although summer-time, it happened to be very wet, and therefore cold; our native force had been allowed to strip the unfortunates of all their possessions, even to their blankets and the leather petticoats of the women. The sufferings of these poor creatures many of them with infants a few days old, or born on the march down were very great. A scheme was at first laid, by those in authority, for "giving the women and children out" as servants for a term of years that is to say, for making temporary slaves of them to the white colonists. This additional enormity was vetoed by the home Government, but the fact remains that its perpetration was actually contemplated by those entrusted with the government of the colony, and especially of the natives, and was hailed by the colonists as one of the advantages to accrue to them from the expedition of 1873. Several children were actually given out in the way referred to before the order to the contrary arrived from England, and a considerable time elapsed before they were all recovered by their relatives.

The unhappy women and children of the Langalibalele tribe were mere emaciated skeletons when they reached the various places where they were to live under surveillance. They seemed crushed with misery, utterly ignorant of the cause of their misfortunes, but silent and uncomplaining. Many of the women had lost children few knew whether their male relatives were yet alive. On being questioned, they knew nothing of Mr. Shepstone, not even his name, which was always supposed to command the love and fear of natives throughout the length and breadth of the land. They did not know what the tribe had done to get into such trouble; they only knew that the soldiers had come, and that they had run away and hidden themselves; that some of them were dead, and the rest were ready to die too and have it all over. A considerable number of these poor creatures were permitted by Government to remain upon the Bishop's land, where most of them gradually regained health and spirits, but retained always the longing for their own homes and people and their lost chief which characterises them still.[6]

---

6. It is hard to understand why these people should yet be detained and their harmless old chief still kept prisoner at Cape Town. The common saying that they are all content and the chief better off than he ever was before in his life, is an entirely and cruelly false one. Langalibalele is wearying for his freedom and his own people; the few women with him are tired of their loneliness, and longing to be with their children in Natal. The present writer paid the chief a visit in September of this year (1879), and found him very sad. "I am weary; when will they let me go?" was his continual question.

CHAPTER 3

Trial of Langalibalele

Meanwhile the fugitive chief had at last been captured by the treachery of a Basuto chief named Molappo, who enticed him into his hands, and then delivered him up to Mr. Griffiths, resident magistrate in that part of British Basutoland. When he and his party were first captured they had with them a horse laden with all the coin which the tribe had been able to get together during the last few days before the expedition started from Pietermaritzburg, and which they had collected to send down as a ransom for their chief. Their purpose was arrested by the news that the soldiers had actually started to attack them; when, feeling that all was lost, they fled, carrying the chief and his ransom with them. What became of the money, whether it became Molappo's perquisite, or whether it formed part of the English spoil, has never been publicly known. But it can hardly be denied that the readiness of the people to pay away in ransom for their chief the whole wealth of the tribe earned by years of labour on the part of the working members, is in itself a proof that their tendencies were by no means rebellious.

Langalibalele, with seven of his sons and many *indunas* (captains) and head-men, was brought down to Pietermaritzburg for trial, reaching the town on the 21st December.

So strong was the unreasoning hatred of the colonists against him on account of the death of the three Carbineers which had resulted from the expedition, that the unhappy man, a helpless captive, was insulted and pelted by the populace as he was conveyed in irons to the capital; and again, after sentence had been passed upon him, upon his way to Durban.

It was at this stage of affairs that the Bishop of Natal first came upon the scene, and interfered on behalf of the oppressed. Until 1873, while earnestly endeavouring to do his best as teacher and pastor amongst the natives as well as amongst their white fellow-colonists, he had not found it to be his duty to go deeply into political matters concerning them. He had great confidence at that time in the justice and humanity of their government as carried on by Mr. Shepstone, for whom he had a warm personal regard, based on the apparent uprightness of his conduct; and he had therefore contented himself with accepting Mr. Shepstone's word in all that concerned them.

That so many years should have passed without the Bishop's having discovered how greatly his views and those of his friend differed in first principles as to the government of the people, is due partly to the fact that the two met but seldom, and then at regular expected intervals, and partly because no great crisis had previously taken place to prove the principles of either in that respect. Their regular interviews were upon Sundays, when the Bishop, going into Pietermaritzburg for the cathedral service, invariably spent a couple of hours with his friend. During these comparatively short meetings doubtless Mr. Shepstone's real personal regard for the Bishop caused him temporarily to feel somewhat as he did, and, where he could not do so, to refrain from entering upon political discussion. The sympathy with Mr. Shepstone which existed in the Bishop's mind prevented the latter from looking more closely for himself into matters which he believed to be in good hands, and which did not naturally fall within the sphere of his duties; while the comparatively trivial character of the cases with which the native department had hitherto dealt, was not such as to force their details before a mind otherwise and fully employed.

The Langalibalele expedition, however, opened the Bishop's eyes. While it lasted, although deeply deploring the loss of life on either side, and feeling great indignation at the atrocities perpetrated on ours, he did not doubt that Mr. Shepstone had done all he could to avert the necessity of bloodshed, and expected to find him, upon his return to Pietermaritzburg, much grieved and indignant at the needless amount of suffering inflicted upon his people, the greater portion of whom must be entirely innocent, even although the charges against their chief should be proved.

The discovery that Mr. Shepstone entirely ratified what had been done[1] was the first blow to his friend's reliance on him. The mockery of justice termed a trial, granted to Langalibalele, was the next; and the discovery of how completely he had misconceived Mr. Shepstone's policy closed the intimacy of their friendship.

It soon became apparent that the trial of the chief was indeed to be a farce a pretence, meant to satisfy inquiring minds at home that justice had been done, but which could have but one result, the condemnation of the prisoner, already prejudged by a Government which, having declared him to be a rebel and having treated him as such, was hardly likely to stultify itself by allowing him to be proved innocent of the charges brought against him.

That there might be no doubt at all upon the subject, the prisoner was denied the help of counsel, white or black, in the hearing of his case, even to watch the proceedings on his behalf, or to cross-examine the witnesses; consequently the official record of the trial can only be looked upon as an *ex parte* statement of the case, derived from witnesses selected by the Supreme Chief,[2] examined by the Crown Prosecutor, and not cross-examined at all on the prisoner's behalf, although the assistance of counsel was recognised by the Crown Prosecutor himself as being in accordance with Kafir law.[3]

But the formation of the court and its whole proceedings were palpably absurd, except for the purpose of securing a conviction; and that this was the case was generally understood in Natal. Even those colonists who were most violent against the so-called "rebel," and would have had him hanged without mercy, asserting that he had been "taken red-handed" saw that the authorities

---

1. Not including those individual acts of cruelty which no one could defend, although many speak of them as unavoidable.
2. The Lieut.-Governor of the colony.
3. Kafir law, under which Langalibalele was tried, because most of the offences with which he was charged were not recognisable by English law.

had put themselves in the wrong by granting the prisoner a trial against the justice of which so much could be alleged.

In point of fact, the Lieut.-Governor had no power to form a court such as that by which Langalibalele was tried, consisting of His Excellency himself as Supreme Chief, the Secretary for Native Affairs, certain administrators of native law, and certain native chiefs and *indunas*. Besides which the Lieut.-Governor was not only debarred by an ordinance of the colony[4] from sitting as judge in such a court, from which he would be the sole judge in a court of appeal, but had already committed himself to a decision adverse to the prisoner by having issued the proclamation of November 11th, 1873, declaring that the chief and his tribe had "set themselves in open revolt and rebellion against Her Majesty's Government in this colony," and "proclaiming and making known that they were in rebellion, and were hereby declared to be outlaws," and that "the said tribe was broken up, and from that day forth had ceased to exist," and by further seizing and confiscating all the cattle and property of the said tribe within reach, deposing Langalibalele from his chieftainship, and otherwise treating him and his tribe as rebels.

His Excellency, therefore, could not possibly be looked upon as an unprejudiced judge of the first instance in the prisoner's case; nor could the Secretary for Native Affairs, Mr. Shepstone, by whose advice and with whose approval the expedition had been undertaken. As to the minor members of the court, they could hardly be expected to have an independent opinion in the matter, especially the "native chiefs and *indunas*," who knew very well that they would be liable to the accusation of disaffection themselves if they ventured to show any bearing towards the prisoner, or to do otherwise than blindly follow the lead of their white "brother-judges" and masters.

The native names gave a satisfactory air of justice to the proceedings of the court in English eyes, but in point of fact they were but dummy judges after all.

Not only, however, was the court wrongly constituted, but its proceedings were irregular and illegal. It was called, and considered

4. Ordinance No. 3, 1849.

39

to be, a native court, but in point of fact it was a nondescript assembly, such usages of either native or supreme court as could possibly tell on the prisoner's side (notably the use of counsel) being omitted, and only those which would insure his conviction admitted.

It was not the practice of the colony for serious crimes to be tried before a native court. But in this case they were obliged to run counter to custom for the reason given in a previous note, that most of the separate charges against the chief could not be recognised as crimes at all in an English court of law. At the same time the sentence finally given was one quite beyond the power of the court to pronounce. Clause 4 of the ordinance limits the power of the Supreme Chief to "appointing or removing the subordinate chiefs or other authorities" among the natives, but gives him no power to sentence to death, or to "banishment or transportation for life to such place as the Supreme Chief or Lieut.-Governor may appoint." When Langalibalele had been "removed "from his chieftainship, and himself and the bulk of his tribe "driven over the mountain out of the colony "by the Government force, as announced in the bulletin of November 13th, 1873, the cattle within the colony seized, and many of the tribe killed in resisting the attempt to seize them, the Supreme Chief, under native law, had expended his power; while banishment is a punishment wholly unknown to Kafir law, as is plainly stated in "Kafir Laws and Customs," p. 39.

Again, throughout the trial, the prisoner was assumed to have pleaded guilty, although in point of fact he had merely admitted that he had done certain acts, but desired witnesses to be called whose "evidence would justify or extenuate what he had done," a plea which in any ordinary court would be recorded as a plea of "not guilty."

The native members of the court, also, were made to sign a judgment, the contents of which had been "interpreted" to them, and their signatures "witnessed," by which the prisoner is declared to have been "convicted, on clear evidence, of several acts, for some of which he would be liable to forfeit his life under the law of every civilised country in the world." The absurdity of this is palpable, since it was impossible that these men should know anything of the law of any civilised land; it is plain, therefore, that in pretending to agree with assertions, of the meaning of which they were totally ignorant, they were under some strong influence, such as prejudice against the prisoner, undue fear of the Supreme Chief, or desire to please him one of them being "Head *Induna* of the Natal Government," and another the "*Induna* to the Secretary for Native Affairs."

To turn to these crimes, "for some of which he would be liable to forfeit his life under the law of every civilised country in the world" to which statement His Excellency the Supreme Chief, the Secretary for Native Affairs, and the Administrators of Native Law have also signed their names we find that the charges run as follows:

1. Setting at naught the authority of the magistrate in a manner[5] *not indeed sufficiently palpable to warrant the use of forcible coercion to our* (civilised) laws and customs.

Which charge we may at once dismiss as absurd.

2. Permitting, or *probably* encouraging, his tribe to possess fire-arms, and retain them contrary to law.
3. With reference to these fire-arms, defying the authority of the magistrate, and once insulting the messenger.
4. Refusing to appear before the Supreme Chief when summoned, excusing this refusal by evasion and falsehood, and insulting the Supreme Chief's messenger.
5. Directing his cattle and other effects to be taken out of the colony under an armed escort.
6. Causing the death of Her Majesty's subjects at the Bushman's River Pass.

It is plain to the most casual observation that none of the first five accusations, even if fully proved, refer to crimes punishable by death in any civilised land; and it is difficult to see how the Chief could reasonably be considered responsible for the sixth and last, seeing that the action took place in his absence, against his express commands, and to his great regret.

Returning to the five first-named offences, we find that the

---

5. The italics are the Author's own in this and the following charge.

statements contained in the second and third charges are the only proofs alleged of the truth of the first to which therefore we need give no further attention the magistrate himself stating that "this was the first time the prisoner ever refused to appear before him when ordered to do so;" and this was the first time for more than twenty years that he had been reported for any fault whatever.

Proceeding to charge No. 2, we find that the prisoner entirely denied having encouraged his young men to possess themselves of guns; nor could he justly be said to have even "permitted" them to do so merely because he did not actively exert himself to prevent it. The men went away from home, worked, were paid for their services in guns, or purchased them with their earnings, without consulting him. He had never considered it to be part of his duty to search the huts of his people for unregistered guns, but had simply left them to suffer the consequences of breaking the laws of the colony, if discovered. It is also to be observed that amongst the seven sons captured with him only one had a gun at a time when certainly, if ever, they would have carried them; which does not look as though he had greatly encouraged them to possess themselves of fire-arms.

But if the second charge, in a very modified form, might be considered a true one, yet Langalibalele had done no worse in that respect than most of the other chiefs in the colony. In proof of this assertion may be brought *Perrin's Register* for the years 1871-3 the years during which a large number of natives received payment for their services at the diamond fields in guns. From this register it appears that the total number of guns registered in eight of the principal northern tribes of the colony the two first-named chiefs being *indunas* to the very magistrate who complained of Langalibalele was as follows:

| Huts | | Guns Registered | | |
		1871	1872	1873
Ndomba	1190	—	—	—
Faku	2071	—	2	—
Mganu	1277	—	—	—
Pakade	2222	1	—	1

Zikali	1651	—	1	—
Nodada	3000	—	1	2
Putini	1239	—	1	—
Langalibalele	2244	—	9	4

Furthermore, any fault with respect to the guns was not an offence under Kafir Law, and could only have been tried in the Colonial Court under the ordinary law of the colony.

The third and fourth charges were those which, when first reported in Natal, produced considerable alarm and indignation in the minds of the colonists. A defiance of the authority, both of magistrate and Supreme Chief, and insult offered to their messengers, looked indeed like actual rebellion. The charges, however, dwindled down to very little when properly examined. The "defiance" in question consisted only in an answer made to the magistrate to the effect that he could not send in as desired five young men in possession of unregistered guns because they had run away, he knew not whither, being frightened by the course pursued by the magistrate's messenger; and that he could not find eight others, said to have come into the colony with guns, and to belong to his tribe, upon such insufficient data, and unless their names were given to him. The sincerity of which reasoning was shortly proved by the fact that, as soon as their names were notified to him, he did send in three of those very lads, with their guns, and two more belonging to other members of their party, besides sending in with their guns those who had worked for Mr. W. E. Shepstone, and who probably thought that the name of their master was a sufficient guarantee for their right to possess fire-arms.

The charge of insulting the native messengers from Government, of which a great deal was made at first, proved to be of very little consequence when investigated, but it is one to which special attention should be given because, indirectly, it is connected with the Zulu War.

The facts are as follows: One of the chief witnesses for the prosecution, Mawiza, a messenger of the Government, stated in his evidence-in-chief on the second day of the trial, that on the occasion of his carrying a message from Government, the prisoner's people had "taken all his things from him," and had "stripped, and taken him naked" into the Chief's presence. But on the fourth day, in answer to a question from His Excellency, he said "that they had *intended* to strip him but had allowed him to retain his trousers and boots" thereby contradicting himself flatly. Nevertheless the court being asked by His Excellency whether it required further evidence on this point, replied in the negative. They did not even ask a question, on the subject, of Mawiza's two companion messengers, Mnyembe and Gayede, though both these were examined; Mnyembe's evidence-in-chief being cut short *before* he came to that part of the story, and Gayede's taken up just *after* it.

The chief was kept in solitary confinement from the day when he was brought down to Pietermaritzburg, December 31st, till the day when his sons were sentenced, February 27th; not being allowed to converse with any of his sons, or with any members of his tribe, or with any friend or adviser, white or black. It was therefore quite out of his power to find witnesses who would have shown, as Mnyembe and Gayede would have done, that Mawiza's statements about the "stripping" were false; that he still wore his waistcoat, shirt, trousers, boots, and gaiters, when he was taken to the chief; and that the "stripping" in question only amounted to this, that he himself put off his two coats, by the chief's orders, "as a matter of precaution caused by fear" and not for the purpose of insulting the messenger, or defying the Supreme Chief. They would have satisfied the court also that other acts charged against the prisoner arose from fear, and dread of the Supreme Chief, and not from a spirit of defiance.

This affair of the messenger, explained by fear and suspicion on the part of Langalibalele, by which, also, he accounted for his refusal to "appear before" the Supreme Chief (which is to say that, being desired to give himself up into the hands of the Government, he was afraid to do so, and ran away), was the turning point of the whole trial. What special reason he had for that fear and distrust will be inquired into shortly. Meanwhile the court considered that such expressed distrust of the good faith

of the authorities was an added offence on the part of the prisoner, who was formally condemned to death, but his sentence
commuted to banishment for life to Robben Island, the abode
of lunatics and lepers, in which other captive native chiefs had
languished and died before him.[6]

6. The other rebel chiefs of the Cape Colony here alluded to, however, were not
"banished," but merely imprisoned in a portion of their own Supreme Chiefs territory, where, at proper times, they could be visited by members of their families and
tribes; moreover, they were duly tried and convicted before the ordinary courts of
serious crimes committed by themselves individually, and they had actually resisted
by force their Supreme Chief within his territory; whereas Langalibalele had made
no resistance—he was a runaway, but no rebel; he had not been tried and condemned for any crime in the Colonial Court, and banishment for life to Robben
Island, away from all his people, was a fate worse than death in his and their eyes.

The Bishop's Defence

The daily accounts of the trial which appeared in the local papers were read with great interest and attention by the Bishop, who quickly discerned the injustice of the proceedings. Mawiza's manifest contradiction of his own evidence first attracted his attention, and led to his hearing from some of his own natives what was not allowed to appear at the trial, that Mawiza's story was entirely false. Seeing how seriously this fact bore upon the prisoner's case, he went to Mr. Shepstone and told him what he had heard.

The Secretary for Native Affairs was at first very indignant with the Bishop's informant, doubting the truth of his statement, and declaring that the man must be severely punished if it were proved that he had lied. The Bishop, confident in the integrity of his native,[1] assented, saying, however, that the same argument should apply to Mawiza. The matter was at once privately investigated by Mr. Shepstone—the Bishop, Mawiza, Magema, and others being present—with the result that Mr. Shepstone himself was obliged to acknowledge the untrustworthiness of Mawiza, who was reproved in the severest terms for his prevarications by the other native *indunas*.[2]

Singularly enough, however, *this discovery made no difference whatever in the condemnation and sentence of the prisoner*, although

---

1. The same Magema, the Bishop's printer, before mentioned.
2. Although Mawiza's lies were plainly exposed, he was never punished, but remains to this day in charge of a large tribe, over which he has been placed by the Government.

the charge thus, to a great extent, disposed of, was the most serious of those brought against him.

But this was not all. Another point struck the Bishop very forcibly, namely, the perpetual recurrence of one phrase from various witnesses. "He (Langalibalele) was afraid, remembering what was done to Matshana," and "he was afraid that he should be treated as Matshana was, when he was summoned to appear by Government." Such expressions, used in excuse of the Chief's conduct, would, of course, have been inquired into had the prisoner been allowed counsel, or had anyone watched the case on his behalf. But although the court judged the excuse of "fear" to be an added fault on the Chief's part, and although perpetual allusions were made by witnesses to a specific cause for this fear, no question was asked, and no notice taken by those present of the perpetually recurring phrase. The Bishop, however, in the interests of justice and truth, made inquiries amongst his own natives as to the meaning of these allusions. He knew, of course, in common with the rest of the inhabitants of Natal, that, in the year 1858, a native chief named Matshana had got into some trouble with the Government of Natal. A commando had gone out against him, and, after a skirmish with some native troops under Mr. John Shepstone, in which Mr. Shepstone was wounded, and some men on the other side killed, he had escaped with his people into Zululand, where he had lived ever since. The Bishop had never heard the details of the affair, and knew of nothing in connection with this incident which could account for the "fear because of what was done to Matshana."

"Can you tell me anything of the story of Matshana's escape from Natal?" was the question put by him at different times to different natives; and everyone thus questioned gave substantially the same account, of what was plainly among them a well-known, and well remembered incident in the history of the colony.

Matshana, they said, was accused of some offence, and being summoned before the authorities to answer for it, had refused to appear. Mr. John Shepstone, with a native force, of whom this very Langalibalele, then a young chief, with his followers formed a portion, was sent out to endeavour to reduce him to obedience. Mr. Shepstone invited him to a friendly interview, in which they might talk over matters, but to which Matshana's men were to bring no weapons. In consequence of the reluctance of Matshana to fulfil this condition, the proposed interview fell through several times before it was finally arranged. Matshana's people, even then, however, brought their weapons with them, but they were induced to leave them at a certain spot a short distance off. The meeting took place; Mr. Shepstone being seated in a chair with his people behind him, Matshana and his men crouched native fashion upon the ground, suspicious and alert, in a semicircle before him. Suddenly Mr. Shepstone drew a gun from beneath the rug at his feet, and fired it (he says, as a signal), whereupon his men, some of whom had already ridden between Matshana's party and their arms, fell on, and the struggle became general, resulting in the death of many of Matshana's people. The chief himself, who seems to have been on the look-out for a surprise, escaped unhurt. He was resting upon one knee only when the first shot was fired, and sprang over the man crouching behind him. Another man, named Deke, who was sitting close to him, was wounded in the knee, but is alive to this day.

This story, which in varied form, but substantially as given above, was generally known and believed by the natives, furnished a very complete explanation of why Langalibalele ventured to distrust the good faith and honour of the Government, having himself taken part in, and been witness of, such a disgraceful transaction; which, when it came to the knowledge of the Secretary of State, was emphatically condemned by him. Remembering this circumstance, it is not wonderful that Langalibalele should have taken the precaution of searching the Government messengers for concealed weapons.

It seemed strange that Mr. Shepstone, sitting as judge upon the bench to try a man for his life, should silently allow so great a justification of his chief offence to remain concealed. But it seemed stranger still to suppose him ignorant of any part of an affair carried out under his authority, and by his own brother.

However, the Bishop took the matter privately to him in the

first instance, telling him what he had heard, and pointing out what an important bearing it had upon the unfortunate prisoner's case. He was met by a total denial on Mr. Shepstone's part that any such act of treachery had ever taken place, or that there were any grounds for the accusation.

Nevertheless, after careful consideration, and on thoroughly sifting the obtainable evidence, the Bishop could not avoid coming to the painful conclusion that the story was substantially true, and was a valid excuse for Langalibalele's fear. Finding that further appeal on behalf of the prisoner to those on the spot was in vain, he now wrote and printed a pamphlet (giving the usual native version that the first shot fired was at Matshana) on the subject for private circulation, and especially for Lord Carnarvon's information.[3]

One of the first results of the appearance of this pamphlet was a demand on the part of Mr. J. Shepstone's solicitor for "an immediate, full, and unqualified retraction of the libel falsely and maliciously published in the pamphlet, with a claim for £1000 damages for the injury done to Mr. J. Shepstone by the same."

Such an action would have had but a small chance of a decision upon the Bishop's side at that time in Natal, so, to defend himself and not, as generally supposed, out of enmity to the Shepstones he appealed to Lord Carnarvon in the matter, on the grounds that his action had been taken for the public good, and in the interests of justice.

Meanwhile the unfortunate chief and his eldest son Malambule were sent to Robben Island, the former as a prisoner for life, the latter for five years. They were secretly conveyed away from Pietermaritzburg to the port, and every effort made to prevent the Bishop from seeing them, or interfering on their behalf. Other sons, two of them mere lads, who had as yet held no more

---

3. On June 24th, 1874, the Bishop presented this "Appeal on behalf of Langalibalele" to His Excellency the Lieut.-Governor of Natal and the executive committee of the Colony. The appeal was made in the first instance to Sir B. C. C. Pine, who altogether refused to listen to it. On this the Bishop forwarded a letter through the Lieut.-Governor to the Earl of Carnarvon, enclosing a copy of his correspondence with Sir B. C. C. Pine, and stating his reasons for acting as he had done in the matter. This letter was dated August 6th, 1874, and on August 16th the Bishop left home *en route* to England.

important position in the tribe than that of herd-boys to their father's cattle, and many of the head men and *indunas*, were condemned to imprisonment in the gaol at Pietermaritzburg for terms varying in length from six months to seven years. The two young sons, lads named Mazwi and Siyepu, were kept prisoners for the shortest period named, six months; but it was some little time after they left the gaol before they were really set at liberty. The family at Bishopstowe, where their mothers and many of their other relatives were located, were naturally anxious to have the two boys also, and, as soon as their term of imprisonment was up, applied for the charge of them. Somewhat to their surprise all sorts of difficulties were raised on the point—one would have thought a very simple one—and they were at last curtly informed that the boys did not wish to go to Bishopstowe, and would remain where they were, under surveillance in another district. The Bishop himself was away at the time, but his eldest daughter, acting for him, soon discovered through native sources that in point of fact the boys were extremely anxious to go to Bishopstowe, but were in too terrified a condition to express a wish. The question had been put to them in this form:

"So! you have been complaining! you say you want to leave the place you have been sent to, and go to Bishopstowe?"

Whereupon the frightened lads, their spirits crushed by all that had befallen them, naturally answered:

"We never complained, nor asked to go anywhere" which, was perfectly true.

By dint of a little determination on the part of Miss Colenso, however, the desired permission was at last obtained, and Mazwi and Siyepu entered the Bishopstowe school, which had already been established for the boys of the scattered tribe. Under the treatment which they there received they soon began to recover from their distress, and to lose the terrified expression in the eyes which characterised them painfully at first. But the health of Mazwi, the elder, was broken by hardship and confinement, and he died of consumption a few years after.[4]

4. He was a bright intelligent lad, keenly anxious for self-improvement, and with a great desire, unusual amongst his kind, to go to England, and see a civilised country.

It soon became apparent that there must be something specially injurious to the prisoners in their life in gaol beyond the mere fact of confinement. Nearly all the men of the Hlubi tribe left it labouring under a dreadful complaint of a complicated form (said to be some species of elephantiasis), of which a considerable number died; others, as in Mazwi's case, falling victims to consumption. On inquiry it appeared that the fault lay in the *excessive washing* to which every part of the building was habitually subjected—floors and bed-boards being perpetually scrubbed, and therefore seldom thoroughly dry. This state of things was naturally a trial to the constitutions of people accustomed to life in the warm smoke-laden atmosphere of a native hut. However beneficial it might be to the natives to instruct them in habits of cleanliness,[5] this was hardly the way to do it, and the results were disastrous. The peculiar complaint resulting from confinement in the city gaol was commonly known amongst the natives as the "gaol-disease," but it had not attracted the same attention while the victims to it were occasional convicts, as it did when it attacked a large number of innocent prisoners of war!

After the chief had been sent to Robben Island, it was represented, by those interested in his welfare, that to leave him there for the rest of his life without any of his family or people near him—except his son Malambule, who was to be released in five years' time—would be a great and unnecessary addition to the hardship of his position; and it was finally decided that one of his wives and a servant of his own should be sent to join him in captivity. A few days after this decision a story was circulated in the colony, causing some amusement, and a little triumph on the part of the special opponents of the chief and his cause: it was to the effect that "out of all Langalibalele's wives not one was willing to go to him," and many were the sarcastic comments made upon the want of family affection thus evinced by the natives. On due inquiry it turned out that the manner in which the question had been put to them was one highly calculated

---

5. The Zulus and Zulu-Kafirs bathe their persons frequently, but they have not our ideas of cleanliness in respect to dress and habitations, although they are very particular about their food, utensils, and other matters.

to produce a negative answer. Native policemen, who were sent to the *kraals* where they were living, to inquire which of them would be willing to go, accosted them with "Come along! come along and be killed with your chief!" Which proposition was not unnaturally looked upon with considerable disfavour. When, however, the matter was properly explained to them, they all expressed their willingness to go, although a journey across the (to them) great unknown element was by no means a trifling matter in their eyes. The woman selected in the first instance was one Nokwetuka, then resident at Bishopstowe, where she was fitted out for her journey, and provided with suitable clothes.[6] She joined her husband upon the island as proposed, as also did a lad of the tribe Fife, who happened to be residing (free) at the Cape, and obtained permission to attend upon his chief. It was not until some time after, when Langalibalele had been removed to an adjoining portion of the mainland, bleak and barren indeed, but an improvement upon Robben Island, that two other women and a little son were added to the party.[7]

For the son, Malambule, however, there was no possibility of making any such arrangements during the five years of his captivity, as he was a bachelor; although when he was captured he had a bride in prospect, the separation from and probable loss of whom weighed greatly upon his mind. He could not even learn whether she was yet alive, as so many women had been killed,

---

6. This was done at the expense of Government, which likewise allowed certain supplies of meal, salt, and a little meat to the captives.

7. The boy was one of those who in the meanwhile had learnt at Bishopstowe to read and write, and who therefore could be of some use to his father as scribe, although his usefulness in that respect is much curtailed by the exceeding caution of the Government, which in its absurd and causeless fear of "treasonable correspondence," will not allow written words of any description to reach or leave the poor old chief without official inspection. This precaution goes so far that in one instance some mats made by the women for Miss Colenso, and sent from Uitvlugt (the place of Langalibalele's confinement after he was removed from the island), never reached their destination, owing to the paper attached, signifying for whom they were intended, being removed, as coming under the head of prohibited liberties. Another case is that of a lady who visited the family in September, 1879, and asked them to tell her what trifles they would like her to send them from Cape Town, but found that she had no power to send some babies' socks which the women had chosen, and a comforter for the old man's neck, except through an official individual and by formal permission.

and others had died since from the effects of the hardships they had undergone; while it was more than probable, supposing her to be yet living, that she might be given in marriage to some other more fortunate individual, either by the authority of her relatives, or, as happened in another case, by that of the Government of Natal.[8]

Towards the end of his imprisonment, Malambule grew very restless and morose; and, when he found himself detained some time after the term of years had elapsed, he became extremely indignant and difficult to manage, being in fact in a far more "rebellious" frame of mind than he ever was before. On one occasion he showed so much temper that it was thought necessary to put him under temporary restraint in the gaol. Apparently he was very wise in giving so much trouble, for it was shortly found expedient to let him go, though it remains unexplained why he should not have been set free immediately upon the expiration of his sentence. He was sent back to Natal, but still treated as a prisoner until he reached Pietermaritzburg, where he was finally set at liberty; putting in a sudden and unexpected appearance at Bishopstowe, where he was joyfully welcomed by his own people. He did not, however, spend much time amongst them, but hurried off as soon as possible up-country to find his bride. It is pleasant to be able to record that he found her just in time to prevent another marriage being arranged for her, and that his return was as satisfactory an event to her as to himself.

---

8. A woman, wife of one of the fugitives, being taken prisoner during the expedition, found favour, much against her will, in the eyes of one Adam (a follower of the Secretary for Native Affairs), who asked to be allowed to take her as his wife. Permission was granted, but the woman refused, saying that she had a husband already, to whom she was attached. Her wishes were disregarded, and she was conveyed home by Adam, from whom she shortly escaped. Adam applied to the nearest magistrate for an order to take forcible possession of the fugitive, and the woman was thrown into gaol by the magistrate, until she should consent to be Adam's wife. The man took her home a second time, and she again escaped from him; in fact her determination was so great that the matter was finally given up altogether. Eventually she rejoined her own husband, who received her and her child with the kindness which her constancy deserved.

CHAPTER 5

The Putini Tribe

To assist in paying the expenses of the expedition, "Government" had "eaten up" the small tribe commonly known as the "Putini," but properly called the "Amangwe" tribe, "Putini" being, in reality, the name of their late chief, who died shortly before the disturbances, leaving the sole custody of their infant son and heir to his young widow, who accordingly held the position and dignity of chieftainess in the tribe.

To say that the "eating up" of these people was an utter mistake is to say no more than can honestly be said concerning Langalibalele's tribe, the Ama-Hlubi; but, in the case of the Putini people, the mistake was a more flagrant one, and, when all was said and done, there was no possibility of making out a charge against them at all. Finally the fact stared the Government (both at home and in Natal) in the face that a tribe had been attacked, members of it killed, the people taken prisoners and stripped of all their possessions, without even the shadow of a reason for such treatment being forthcoming.

Major (by this time Lieutenant-Colonel) Durnford specially took up the cause of this injured and innocent people. It was plain enough that the Government at home would never ratify the action taken against the Amangwe tribe by the Government in Natal; and that sooner or later the latter would be forced, in this instance, to undo their work as far as possible to restore the people to their location, and to disgorge at least part of their plunder: and it was evident to Colonel Durnford that the sooner this was done the better for all parties. The Natal Government would put itself in a more dignified position by voluntarily and speedily making full amends for the wrong done, and doing of its own accord what eventually it would be obliged to do at the command of the home Government. It was also of special importance to the people themselves that they should be allowed to return to their homes in time to plant their crops for the following year.

About May, 1874, it had been decided by the Government that Lieutenant-Colonel Durnford, in his capacity of Colonial Engineer, should take a working party to the Draakensberg Mountains, and blow up, or otherwise destroy, all the passes by which ingress or egress could be obtained. The chief object of this demolition was that of giving confidence to the up-country districts, the inhabitants of which were in perpetual fear of inroads from the scattered members of the outlawed tribe. They had indeed certain grounds for such apprehensions, as one or two attacks had been made upon farmhouses since the expedition. Even these demonstrations were not evidence of organised resistance, but mere individual acts of vengeance committed by single men or small parties, in return for brutalities inflicted upon the women and children belonging to them. They were, however, sufficient to keep the country in perpetual alarm, which it was highly advisable should be checked.

The demolition of the passes being decided upon, Colonel Durnford applied for the services of the male Putini prisoners, some eighty in number, and induced the Government to promise the men their liberty, with that of the rest of the tribe, if, on their return, when the work should be finished, the Colonel could give them a good character.

He left Pietermaritzburg with his party of pioneers and a company of the 75th Regiment, under Captain Boyes and Lieutenant Trower, in May, and spent some months in the complete destruction of the Draakensberg passes, returning to the capital in September. The movement at first raised violent though unavailing opposition amongst the colonists, who persisted in looking upon the Putini men as bloodthirsty rebels, who might at any moment break loose upon them and ravage the country. But when the whole party returned from the mountains, without a single case of misconduct or desertion amongst them although they had had hard work and undergone great hardships (shared to the full by Colonel Durnford, who suffered to the end of his life from the effects of intense cold upon his wounded arm) the colonists ceased to look upon them as desperate ruffians, and soon forgot their fears. Meanwhile the Colonel found considerable difficulty in obtaining the actual freedom of the tribe, for which he and his eighty pioneers had worked so hard and suffered so much. Any less resolute spirit would have been beaten in the contest, for "Government" was determined not to give way an inch more than could possibly be helped.

However, the matter was carried through at last, and the whole tribe returned to their devastated homes including the eighty pioneers, to whom the Colonel had paid the full wages of free labourers for the time during which they had worked in good time to plant their crops for the coming year. Eventually they also received some small compensation for the property of which they had been robbed, though nothing even approaching to an equivalent for all that had been taken from them or destroyed by the Government force in 1873.

The same party of mounted Basutos who were with Colonel Durnford at the Bushman's River Pass affair, accompanied him throughout this second more peaceful expedition, and remained his devoted followers for the rest of his life.

The colony was tranquil again, and gradually the immediate consequences of the expedition vanished below the surface of everyday life, except in the minds of those who had suffered by it. But one important result was obtained. England was once more convinced that the time for withdrawing her troops from the colony and leaving it to protect itself had not yet arrived. Some such project had been entertained during the previous year, and its speedy accomplishment was frequently foretold; but such a proceeding would have been fatal to the plans of the empire-making politicians. The impossibility of withdrawing the troops was clearly established by turning a mole-hill into a mountain by proving how critical the condition of the native mind within the colony was considered to be by those who should be the best judges so that it was thought necessary to turn out the whole available European force, regular and irregular, upon the slightest sign of disturbance; and most of all by creating such a panic in the colonial mind as had not existed since the early days of Natal.

It is doubtful how soon the Secretary of State for the Colonies himself knew the extent to which the operations of 1873-4 could be made subservient to his great confederation scheme; or rather, to speak more correctly, how seriously the latter must be injured by any attempt to set right the injustice done to the Hlubi tribe. When the Bishop went to England[1] and pleaded in person the cause of the injured people, there can be no doubt that Lord Carnarvon was fully impressed by the facts then made known to him. None of the despatches sent home could in the least justify the proceedings of his subordinates in Natal. Lord Carnarvon's own words, expressing his disapproval of the action taken against the two tribes, and requiring that all possible restitution should be made to them, show plainly enough that at the period of the Bishop's visit to him, with all the facts of the case before him, his judgment in the matter coincided with that of the Bishop himself. The latter returned to Natal, satisfied that substantial justice would now be done, or at all events that the suffering already inflicted upon the innocent Hlubi and Amangwe tribes, by the rash and mistaken action of the Government, would be alleviated to the utmost extent considered possible without lowering that Government in the eyes of the people.

Certain steps, indeed, were immediately taken. Orders were sent out for the release of the Putini people, which order Colonel Durnford had already induced the Natal Government to anticipate; and a further order was notified that the tribe should be compensated for the losses sustained by them during the late expedition. In the case of Langalibalele and his tribe, although it was not thought advisable to reinstate them in their old position, every effort was to be made to mitigate the severity with

---

1. Reaching home early in October, 1874.

which they had been treated. A few extracts from the Earl of Carnarvon's despatch on the subject will best show the tone in which he wrote, and that the Bishop might reasonably feel satisfied that mercy and consideration would be shown to the oppressed people.

The Earl of Carnarvon, after reviewing the whole proceeding, comments somewhat severely upon the manner in which the trial had been conducted. On this point he says: "I feel bound to express my opinion that there are several points open to grave observation and regret." He speaks of the "peculiar and anomalous" constitution of the court, the equally "peculiar" law by which the prisoner was tried, and of "the confusion and unsatisfactory result to which such an anomalous blending of civilised and savage terms and procedure must lead." He remarks that it was in his judgment "a grave mistake to treat the plea of the prisoner as one of guilty;" and he says, "still more serious, because it involved practical consequences of a very grave nature to the prisoner, was the absence of counsel on his behalf." Entering into the various charges brought against the prisoner, and the evidence produced to support them, he dismisses the magistrate's accusation of "general indications, of which, however, it is difficult to give special instance, of impatience of control;" and the Governor and Secretary for Native Affairs comments on the same as unimportant, with the words, "I am bound to say that the evidence does not appear to me fully to support these statements."[2]

Reviewing the circumstances and evidence concerning the unregistered guns, he says: "I am brought to the conclusion that, though there was probably negligence it may be more or less culpable in complying with the law, there was no sufficient justification for the charge in the indictment that Langalibalele did encourage and conspire with the people under him to procure firearms and retain them, as he and they well knew contrary to law, for the purpose and with the intention of, by means of such firearms, resisting the authority of the Supreme Chief." Of the

---

2. Acts of "defiance" and "resistance," too vague for any special instance to be given, probably striking his lordship as being of a slightly imaginary character.

extent to which the chief's disobedience, in not appearing when summoned by Government, was due to a "deliberately-planned scheme of resistance in concert with others, or the mere effect of an unfounded panic," the Earl remarks: "Unfortunately this was not made clear." And, finally, referring to the charge of insulting the Government messengers, he says:

> I am obliged, with great regret, to conclude that this very important portion of the evidence given against the prisoner at the trial was so far untrustworthy as to leave it an open question whether the indignities of which the witness complained may not have amounted to no more than being obliged to take off his coat, which might be a precaution dictated by fear, and nothing else.

Having thus censured the proceedings of his subordinates on every point, he says:

> That the Amahlubi tribe should be removed from its location may have been a political necessity which, after all that had occurred, was forced upon you, and I fear[3] it is out of the question to reinstate them in the position, whether of land or property, which they occupied previously. The relations of the colony with the natives, both within and without its boundaries, render this impossible. But every care should be taken to obviate the hardships and to mitigate the severities which, assuming the offence of the chief and his tribe to be *even greater than I have estimated it, have far exceeded the limits of justice.*[4] Not only should the terms of the amnesty of the 2nd May last be scrupulously observed, but as far as possible means should be provided by which the members of the tribe may be enabled to re-establish themselves in settled occupations.[5] With respect to the Putili tribe, I have in their case also expressed my opinion that no sufficient cause has been shown for removing them from their location. I can discover no indication of their conspiracy or combination with Langalibalele, beyond the vague and wholly un-

---

3. Implying plainly that strict justice would demand it.
4. Author's italics.
5. No notice was ever taken of the recommendation.

corroborated apprehension of some movement on their part in connection with the supposed tendencies of his tribe; and therefore I can see no good reason for any punishment on this ground.

The proclamation to the native population enclosed in this despatch contained the following sentences:

> Langalibalele we release from imprisonment on the island in the sea, but he shall not return to Natal. The Amahlubi may, if they choose, when that is prepared which is to be prepared, go to him, but he will not be allowed to go to the Amahlubi.

In all that Lord Carnarvon thought fit to say on this occasion he does not express the slightest approval of any person concerned, or action taken, except of the "conduct of Colonel Durnford, whose forbearance and humanity towards the natives has attracted my attention." A despatch of the same date (3rd December, 1874) recalls Sir Benjamin Pine from the government of Natal.

Anything more thoroughly condemnatory could hardly be imagined, although it may be reasonably questioned how far justice was done to Sir Benjamin Pine[6] by the whole weight of mismanagement being placed upon his shoulders, while his coadjutor and adviser, Mr. Shepstone, on whose opinion he had acted throughout, and whose word, by his supposed knowledge of native ways and character, was law throughout the affair, was promoted and rewarded.

After perusing Lord Carnarvon's remarks and directions, my readers may imagine that some very good result would be produced on the fortunes of both tribes, but in this supposition they would be greatly mistaken. Nor, unless they had been in the habit of perusing South African despatches with attention, would it occur to them how easily the proclamation quoted

---

6. It is reported that Sir B. Pine has felt the injustice to himself so keenly that he refuses longer to acknowledge his title of K.C.M.G., and styles himself simply Mr. Pine. There can be little doubt that in point of fact Mr. Shepstone was mainly responsible for all that happened; but "the right man to annex the Transvaal" could not well be spared, and a scapegoat was found for him in Sir Benjamin Pine.

from, drawn up by Mr. Shepstone, could be evaded. The proclamation itself is almost childish in its foolish way of informing the people that they had behaved very badly, and deserved all they had got, but would be relieved of their punishment by the mercy of the Queen, and must behave very well and gratefully in future. Such exhortations to people who were perfectly aware that they had been treated with the utmost injustice were rather likely to raise secret contempt than respect in the minds of an intelligent people, who would have far better understood an honest declaration that "we have punished you, under the impression that you had done what we find you did not do, and will therefore make it up to you as much as possible."

The two important sentences of the proclamation, however, were capable of being adapted to an extent of which Lord Carnarvon probably did not dream. His lordship can hardly have intended the first sentence by which Langalibalele was released "from imprisonment on the island in the sea," simply to mean that he was to be conveyed to the nearest (most dreary) mainland, and imprisoned there, within the limits of a small and barren farm, where every irritating restriction and annoying regulation were still imposed five years after. The words "he shall not return to Natal," certainly do not imply rigid confinement to a small extent of land, where friends, white or black, are not allowed to visit him, or send the most innocent presents without tedious delay and official permission. The second sentence is an admirable specimen of South African art. The people might go to their chief if they chose, *"when that is prepared which is to be prepared"* but which never has been yet.

We give Lord Carnarvon full credit for not having the slightest notion that this clause would have no result whatever, as nothing ever would be "prepared." Year after year has dragged on—one or two women[7] and a couple of boys being allowed, as a great favour, to join the old chief during that time. But every difficulty has always been raised about it, and not the slightest attempt has been made to enable or permit the tribe or any part of it to follow.

---

7. Three at last.

When the chief and his son were first removed from Robben Island to Uitvlugt, a desolate and unfruitful piece of ground
on the adjoining mainland, at a considerable distance from the
nearest dwelling-place of any description, it was understood
that the family would live in comparative liberty, being merely
"under surveillance;" that is to say, that some suitable person or
persons would be appointed by the Cape Government to live
within reach of them, and to be answerable for their general
good behaviour, for their gratification in every reasonable wish
or request, and for their making no attempt to escape from the
Cape Colony and return to their homes in Natal.

Strict justice would have required that the chief and his people—those that were left of them—should be restored to their
location, as was done in the case of the other tribe, and that both
should be repaid the full ascertainable value of the property tak-
en from them or destroyed; but politicians place "expediency"
so far above justice and truth, that men who are fighting for the
latter out-of-date objects may well be thankful for the smallest
concession to their side.

The Bishop accordingly was satisfied that the new arrangement proposed for the captive chief's comfort was as good a one
as he could expect from Lord Carnarvon, although not what
he might have done himself had the power lain with him. But
when he signified his satisfaction in the matter, it was certainly
on the assumption that Langalibalele was to be made to feel his
captivity as little as possible upon the mainland—in fact that it
was to consist *merely* in his inability to leave the colony, or, without permission, the land assigned to him in it. But that such reasonable permission should be easily obtainable—that as many of
his family and tribe as desired to do so should be allowed to join
him there—that no galling restraints (such as still exist) should
be imposed upon him, were certainly conditions proposed by
Lord Carnarvon and accepted by the Bishop.

When the Bishop returned to Natal, however, he left behind
him in England one who, closely following upon his steps, undid
much of the work which the other had done. Mr. Shepstone
could have brought no new light to bear upon the subject—he

could have given Lord Carnarvon no fresh facts which had not appeared already in the despatches, through which the Natal Government had been in constant communication with him. It was not likely that Mr. Shepstone should possess information hitherto unknown to the rest of the world, including Lord Carnarvon himself, which should have the power of entirely altering the latter's deliberately formed judgment upon the subject under consideration. But had this been so, Lord Carnarvon would assuredly have communicated the fact to the Bishop, with whom he had parted in complete unanimity of opinion, and to whom, and through whom to the unhappy chief, promises had been made and hopes held out, destined, apparently, never to be fulfilled.

It is needless to conjecture what may have passed between Lord Carnarvon and the man who reached England somewhat under a cloud, with certain errors to answer for to a chief who was well up in facts beforehand, but who, in 1876, appears as Sir Theophilus Shepstone, K.C.M.G., with a commission as administrator of the Transvaal hidden in the depths of his pocket. The facts speak for themselves. The desire of the Secretary of State to achieve confederation in South Africa (the South African Empire!), the peculiar capabilities of Mr. Shepstone for dealing with the native and Dutch races of the country, and the considerable check which "strict justice" to the injured tribes would be to the great confederation scheme, are sufficient grounds for believing that absolution for the past, and immunity from the consequences of his acts were purchased by the engagement, on Mr. Shepstone's part, to carry out in quiet and successful manner the first decided step towards the great project of confederation and empire, namely, the annexation of the Transvaal. In the light cast by succeeding events, it is plain that nothing would have been much more inconvenient in the scheme of South African politics than any measure which would be a censure upon Mr. Shepstone, or prevent his promotion to a higher office in the State.

That no such alteration in the opinion of the Secretary of State ever took place may be gathered from his very decided though courteous replies to the appeals made to him from the colony, to the addresses from the Legislative Council and other colonists, containing protests against Lord Carnarvon's decisions, and professing to give additional evidence against the tribes in question which would completely justify the proceedings of the colonial Government, and the severities of their punishment.

To all that could be thus alleged Lord Carnarvon replies:

> I did not form my opinion until I had received and considered the fullest explanation which the Government whose acts are questioned desired to place before me, and in considering the case I had the advantage of personal communication with an officer who was specially deputed to represent the Government of Natal before me, and who, from his knowledge, ability, and experience, was perhaps better qualified than any other to discharge the duty which was confided to him. I fail to find in the present documents the explanations which are promised in the address to Her Majesty, or indeed any evidence so specific or conclusive as to affect the opinion which, after the most anxious consideration, Her Majesty's Government formed upon this case.[8]

In another despatch of the same date,[9] addressed to the officer administering the Government, Natal, he concludes:

> As there is apparently no prospect of arriving at an agreement of opinion on several points, there is, perhaps, no advantage in continuing the discussion of them.

Nevertheless, although holding so clear and decided a judgment, Lord Carnarvon permitted his just and humane directions for the treatment of the injured tribes to be practically set aside by those in authority under him.[10]

---

8. P. P. (C. 1342-1) p. 45.
9. July 27, 1875, (C. 1342-1) p. 46.
10. It would be an injustice to an association, called into existence and maintained by a true spirit of Christian charity, to pass over in silence the active, if seemingly ineffectual, efforts of the Aborigines Protection Society to obtain justice for the unfortunate people of the Putini tribe.

Sir Garnet Wolseley

England, however, was beginning to feel that her South African possessions were in an unsettled condition, although in point of fact they were quiet enough until she meddled with them in the blundering well-meaning fashion in which she has handled them ever since. It was patent, indeed, that some interference was required, when innocent tribes were liable to such cruel injustice as that inflicted upon the Ama-Hlubi and Amangwe in 1873, and, if her interference was honestly intended on their behalf, she has at least the credit of the "well-meaning" attributed to her above. Whatever her intentions may have been, however, the result has been a progress from bad to worse, culminating at last in the late unhappy Zulu War.

It is believed by many that England possesses but one man upon whom she can place any reliance in times of difficulty and danger, and accordingly Natal shortly received notice that Sir Garnet Wolseley was coming to "settle her affairs;" and the Natalians, with feelings varying from humble and delighted respect to bitter and suspicious contempt, prepared themselves to be set straight— or not—according to their different sentiments. The great man and his "brilliant staff," as it was soon popularly called by the colonists not without a touch of humour arrived in Natal upon the last day of March, 1875, and on the 1st of April he took the oaths as Administrator of the Government at Pietermaritzburg.

He immediately commenced a series of entertainments, calculated by their unusual number and brilliancy to dazzle the eyes of young Natalian damsels. These latter, accustomed as they were to very occasional and comparatively quiet festivities, and balls at which a few of the subalterns of the small garrison at Fort Napier were their most valued partners, found themselves in a new world of a most fascinating description, all ablaze with gold and scarlet, V.Cs, C.Bs, titles, and clever authors. And, what was more, all these striking personages paid them the most gracious attentions attentions which varied according to the importance of the young ladies' male relatives to the political scheme afoot. Meanwhile dinner after dinner was given to the said relatives; Sir Garnet Wolseley entertained the whole world, great and small, and the different members of his staff had each his separate duty to perform his list of people to be "fascinated" in one way or another. For a short time, perhaps, the popularity desired was achieved in consequence of their united and persevering efforts, although from the very first there were voices to be heard casting suspicion upon those who were "drowning the conscience of the colony in sherry and champagne;" and there were others, more far-sighted still, who grimly pointed out to the gratified and flattered recipients of this "princely hospitality" the very reasonable consideration: "You will have to pay for the sherry and champagne yourselves in the end."

Undoubtedly the conviction that the colony would pay dear for its unwonted gaiety that it was being "humbugged" and befooled soon stole upon the people. While the daughters enjoyed their balls, their fathers had to buy their ball-dresses; and while the legislative councillors and all their families were perpetually and graciously entertained at Government House, the question began to arise: "What is the object of it all?"

All unusual treatment calls forth special scrutiny, and it is to be doubted whether Sir Garnet's lavish hospitality and (almost) universally dropped honey, with all the painful labours of his brilliant staff combined, did more than awaken the suspicions which a course of proceedings involving less effort would have failed to evoke. Even the most ignorant of Dutch councillors would be wise enough to know that when a magnate of the land treated him and his family as bosom friends and equals of his own, the said magnate must want to "get something out of him" even the most untaught and ingenuous of colonial maidens would soon rate at their true value the pretty speeches of the "men of note," who would have had them believe that, after frequenting all the gayest and most fashionable scenes of the great world, they had come to Natal and found their true ideal upon its distant shores.

A vast amount of trouble and of energy was thrown away by all concerned, while the few whose eyes were open from the first stood by and watched to see what would come of it. The question remains unanswered to this day. That the annexation of the Transvaal by Sir Garnet Wolseley did *not* come of it, is to that discreet general's great credit. And had his decision—that the work which he was specially sent out to do[1] was one for which the country was not ripe, and would not be for many years—been accepted and acted upon by England, the expense of his six months' progress through Natal would have been well worth incurring indeed, for in that case there would have been no Zulu War. But this, unfortunately for all parties, was not the case.

The popular answer in Natal to the question, "What did Sir Garnet Wolseley do for you?" is, "He got us up an hour earlier in the morning;" an excellent thing truly, but a costly hour, the history of which is as follows: For many years the city of Pietermaritzburg, known as "Sleepy Hollow" to its rivals of another and, in its own opinion, a busier town, had set all its clocks and watches, and regulated all its business hours by the sound of a gun, fired daily from Fort Napier at nine o'clock a.m., the signal for which came from the town itself. The gun was frequently credited with being too fast or slow by a few seconds or even minutes, and on one occasion was known to have been wrong by half-an-hour; a mistake which was remedied in the most original fashion, by setting the gun

---

1. The annexation of the Transvaal: so stated by one of his own staff.

back a minute and a half daily till it should have returned to the proper time; to the utter confusion of all the chronometers in the neighbourhood. But, right or wrong, the nine o'clock gun was the regulator of city time, including that of all country places within reach of its report. The natives understood it, and "gun-fire" was their universal hour of call; the shops were opened at its sound, and but little business done before it. But during Sir Garnet Wolseley's reign in Natal it occurred, not without reason, to the member of his staff whom he placed in temporary authority over the postal and other arrangements of the colony, that nine o'clock was too late for a struggling community to begin its day, and he therefore altered the original hour of gun-fire to that of eight a.m. How far the alteration really changed the habits of the people it is hard to say, or how many of them may now let the eight-o'clock gun wake them instead of sending them to work, but the change remains an actual public proof of the fact that in 1875 Sir Garnet Wolseley visited Natal.

A more important measure was the bill which he carried through the Legislative Assembly for the introduction of eight nominee members to be chosen by the Government, thereby throwing the balance of power into the hands of the executive, unless, indeed, nominee members should be chosen independent enough to take their own course. Whether this measure was looked upon as very important by those who proposed it, or whether the energy displayed was for the purpose of convincing the public mind that such really was Sir Garnet's great object in Natal, it is not so easy to decide. But looking back through the events of the last few years one is strongly tempted to suspect that the whole visit to Natal, and all the display made there, was nothing but a pretence, a blind to hide our designs upon the Transvaal, for which Sir Garnet wisely considered that the country was not ripe.

But if in this instance we are bound to admire Sir Garnet Wolseley's good sense, we must, on the other hand, greatly deprecate his behaviour towards the two unfortunate tribes whose sorrows have been recorded, and towards those who took an interest in their welfare and just treatment more especially towards the Bishop of Natal.[2]

From the very first Sir Garnet's tone upon native matters, and towards the Bishop, were entirely opposed to that used by Lord Carnarvon. Every attempt made by the Bishop to place matters upon a friendly footing, which would enable the new Governor to take advantage of his thorough, acquaintance with the natives, was checked; nor through the whole of his governorship did he ever invite the Bishop's confidence or meet him in the spirit in which he was himself prepared to act; a course of proceeding most unfortunately imitated by some of his successors, especially Sir Bartle Frere, who only "invited criticism of his policy"—and received it—when too late to be of any avail except to expose its fallacies.

It is impossible to rise from a perusal of the despatches written by Sir Garnet after his arrival in Natal, in answer or with reference to matters in which the Bishop was concerned, without coming to the conclusion that from the very beginning his mind was prejudiced against the Bishop's course, and that he had no sympathy with him or the people in whom he was interested. Far from attempting to carry out Lord Carnarvon's instructions in the spirit in which they were undoubtedly given, he set aside some, and gave an interpretation of his own to others, which considerably altered their effect; while his two despatches, dated May 12th and 17th, show plainly enough the bias of his mind.

The first is on the subject of the return of Langalibalele, which

---

2. It is neither customary nor convenient to speak publicly of a parent, and I desire to let facts speak for themselves as much as possible. I feel, however, bound to remark that of all the mistakes made by a succession of rulers in Natal, perhaps the most foolish and unnecessary has been that jealousy of episcopal or "unofficial" interference, which has blinded them to the fact that the Bishop has always been ready to give any assistance in his power to the local Government in carrying out all just and expedient measures towards the natives, without claiming any credit or taking any apparently prominent position beyond his own; and, so long as justice is done, would greatly prefer its being done by those in office. He has never interfered, except when his duty as a man, and as the servant of a just and merciful Master, has made it imperatively necessary that he should do so; nor does he covet any political power or influence. To a government which intends to carry out a certain line of policy in defiance of justice and honour, he would ever be an opponent; but one which honestly aims at the truth would assuredly meet with his earnest support.

the Bishop had recommended, offering to receive him upon his own land at Bishopstowe, and to make himself responsible, within reasonable limits, for the chiefs good behaviour. Sir Garnet "would deprecate in the strongest terms" such return. He says:

> Langalibalele, as I am informed by all classes here, official and non-official (a very small knot of men of extreme views excepted), is regarded by the native population at large as a chief who, having defied the authorities, and in doing so occasioned the murder of some white men, is now suffering for that conduct.

While thus avoiding the direct responsibility of sitting "in judgment upon past events," by quoting from "all classes here," he practically confirms their opinion by speaking of those who differ from them as "a very small knot of men of extreme views;" and he further commits himself to the very unsoldierlike expression of "murder" as applied to the death of the five men at the Bushman's River Pass, by speaking in the same paragraph of the punishment of the chief as "a serious warning to all other Kafir chiefs ... to avoid imitating his example." Without mentioning the Bishop by name, he makes repeated allusions to him in a tone calculated to give an utterly false impression of his action and character.

> To secure these objects[3] it is essential that a good feeling should exist between the two races; and I am bound to say that in my opinion those who, by the line of conduct they adopt, keep alive the recollection of past events[4] .... I have no wish to attribute to those who adopt this policy any interested motives. I am sure that they are actuated by feelings of high philanthropy,[5] and nothing is farther from my mind than a wish to cast any slur upon them. Yet I must say that from the

---

3. The future safety of the colony and the true interests of white and black.
4. "The recollection of past events," that is to say, of the slaughter of many men, women, and children, the destruction of homes, and the sufferings of the living; —this can hardly with reason be said to be *kept alive* by attempts to ameliorate the condition of those that remained, and to show them some small kindness and pity. How "a good feeling" was to be restored between the victims and their conquerors by other means, Sir Garnet does not suggest.
5. Simple justice and honesty?

manner in which they refuse to believe all evidence that does not coincide with their own peculiar views, and from the fact of their regarding the condition of affairs in Natal from one standpoint alone, I am forced to consider them impractical (sic), and not to be relied on as advisers by those who are responsible for the good government of all classes.

In the following paragraphs he speaks of "sensational narratives oftentimes based upon unsifted evidence," "highly-coloured accounts," and "one-sided, highly-coloured, and, in some instances, incorrect statements that have been made public in a sensational manner," all which could refer to the Bishop alone.

If by regarding the condition of affairs in Natal from one standpoint alone, Sir Garnet Wolseley means the standpoint of British honour and justice, and looks upon those who hold it as "impractical," there is little more to say. But Sir, Garnet can never have given his attention to the Bishop's printed pamphlets, and could therefore have no right to an opinion as to his reception or treatment of evidence, or he would not venture to use the expressions just quoted of one who had never made an assertion without the most careful and patient sifting of the grounds for it, whose only object was to establish the truth, *whatever that might be*, and who was only too glad whenever his investigations threw discredit upon a tale of wrong or oppression. That principles of strict honour and justice should in these our days be characterised as "peculiar views," is neither to the credit of the English nation nor of its "only man."

In the second despatch mentioned Sir Garnet makes the following singular remark:

> In the meantime I take the liberty of informing your lordship that the words 'the Amahlubi may, if they choose, when that is prepared which is to be prepared, go to him,' are interpreted, by those who have taken an active part in favour of the tribe, as binding the Government to convey all members of the Amahlubi tribe who may wish to join Langalibalele, to whatever place may be finally selected for his location. I do not conceive that any such meaning is intended, and. should not recommend that such an interpreta-

tion should be recognised. I think, however, it may fairly be matter for consideration whether Langalibalele's wives and children, who have lost all their property,[6] might not be assisted with passages by sea to join Langalibalele.[7]

It is difficult to imagine what other interpretation can be placed on the words of the proclamation, or how, after it had once been delivered, any narrower measures could be fairly considered, or require further "instructions."

In subsequent letters Sir Garnet scouts altogether representations made by the Bishop of the destitute condition of members of the Hlubi tribe, replying to Lord Carnarvon on the subject by enclosing letters from various magistrates in different parts of the country denying that destitution existed; saying that the people were "in sufficiently good circumstances;" and most of them suggesting that, should anything like starvation ensue, the people have only to hire themselves out as labourers to the white people. The Bishop would certainly never have made representations unsupported by facts; but in any case it is a question whether we had not some further duties towards a large number of innocent people whom we had stripped of all their possessions, and whose homes and crops we had destroyed, than that of allowing them to labour for us at a low rate of wages; or whether the mere fact of its being thus possible for all to keep body and soul together relieved us of the responsibility of having robbed and stripped them.

These facts in themselves prove how different from Lord Carnarvon's feelings and intentions were those of his subordinate, and how real Sir Garnet's antagonism. It is not therefore surprising that the commands of the former were not, and have never been, carried out.

---

6. In common only with the rest of the tribe.
7. Three women and two children only have been allowed to join him.

CHAPTER 7

The Matshana Inquiry
and Colonel Colley

In consequence of the threatened action for libel against the Bishop of Natal on account of statements made in his defence of Langalibalele, which Mr. John Shepstone considered to be "of a most libellous and malicious nature," the Bishop had laid the matter before the Lieut. Governor, Sir B. Pine, requesting him to direct an inquiry to be made into the truth of the said statements. This was refused by His Excellency through the acting Colonial Secretary in the following terms—thereby prejudging the case without inquiry:

> Your lordship has thought it right to make the most serious charges against an important and long-tried officer of this Government—charges, too, relating to a matter which occurred sixteen years ago.[1] That officer has, in His Excellency's opinion, very properly called upon your lordship to retract those charges. Instead of doing this, you have appealed to the Lieut.-Governor to institute an inquiry as to the truth of the charges you have made. This the Lieut.-Governor has no hesitation in declining to do.

The Bishop's next action was an appeal to the Secretary of State for the Colonies, which he requested the Lieut.-Governor to forward with a copy of the correspondence which had

---

1. Which did not prevent their being of the utmost importance in considering the case of the chief under trial at the time the statements were made.

already taken place on the subject, in order that His Excellency might be fully aware of what steps he was taking.

This appeal contained a short account of the facts which had led to his making the statements complained of—the trial of Langalibalele, and the "fear of treachery" perpetually pleaded by many witnesses in excuse of the chiefs conduct, but treated with contempt both by the court below and the council, each including the Secretary for Native Affairs, and presided over by His Excellency. The statements made by the Bishop—not mere "charges" unsupported by evidence, but the deposition of four eye-witnesses who might be cross-examined at will—would, if proved to be true, greatly tend to palliate the offences imputed to the chief, and should therefore not have been suppressed by the officer concerned, who had kept silence when a word from his mouth would have cleared a prisoner on trial for his life from a very serious part of the charge against him. The Bishop therefore submitted that the fact of the events in question having taken place sixteen years before was no reason why they should not be brought to light when required for the prisoner's defence.

The correspondence which ensued including a very curious circumstance relating to a missing despatch, recorded in the despatch-book at Pietermaritzburg, but apparently never received, in Downing Street—will be found by those interested in the subject in the Bishop's pamphlet, *The History of the Matshana Inquiry*.

For our present purpose it is sufficient to remark that on the 22nd of April, 1875, Lord Carnarvon directed Sir Garnet Wolseley to institute a careful inquiry into the matter, and suggested that under all the circumstances this inquiry might be best conducted by one or more of the senior officers of Sir Garnet's staff, who had accompanied him on special service to Natal. The correspondence which followed between the parties concerned, with arrangements for the summoning of witnesses and for the management of the trial, are also all to be found in the above-mentioned pamphlet. The inquiry was to be of a private nature, no reporters to be admitted, nor counsel on either side permitted.[2] The Bishop and Mr. Shepstone were each to be allowed the presence of one friend during the inquiry, who, however, was not to speak to the witnesses, or to address the officer holding the inquiry. In addition the Bishop asked, and received, permission to bring with him the native interpreter, through whom he was in the habit of conducting important conversations with natives, as his own Zulu, although sufficient for ordinary purposes, was not, in his opinion, equal to the requirements of the case, while Mr. J. Shepstone was familiar from childhood with colloquial Kafir.

In the Bishop's pamphlet he points out that the course which Lord Carnarvon had thought proper to adopt in this case was wholly his own, and proceeds as follows: a passage which we will quote entire:

> And I apprehend that this inquiry, though of necessity directed mainly to the question whether Mr. John Shepstone fired at Matshana or not, is not chiefly concerned with the character of the act imputed to him, described by the Secretary for Native Affairs as of a treacherous murderous nature, but involves the far more serious question whether that act, if really committed, was suppressed by Mr. John Shepstone at the time in his official report, was further suppressed by him when he appeared last year as Government prosecutor against a prisoner on trial for his life who pleaded it as a very important part of his defence, but found his plea treated by the court, through Mr. John Shepstone's silence, as a mere impudent 'pretext' and has been finally denied by him to the Secretary of State himself, and is still denied down to the present moment. Such an act as that ascribed to him, if duly reported at the time, might, I am well aware, have been justified by some, or at least excused, on grounds of public policy under the circumstances; though I, for my part, should utterly dissent from such a view. In that case, however, it would

---

2. Sir B. Pine complains in his despatch, December 31st, 1874, of the "intolerable injustice" of charges being made against Mr. J. Shepstone, upon evidence taken by the Bishop *ex parte*, without the safety of publicity and the opportunity of cross-examination. Yet Sir Garnet Wolseley refused to allow publicity or searching cross-examination by experienced advocates.

have been unfair and unwarrantable to have reproached Mr. Shepstone at the present time for an act which had been brought properly under the cognizance of his superiors. But the present inquiry, as I conceive, has chiefly in view the question whether the facts really occurred as Mr. John Shepstone reported at first officially, and has since reaffirmed officially, or not.

Colonel Colley, C.B., was the officer appointed to conduct the inquiry, the commencement of which was fixed for August 2nd, 1875.

The intervening period granted for the purpose was employed by the Bishop in summoning witnesses from all parts of the land; from Zululand, from the Free State, and distant parts of the colony. Matshana himself was summoned as a witness under an offer of safe-conduct from the Government. He, however, did not find it convenient, or was afraid, to trust himself in person; but Cetshwayo sent some of his men in his place. The Bishop's object was to summon as many *indunas*, or messengers, or otherwise prominent persons in the affair of 1858; men who were thoroughly trustworthy, and "had a backbone," and would not be afraid to speak the truth; his desire being to get at that truth, whatever it might be. Thirty-one men responded to his call, of whom, however, only twenty were examined in court, the Bishop giving way to Colonel Colley's wish in the matter, and to save the court's time. Four other witnesses summoned by *both* the Bishop and Mr. Shepstone were examined, and nine more on Mr. Shepstone's behalf, called by him. The Bishop had considerable difficulty in procuring the attendance of the witnesses he required. The simple order of Mr. John Shepstone would suffice, by the mere lifting up of his finger, to bring down to Pietermaritzburg at once any natives whom he desired as witnesses, invested as he was in the native mind with all the weight and all the terrors of the magisterial office; and with the additional influence derived from the fact of his having only recently filled, during his brother's absence in England, the office of Secretary for Native Affairs, with such great—almost despotic—authority over all the natives in the colony. The Bishop, on the contrary, had no such influence. He had no power at all to insist upon the attendance of witnesses. He could only *ask* them to come, and if they came at his request, they would know that they were coming, as it were, with a rope around their necks; and if they were proved to have borne false witness, calumniating foully so high an official, they had every reason to fear that their punishment would be severe, from which the Bishop would have had no power—even if, in such a case, he had the will—to save them.

When, upon the 2nd August, the inquiry began, out of the many witnesses called by the Bishop, upon whom lay the *onus probandi*, only three were at hand; and two of these, as will be seen, were present merely through the wise forethought of *the* intelligent Zulu, William Ngidi. But for this last, the inquiry would have begun, and—as the Commissioner was pressed for time, having other important duties on his hands in consequence of Sir Garnet Wolseley and staff being about immediately to leave the colony—might even (as it seemed) have ended, with only a single witness being heard in support of the Bishop's story. No others were seen or even heard of for some days, and then by accident only. The Secretary for Native Affairs, it is true, by direction of Sir Garnet Wolseley, had desired Cetshwayo to send down Matshana, and the Bishop fully expected that this intervention of the Government with a promise of safe conduct for him, would have sufficed to bring him. But Mr. John Dunn, "Immigration Agent" of the Government in Zululand, and Cetshwayo's confidential adviser, whom the Bishop met in Durban on July 8th, told him at once that he did not think there was the least chance of Matshana's coming, as the Secretary for Native Affairs' words in 1873, when he went up to crown Cetshwayo (who asked very earnestly that Matshana might be forgiven and allowed to return to Natal) were so severe—"He had injured the Secretary for Native Affairs' own body;" that is, one of his men had wounded his brother (Mr. John Shepstone) fifteen years previously, when thirty or forty of Matshana's men had been killed—that he would be afraid to come at a mere summons like this, notwithstanding the promise of safety, the value of which he would naturally appreciate by his own experience in former days. Mr. Dunn promised to do his best to persuade him to go down, but did not expect to succeed. And, in point of fact, he never came, alleging the usual "pain in the leg;" and the discussion in Zululand about his coming had only the result of delaying for some days the starting of the other witnesses whom the Bishop had asked Cetshwayo to send. On August 4th, however, Zulu messengers arrived, reporting to the Secretary for Native Affairs the sickness of Matshana, and to the Bishop the fact that six witnesses from Zululand were on the way, and they themselves had pushed on ahead to announce their coming, as they knew they were wanted for August 2nd. Accordingly five of them arrived on August 8th, and the sixth, Maboyi, on August 5th, under somewhat singular circumstances, as will presently appear. Meanwhile most important witnesses in support of the Bishop's story were expected by him from Matshana's old location Kwa' Jobe (at the place of Jobe) —partly in consequence of a letter written by Magema to William Ngidi, partly in compliance with the Bishop's request sent through Cetshwayo to Matshana himself in Zululand. William Ngidi replied to Magema, as follows:

Your letter reached me all right, and just in the very nick of time, for it came on Saturday, and the day before Mr. John arrived here (Kwa' Jobe), and called the men to come to him on Monday, that they might talk together about Matshana's affair. On Sunday my friend Mlingane came, and we took counsel together; for by this time it was well known that Mr. John had come to speak with the people about that matter of Matshana. So we put our heads together, and I got up very early on Monday morning and hurried off to Deke, and told him that he was called by Sobantu (the Bishop) to go before the Governor. He readily agreed to go, and went down at once, on the very day when Matshana's people came together to Mr. John, so that he never went to him; but, when I arrived, there had just come already the messenger to call him to go to Mr. John, and another came just as he was about to set off for 'Maritzburg. I told him to call for Mpupama on his way, and take him on with him. I see that you have done well and wisely in sending that letter without delay to me.

Accordingly these two men, Deke and Mpupuma, reached Bishopstowe safely in good time. Also Ntanibama, Langalibalele's brother, of whom the Bishop had heard as having been present on the occasion, readily came at his summons, though he was not asked to give his evidence, nor did the Bishop know what it would be before he made his statement in court. But for the prudent action of William Ngidi, Ntambama would have been the only witness whose testimony would have sustained the Bishop's statements during the first days of the inquiry; and his evidence, unsupported, might have been suspected, as that of Langalibalele's brother, of not being disinterested, and would have been contradicted at once (see below) by Ncamane's.

On Saturday, July 31st, the inquiry being about to begin on the Monday, Magema received a doleful letter from William Ngidi to the effect that the 'Inkos Sobantu must take care what he was about, for that all the people were afraid, and would not venture to come forward and give evidence against a high government official. He spoke, however, of one man "whom I trust most of all the people here," and who had the scar upon his neck of a wound received upon the day of Matshana's arrest.

Discouraging, indeed, as it was to find on the very eve of the inquiry that all his efforts through William Ngidi had failed to procure witnesses, except the two sent down by him at the first, the Bishop was utterly at a loss to understand how his message to Cetshwayo had, to all appearance, also entirely failed with respect to those men of Matshana still living Kwa' Jobe, as well as (it seemed) those living in Zululand.

On August 5th the mystery with respect to the witnesses Kwa' Jobe was explained. Deke, Mpupuma, Ntambama, and Njuba, who had come from Zululand, had all been examined, as well as Ncamane, who, when called by the Bishop, had replied that he would only come if called by the Government; and when summoned through the Secretary for Native Affairs, at the Bishop's request, withdrew or modified important parts of his printed statement. The Bishop had actually no other witness to call, and all his efforts to obtain a number of well-informed and trustworthy eye-witnesses from Zululand, Kwa' Jobe, and

Basutoland, seemed likely to end in a complete fiasco. But on the evening of Thursday, August 5th, a native came to him in the street and said that his name was Maboyi, son of Tole (Matshana's chief *induna*, who was killed on the occasion in question), and that he had been sent by Matshana to Mr. Fynn, the superintendent, and Lutshungu, son of Ngoza, the present chief, of the remnant of his former tribe living Kwa' Jobe, to ask to be allowed to take down to 'Maritzburg as witnesses those men of his who were present on the day of the attempt to seize Matshana. Mr. Fynn said that "He did not refuse the men, but wished to hear a word by a letter coming from the Secretary for Native Affairs—it was not proper that he should hear it from a man of Matshana coming from Zululand," and sent him off under charge of a policeman to 'Maritzburg, where he was taken to the Secretary for Native Affairs, who said to him: "If Matshana himself had come, this matter might have been properly settled; it won't be without him!" But the Secretary for Native Affairs said nothing to Maboyi about his going to call the witnesses Kwa' Jobe; he only asked by whom he had been sent, and when informed, he told him to go home to Zululand, as he had not been summoned and had nothing to do with this affair. Maboyi had reached 'Maritzburg on Monday, August 2nd, the day on which the inquiry began. He saw the Secretary for Native Affairs on Tuesday, and on that day was dismissed as above.

Not a word was said to the Bishop about his being brought down in this way under arrest, which fully explained the non-arrival of his witnesses from the location; since, first, their fear of giving witness against a government official, and now the arrest of Maboyi, had spread a kind of panic among them all, and deterred them from coming to give evidence against Mr. John Shepstone—himself a resident magistrate, only lately acting as Secretary for Native Affairs, and the brother of the Secretary for Native Affairs himself—merely in answer to the Bishop's unofficial summons. Hearing, however, on Thursday from natives that the case was then going on at Government House, Maboyi went up to speak with the Bishop, but arrived when the court had adjourned. He found him out in town, however, just as he was on the point of leaving for Bishopstowe, and was, of course, told to wait and give his evidence. Accordingly, he went to Bishopstowe, and Magema was charged to bring him in for examination on Saturday, the next day of the inquiry. On the way into town for that purpose, Mr. Fynn's policeman most positively refused to let him stay, and went off ultimately in great wrath, as Maboyi and Magema insisted that he must give his evidence before leaving town to return to Zululand.

On that day, Saturday, August 7th, the Bishop explained the whole affair to the Commissioner, and, having obtained a list of names from Maboyi, requested that a Government messenger might be sent for the men at once, and the Secretary for Native Affairs was instructed to summon them. On Monday, August 9th, the Secretary for Native Affairs replied that he had summoned all these men, except seven, who were already in town, having been called by Mr. John Shepstone, and having been, in fact, under his hands—in charge of his *induna* Nozitshina—from the very first day of the inquiry. It seemed as if William Ngidi's statement was really to be verified, and that these men had all succumbed to their fears. On the other hand, among these seven was Matendeyeka, whom William Ngidi "trusted most of all;" and there might be amongst them some who would have the courage to speak out and to describe the facts connected with the arrest of Matshana to the best of their ability. At all events the Bishop resolved to call them, and do his best to bring the truth out of them; and Magema afterwards whispered that he had heard from one of Mr. John's men, who was present when he spoke with the people (Kwa' Jobe), that the men there had said: "It was of no use to discuss it beforehand; they would say nothing about what they remembered now; but before the Governor they would speak the plain truth as they knew it." Accordingly the Bishop called four of these men—Matendeyeka, Faku (son of Tole), Magwaza, Grwazizulu—and they all confirmed the story as told by his other witnesses. He left the other three to be called by Mr. John Shepstone, but he never called them. That these witnesses should have been called by Mr. John Shepstone, as well as by the Bishop, was satisfactory, showing that they were witnesses to whom no objection could be made on the score of character or position in the tribe, or as having been in any way, directly or indirectly, influenced by the Bishop.

But the result was that, as these men were in the hands of the other side from the time they reached until they left; 'Maritzburg, the Bishop had never even seen them, or had any communication with them, until they appeared to give their evidence. He was wholly ignorant beforehand of what they *would* say or what they could say; he knew not whether they would confirm or contradict the story told by his other witnesses; and he knew not on what particular points, if any, they could give special evidence, and was therefore unable to ask the questions which might have elicited such evidence.

By this time (August 8th) the witnesses from Zululand had arrived, from whom the Bishop learned the names of other important witnesses living Kwa' Jobe, and at his request these also were sent for by Government messengers. Unfortunately, through Maboyi's arrest, some of the Bishop's witnesses summoned by the Secretary for Native Affairs arrived too late on the very day (August 21st) on which the evidence was closed, and others a day or two afterwards—twelve altogether—of whom only one could be heard, whom the Bishop had expressly named as a man whose testimony he especially desired to take. Upon the whole, Sir Garnet Wolseley, who began by "leaving entirely in the Bishop's hands" the difficult and not inexpensive business of "obtaining his witnesses," summoned ultimately twenty-two of them, of whom, however, four only could be heard by the Commissioner; two (Matshana and Ngijimi) did not come at all; and three, including a most important witness, were called too late to be able to arrive till all was over; while four more out of the seven who had been called by Mr. John Shepstone gave their evidence in support of the Bishop, as doubtless the three others would have done, if Mr. John Shepstone had called them.

In the despatch to the Earl of Carnarvon, already quoted from, Sir B. Pine remarks:

I think it further my duty to point out to your lordship that much of the evidence adduced by the Bishop in this case has been taken in this way (*ex parte*, without the safety of publicity, and the opportunity of cross-examination); evidence so taken is peculiarly untrustworthy, for everyone moderately acquainted with the native character is aware that when a question is put to a native, he will intuitively perceive what answer is required, and answer accordingly.

The above is a common but insufficiently supported accusation against the natives, denied by many who are more than "moderately acquainted" with their character; although of course it is the natural tendency of a subservient race in its dealings with its masters, and possible tyrants. But granting for the nonce its truth, it would, in the case of the Matshana inquiry, tell heavily on the Bishop's side. Sir B. Pine was not present at the private investigation made by the Bishop, to which he alludes in the above sentence, and therefore can be no judge of the "cross-examination," which the four original witnesses underwent; and they, if they did "intuitively perceive" what answer was required, and "answer accordingly," must merely have spoken the truth; a truth which, at that early period of his investigations, the Bishop was *most reluctantly* receiving, and would gladly have had disproved.

The evidence before the court, however, was given under circumstances which, if Sir B. Pine's account of native witnesses be correct, adds enormously to the value of the fact that out of these twenty-four witnesses, summoned from various quarters, many of them without opportunity of communicating either with the Bishop or with each other, but one[3] failed when it came to the point; and he, a feeble old man, just released from prison (one of the captured tribe), was manifestly in a state of abject alarm at finding himself brought up to witness against the Government whose tender mercies he had so lately experienced, and contradicted before Colonel Colley the greater part of the story which he had originally told the Bishop. This poor creature had been intimidated and threatened by a certain man named Adam, under whose surveillance he lived after being re-

3. One of the original four.

leased from gaol, and who actually turned him and his family out at night as a punishment for his having obeyed a summons to Bishopstowe. He was manifestly ready to say anything which would relieve him from the fear of the gaol, which he pleaded to Mr. Shepstone a day or two later; on which occasion he unsaid all he had previously said, having, as he afterwards confessed, been warned by Mr. Shepstone's policeman Ratsha, who asked him for what purpose he had been summoned by the Bishop, *not to speak a word about* "Mr. John's" treatment of Matshana. But, with the best intentions, the man did not succeed in making his story tally entirely with that of Mr. Shepstone's other witnesses, nor with Mr. Shepstone's own.

With this one exception the Bishop's witnesses told the same story in all essential respects. They were men arriving from many different and distant parts of the colony, from Zululand, and from the Free State, who could not possibly have combined to tell the same story in all its details, which, if false, would have been torn to pieces when so many men of different ages and characters were cross-examined by one so thoroughly acquainted with all the real facts of the case as Mr. Shepstone—men who had nothing to expect from the Bishop, but had everything to dread from the Government if proved to have brought a false and foul charge against an officer so highly placed and so powerfully protected; *yet not the least impression was made upon the strength of their united evidence.*

The case, however, is very different when we turn to Mr. Shepstone's witnesses. Of these, nine in number (besides the four natives called by both the Bishop and Mr. Shepstone), seven were natives; the other two being the Secretary for Native Affairs and Mr. John Taylor a son of Mr. John Shepstone's first wife by her former husband. Mr. Taylor was a lad of nine at the time, but, having been present with his mother and little sister on the occasion of the attack upon Matshana, was summoned as a witness by Mr. Shepstone. His evidence was chiefly important as helping to prove that Matshana's party had not the concealed weapons which Mr. Shepstone's chief native witness Nozitshina said were left by them in immense numbers upon the ground; as he stated that he and his sister went over the ground, after the affair was over, and picked up the *assegais*, "about eight or nine" in number.

But it is important to remark that the very fact of the presence at this meeting of Mrs. Shepstone with her two children, goes far to disprove the account given by Mr. Shepstone in his second "statement," prepared by him on the occasion of this trial, but which is greatly at variance on some vital points with the narrative written by him on the day after the event, dated March 17th, 1858, for the information of His Excellency the Lieut. Governor. It seems almost incredible that Mr. John Shepstone should have, as he says in his second statement, "made up his mind to face almost certain" death, not only for himself and all his men, but for *his wife and her two young children*, on the grounds that it was "too late to withdraw at this stage" (same report), when at any time since the "day or two previous" (*ibid.*), when the information in question[4] reached him; according to his account he might have put off the meeting, or at all events have sent his wife and her children to a place of safety. The Secretary for Native Affairs's evidence could of course be of a merely official character, as he was not present on the occasion. He stated that Mr. John Shepstone's letters of February 16th and 24th, 1858, asked for by the Bishop, on the subject of the approaching interview with Matshana, could not be found, although they "must have been recently mislaid," as he himself (the Secretary for Native Affairs) had quoted from one of them in his minute for the Secretary of State in June, 1874. Of Mr. Shepstone's native witnesses it can only be said that, amongst the seven called by him only, six contradicted themselves and each other to so great an extent as to make their evidence of no value, while the evidence of the seventh was unimportant, and the four witnesses called by both Mr. Shepstone and the Bishop told the same story as did the witnesses of the latter, most unexpectedly to him.

---

4. Mr. Shepstone says in his second report that a day or two previous to the meeting with Matshana, he had received information to the effect that the chief's intentions were to put him and his people to death at the expected interview, and all the efforts made by Mr. Shepstone and his witnesses were to prove, first, the murderous intentions of Matshana; and, secondly, that nevertheless Mr. Shepstone had no counter-plans for violence, and did not fire upon the people.

Nevertheless Colonel Colley's judgment, although convicting Mr. John Shepstone of having enticed the chief Matshana to an interview with the 'intention of seizing him, was received and acted upon in Natal as an acquittal of that officer. So far was this the case, that, although Lord Carnarvon directed that the Bishop's costs should be placed upon the colonial estimates, the Legislative Council of the colony refused to pay them on the grounds that they were the costs of the losing party. In his report Colonel Colley gives his opinions as follows:

That Matyana was enticed to an interview, as stated by the Bishop, and was induced to come unarmed, under the belief that it was a friendly meeting, such as he had already had with Mr. Shepstone, for the purpose of discussing the accusations against him and the question of his return to his location.

That Matyana, though very suspicious and unwilling, came there in good faith; and that the accusations against him of meditating the assassination of Mr. Shepstone and his party, of a prearranged plan and signal for the purpose, and of carrying concealed arms to the meeting which are made in Mr. J. Shepstone's statements, are entirely without foundation.

That Mr. Shepstone at that time held no magisterial position, but was simply the commander of a small armed force charged with the execution of a warrant; and that the manner in which he proposed to effect the seizure, *viz.* at a supposed friendly meeting, was known to and sanctioned by, if not the Government, at least the immediate representative of the Government and Mr. Shepstone's superior, Dr. Kelly, the resident magistrate of the district.

That Mr. Shepstone did not attempt to shoot Matyana, as described by the Bishop, but fired into the air after the attempt to seize Matyana had failed, and in consequence of the attempt made almost simultaneously by some of Matyana's men to reach the huts and seize the arms of Mr. Shepstone's men.

The concealment of the gun, and the fact that a number of Matyana's men were killed in the pursuit, is not disputed by Mr. Shepstone.

I confess that I have had the greatest difficulty in forming my opinion on this latter point, and especially as to whether Mr. Shepstone fired into the air as he states. *The weight of direct evidence adduced at the inquiry lay altogether on the other side.*[5]

Colonel Colley then proceeds to give the considerations by which he has been influenced in coming to a conclusion directly opposed to the side on which, as he himself says, lay the weight of direct evidence. These considerations were threefold. The first is an opinion of his own, considerably at variance with most people's experience, namely, that a story handed down by oral tradition "crystallises into an accepted form," by which he explains away the fact that so many witnesses told the same story, and one which stood the test of cross-examination, without any important variations.

The second consideration was even more singular, namely, that allowance must be made on Mr. John Shepstone's side for the greater ability with which the Bishop conducted his case; and the third lay in the statement that "Mr. J. W. Shepstone is a man of known courage, and a noted sportsman and shot," and "was not likely to have missed" Matyana if he had fired at him; "and, if driven to fire into the crowd in self defence, it is more probable that he would have shot one of the men on the right."

The Bishop's opponents from the very first persistently put forward the notion that he had "brought a charge against Mr. J. W. Shepstone," and this was countenanced by the Government when they threw upon him the serious task of prosecuting before a Court of Enquiry, whereas in point of fact the real question at issue was not whether or no a certain shot was actually fired, but whether, on a certain occasion, a Government official had acted in a treacherous manner towards a native chief, thereby giving reason for the excuse of fear on the part of Langalibalele, treated as a false pretence by the court, some members of which were fully aware of the facts, and the prosecutor himself the official concerned. And, further, whether the said facts had been concealed by high Government officers, and denied by them repeatedly to their superiors in England.

---

5. Author's italics.

On the former questions Colonel Colley's report leaves no doubt, and Lord Carnarvon's comments upon it are of a very decided nature. After signifying his acceptance of the decision as a "sound and just conclusion," and complimenting Colonel Colley on the "able and conscientious manner in which" he "has acquitted himself of an arduous and delicate task," he continues:

> On the other hand, I must, even after the lapse of so many years, record my disapprobation of the artifices by which it is admitted Matyana was entrapped into the meeting with a view to his forcible arrest. Such underhand manoeuvres are opposed to the morality of a civilised administration; they lower English rule in the eyes of the natives; and they even defeat their own object, as is abundantly illustrated by the present case.

Mr. J. W. Shepstone, however, was a subordinate officer, and if his mode of executing the warrant was approved by the superior authorities in the colony, the blame which may attach to the transaction must be borne by them at least in equal proportion. The gist of Colonel Colley's decision is altogether condemnatory of Mr. J. Shepstone, some of whose statements, he says, "are entirely without foundation," and, by implication, also of his brother, the Secretary for Native Affairs; yet virtually, and in the eyes of the world, the decision was in their favour. To quote from The Natal Mercury of November 2nd, 1875:

> It is still understood that Mr. Shepstone, in the minds of impartial judges, stands more than exonerated from the Bishop's charges.

Mr. John Shepstone was retained in his responsible position, and received further promotion; and his brother was immediately appointed to the high office of Administrator of Government, and sent out with power to annex the Transvaal if he thought proper.

We have dwelt at some length upon the inquiry into the Matshana case; for, since the annexation of the Transvaal was one of the direct and immediate causes of the Zulu War, and since it seems improbable that any other man than Sir Theophilus

Shepstone could at the moment have been found equally able to undertake the task, it becomes a serious question to what extent an inquiry which had no practical effect whatsoever upon the position of men whose conduct had been stigmatised by the Secretary of State himself as "underhand manoeuvres, opposed to the morality of a civilised administration," may not be considered chargeable with the disastrous results. And, further, we must protest against the spirit of the last sentence of Lord Carnarvon's despatch on the subject, in which he expresses his "earnest hope that his (Colonel Colley's) report will be received by all parties to this controversy in the spirit which is to be desired, and be accepted as a final settlement of a dispute which cannot be prolonged without serious prejudice to public interests, and without a renewal of those resentments which, for the good of the community—English as well as native—had best be put to rest."

A dislocated joint must be replaced, or the limb cannot otherwise be pressed down into shape and "put to rest;" a thorn must be extracted, not skinned over and left in the flesh; and as, with the dislocation unreduced or the thorn unextracted, the human frame can never recover its healthful condition, so it is with the state with an unrighted wrong, an unexposed injustice.

The act of treason towards Matshana, hidden for many years, looked upon by its perpetrators as a matter past and gone, has tainted all our native policy since—unknown to most English people in Natal or at home—and has finally borne bitter fruit in the present unhappy condition of native affairs.

CHAPTER 8

The Annexation of the Transvaal

On the 5th of October, 1876, Sir Theophilus Shepstone, K.C.M.G., was appointed "to be a Special Commissioner to inquire respecting certain disturbances which have taken place in the territories adjoining the colony of Natal, and empowering him, in certain events, to exercise the power and jurisdiction of Her Majesty over such territories, or some of them."[1]

The commission stated:

> Whereas grievous disturbances have broken out in the territories adjacent to our colonies in South Africa, with war between the white inhabitants and the native races, to the great peril of the peace and safety of our said colonies . . . and, if the emergency should seem to you to be such as to render it necessary, in order to secure the peace and safety of our said colonies and of our subjects elsewhere, that the said territories, or any portion or portions of the same, should provisionally, and pending the announcement of our pleasure, be administered in our name and on our behalf; then, and in such case only, we do further authorise you, the said Sir Theophilus Shepstone, by proclamation under your hand, to declare that, from and after a day to be therein named, so much of any such territories as aforesaid, as to you after due consideration, shall seem fit, shall be annexed to and form part of our dominions. . . . Provided, first, that no such proclamation shall be issued by you with respect to any dis-

---

1. P. P. (C. 1776) p. 1.

trict, territory, or state unless you shall be satisfied that the inhabitants thereof, or a sufficient number of them, or the Legislature thereof, desire to become our subjects, nor if any conditions unduly limiting our power and authority therein are sought to be imposed.

Such was the tenor of the commission which, unknown to the world at large, Sir Theophilus Shepstone brought with him when he returned to Natal in November, 1876. The sudden annexation which followed was a stroke which took all by surprise except the few already in the secret; many declaring to the last that such an action on the part of the English Government was impossible—because, they thought, unjust. It is true that the Republic had for long been going from bad to worse in the management of its own affairs; its Government had no longer the power to enforce laws or to collect taxes; and the country was generally believed to be fast approaching a condition of absolute anarchy. Nevertheless it was thought by some that, except by the request of those concerned, we had no right to intrude our authority for the better control of Transvaal affairs so long as their bad management did not affect us.

On one point, however, we undoubtedly had a right to interfere, as the stronger, the juster, and more merciful nation—namely, the attitude of the Transvaal Boers towards, and their treatment of, the native tribes who were their neighbours, or who came under their control. On behalf of the latter unfortunates (Transvaal subjects), we did not even profess to interfere; but one of the chief causes alleged by us for our taking possession of the country was a long and desultory war which was taking place between the Boers and Sikukuni, the chief of the Bapedi tribe living upon their northern borders, and in the course of which the Boers were behaving towards the unhappy natives with a treachery, and, when they fell into their power, with a brutality unsurpassed by any historical records. The sickening accounts of cruelties inflicted upon helpless men, women, and children by the Boers, which are to be found on official record in the pages of the *Blue Book*, should be ample justification in the eyes of a civilised world for English interference, and forcible protection

91

of the sufferers; and it is rather with the manner in which the annexation was carried out, and the policy which followed it, than with the intervention of English power in itself, that an objection can be raised.

The war between the Boers and the Bapedi arose out of similar encroachments on the part of the former, which led, as we shall presently show, to their border disputes with the Zulus. Boer farmers had gradually deprived of their land the native possessors of the soil by a simple process peculiarly their own. They first rented land from the chiefs for grazing purposes, then built upon it, still paying a tax or tribute to the chief; finally, having well established themselves, they professed to have purchased the land for the sum already paid as rent, announced themselves the owners of it, and were shortly themselves levying taxes on the very men whom they had dispossessed. In this manner Sikukuni was declared by the Boers to have ceded to them the whole of his territory—that is to say, hundreds of square miles, for the paltry price of a hundred head of cattle.

An officer of the English Government, indeed (His Excellency's Commissioner at Lydenburg, Captain Clarke, R.A.), was of opinion[2] that, "had only the Boer element in the Lydenburg district been consulted, it is doubtful if there would have been war with Sikukuni," as the Boers, he said, might have continued to pay taxes to the native chiefs. And the officer in question appears to censure the people who were "willing to submit to such humiliating conditions, and ambitious of the position of prime adviser to a native chief." It is difficult to understand why there should be anything humiliating in paying rent for land, whether to white or black owners, and the position of prime adviser to a powerful native chief might be made a very honourable and useful one in the hands of a wise and Christian man. Captain Clarke continues thus:

> It was the foreign element under the late President which forced matters to a crisis. Since the annexation the farmers have, with few exceptions, ceased to pay tribute to the Chiefs; their relations with the natives are otherwise unchanged.

2. C. 2316, p. 29

Culture and contact with civilisation will doubtless have the effect of re-establishing the self-respect of these people, and teaching them the obligation and benefits imposed and conferred on them by their new position.

That is to say, apparently, teaching them that it is beneath their dignity to pay taxes to native landowners, but an "obligation imposed" upon them to rob the latter altogether of their land, the future possession of which is one of the "benefits conferred on them by their new position" (i.e. as subjects of the British Crown). In the same despatch Captain Clarke says:

> The Bapedi branch of the Basuto family, essentially agricultural and peaceful in its habits and tastes, even now irrigate the land, and would, if possible, cultivate in excess of their food requirements. The friendly natives assure me that their great wish is to live peacefully on their lands, and provide themselves with ploughs, wagons, etc. The experience of the Berlin missionaries confirms this view. Relieved of their present anomalous position, into which they have been forced by the ambition of their rulers,[3] and distrust of the Boers, encouraged to follow their natural bent, the Basutos would become a peaceful agricultural people, capable of a certain civilisation.

How well founded was this "distrust of the Boers," may be gathered from the accounts given in the *Blue Book* already mentioned.

The objects of the Boers in their attacks upon their native neighbours appear to have been twofold the acquisition of territory, and that of children to be brought up as slaves.

The Cape Argus of December 12th, 1876, remarks:

> Through the whole course of this Republic's existence, it has acted in contravention of the Sand River Treaty;[4] and that slavery has occurred not only here and there in isolated cases, but as an unbroken practice, has been one of the peculiar institutions of the country, mixed up with all its

---

3. Rather by the determination of their rulers to preserve their land from Boer encroachments.

social and political life. It has been at the root of most of its wars. . . . The Boers have not only fallen upon unsuspecting *kraals* simply for the purpose of obtaining the women and children and cattle, but they have carried on a traffic through natives, who have kidnapped the children of their weaker neighbours, and sold them to the white man. Again, the Boers have sold and exchanged their victims amongst themselves. Wagon-loads of slaves have been conveyed from one end of the country to the other for sale, and that with the cognizance and for the direct advantage of the highest officials of the land. The writer has himself seen in a town situated in the south of the Republic the children who had been brought down from a remote northern district. . . . The circumstances connected with some of these kidnapping excursions are appalling, and the barbarities practised by cruel masters upon some of these defenceless creatures during the course of their servitude are scarcely less horrible than those reported from Turkey, although they are spread over a course of years instead of being compressed within a few weeks.

This passage is taken from a letter to The Argus (enclosed in a despatch from Sir Henry Barkly to the Earl of Carnarvon, December 13th, 1876), which, with other accompanying letters from the same source, gives an account of Boer atrocities too horrible for repetition. A single instance may be mentioned which, however shocking, is less appalling than others, but per-

---

4. (see facing page) *Sand River Treaty*—"Evidence was adduced that the Transvaal Boers, who, by the Sand River Convention, and in consideration of the independence which that convention assured to them, had solemnly pledged themselves to this country (England) not to reintroduce slavery into their Republic, had been in the habit of capturing, buying, selling, and holding in forced servitude, African children, called by the cant name of *black ivory*, murdering the fathers, and driving off the mothers; that this slave trade was carried on with the sanction of the subordinate Transvaal authorities, and that the President did actually imprison and threaten to ruin by State prosecution a fellow-countryman who brought it to the notice of the English authority—an authority which, if it had not the power to prevent, had at any rate a treaty right to denounce it. This and more was done, sometimes in a barbarous way, under an assumed divine authority to exterminate those who resisted them. So much was established by Dutch and German evidence. But it was supplemented and carried farther by the evidence of natives as to their own sufferings, and of English officers as to that general notoriety which used to be called *publica fama*." From an article by Lord Blachford in *The Nineteenth Century Review*, August 1879, p. 265.

haps shows more plainly than anything else could do what the natives knew the life of a slave in the Transvaal would be. The information is given by a Boer, he says:

> In 1864, the Swazis accompanied the Boers against Males[5] The Boers did nothing but stand by and witness the fearful massacre. The men and women were also murdered. One poor woman sat clutching her baby of eight days old. The Swazis stabbed her through the body; and when she found that she could not live, she wrung her baby's neck with her own hands, to save it from future misery. On the return of that commando the children who became too weary to continue the journey were killed on the road. The survivors were sold as slaves to the farmers.

Out of this state of things eventually proceeded the war between the Boers and Sikukuni, the result of which was a very ambiguous one indeed; for although Sikukuni was driven out of the low-lying districts of the country, he took refuge in his stronghold, which affords such an impregnable position in a thickly-populated range of mountains as hitherto to have defied all attempts, whether made by Boers or by English, to reduce it.[6]

Another important reason alleged at the time for taking possession of the Transvaal was that the border troubles between it and Zululand were becoming more serious every day; that, sooner or later, unless we interposed our authority, a war would break out between the Boers and the Zulus, into which we should inevitably be drawn. The Zulus, having continually entreated our protection, while at our desire they refrained from defending themselves by force of arms, were naturally rejoiced at an action on our part which looked like an answer to their oft-repeated prayer, and eagerly expected the reward of their long and patient waiting.

But, however strongly we may feel that it was the duty of the more powerful nation to put a stop to the doings of the Transvaal Boers, even at considerable expense to ourselves, the

---

5. A native chief.
6. Written in October, 1879.

manner in which we have acted, and the consequences which followed, have been such as to cause many sensible people to feel that we should have done better to withdraw our prohibition from Cetshwayo, and allow him and the Boers "to fight it out between them."[7]

We might have honestly and openly interfered and insisted upon putting a stop to the atrocities of the Boers, annexing their country if necessary to that end, but then we ourselves should have done justice to the natives on whose behalf we professed to interfere, instead of taking over with the country and carrying on those very quarrels and aggressions which we alleged as a sufficient reason for the annexation.

When Sir Theophilus Shepstone went up to Pretoria it was, ostensibly, merely to advise the President and Volksraad of the Transvaal Republic as to the best means of extricating themselves and the country from the difficulties into which they were plunged, and with the expressed intention of endeavouring to produce a peaceful settlement with Sikukuni, which should pro-

---

7. Lord Blachford says in the article already quoted from: "The citizens of these Republics have gone out from among us into a hostile wilderness, because they could not endure a humanitarianism which not only runs counter to their habits and interest, but blasphemes that combination of gain with godliness which is part of their religion. While that humanitarianism forms a leading principle of our government they will not submit to it. Why should we bribe or force them to do so? It is no doubt right and wise to remain, if possible, on good terms with them. It is wise and generous to save them, if possible, in their day of calamity as, with our own opposite policy, we have been able to save them—by a wave of the hand—twice from the Basutos, and once from the Zulus. (Once for all rather, through the course of many years, during which we have restrained the Zulus from asserting their own rights to the disputed territory, by promises that we would see justice done. Author.) But it is neither wise nor necessary to embroil ourselves in their quarrels until they call for help, until they have had occasion to feel the evil effects of their own methods, and the measure of their weakness, and are ready, not in whispers or innuendos and confidential corners, but outspokenly in public meetings, or through their constituted authorities, to accept with gratitude our intervention on our own terms, until they are, if they ever can be, thus taught by adversity. I do not myself believe that we could enter into any political union with them except at the sacrifice of that character for justice to which, I persist in saying, we owe so much of our power and security in South Africa. Nor so long as we observe the rules of justice to them shall we do any good by disguising our substantial differences, or refraining from indignant remonstrances against proceedings which are not only repugnant to humanity, but violate their engagements with us and endanger our security."

tect him and his people for the future from the tyranny of the Boers. Up to the last the notion that there was any intention of forcibly annexing the country was indignantly repudiated by the members of the expedition, although their chief meanwhile was in possession of his commission as Administrator of the British Government in the Transvaal. There were some who suspected that there was more in the movement than was confessed to by those concerned. It was argued that, were Sir Theophilus Shepstone's visit of a purely friendly nature, no armed force would have been sent to escort him, as he was going, not into a savage country, but into one which, at all events, professed to have a civilised government and an educated class. The unsettled state of feeling amongst the Boers was pleaded in answer to this argument, but was commonly met by the suggestion that if, under the circumstances, the armed force of mounted police which accompanied the important visitor might be looked upon as a justifiable precaution, yet the possible danger to strangers from the violence of a few lawless men in a country in which the government was not strong enough to keep them in check, was not great enough to account for the fact that a regiment of British infantry was hastily moved up to Newcastle, from whence they could speedily be summoned into the Transvaal. The presence of a Zulu army upon the other border, where it lay quiet and inoffensive for weeks during Sir Theophilus Shepstone's proceedings in the Transvaal, was naturally looked upon as a suspicious circumstance. There can be little doubt that—whether or no Cetshwayo obeyed a hint from his old friend the Secretary for Native Affairs, and sent his army to support him, and to overawe the Boers by a warlike demonstration—the Zulus were present in a spirit, however inimical to the Boers, entirely friendly to the English. The mere fact that the army lay there so long in harmless repose, and dispersed promptly and quietly immediately upon receiving orders to do so from Sir Theophilus Shepstone, proves that, at all events, they and their king thought that they were carrying out his wishes. The feeling expressed at the time by a British officer,[8] in speaking of this Zulu army, and

8. Colonel Durnford, R.E., who paid a flying visit to Pretoria at the time.

recommending that it should be dispersed, that "it were better the little band of Englishmen (including, of course, himself) should fall by the hand of the Boers than that aught should be done by the former to bring about a war of races" can hardly have been shared by Sir Theophilus Shepstone himself, or the message to the Zulu king to withdraw his army would have been despatched some weeks earlier.

In face of these facts it strikes one as strange that the temporary presence of this Zulu army on the Transvaal borders, manifestly in our support (whether by request or not), and which retired without giving the least offence, or even committing such acts of theft or violence as might be expected as necessary evils in the neighbourhood of a large European garrison, should have been regarded, later, as a sign of Cetshwayo's inimical feeling towards *the English*.[9]

Mr. Pretorius, member of the Dutch executive council, and other influential Transvaalers, assert that Sir T. Shepstone threatened to let loose the Zulus upon them, in order to reduce them to submission; but the accusation is denied on behalf of the Administrator of the Transvaal. And Mr. Fynney (in the report of his mission to Cetshwayo from Sir T. Shepstone, upon the annexation of the Transvaal, dated July 4, 1877) gives the king's words to him, as follows:

> I am pleased that Somtseu (Sir Theophilus Shepstone) has sent you to let me know that the land of the Transvaal Boers has now become part of the lands of the Queen of England. I began to wonder why he did not tell me something of what he was doing. I received one message from him, sent by Unkabano, from Newcastle, and I heard the Boers were not treating him properly, and that they intended to put him into a corner. If they had done so, I should not have wanted for anything more. Had one shot been fired, I should have said, 'What more do I wait for? they have touched my father.'

9. Mr. John Dunn is said to have stated to the Special Correspondent of *The Cape Argus*, and to have since reaffirmed his statement, that Sir T. Shepstone "sent word to Cetshwayo that he was being hemmed in, and the king was to hold himself in readiness to come to his assistance." This assertion has also been denied by Sir T. Shepstone's supporters.

But all doubt upon the subject of Sir T. Shepstone's intention was quickly and suddenly set at rest the silken glove of friendly counsel and disinterested advice was thrown aside, and the mailed hand beneath it seized the reins of government from the slackened fingers of the President of the Transvaal. On the 22nd January, 1877, Sir Theophilus Shepstone entered Pretoria, the capital of the country, where he was received with all kindness and attention by the president, Mr. Burgers, and other important men, to whom he spoke of his mission in general terms, as one the object of which was "to confer with the Government and people of the Transvaal, with the object of initiating a new state of things which would guarantee security for the future."[10]

On April 9th, 1879, Sir T. Shepstone informed President Burgers that "the extension over the Transvaal of Her Majesty's authority and rule" was imminent.

The following protest was officially read and handed in to Sir T. Shepstone on the 11th April:

> Whereas I, Thomas François Burgers, State President of the South African Republic, have received a despatch, dated the 9th instant, from Her British Majesty's Special Commissioner, Sir Theophilus Shepstone, informing me that his Excellency has resolved, in the name of Her Majesty's Government, to bring the South African Republic, by annexation, under the authority of the British Crown:
>
> And whereas I have not the power to draw the sword with good success for the defence of the independence of the State against a superior power like that of England, and in consideration of the welfare of the whole of South Africa, moreover, feel totally disinclined to involve its white inhabitants in a disastrous war, without having employed beforehand all means to secure the rights of the people in a peaceable way:
>
> So, I, in the name and by the authority of the Government and the people of the South African Republic, do hereby solemnly protest against the intended annexation.

---

10. P. P. (C. 1776) p. 88.

Given under my hand and under the Seal of the State at the Government Office at Pretoria, on this the 11th day of April, in the year 1877.

Thomas Burgers
State President

A strong protest was handed in on the same date by the Executive Council, in which it was stated "the people, by memorials or otherwise, have, by a large majority, plainly stated that they are averse to it" (annexation). On April 17th, 1877, Sir T. Shepstone writes to Lord Carnarvon:

> On Thursday last, the 12th instant, I found myself in a position to issue the proclamations necessary for annexing[11] the South African Republic, commonly known as the Transvaal, to Her Majesty's dominions, and for assuming the administration thereof.[12]

His intentions had been so carefully concealed, the proclamation took the people so completely by surprise; that it was received in what might be called a dead silence, which silence was taken to be of that nature which "gives consent."

It has been amply shown since that the real feeling of the country was exceedingly averse to English interference with its liberties, and that the congratulatory addresses presented, and demonstrations made in favour of what had been done, were but expressions of feeling from the foreign element in the Transvaal, and got up by a few people personally interested on the side of English authority. But at the time they were made to appear as genuine expressions of Boer opinions favourable to the annexation, which was looked upon as a masterstroke of policy and a singular success.

It was some time before the Transvaalers recovered from the stunning effects of the blow by which they had been deprived of their liberties, and meanwhile the new Government made rapid advances, and vigorous attempts at winning popularity amongst

---

11. It may be interesting to compare the above with the wording of Sir T. Shepstone's "Commission". —P. P. (C. 1776) p. 111.
12. P. P. (C. 1776) pp. 152-56.

the people. Sir T. Shepstone hastened to fill up every office under him with his own men, although there were great flourishes of trumpets concerning preserving the rights of the people to the greatest extent possible, and keeping the original men in office wherever practicable. The first stroke by which popularity was aimed at was that of remitting the war taxes levied upon the white population (though unpaid) to meet the expenses of the war with Sikukuni. It became apparent at this point what an empty sham was our proposed protection of Sikukuni, and how little the oppression under which he and his people suffered had really called forth our interference. Sir T. Shepstone, while remitting, as stated, the tax upon the Boers, insisted upon the payment in full of the fine in cattle levied by them upon Sikukuni's people. So sternly did he carry out the very oppressions which he came to put an end to, that a portion of the cattle paid towards the fine (two thousand head, a large number, in the reduced and impoverished state of the people) were sent back, by his orders, on the grounds that they were too small and in poor condition, with the accompanying message that better ones must be sent in their place.

A commission (composed of Captain Clarke, R.A., and Mr. Osborne) was sent, before the annexation, by Sir T. Shepstone, to inquire into a treaty pressed by the Boers upon Sikukuni, and rejected by him, as it contained a condition by which he was to pay taxes, and thereby come under the Transvaal Government.[13] To these gentlemen "Sikukuni stated that the English were great and he was little,[14] that he wanted them to save him from the Boers, who hunted him to and fro, and shot his people down like wild game. He had lost two thousand men" (this included those who submitted to the Boers) "by the war, ten brothers, and four sons. . . . He could not trust the Boers as they were always deceiving him." After saying that "he wished to be like Moshesh" (a British subject), and be "happy and at peace," he

13. The chief repeatedly refused to sign any paper presented to him by the Boers, on the grounds that he could not tell what it might contain, beyond the points explained to him, to which he might afterwards be said to have agreed; showing plainly to what the natives were accustomed in their dealings with the Transvaal.
14. C. 1776, p. 147.

"asked whether he ought to pay the two thousand head of cattle, seeing that the war was not of his making."

"To this we replied," say the Commissioners, "that it was the custom of us English, when we made an engagement, to fulfil it, cost what it might; that our word was our word."

Small wonder if the oppressed and persecuted people and their chief at last resented such treatment, or that some of them should have shown that resentment in a manner decided enough to call for military proceedings on the part of the new Government of the Transvaal. In point of fact, however, it was not Sikukuni, but his sister—a chieftainess herself—whose people, by a quarrel with and raid upon natives living under our protection, brought on the second or English "Sikukuni war."

Turning to the other chief pretext for the annexation of the Transvaal, the disturbed condition of the Zulu border, we find precisely the same policy carried out. When it was first announced that the English had taken possession of the country of their enemies, the Zulus, figuratively speaking, threw up their caps, and rejoiced greatly. They thought that now at last, after years of patient waiting, and painful repression of angry feelings at the desire of the Natal Government, they were to receive their reward in a just acknowledgment of the claims which Sir T. Shepstone had so long supported, and which he was now in a position to confirm.

But the quiet submission of the Boers would not have lasted, even upon the surface, had their new Governor shown the slightest sign of leaning to the Zulu side on the bitter boundary question; and as Sir T. Shepstone fancied that the power of his word was great enough with the Zulus to make them submit, however unwillingly, there was small chance of their receiving a rood of land at his hands. He had lost sight of, or never comprehended the fact, that that power was built upon the strong belief which existed in the minds of the Zulu king and people with regard to the justice and honesty of the English Government. This feeling is amply illustrated by the messages from the Zulu king, quoted in our chapter upon the Disputed Territory, and elsewhere in this volume, and need therefore only be alluded to here.

But this belief, so far as Sir T. Shepstone is concerned, was destroyed when the Zulus found that, far from acting according to his often-repeated words, their quondam friend had turned against them, and espoused the cause of their enemies, whom, at his desire, they had refrained these many years from attacking, when they could have done so without coming into collision with the English.

The Zulus, indeed, still believed in the English, and in the Natal Government; but they considered that Sir T. Shepstone, in undertaking the government of the Boers, had become a Boer himself, or, as Cetshwayo himself said, his old friend and father's back, which had carried him so long, had become too rough for him—if he could carry him no longer he would get down, and go to a man his equal in Pietermaritzburg (meaning Sir Henry Bulwer, Lieut.-Governor of Natal), who would be willing and able to take him up.

It is a curious fact, and one worthy of note, that Sir T. Shepstone, who for so many years had held and expressed an opinion favourable to the Zulus on this most important boundary question, should yet have studied it so little that, when he had been for six months Administrator of the Transvaal, with all evidence, written or oral, official or otherwise, at his command, he could say, speaking of a conversation which he held with some Dutch farmers at Utrecht:[15]

I then learned for the first time, what has since been proved by evidence the most incontrovertible, overwhelming, and clear, that this boundary line[16] had been formally and mutually agreed upon, and had been formally ratified by the giving and receiving of tokens of thanks, and that the beacons had been built up in the presence of the President and members of the Executive Council of the Republic, in presence of Commissioners from both Panda and Cetshwayo, and that the spot on which every beacon was to stand was indicated by the Zulu Commissioners themselves placing the first stones on it. I shall shortly transmit to your Lordship[17] the further evidence on the subject that has been furnished to me.

This "further evidence," if forwarded, does not appear in

---

15. Parl. p. (2079, p. 51-4).
16. That claimed by the Boers.
17. The Secretary of State for the Colonies.

the *Blue Books*. It is plain that the Border Commissioners of 1878 found both the "evidence the most incontrovertible, overwhelming, and clear," and the "further evidence" promised, utterly worthless for the purpose of proving the case of the Boers; but, even had it been otherwise, Sir T. Shepstone's confession of ignorance up to so late a date on this most vital question is singularly self-condemnatory. He says:[18]

> When I approached the question I did so supposing that the rights of the Transvaal to land on the Zulu border had very slender foundation. I believed, from the representations which had been systematically made by the Zulus to the Natal Government on the subject, of which I was fully aware from the position I held in Natal, that the beacons along the boundary line had been erected by the Republican Government, in opposition to the wishes, and in spite of the protests, of the Zulu authorities.[19]
>
> I, therefore, made no claims or demand whatever for land. I invited Cetshwayo to give me his views regarding a boundary, when I informed him from Pretoria that I should visit Utrecht on the tour I then contemplated making. When I met the Zulu prime minister and the *indunas* on the 18th October last[20] on the Blood River, I was fully prepared, if it should be insisted on by the Zulus, as I then thought it might justly be, to give up a tract of country which had from thirteen to sixteen years been occupied by Transvaal farmers, and to whose farms title-deeds had been issued by the late Government; and I contemplated making compensation to those farmers in some way or another for their loss. I intended, however, first to offer to purchase at a fair price from the Zulu king all his claims to land which had for so many years been occupied and built upon by the subjects of the Transvaal, to whom the Government of the country was distinctly liable.[21]

18. P. P. (2079, pp. 51-54).

19. The conclusion arrived at, after a careful consideration of all producible evidence, by the Rorke's Drift Commission, in 1878.

20. Six weeks before he discovered, in conversation with some Boers, the "evidence incontrovertible, overwhelming, and clear."

21. A liability transferred to the Zulu king by Sir Bartle Frere in his correspondence with the Bishop of Natal.

Sir T. Shepstone, when he met the Zulu *indunas* at the Blood River, was prepared to abandon the line of 1861 (claimed by the Boers), for that of the Blood River and the Old Hunting Road ("if it should be insisted on by the Zulus," as he "then thought it might justly be "), which, in point of fact, would have satisfied neither party; but he does not say by what right he proposed to stop short of the old line of 1856-7 *viz.* the Blood River and insist upon the "Old Hunting Road." If the half-concession were just, so was the whole—or neither.

To these half-measures, however, the Zulus would not submit, and the conference failed of its object. Sir T. Shepstone says:

> Fortunately, therefore, for the interests of the Transvaal, I was prevented by the conduct of the Zulus themselves from surrendering to them at that meeting what my information on the subject then had led me to think was after all due to them, and this I was prepared to do at any sacrifice to the Transvaal, seeing, as it then appeared to me, that justice to the Zulus demanded it.

In spite, however, of the concession to the Boers, made in Sir T. Shepstone's altered opinion on the border question, they were by no means reconciled to the loss of their independence, although Captain Clarke says[22] in speaking of the Boers in Lydenburg district, "they, in the majority of cases, would forget fancied wrongs if they thought they had security for their lives and property, education for their children, and good roads for the transport of their produce."[23]

The following "agreement signed by a large number of farmers at the meeting held at Wonderfontein," and translated from a Dutch newspaper, the *Zuid Afrikaan*, published at Cape Town on the 15th February,[24] gives a different impression of the state of feeling amongst the Boers:

> In the presence of Almighty God, the Searcher of all hearts, and prayerfully waiting on His gracious help and pity, we,

---

22. C. 2316, p. 28.
23. That is to say, that they may be bribed by substantial benefits to acquiesce in the loss of their liberties.
24. C. 2316, p. 1.

burghers of the South African Republic, have solemnly agreed, and we do hereby agree, to make a holy covenant for us, and for our children, which we confirm with a solemn oath.

Fully forty years ago our fathers fled from the Cape Colony in order to become a free and independent people. Those forty years were forty years of pain and suffering.

We established Natal, the Orange Free State, and the South African Republic, and three times the English Government has trampled our liberty and dragged to the ground our flag, which our fathers had baptised with their blood and tears.

As by a thief in the night has our Republic been stolen from us. We may nor can endure this. It is God's will, and is required of us by the unity of our fathers, and by love to our children, that we should hand over intact to our children the legacy of the fathers. For that purpose it is that we here come together and give each other the right hand as men and brethren, solemnly promising to remain faithful to our country and our people, and with our eye fixed on God, to co-operate until death for the restoration of the freedom of our Republic.

So help us Almighty God.

These pious words, side by side with the horrible accounts of the use made by the Boers of their liberty while they had it, strike one as incredibly profane; yet they are hardly more so than part of the speech made by Sir T. Shepstone to the burghers of the Transvaal on the occasion of the annexation. He asks them:

Do you know what has recently happened in Turkey? Because no civilised government was carried on there, the Great Powers interfered and said, 'Thus far and no farther.' And if this is done to Empire, will a little Republic be excused when it misbehaves? Complain to other powers and seek justice there? Yes, thank God! justice is still to be found even for the most insignificant, but it is precisely this justice which will convict us. If we want justice we must be in a position to ask it with unsullied hands.[25]

---

25. Was it by inadvertence that Sir T. Shepstone speaks of "us" and "we," thus producing a sentence so strangely and unhappily applicable?

Our first quotation was from the words of ignorant Boers, our second from those of a man South African born and bred, South African in character and education. But perhaps both are surpassed by words lately written by an English statesman of rank. Let us turn to a "minute" of Sir Bartle Frere's, forwarded on November 16th, 1878[26], and see what he says in defence of Boer conquests and encroachments.

The Boers had force of their own, and every right of conquest; *but they had also what they seriously believed to be a higher title, in the old commands they found in parts of their Bible to exterminate the Gentiles, and take their land in possession.*[27] We may freely admit that they misinterpreted the text, and were utterly mistaken in its application. But *they had at least a sincere belief in the Divine authority for what they did, and therefore a far higher title than the Zulus could claim for all they acquired.*[27/28]

If the worship of the Boers for their sanguinary deity is to be pleaded in their behalf, where shall we pause in finding excuses for any action committed by insane humanity in the name of their many gods? But the passage hardly needs our comments, and we leave it to the consideration of the Christian world.

A paragraph from The Daily News of this day, November 8th, 1879, will suitably close our chapter on the Transvaal. It is headed "Serious Disturbance in the Transvaal," and gives a picture of the disposition of the Boers, and of the control we have obtained over them.

Pretoria, October 13th

A somewhat serious disturbance has occurred at Middleberg. A case came in due course before the local court, relating to a matter which took place last July. A Boer, by name Jacobs, had tied up one of his Kaffir servants by his wrists to a beam, so that his feet could not touch the ground. The man was too ill after it to move for some days. The case against the Boer came on on October 8th. A large number of Boers attended *from sympathy with the defendant*[28] and anx-

26. 2222, p. 45.
27. Italics not Sir B. Frere's.
28. P. P. (0. 2222) p. 45.
28. Author's italics throughout.

ious to *resist any interference between themselves and their Kaffirs.* The Landrost took the opportunity to read out Sir Garnet's proclamation, declaring the permanency of the annexation of the Transvaal. The attitude of the Boers appeared to be so threatening that after a time the Landrost *thought it better to adjourn the hearing for a couple of hours.*

On the court's reassembling, he was informed that five-and-twenty Boers had visited two of the stores in the town, and had seized gunpowder there, gunpowder being a forbidden article of sale. The following day a much larger attendance of Boers made their appearance at the court. Seventy of them held a meeting, at which they bound themselves to protect those who had seized the gunpowder, and their attitude was so threatening that the Landrost, on the application of the public prosecutor, *adjourned the case sine die.* A fresh case of powder seizing was reported on the same day. Colonel Lanyon has already gone to the scene of disturbance, which will be dealt with purely, *at all events at present,* as a civil case of violence exercised against the owners of the stores. At the same time a troop of dragoons will be there about the day after tomorrow, and a company of infantry in a few days more, while a considerable number of the 90th Regiment will in a short time be, in regular course, passing that way. The spark will therefore no doubt be stamped out quickly where it has been lighted. The only danger is in the tendency to explosion which it perhaps indicates in other directions.

CHAPTER 9

The Disputed Territory

We must now look back and gather up the threads hitherto interwoven with accounts of other matters connected with what has been rightly called the "burning question" of the disputed territory, which led eventually to the Zulu War.

The disputes between the Boers and Zulus concerning the boundary line of their respective countries had existed for many years, its origin and growth being entirely attributable to the well-known and usually successful process by which the Dutch Boers, as we have already said, have gradually possessed themselves of the land belonging to their unlettered neighbours. This process is described by Mr. Osborn, formerly resident magistrate of Newcastle, now Colonial Secretary of the Transvaal Government, September 22nd, 1876[1].

> I would point out here that this war (with Sikukuni) arose solely out of dispute about land. The Boers as they have done in other cases, and are still doing encroached by degrees upon native territory; commencing by obtaining permission to graze stock upon portions of it at certain seasons of the year, followed by individual graziers obtaining from native headmen a sort of license to squat upon certain defined portions, ostensibly in order to keep other Boer squatters away from the same land. These licenses, temporarily extended, as friendly or neighbourly acts, by unauthorised headmen, after a few seasons of occupation by the Boer, are construed by him as title,

---

1. 1748, p. 196.

and his permanent occupation ensues. Damage for trespass is levied by him upon the very men from whom he obtained right to squat, to which the natives submit out of fear of the matter reaching the ears of the paramount Chief, who would in all probability severely punish them for opening the door of encroachment to the Boer. After awhile, however, the matter comes to a crisis, in consequence of the incessant disputes between the Boers and the natives; one or other of the disputants lays the case before the paramount Chief, who, upon hearing both parties, is literally frightened with violence and threats by the Boer into granting him the land. Upon this, the usual plan followed by the Boer is at once to collect a few neighbouring Boers, including an Acting Field Cornet, or even an Acting Provisional Field Cornet, appointed by the Field Cornet or Provisional Cornet, the latter to represent the Government, although without instructions authorising him to act in the matter. A few cattle are collected among themselves, which the party takes to the Chief, and his signature is obtained to a written instrument, alienating to the Republican Boers a large slice of, or all, his territory. The contents of this document are, so far as I can make out, never clearly or intelligibly explained to the Chief, who signs it and accepts of the cattle, under the impression that it is all in settlement of hire for the grazing licenses granted by his headmen.

This, I have no hesitation in saying, is the usual method by which the Boers obtain what they call cessions of territories to them by native Chiefs. In Sikukuni's case, they say that his father, Sikwata, ceded to them the whole of his territory (hundreds of square miles) for one hundred head of cattle.

Also Sir H. Barkly, late Governor of the Cape, writes as follows, October 2nd, 1876:[2]

The following graphic description of this process (of Boer encroachment) is extracted from a letter in the *Transvaal Advocate* of a few weeks ago:

Frontiers are laid down, the claim to which is very doubtful. These frontiers are not occupied, but farms

2. 1748, p. 140.

are inspected (*guessed at* would be nearer the mark), title-deeds for the same are issued, and, when the unlucky purchaser wishes to take possession, he finds his farm (if he can find it) occupied by tribes of Kafirs, over whom the Government has never attempted to exercise any jurisdiction. Their Chief is rather bewildered at first to find out that he has for years been a subject of the Transvaal. The Chief in question is one Lechune, living on the north-west of the Republic. But the account is equally applicable to the case of Sikukuni, or Umswazi, or half-a-dozen others, the entire circuit of the Republic, from the Barolongs and Batlapins on the west, to the Zulus on the east, being bordered by a series of encroachments disputed by the natives.

A memorandum from Captain Clarke, R.A., Special Commissioner at Lydenburg, dated April 23rd, 1879[3], also gives an account of the way in which the Boers took possession of the Transvaal itself, highly illustrative of their usual practice, and of which the greater part may be quoted here, with a key to the real meaning of phrases which require some study to interpret.

On the entrance of the Fou Trekkers into the Transvaal, they were compelled against their hereditary instincts to combine for self-defence against a common foe. (That is to say, that, having forced themselves into a strange country, they necessarily combined to oust those they found there.)[4] External pressure was removed by success, and the diffusive instinct asserted itself—(which being translated into ordinary English simply signifies that, having conquered certain native tribes, they settled themselves upon their lands, and returned to their natural disunited condition.) Isolated families, whose ambition was to be out of sight of their neighbours' smoke, pushed forward into Kafir-land (as yet unconquered). Boundaries were laid down either arbitrarily or by unsatisfactorily recorded treaty with savage neighbours. The natives, forced back, acquired the powers of coalition lost by the Boers, and in their

---

3. C. 2367, p. 152.
4. Bracketed comments are the author's.

turn brought pressure to bear on their invaders and whilom conquerors; farm after farm had to be abandoned, and many of the Boers who remained acknowledged by paying tribute that they retained their lands by the permission of neighbouring chiefs. The full importance of this retrograde movement was not at once felt, as a natural safety-valve was found.

A considerable portion of the east of the Transvaal is called the High Veldt, and consists of tableland at a considerable elevation, overlying coal-measures; this district appears bleak and inhospitable, overrun by large herds of game and watered by a series of apparently stagnant ponds which take the place of watercourses. . . . From various sources, within the last six years, it has been discovered that the High Veldt is most valuable for the grazing of sheep, horses, and cattle; and farms which possess the advantage of water are worth from £1,000 to £1,200, where formerly they could have been bought for as many pence.

This discovery has opened a door of escape for many of the *native-pressed borderers. The pressure* on those that remain increases, and on the north-east and west of the Transvaal is a fringe of farmers who live by the sufferance or in fear of the interlacing natives.

The phrases which I have italicised seem to indicate that the writer has lost sight of the fact that, if the border farmers are "native-pressed," it is because they have intruded themselves amongst the natives, from which position a just and wise government would seek to withdraw them, instead of endeavouring to establish and maintain them in it by force. This latter course, however, is the one which Captain Clarke recommends. The remainder of his memorandum is a series of suggestions for this purpose, one of which runs as follows:

To take away the immediate strain on the border farmer, and the risk of collision which the present state of affairs involves, I would suggest the establishment of Government Agents, who should reside *on or beyond the border now occupied by the farmers*[5] . . . . Each Residency should be a fortress, built of stone, and prepared for defence against any, native force.

---

5. Author's italics.

Sir Bartle Frere's version of Captain Clarke's account, given to the Secretary of State in a despatch enclosing the above, runs as follows:

> Most of the native chiefs now there have gradually crept in, under pressure from the northward, and finding no representatives of the Transvaal Government able to exercise authority on the spot, have gradually set up some sort of government for themselves, before which many of the Boers have retired, leaving only those who were willing to pay a sort of tribute for protection, or to avoid being robbed of their cattle.

With whatever oblique vision Sir Bartle Frere may have perused the enclosure from which he gathers his facts, no unbiased mind can fail to detect the singular discrepancy between the account given by Captain Clarke and that drawn from it by the High Commissioner in his enclosing letter.

He makes no mention of the *driving out* of the natives which preceded their *creeping in*, and which figures so largely in Captain Clarke's memorandum, of which he professes to give a sketch. And he introduces, entirely on his own account, the accusation against the natives implied in the phrase "or to avoid being robbed of their cattle.," of which not a single word appears in the memorandum itself.

Properly speaking, there were two disputed boundary lines up to 1879, the one being that between Zululand and the Transvaal, to the south of the Pongolo River; the other that between the Zulus and the Swazis, to the north of, and parallel to, that stream.[6] The Swazis are the hereditary enemies of the Zulus, and there has always been a bitter feeling between the two races, nevertheless the acquisitiveness of the Transvaal Boers was at the bottom of both disputes. They profess to have obtained, by cession from the Swazi king in 1855, a strip of land to the northeast of the Pongolo River and down to the Lebomba Mountains, in order that they might form a barrier between them and the Zulus; but the Swazis deny having ever made such cession.

---

6. "*Ama*-Swazi" for the plural correctly, as also "*Ama*-Zulu."

In addition to the doubt thrown upon the transaction by this denial, and the well-known Boer encroachments already described, it remains considerably open to question whether the Swazis had the power to dispose of the land, which is claimed by the Zulus as their own. The commission which sat upon the southern border question was not permitted to enter upon that to the north of the Pongolo, which therefore remains uncertain. The one fact generally known, however, is undoubtedly favourable to the Zulu claim. The territory in question was occupied until 1848 by two Zulu chiefs, Putini of the Ama-Ngwe, and Langalibalele of the Ama-Hlubi tribe, under the rule of the Zulu king Umpande. These chiefs, having fallen into disgrace with the king, were attacked by him, and fled into Natal. They were ultimately settled in their late locations under the Draakensberg, leaving their former places in Zululand, north and south of the Pongolo, the inNgcaka (Mountain), and inNgcuba (River) vacant.

Sir Henry Bulwer remarks on this point:[7]

> Sir T. Shepstone says indeed, that there is no dispute between the Transvaal and the Ama-Swazi; but, as he adds that, should questions arise between them, they may be settled on their own merits, it is not impossible that questions may arise; and I am certainly informed that the Ama-Swazi used formerly to deny that they had ever ceded land to the *extent* claimed by the Republic.

But that the western portion, at all events, of the land in dispute was at that time under Zulu rule, is apparent from an account given by members of the house of Masobuza, principal wife of Langalibalele, and sister to the Swazi king, who was sheltered at Bishopstowe after the destruction of the Hlubi tribe, and died there in 1877.

> In Chaka's time, Mate, father of Madhlangampisi, who had lived from of old on his land north of the Pongolo, as an *independent* chief, not under Swazi rule, gave, without fighting, his allegiance to Chaka; and from that time to this the

---

7. P. P. 2220, pp. 400-2.

district in question has been under Zulu rule, the Swazi king having never at any time exercised any authority over it.

The same statement applies to several other tribes living north, and on either side of the Pongolo, amongst them those of Langalibalele and Putini.

> Madhlangampisi's land was transferred by the Boer Government as late as January 17th, 1877, to the executors of the late Mr. M'Corkindale, and now goes by the name of Londina, in which is the hamlet of Derby . . . We are perfectly aware that the southern portion of the block is held by command of the Zulu chief, and the executor's surveyors have been obstructed in prosecuting the survey.[8]

In 1856 a number of Boers claimed *Natal* territory west of the Buffalo, as far as the Biggarsberg range, now the south-west boundary of the Newcastle County, and some of them were in occupation of it; and, a commission being sent to trace the northern border of the colony along the line of the Buffalo, these latter opposed and protested against the mission of the Commissioners; but their opposition spent itself in threats, and ended in the withdrawal from Natal of the leaders of the party.

Other Boers had settled *east* of the Buffalo, in the location vacated by the tribe of Langalibalele, as to whom the aforesaid Commissioners write:

> During our stay among the farmers it was brought to our notice by them that they had obtained from Panda the cession of the tract of country beyond the Buffalo (inNcome), towards the north-west; they had subscribed among themselves, one hundred head of cattle for this land, which had been accepted by Panda.

And Sir T. Shepstone says:

> Panda never denied this grant,[9] but repudiated the idea that he had sold the land. His account was that, when the farmers were defeated by Her Majesty's troops in Natal, some

---

8. Natal Mercury, July 23rd, 1878.
9. In respect of what lay west of the Draakensberg.

of them asked him for land to live upon outside the jurisdiction of the British Government, and that he gave them this tract 'only to live in, as part of Zululand under Zulu law'.[10] The cattle they say they paid for it, Panda looked upon as a thank-offering, made in accordance with Zulu custom.[11]

In reply to messages sent by the Zulu king to the Natal Government, complaining of the encroachments of the Boers on the *north*, as well as the west of Zululand, and begging the friendly intervention and arbitration of the English, the advice of the Natal authorities was always to "sit still," and use no force, for England would see justice done in the end.[12]

From all this it would appear that the claim of Cetshwayo to land north of the Pongolo was not an "aggressive act," without any real foundation in right, and merely a defiant challenge intended to provoke war; but was a just claim, according to the tests applied by Sir Bartle Frere *viz.* "actual occupation and exercise of sovereign rights."[13]

The subject is fully gone into, and further evidence produced, in the Bishop of Natal's pamphlet, *Extracts from the Blue-Books*; but the main facts are as here stated.

On turning to the subject of the better known border dispute, between the Zulus and the Transvaal Boers on the east, we are confronted at once by the fact that the decision of the Commissioners, chosen by Sir H. Bulwer to investigate the matter, was decidedly favourable to the Zulu claim; which, after careful consideration of all the evidence on either side, they found to be a just

---

10. (P. p. 1961, p. 28)

11. 1961, pp. 1–5.

12. Sir Henry Bulwer, speaking of the disputed territory generally, writes as follows: "The Zulu king had always, in deference very much to the wishes and advice of this Government (Natal), forborne from doing anything in respect of the question that might produce a collision, trusting to the good offices of this Government to arrange the difficulty by other means. But no such arrangement had ever been made; and thus the question had drifted on until the formal annexation of the disputed territory by the Government of the Republic last year, and their subsequent attempt to give a practical effect to their proclamation of annexation by levying taxes upon the Zulus residing in the territory, provoked a resistance and a feeling of resentment which threatened to precipitate a general collision at any moment." Sir H. Bulwer, June 29th, 1876 (C. 1961, p. 1).

13. P. p. 2222, p. 29.

and good one. This decision should, in itself, have been sufficient to relieve the Zulu king from the accusation of making insolent demands for territory with aggressive and warlike intentions. But as, up to July, 1878, the above charge was the sole one brought against him, and on account of which troops were sent for and preparations made for war; and as, also, Sir Bartle Frere has thought fit to cast a doubt upon the judgment of the Commissioners by the various expressions of dissatisfaction which appear in his correspondence with the Bishop of Natal; it will be necessary for us to enter fully into the matter, in order to understand the extent to which the question bore fruit in the Zulu War.

In 1861 Cetshwayo demanded from the Transvaal Government the persons of four fugitives, who had escaped at the time of the Civil War of 1856, and had taken refuge amongst the Boers. One of these fugitives was a younger son of Umpande, by name Umtonga, who took refuge at first in Natal; from whence, however, he carried on political intrigues in Zululand, with the assistance of his mother, which resulted in the death of the latter and in a message from Cetshwayo to the Natal Government, complaining of Umtonga's conduct, and requesting that he should be placed in his hands. This was refused, but the Government undertook to place the young man under the supervision of an old and trusted colonial chief, Zatshuke, living in the centre of the colony. Umtonga professed to accept and to be grateful for this arrangement; but, upon the first step being taken to carry it out, he fired twice at the policeman who was sent to conduct him to Zatshuke, but missed him, and then escaped to the Transvaal territory.

From thence he, with another brother, and two *indunas* (captains) were given up to Cetshwayo by the Boers, who required, in return for their surrender, the cession of land east of the Blood River, and a pledge that the young princes should not be killed. Cetshwayo is said by the Boers to have agreed to both conditions, and he certainly acted up to the latter, three of the four being still alive, and the fourth having died a natural death.[14] It

---

14. Umtonga escaped again, and is now living in the Transvaal. His brother was still living in Zululand, as head of Umtonga's *kraal*, at the beginning of the war, and no injury appears to have been done to any of the four.

is this alleged bargain with Cetshwayo (in 1861) on which the Boers found their claim to the main portion of the disputed territory a "bargain in itself base and immoral; the selling of the persons of men for a grant of land, and which no Christian government, like that of England, could recognise for a moment as valid and binding," even if it were ever made. But it is *persistently denied by the Zulus* that such a bargain was ever consented to by them *or by their prince*. On this point Cetshwayo himself says:

> I have never given or sold any land to the Boers of the Transvaal. They wished me to do so when I was as yet an *umtwana* (child, prince). They tried to get me to sign a paper, but I threw the pen down, and never would do so, telling them that it was out of my power to either grant or sell land, as it belonged to the king, my father, and the nation. I know the Boers say I signed a paper, and that my brothers Hamu and Ziwedu did also. I never did, and if they say I held the pen or made a mark, giving or selling land, it is a lie!

The Prince Dabulamanzi, and chiefs sitting round, bore out the king in this statement.[15] And so says Sir T. Shepstone:[16]

> Panda, who is still living, repudiated the bargain, and Cetshwayo denied it. The emigrant farmers, however, insisted on its validity, and proceeded to occupy. The Zulus have never ceased to threaten and protest. And the Government of Natal, to whom these protests and threats have been continually made, has frequently, during a course of fifteen years, found it very difficult to impress the Zulus with the hope and belief that an amicable solution of the difficulty would some day be found, provided that they refrained from reprisals or the use of force.

The first message from the Zulus on the subject of the disputed territory was received on September 5th, 1861, in the very year in which (according to the Boers) the cession in question was made.[17] The Bishop of Natal, in his *Extracts* already mentioned,

---

15. From Report of Mr. Fynney on July 4th, 1877 (P. p. 1961, p. 45.)
16. 1961, p. 5.
17. 1961, p. 7.

records eighteen messages on the same subject, commencing with the above and concluding with one brought on April 20th, 1876,[18] showing that for a period of fifteen years the Zulu king (whether represented by Umpande or by Cetshwayo) had never ceased to entreat "the friendly intervention and arbitration of this Government between them and the Boer Government".[19] These eighteen messages acknowledge the virtual supremacy of the English, and the confidence which the Zulus feel in English justice and honour, and they request their protection, or, failing that, their permission to protect themselves by force of arms; they suggest that a Commission sent from Natal should settle the boundary, and that a Resident or Agent of the British Government should be stationed on the border between them and the Boers, to see that justice was done on both sides. They report the various aggressions and encroachments by which the Zulus were suffering at the hands of their neighbours, but to which they submitted because the question was in the hands of the Government of Natal; and they repeatedly beg that the English will themselves take possession of the disputed country, or some part of it, rather than allow the unsettled state of things to continue.

> They (the Zulus) beg that the Governor will take a strip of country, the length and breadth of which is to be agreed upon between the Zulus and the Commissioners (for whom they are asking) sent from Natal, the strip to abut on the Colony of Natal, and to run to the northward and eastward in such a manner, in a line parallel to the seacoast, as to interpose in all its length between the Boers and the Zulus, and to be governed by the Colony of Natal, and form a portion of it if thought desirable.
>
> The Zulu people earnestly pray that this arrangement may be carried out immediately, because they have been neighbours of Natal for so many years, separated only by a stream of water, and no question has arisen between them and the Government of Natal; they know that where the boundary is fixed by agreement with the English there it will remain.

---

18. 1748, p. 49.
19. 1961, p. 9.

Panda, Cetshwayo, and all the heads of the Zulu people assembled, directed us to urge in the most earnest manner upon the Lieutenant-Governor of Natal the prayer we have stated.

This is the concluding portion of the fourth message, received on June 5th, 1869.[20] The fifth, reporting fresh Boer aggressions, was received on December 6th, 1869.

In the course of the same year Lieutenant-Governor Keate addressed the President of the South African Republic on the subject, and suggested arbitration, which suggestion was accepted by the President, provided that the expenses should be paid by the losing party; and during the following two years repeated messages were sent by Mr. Keate reminding the President that being "already in possession of what the Zulu authorities put forward as justifying their claims," he only awaits the like information from the other side before "visiting the locality and hearing the respective parties."[21]

On August 16th, 1871, the Government Secretary of the South African Republic replies that he has "been instructed to forward to the Lieutenant-Governor of Natal the necessary documents bearing on the Zulu question, together with a statement of the case, and hopes to do so by next post; but that, as the session of the Volksraad had been postponed from May to September, it would be extremely difficult to settle the matter in 1871," he therefore proposed January, 1872, as a convenient time for the purpose.

Nearly eight weeks later (October 9th) Lieutenant-Governor Keate informs the President that the documents promised, upon the Zulu-border question, have not yet reached him; but sees nothing, at present, likely to prevent his "proceeding, in January next, to the Zulu-border for the purpose of settling the matter at issue."

But the promised papers appear never to have been sent. The arbitration never took place. Lieutenant-Governor Keate was relieved from the government of Natal in 1872; and the next stage of the question is marked by the issue on May 25th, 1875, of a proclamation by Acting-President Joubert, annexing to the

20. (1961, p. 9)
21. (P. p. 1961, p. 24).

dominion of the South African Republic the territory, the right to which was to have been decided by this arbitration.

In this proclamation no reference is made to the (alleged) Treaty of 1861, by which "what is now and was then disputed territory had been ceded to the South African Republic," though it certainly annexes to the Republic all the country included in the Treaty, and seems to annex more. But no ground of claim is set forth or alluded to upon which the right to annex is founded, "with reservation of all further claims and rights of the said Republic," nor any reason assigned for the act, except to "prevent disagreement" between the Boers and the Zulus. And Sir T. Shepstone goes on to say:[22]

> The officers of the South African Republic proceeded to exercise in this annexed territory the ordinary functions of government, and among these, the levying taxes on natives. The Zulus, who had been persistent in repudiating the cession, and who have continued to occupy the territory as theirs, resisted the demand by Cetshwayo's directions, and a collision appeared imminent, when the difficulty was avoided by the officers withdrawing the order they had issued.

Nevertheless, in spite of the repeated disappointments with which they met, the Zulus continued to send complaints and entreaties to the Government of Natal; which messages, although they never varied in their respectful and friendly tone towards the English, show plainly how deeply they felt the neglect with which they were treated. The English "promises" are spoken of again and again, and the thirteenth message contains a sentence worth recording, in its simple dignity.

> Cetshwayo desired us to urge upon the Governor of Natal to interfere, to save the destruction of perhaps both countries—Zululand and the Transvaal. He requests us to state that he cannot and will not submit to be turned out of his own houses. It may be that he will be vanquished; but, as he is not the aggressor, death will not be so hard to meet.[23]

---

22. (1961, p. 5)
23. (1748, p. 14)

Sir Henry Bulwer's answers to these messages contain passages which sufficiently prove that up to this time the Government of Natal had no complaints to make against the Zulu king.

> This is the first opportunity the Lieutenant-Governor has had of communicating with Cetshwayo since his (Sir H. Bulwer's) arrival in the Colony. He therefore takes the opportunity of sending him a friendly greeting, and of expressing the pleasure with which he had heard of the satisfactory relations that have existed between this Colony and the Zulus. (November 25th, 1875).[24]

This Government trusts that Cetshwayo will maintain that moderation and forbearance which he has hitherto shown, and which the Government has great pleasure in bringing to the notice of the councillors of the great Queen, and that nothing will be done which will hinder the peaceful solution of the Disputed Territory question. (July 25th, 1876).[25]

Meanwhile repeated acts of violence and brutality on the part of the Boers are reported, and in the *Blue Books* before us the Zulu complaints are confirmed from various official sources, by Mr. Fynn, Resident Magistrate of the Umsinga Division,[26] by Sir Henry Bulwer,[27] by Sir T. Shepstone himself,[28] by Mr. Osborn,[29] and by Sir Henry Barkly.[30] No attempt at settlement, however, had been made in answer to these appeals up to the time of the annexation of the Transvaal, in 1877, by Sir T. Shepstone; after which so great a change took place in the tone of the latter upon the subject of the disputed territory.

Upon this question we may quote again from Mr. Fynney's report of the king's answer to him upon the announcement of the annexation of the Transvaal:

> "I hear what you have said about past disputes with the

---

24. (1748, p. 15)
25. (1748, p. 97)
26. (1748, p. 10)
27. (1748, pp. 8, 11, 12, 25)
28. (1748, pp. 10, 24, 29, 52, 56)
29. (1748, p. 82)
30. (1748, p. 25)

Boers, and about the settlement of them, the land question is one of them, and a great one. I was in hopes, when I heard it was you who visited me, that you had brought me some final word about the land, as Somtseu had sent from Newcastle by Umgabana to say that his son would come with the word respecting the land so long in dispute, and I felt sure it had come today, for you are his son. Now the Transvaal is English ground, I want Somtseu to send the Boers away from the lower parts of the Transvaal, that near my country. The Boers are a nation of liars; they are a bad people, bad altogether; I do not want them near my people; they lie, and claim what is not theirs, and ill-use my people. Where is Thomas (Mr. Burgers)?"

I informed him that Mr. Burgers had left the Transvaal.

"Then let them pack up and follow Thomas," said he, "let them go. The Queen does not want such people as those about her land. What can the Queen make of them or do with them? Their evil ways puzzled both Thomas and Rudolph (Landrost of Utrecht); they will not be quiet. They have laid claim to my land, and even down to N'Zalankulu (you saw the line), burned it with fire, and my people have no rest."

Umnyamana (Prime Minister) here remarked:

"We want to know what is going to be done about this land; it has stood over as an open question for so many years. Somtseu took all the papers to England with him to show the great men there, and we have not heard since."

To which Mr. Fynney, of course, had no reply to make.

Within a fortnight of the annexation the Boers on the Zulu border presented Sir T. Shepstone with an address, stating that during the last ten or twelve years (*i.e.* from 1861, when this encroachment was begun by the Boers) they had "suffered greatly in consequence of the hostile behaviour of the Zulu nation, but more so for the last two years" (*i.e.* from 1875, when the Boer Government proclaimed the disputed territory to belong to the Transvaal, and proceeded to levy taxes upon its Zulu inhabitants), so that, they said, their lives and goods were in danger.[31] Accordingly Sir T. Shepstone writes to Lord Carnarvon as follows:

---

31. (1814, p. 14)

I shall be forced to take some action with regard to the Disputed Territory, of which your lordship has heard so much, but I shall be careful to avoid any direct issue.[32] It is of the utmost importance, that all questions involving disturbance outside of this territory should be, if possible, postponed until the Government of the Transvaal is consolidated, and the numerous tribes within its boundaries have begun to feel and recognise the hand of the new administration.

These remarks already show the change in sentiment, on Sir T. Shepstone's part, which was more markedly displayed at the Blood River meeting between him and the Zulu *indunas*. The conference proved an utter failure, as also did several other attempts on Sir T. Shepstone's part to persuade the Zulus to relinquish to him, on behalf of the Transvaal, the claims upon which they had so long insisted.

On December 5th, 1877, two *indunas* came from Cetshwayo to the Bishop of Natal with a request that he would put the Zulu claim in writing, to be sent to Sir H. Bulwer and the Queen. The same *indunas*, a few days later, with Umfunzi and Nkisimane—messengers from Cetshwayo—appointed, before a notary public, Dr. Walter Smith and Mr. F. E. Colenso to be "diplomatic agents" for Cetshwayo, "who should communicate on his behalf in the English language, and, when needful, in writing," and especially to "treat with the British Government on the boundary question;"[33/34] which appointment, however, Sir H. Bulwer and Sir T. Shepstone refused to recognise; and the former, having proposed the Border Commission before receiving notice of this appointment—though the Commissioners had not yet started from 'Maritzburg— did not feel it advisable, as "no such appointment had been

32. Thereby pointing the truth of his own remark at a previous date March 30th, 1876 (1748, p. 24). "But messages from the Zulu king are becoming more frequent and urgent, and *the replies he receives seem to him to be both temporising and evasive.*" (Author's italics.)
33. (2000, p. 58)
34. Immediately after they had signed the instrument of appointment the two Zulu messengers were sent in to the Government by Messrs. Smith and Colenso, and took with them a letter (C. 2000) which mentioned them as its bearers, and announced what they had done.

made by the Zulu king,"[35] to communicate to Messrs. Smith and Colenso Lord Carnarvon's despatch (January 21st, 1.878), which said:

> I request that you will inform Mr. Smith and Mr. Colenso that the desire of Her Majesty's Government in this matter is that the boundary question shall be fully and fairly discussed, and a just arrangement arrived at, and that you will refer them to Sir T. Shepstone, to whom has been committed the duty of negotiating on the subject.[36]

---

35. Mfunzi and Nkisimane were sent down again to 'Maritzburg by Cetshwayo, at the request of Sir H. Bulwer, and denied the whole transaction, though it was attested by the signatures of the notary and two white witnesses. It was afterwards discovered that they had been frightened into this denial by a Natal Government messenger, who told them that they had made the Governor very angry with them and their king by making this appointment; and John Dunn also, after receiving letters from 'Maritzburg, told them that they had committed a great fault, and that he saw that they would never all come home again.

36. Messrs. Smith and Colenso's explanatory letter to Sir M. Hicks-Beach, dated June 9th, 1878, concludes as follows: "This business, as far as we are concerned, is, therefore, ended. We had hoped to be instrumental in embodying in a contract a proposal which we knew was advantageous to both parties. To do so only required the intervention of European lawyers trusted by Cetewayo. We knew that he trusted us, and would trust no others. The task of acting for the king was, therefore, imposed on us as lawyers and as gentlemen. Of pecuniary reward, or its equivalent, our labours have brought us nothing. We do not require it. Honour we did not desire, nor had a savage prince any means of conferring it. The duty thus undertaken we give up only in despair, and we have nothing to regret. Such information, however, as we have gleaned in the course of our agency you are entitled to hear from us, as we are British subjects. The Zulus are hostile to the Boers of the Transvaal, and would fight with them but for fear of being involved in a quarrel with the English. But neither Cetywayo himself, who is wise and peaceful, nor the most hot-blooded of his young warriors have any desire to fight with England, i.e. Natal. If they wished to do so there is nothing to prevent them, and never has been. As they march, they could march from their border to this city or to Durban in a little more than twenty-four hours. Their only fear is, that the English will come with an army 'to make them pay taxes.' They say they will rather die than do so. The king says the same. Almost every man has a gun. Guns and ammunition are cheaper at any military kraal in Zululand than at Port Natal. These goods are imported by Tonga men, who come in large gangs from Delagoa Bay, for white merchants. An Enfield rifle may be had for a sheep of a Tonga man; many have breech-loaders. The missionaries, whose principal occupation was trading, deal in ammunition. The missionaries have recently lost most of their converts, who have gone trading on their own account. Without these converts the missionaries cannot do business, and they have left the country, except Bishop Schreuder, who has gone back, that it may not be said that a white man is not safe there. Cetywayo says that he has asked the (continued on next page)

Meanwhile, however, Sir T. Shepstone's *negotiations* had proved unsuccessful, and Sir Henry Bulwer writes to Sir Bartle Frere:[37]

> It seems but too clear, from all that has now happened, that the prospect of a settlement of the question by direct negotiations between the Government of the Transvaal and the Zulu king is at an end. The feeling against the Boers on the part of the Zulu king and people is too bitter, and they are now scarcely less angry against the new Government of the Transvaal than they were against the old Government.

He then suggests arbitration as a way by which the Zulu king "can escape the alternative of war, by which he can obtain justice, and by which, at the same time, he can avoid direct negotiations with the Government of a people whom he dislikes and distrusts."

The diplomatic agents were never recognised by the colonial authorities, or allowed to exercise their functions; but a visit which Mr. Colenso paid to the Zulu king in connection with the appointment is worth recording for the sake of the glimpse it gives of Cetshwayo's habits and daily life, as told by a disinterested eye-witness.

The king, it appears, whom so many have delighted to represent as a corpulent unwieldy savage, to whom movement must be a painful exertion, was in the habit of taking a daily constitutional of about six miles out and back. Mr. Colenso observed that this was his regular habit, and during his stay at the royal *kraal* he daily saw Cetshwayo start, and could trace his course over the hills by the great white shield carried before him as the emblem of kingship.

On his return the king regularly underwent a process of ablution at the hands of his attendants, who poured vessels of water over him, and rubbed the royal person down with a species of soft stone. This performance over, Cetshwayo ascended

---

missionaries to stop. They have certainly not been turned out or threatened. Their going makes the Zulus think that we are about to invade the country. Nothing but gross mismanagement will bring about a quarrel between England and the Zulus. (P. p. (C. 2U4) pp. 215, 216).

37. (2000, p. 68)

his throne or chair of state, upon which he remained, hearing causes, and trying cases amongst his people, until the shades of evening fell, before which time he did not break his fast.

This description, of the accuracy of which there can be no question, gives a picture of a simple, moderate, and useful kingly existence, very different from the idea commonly received of a savage monarch, wallowing in sloth and coarse luxury, and using the power which he holds over his fellow-creatures only for the gratification of every evil or selfish human passion. Cetshwayo ruled his people well according to his lights: let us hope that, now we have wrested his kingdom from him, our government may prove a more beneficent one.

CHAPTER 10

The Boundary Commission

Sir Henry Bulwer's message proposing arbitration was sent to Cetshwayo on December 8th, 1877).[1] In this message he makes it plain to the king that "the Governments of Natal and the Transvaal are now brothers, and what touches one touches the other." He continues:

Therefore the Lieut.-Governor of Natal sends these words to Cetshwayo that he may know what is in his mind, and that Cetshwayo may do nothing that will interrupt the peaceful and friendly relations that have existed for so many years between the English and the Zulus.

He then proposes that he should write to. . . .

. . . . the Ministers of the great Queen in England, and also to the Queen's High Commissioner who resides at Cape Town, in order that they may send fit and proper persons, who will come to the country with fresh minds, and who will hear all that the Zulus have to say on the question, and all that the Transvaal Government has to say, and examine and consider all the rights of the question, and then give their decision in such manner that all concerned may receive and abide by that decision, and the question be finally set at rest.

Meanwhile, no action should be taken to interfere with the existing state of things or to disturb the peace. But the disputed territory should be considered and treated as neutral between the two countries for the time being.

---

1. (2000, p. 67)

Before this communication reached him, Cetshwayo had already sent messengers to the Bishop of Natal, asking advice how to act in his present difficulties. And they had carried back "a word," which would reach the king about November 19th, to the effect that he must on no account think of fighting the Transvaal Government, and that he had better send down some great *indunas* to propose arbitration to Sir Henry Bulwer, in whose hands he might leave himself with perfect confidence, that the right and just thing would be done by him. The Bishop knew nothing of Sir Henry's intentions when he sent this reply; and, in point of fact, the two had separately come to the same conclusion as to what would be the wisest course to follow.

Cetshwayo therefore was prepared to receive Sir Henry's proposition, which he did, not only with respect, but with delight and relief.[2] His answer to the message contained the following passages:

> Cetshwayo hears what the Governor of Natal says . . . . and thanks him for these words, for they are all good words that have been sent to Cetshwayo by the Governor of Natal; they show that the Natal Government still wishes Cetshwayo to drink water and live.

He suggests, however, that before sending for people from across the sea to settle the boundary, he should be glad if the Governor would send his own representatives to hear both sides of the dispute, and if they cannot come to a decision, "a letter can be sent beyond the sea" for others to come. The message continues:

> Cetshwayo thanks the Governor for the words which say the ground in dispute should not be occupied while the matter is talked over.
>
> Cetshwayo says he hears it said that he intends to make war upon the Transvaal. He wishes the Natal Government to watch well and see when he will do such a thing. For, if he attended to the wish of the English Government in Natal when it said he must not make war on the Transvaal Boers,

2. (2000, p. 138).

why should he wish to do so upon those who are now of the same Great House as Natal, to whose voice he has listened?

Cetshwayo is informed that he is to be attacked by the Transvaal people. If so, and if he is not taken by surprise, he will, as soon as he hears of the approach of such a force, send men who will report it to the Natal Government before he takes any action.

Cetshwayo says he cannot trust the Transvaal Boers any longer; they have killed his people, they have robbed them of their cattle on the slightest grounds. He had hoped Somtseu would have settled all these matters. But he has not done so; he wishes to cast Cetshwayo off; he is no more a father, but a firebrand. If he is tired of carrying Cetshwayo now, as he did while he was with the Natal Government, then why does he not put him down, and allow the Natal Government to look after him, as it has always done?

Sir Henry Bulwer expressed his satisfaction at this reply, speaking of it as a far more satisfactory one than they had been led to expect,[3] and he writes of it to Sir T. Shepstone thus:

You will see by the king's reply that he has met my representations in a very proper spirit. . . . I have no reason to think that what the king says is said otherwise than in good faith; and, if this be so, there seems to me to be no reason why this dispute should not be settled in a peaceable manner.[4]

To Cetshwayo himself he says:

The Lieutenant-Governor has heard the words of Cetshwayo. He is glad that the words which he lately sent to Cetshwayo were welcome. They were words sent in a friendly spirit, and Cetshwayo received them in a friendly spirit. This is as it should be.

He then agrees to the king's proposal concerning commissioners from Natal, provided that the Transvaal Government agree also.

The following is the account given by the Government mes-

---

3. (2000, p. 138)
4. (2097, p. 26)

sengers, who carried Sir H. Bulwer's message to Cetshwayo of the manner in which it was received by the king and his *indunas*:[5]

> While we spoke to Cetshwayo, we saw that what we were saying lifted a great weight from his heart, that they were words which he was glad to hear; and what he said to us as we finished showed us we were right in this belief. . . .
>
> We could see, when we arrived at the great *kraal*, that the *indunas*, and even the king, were not easy in their hearts, and from all we could see and gather, the chief men under the king did not wish for war. After the message was delivered, all of them appeared like men who had been carrying a very heavy burden, and who had only then been told that they could put it down and rest.

It is best known to himself how, in the face of these words, and with nothing to support his statement, Sir Bartle Frere could venture to assert in his fourth letter to the Bishop:

> The offers to arbitrate originated with the Natal Government, and were by no means willingly accepted by Cetshwayo.

Cetshwayo having, in point of fact, earnestly asked for arbitration again and again, as we have already shown, and rejoicing greatly when at last it was offered him. Mr. J. Shepstone's observation also,[6] that "to this suggestion Cetshwayo replied 'that he had no objection'" hardly gives a fair view of the state of the case.

But, before this satisfactory agreement had been arrived at, Sir T. Shepstone had managed still further to exasperate the feelings of the Zulus against the new Government of the Transvaal, while the fact that Natal and the Transvaal were one, and that to touch one was to touch the other, and to touch England also, had not been brought home to the king's mind until he received Sir H. Bulwer's message.

Before the receipt of that message, Cetshwayo had every reason to believe that the negotiations concerning the disputed territory were broken off. Sir T. Shepstone's tone on the subject had altered; he had parted with the king's *indunas* at the Blood River

---

5. (2079, p. 25)
6. (2144, p. 184)

in anger, and the messenger whom he had promised to send to the king himself had never appeared. Meanwhile, the Boers had gone into *laager*, by direction, they say, of Sir T. Shepstone himself, and with the full expectation that he was about to make war upon the Zulus. No offer of arbitration had yet been made. Cetshwayo had been played with and baffled by the English Government for sixteen years, and to all appearance nothing whatever was done, or would be done, to settle in a friendly manner this troubled question, unless he took steps himself to assert his rights, and he seems to have taken the mildest possible way of so doing under the circumstances. According to the official reports at the time, he sent a large force of armed men to build a military *kraal* near Luneburg, north of the Pongolo, in land which was also disputed with the Transvaal Government, but formed no part of the (so called) disputed territory to the south of that river, or as Lord Carnarvon said to a deputation of South African merchants:[7]

He (the Zulu king) had proceeded to construct, in opposition to Sir T. Shepstone's warnings, a fortified *kraal* in a disputed territory abutting upon English soil.

But this was a very exaggerated way of describing a comparative trifling circumstance. The erection of a *kraal*—not, as so frequently asserted, a military one, but merely an ordinary Zulu *kraal* for the residence of a headman, to keep order among the 15,000 Zulus who lived in that district—had long been contemplated, and had once, during Umpanda's lifetime, been attempted, though the Boers had driven away the Zulu officer sent for the purpose, and destroyed the work he had commenced.

Cetshwayo himself explains his reason for sending so large a force for the purpose, on the grounds that he wished the *kraal* to be built in one day, and his men not to be obliged to remain over a night, while, as Colonel Durnford, R.E., says:[8]

The fact that the men at work are armed is of no significance, because every Zulu is an armed man, and never moves without his weapon.

7. *Guardian*, January 9th, 1878.
8. (2144, p. 237)

Sir T. Shepstone, however, was greatly alarmed when he first heard of the building of this *kraal*, and writes concerning it— November 16th, 1877:[9]

> I feel, therefore (because of the irritating effect of it upon the Transvaal), that the building of this *kraal* must be prevented at all hazards.

The "hazards" do not appear to have proved very serious, as a simple representation on the part of Captain Clarke, R.A., and Mr. Rudolph, sent to the spot by Sir T. Shepstone, resulted in the Zulu force retiring, *having made only a small cattle kraal and chopped and collected some poles*, which they left on the ground, to be used for the building of the huts hereafter, but which were very soon carried off and used as firewood by the Luneburg farmers.

But this did not satisfy Sir T. Shepstone, who sent messengers to Cetshwayo, complaining of what had been done, and of "finding," as he says, "a Zulu force in the rear of where he was staying;"[10] and saying that, in consequence, and in order to restore confidence amongst those Boers living on the Blood River border, he (Sir T. Shepstone) had decided to send a military force down to the wagon-drift on the Blood River, to encamp there on our side of the river. Cetshwayo replies that he did not send to have the *kraal* built that trouble might arise, but because his people were already living on the ground in dispute. He admits that of course the administrator could do as he pleased about sending an armed force to encamp on his own borders; but he urges him to think better of it, saying that the Zulus would be frightened and run away, and, if he in his turn should send an armed force to encamp just opposite Sir T. Shepstone's encampment, to put confidence into his people's hearts, he asks, somewhat quaintly, "would it be possible for the two forces to be looking at one another for two days without a row?"

Many expressions are scattered through the *Blue Books* at this period concerning "Zulu aggressions;" and Sir T. Shepstone

---

9. (1961, p. 224)

10. This is apparently a figure of speech, since Luneburg, near which the *kraal* was being built, would seem by the map not to lie "to the rear" —as seen from Zululand—of Utrecht, where Sir T. Shepstone was staying.

makes frequent, though vague and unproven, accusations concerning Cetshwayo's "mischievous humour," and the terror of the Boer frontier farmers.

But, so far as these remarks allude to the border squabbles inseparable from the state of affairs, the score is so heavily against the Boers that the counter-charges are hardly worth considering. The only acts chargeable upon the king himself are, first, the building of this *kraal*, which really amounted to no more than a practical assertion of the Zulu claim to land north of the Pongolo; and, secondly, the execution of a (supposed) Zulu criminal there, which was an exercise of Cetshwayo's authority over his own people living in the district.

For the acts of violence committed by the robber chief Umbilini, the Zulu king could not justly be considered responsible; but of this matter, and of the raid committed by the sons of Sihayo, we will treat in a later chapter.

Sir T. Shepstone himself allows that Cetshwayo's frame of mind was a better one after the reception of Sir Henry Bulwer's message offering arbitration;[11] and says that his (Sir T. Shepstone's) messengers—

> .... describe Cetshwayo as being in a very different temper to that which he had on former occasions exhibited; to use their own expression, "it was Cetshwayo, but it was Cetshwayo born again." ...They gleaned from the Zulus .... that a message from the Governor of Natal had been delivered, and they concluded that the change which they had noticed as so marked in the king's tone must have been produced by that message.

The fact that Cetshwayo joyfully and thankfully accepted Sir Henry Bulwer's promise—not to give him the land he claimed, but to have the matter investigated and justice done—is sufficiently established; but from the Boers the proposal met with a very different reception.

Sir T. Shepstone acknowledged the receipt of Sir H. Bulwer's despatch of December 11th, "transmitting copy of a message"

---

11. (2079, pp. 51-54)

which he "had thought fit to send to the Zulu king," and then summoned a few leading men in the district, and laid the proposition before them. He reports that after some pretty speeches about the "Christian, humane, and admirable proposal," which they should have "no excuse for hesitating to accept, if Cetshwayo were a civilised king and the Zulu Government a civilised government," etc. etc., they proceeded to state their objections. They had, they said, no misgiving regarding the justice of the claim of the State; and they believed that the more it was investigated, the more impartial the minds of the investigators, the clearer and more rightful would that claim prove itself to be. Nevertheless, they professed to fear the delay that must necessarily be caused by such an investigation[12] (the dispute having already lasted fifteen years!) and to doubt Cetshwayo's abiding by any promise he might make to observe a temporary boundary line.

To place the two parties to the dispute on equal terms, they said, the land in question should be evacuated by both, or occupied by both under the control of Sir Henry Bulwer, who, they proposed, as an indispensable condition of the proposed arbitration, should take possession of the land in dispute or of some part of it. And Sir T. Shepstone remarks:

> My view is that the considerations above set forth are both weighty and serious. I do not anticipate that, under the circumstances, Cetshwayo would venture to make or to authorise any overt attack. I do fear, however, the consequences of the lawless condition into which the population all along the border is rapidly falling. Cetshwayo, I fear, rather encourages than attempts to repress this tendency; and, although he will not go to war, he may allow that to go on which he knows will produce war.

The condition of the border seems, as we have already shown, to have been "lawless" for many years, though the fault lay rather, with the Boers whose many acts of violence are recorded in the *Blue Books* than with the Zulus, and Sir T. Shepstone has apparently overlooked the fact that he himself had just sum-

---

12. Compare the account of the delay on the part of the Boer Government when Mr. Keate proposed to arbitrate.

marily put a stop to an attempt on Cetshwayo's part to "repress" any lawless "tendency" amongst his own people (of which the Administrator complains) by placing a headman, or responsible person, amongst them to keep order.

Under the above-mentioned conditions Sir T. Shepstone accepts Sir Henry Bulwer's proposal, and informs him that, under the circumstances, he shall not carry out his expressed intention of placing a military post in the neighbourhood of the Blood River. And again he writes January 17th, 1878:[13]

> It was, however, necessary to point out to Sir H. Bulwer the difficulties and dangers, as well as the loss of property, which the white people (Boers?) feel that they will be subjected to by the acceptance of His Excellency's proposal, unless he can devise some means by which their safety and interests can be protected during the pending of the investigation, *which under existing circumstances it is Cetshwayo's interest to prolong indefinitely.*

The words which I have italicised show that Sir T. Shepstone took for granted beforehand that the decision of the Commissioners would be unfavourable to the Zulus. Sir Henry Bulwer, however, did not see his way to falling in with the conditions of the Boers, and replies as follows:[14]

> I do not see that I am in a position, or that, as the Lieutenant-Governor of this colony, I should have the power to take actual possession of the country in dispute. And if to take over the country, and hold possession of it, is considered by your Government an indispensable condition for the acceptance of the mediating course I have proposed, I feel that my proposal falls short of the requirements of the case.

On January 29th, Sir T. Shepstone writes to Sir Henry again, saying that:

> It was felt that, in consequence of the step which you have thought it right to take in your communication to the Zulu king of the 8th December last, the Government of

13. (2079, p.58)
14. (2079, p. 128)

the Transvaal is placed at a disadvantage, and that the longer action on your part is delayed, the greater that disadvantage grows. It follows, therefore, that any action in the direction of your proposition is better than no action at all; and I was urged to beg your Excellency to take some step in the matter without delay.

Accordingly Sir Henry at once sends a message to Cetshwayo, suggesting the observance of a "neutral belt," pending the settlement of the boundary question,[15] and mentioning the two lines, from point to point, which he proposed for the purpose. The same suggestion was made, of course, to Sir T. Shepstone, who replies as follows:

> You have rightly assumed the concurrence of this Government, and I trust that Cetshwayo will see in your message the necessity that is laid upon him to prove that he was sincere in asking you to undertake the inquiry.

This ready acquiescence is fully accounted for by the fact, shortly apparent, that *both* the lines mentioned by Sir Henry, between which neutrality should be observed, were within what was claimed by the Zulus as their own country, and Sir T. Shepstone says:

> At present the belt of country indicated is occupied solely by Zulus. The whole of it has been apportioned in farms to Transvaal subjects, but has not been occupied by them.

Small wonder that the Zulu king, in reply to this proposal, "informs the Governor of Natal that the two roads mentioned in His Excellency's message are both in Zululand, and therefore the king cannot see how the ground between the roads can belong to both parties."

Nevertheless Sir Henry Bulwer hardly seems to fall in with Sir T. Shepstone's suggestion, that Cetshwayo's consent on this point should be looked upon as a test of his sincerity: "Either," he says,[16] "he has misunderstood the real nature of the proposal, or he is disinclined to accept anything which may in his opinion be taken

---

15. (2079, p. 132)
16. (2100, p. 73)

to signify a withdrawal of one iota of his claim." And, in point of fact, though no "neutral ground" was marked off, the Commission went on just as well without it; all the apprehensions of disturbance and disorder having been falsified by the event.

Sir T. Shepstone repeatedly speaks of the border Boers having been forced by Zulu acts and threats of aggression to abandon their farms and go into *laager*, etc. etc.; but, on investigation, it is apparent that this abandonment of farms, and trekking into *laager*, took place in consequence of an intimation from the Landrost of Utrecht, under instructions from Sir T. Shepstone himself; as appears from the following passages of an address from seventy-nine Boers, protesting against arbitration as "an absurdity and an impossibility," which was presented to Sir T. Shepstone on February 2nd, 1878:[17]

> The undersigned burghers, etc. . . . . take the liberty to bring to your Excellency's notice that they, in consequence of intimation from the Landrost of Utrecht, dated 14th December last, on your Excellency's instructions, partly trekked into *laager*, and partly deserted their farms, in the firm expectation that now a beginning of a war would soon be made. . . . That they have heard with anxiety and understand that arbitration is spoken of, which would have to determine our property and possessions; which we fear will decide in favour of a crowned robber, murderer, and breaker of his word, who knows as well as we that he is claiming a thing which does not belong to him . . . . for which reason we are sure that such arbitration is an absurdity and an impossibility. We therefore hereby protest against all proposed or to be undertaken arbitration; and we will, with all legal means at our disposal, etc., resist a decision, etc., over our property which we know would be unlawful and unjust.

They give as a reason for presenting the address from which these phrases are taken, *"because it is impossible for us to remain any longer in laager without any object"* which hardly looks as though they thought themselves in daily danger from the Zulus, unless the "beginning of a war" should "soon be made" by

---

17. (2079, p. 140)

Sir T. Shepstone. They request His Excellency "to commence without any further delay defending" their "rights and property and lives;" and should His Excellency "not be inclined or be without power" to do so, they further signify their intention of requesting him to assist them with ammunition, and not to hinder them seeking assistance, of fellow-countrymen and friends, to maintain their "rights," and to check their "rapacious enemies and to punish them."

And they conclude: "We, the undersigned, bind ourselves on peril of our honour to assist in subduing the Zulu nation, and making it harmless."

Sir T. Shepstone encloses this in a sympathising despatch, but Sir Henry Bulwer remarks upon it and upon a subsequent memorial[18] of the same description—February 23rd:[19]

> Of course, if the object of the memorialists is war, if what they desire is a war with the Zulu nation, it is not to be wondered at that they should find fault with any steps that have been taken to prevent the necessity for war. Nor, if they desire war, is it to be expected that they should be favourable to arbitration, though I find it difficult to reconcile the expression of the apprehensions of the memorialists that arbitration would decide against them, with the unanimous expression of opinion, previously given to your Excellency by some of the leading men of the district, that the proposal made by me was a Christian, humane, and admirable one; that they had no misgivings regarding the justice of the claim of the State, and that they believed the more it was investigated . . .. the clearer and more rightful would that claim prove itself to be. Your Excellency observes that the deep feeling of distrust shown by the memorialists is scarcely to be wondered at, when it is remembered that they are compelled to occupy with their families fortified camps, while their farms in the neighbourhood are being occupied by Zulus, their crops reaped, and their cultivated lands tilled by Zulus, and the timber of their houses used as Zulu firewood.

---

18. 2144, p. 191.
19. 2100, p. 67.

I do not quite understand what farms and cultivated lands are referred to; because in a previous despatch—your despatch, No. 7, of February 5th—your Excellency, in referring to the disputed territory, states, so I understand, that it *'is at present occupied solely by Zulus'* and that, although the whole of it has been apportioned in farms to Transvaal subjects, *it has not been occupied by them.'*

The matter was referred to the High Commissioner, Sir Bartle Frere, and the appointment of a commission was approved by him. He plainly took it for granted that, as Sir T. Shepstone had said, the Transvaal claim was based on "evidence the most incontrovertible, overwhelming, and clear," and looked to the commission for the double advantage of enabling Sir T. Shepstone "to clear up or put on record, in a form calculated to satisfy Her Majesty's Government, an answer to all doubts as to the facts and equity of the question," and of gaining time for preparing a military force to silence and subjugate the Zulus should they object (as he expected) to such an award. That nothing short of military coercion of the Zulus would settle the matter, was evidently Sir Bartle Frere's fixed idea; in fact that was the foregone conclusion with him from beginning to end.

On February 12th, Sir Henry Bulwer sent a message to Cetshwayo,[20] to this effect:

> The Lieut.-Governor now sends to let Cetshwayo know that he has selected, for the purpose of holding this inquiry, the Queen's Attorney-General in Natal (Hon. M. H. Gallway, Esq.), the Secretary for Native Affairs (Hon. J. W. Shepstone, Esq.), and Colonel Durnford, an officer in the Queen's army.
>
> These gentlemen will proceed by-and-by to the place known as Rorke's Drift, which is on the Buffalo River, and in Natal territory, and they will there open the inquiry on Thursday, March 7th.
>
> The Lieut.-Governor proposes, as the most convenient course to be taken, that the Zulu king should appoint two or three *indunas* to represent the Zulu king and the Zulu case at the inquiry, and that these should be at Rorke's Drift on

20. 2079, p. 140.

March 7th, and meet the Natal Commissioners there. The same thing also the Governor proposes shall be done by the Transvaal Government.

And the king's reply to the messengers was expressive:

I am very glad to hear what you say I shall now be able to sleep.

On March 7th the Commission met at Rorke's Drift, and sat for about five weeks, taking evidence day by day in presence of the representatives deputed, three by the Transvaal Government, and three by the Zulus.

Of the three gentlemen who formed the Commission, one was Sir T. Shepstone's brother, already mentioned in this history, whose natural bias would therefore certainly not be upon the Zulu side of the question; another was a Government official and an acute lawyer; and the third, Colonel Durnford, to the writer's personal knowledge, entered upon the subject with an entirely unbiased mind, and with but one intention or desire, that of discovering the actual truth, whatever it might be. The only thing by which his expectations—rather than his opinions—were in the least influenced beforehand, was the natural supposition, shared by all, that Sir T. Shepstone, who had the reputation of being in his public capacity one of the most cautious of men, must have some strong grounds for his very positive statement of the Transvaal claim.

There was, plainly, some slight confusion in the minds of the three Transvaal delegates, as to their position relative to the Commissioners, with whom they apparently expected to be on equal terms, and in a different position altogether from the Zulu delegates on the other side. This, however, was a manifest mistake. It was particularly desirable that the Zulus should be made to feel that it was no case of white against black; but a matter in which impartial judges treated either side with equal fairness, and without respect of persons. One of the Commissioners was the brother of their chief opponent, one of the Transvaal delegates his son; it would naturally have seemed to the Zulus that the six white men (five out of whom were either Englishmen, or claimed to be such) were combining together to out-wit them, had they seen them, evidently on terms of friendship, seated together at the inquiry or talking amongst themselves in their own language.

The Commissioners, however, were careful to avoid this mistake. Finding, on their arrival at Rorke's Drift, that the spot intended for their encampment was already occupied by the Transvaal delegates, who had arrived before them, they caused their own tents to be pitched at some little distance, in order to keep the two apart. The same system was carried out during the sitting of the Court, at which the Commissioners occupied a central position at a table by themselves, the Transvaal delegates being placed at a smaller table on one hand, mats being spread for the Zulu delegates, in a like position, on the other.[21]

Care was also necessary to prevent any possible altercations arising between the Boer and Zulu attendants of either party of delegates, who, in fact, formed the one real element of danger in the affair. On one occasion, during the sitting of the Commission, Colonel Durnford observed a Boer poking at a Zulu with his stick, in a manner calculated to bring to the surface some of the feelings of intense irritation common to both sides, and only kept under control by the presence of the Commissioners. The Colonel at once put a stop to this, and placing a sentry between the two parties, with orders to insist on either keeping to its own side of the ground, no further disturbance took place. Popular rumour, of course, greatly exaggerated the danger of the situation, catching as usual at the opportunity for fresh accusations against the Zulu king, who, it was once reported from Durban, had sent an *impi* to Rorke's Drift, and had massacred the Commissioners and all upon the spot. Fortunately the same day that brought this report to Pietermaritzburg, brought also letters direct from the Commissioners themselves, of a later date than the supposed massacre, and in which the Zulus were spoken of as "perfectly quiet."

---

21. The Zulus, of course, would not have appreciated the convenience of a table and chairs; they had no "documents" to lay upon the former; and their opinion of the comfort of the latter is best expressed by the well-known Zulu saying that, "Only Englishmen and chickens sit upon perches." The mats provided for them were, therefore, a proper equivalent to the tables and seats placed for the other delegates.

That the impartial conduct of the Commissioners had the desired effect is manifest from Cetshwayo's words, spoken after the conclusion of the inquiry, but before its result had been made known to him. His messengers, after thanking Sir Henry Bulwer in the name of their king and people for appointing the commission, said that:

> Cetshwayo and the Zulu people are perfectly satisfied with the way in which the inquiry was conducted throughout, the way in which everything went on from day to day in proper order, and without the least misunderstanding; but that each party understood the subject that was being talked about.
>
> Cetshwayo says he now sees that he is a child of this Government, that the desire of this Government is to do him justice. . . .
>
> Cetshwayo and the Zulu people are awaiting with beating hearts what the Lieut.-Governor will decide about the land that the Boers have given the Zulus so much trouble about; for the Zulus wish very much now to reoccupy the land they never parted with, as it is now the proper season (of the year) for doing so.

Such was Cetshwayo's frame of mind (even before he knew that the decision was in his favour) at a time when he was popularly represented as being in an aggressive, turbulent condition, preparing to try his strength against us, and only waiting his opportunity to let loose upon Natal the "war-cloud" which he was supposed to keep "hovering on our borders."

The boundary question resolved itself into this:

1. To whom did the land in dispute belong in the first instance?
2. Was it ever ceded or sold by the original possessors?

In answer to the first question, the Commissioners took the treaty made in 1843, between the English and the Zulus, as a standpoint fixing a period when the territory in dispute belonged entirely to one or other. There was then no question but that the Zulu country extended over the whole of it.

In answer to the second question, Zulus deny ever having relinquished any part of their country to the Boers, who on the other hand assert that formal cessions had been made to them of considerable districts. With the latter rested the obligation of proving their assertions, which were simply denied by the Zulus, who accordingly, as they said themselves, "had no witnesses to call," having received no authority from the king to do more than point out the boundary claimed.[22/23]

The Boer delegates brought various documents, from which they professed to prove the truth of their assertions, but which were decided by the Commissioners to be wholly worthless, from the glaring discrepancies and palpable falsehoods which they contained. One of these documents, dated March 16th, 1861, "purporting to give an account of a meeting between Sir T. Shepstone, Panda, and Cetshwayo," they decided to be plainly a fabrication, as Sir T. Shepstone did not arrive at Nodwengu,[24] from Natal, to meet Panda and Cetshwayo, until May 9th, 1861.

Other records of cessions of land professed to be signed by the king, but were witnessed by neither Boer nor Zulu, or else by Boers alone. A definition of boundaries was in one case ratified by one Zulu only, a man of no rank or importance; and in other documents alterations were made, and dates inserted, clearly at another time.

Meanwhile it was apparent, from authentic Boer official papers, that the Zulus were threatened by the Boer Government that, if they dared to complain again to the British Government, the South African Republic "would deal severely with them, and that they would also endanger their lives;" while such expressions used by the Volksraad of the South African Republic as the following, when they resolve—

> .... to direct the Government to continue in the course it had adopted with reference to the policy on the eastern frontier, with such caution as the Volksraad expects from the Government with confidence; and in this matter to give it

22. Sir Bartle Frere gives a very unfair account of this matter-of course fact when he transmits to the Secretary of State the above despatch, "informing me of the incomplete result, in consequence of the attitude of Cetshwayo's representatives at the Commission of Inquiry."
23. 2242, p. 80.
24. The king's *kraal* at that time.

the right to take such steps as will more fully benefit the interests of the population than the strict words of the law of the country lay down. . . .[25]

—convicts them of dishonesty out of their own mouths.

Finally the Commissioners report that in their judgment, east of the Buffalo, "there has been no cession of land at all by the Zulu kings, past or present, or by the nation."

They consider, however, that as the Utrecht district has long been inhabited by Boers, who have laid out the site for a town, and built upon it, and as the Zulu nation had virtually acquiesced in the Boer authority over it by treating with them for the rendition of fugitives who had taken refuge there the Transvaal should be allowed to retain that portion of the land in dispute, compensation being given to the Zulus inhabiting that district if they surrendered the lands occupied by them and returned to Zululand, or permission being given them to become British subjects and to continue to occupy the land.

Sir Bartle Frere's version of this is as follows: "The Commissioners propose to divide the area in dispute between the Blood River and the Pongolo, giving to neither party the whole of its claim."

He then quotes the recommendation of the Commissioners, that compensation should be given to Zulus leaving the Utrecht district, and wants to know what is to be done for the farmers who "in good faith, and relying on the right and power of the Transvaal Government to protect them, had settled for many years past on the tract which the Commission proposes to assign to the Zulus." He wishes to know how they are to be placed on an equality with the Zulus from the Utrecht district. To this Sir Henry Bulwer ably replies by pointing out that compensation to the said farmers lies with their own Government, by whose sanction or permission they had occupied land over which that Government had no power by right. In fact, far from "dividing the area in dispute," and giving half to either party on equal terms, the reservation of the Utrecht district was rather

---

25. 2220, p. 337.

an unavoidable concession to the Boers who had long had actual possession of it—which, with due compensation, the Zulus would have been ready enough to make, while receiving back so much of their own land—than an acknowledgment that they could make good their original claim to it. The Commissioners indeed say distinctly *"there has been no cession of land at all by the Zulu king, past or present, or by the nation."*

But indeed, after the decision in favour of the Zulus was given, Sir Bartle Frere entirely changed the complacent tone in which he had spoken of the Commission before-hand. To all appearance his careful schemes for subjugating the Zulu nation were thrown away—the war and the South African Empire were on the point of eluding his grasp. He had sent to England for reinforcements—in direct opposition to the home policy, which for some years had been gradually teaching the colonies to depend upon themselves for protection, and therefore to refrain from rushing headlong into needless and dangerous wars, which might be avoided by a little exercise of tact and forbearance. He and his friend General Thesiger had laid out their campaign and had sent men-of-war to investigate the landing capabilities of the Zulu coast, and he had recommended Sir Henry Bulwer to inform the Zulu king when the latter expressed his disquietude on the subject of these men-of-war that the ships he saw were "for the most part English merchant vessels, but that the war-vessels of the English Government are quite sufficient to protect his (Cetshwayo's) coast from any descent by any other power".[26]

Sir Henry Bulwer was too honest to carry out this recommendation, even had he not had the sense to know that Cetshwayo was accustomed to the passing of merchantmen, and was not to be thus taken in (supposing him to be likely to fear attacks from "foreign foes"). But the fact remains that, an English official of Sir Bartle Frere's rank has put on record, in an official despatch under his own hand, a deliberate proposal that the Zulu king should be tranquillised, and his well-founded suspicions allayed by—a "figure of speech," shall we say?

Every possible objection was made by Sir Bartle Frere to the

---

26. October 6th, 1878, 2220, p. 307.

decision of the Commissioners, and it was with the utmost difficulty that he was at last persuaded to ratify it, after a considerable period employed in preparing for a campaign, the idea of which he appears never for a minute to have relinquished. Sir T. Shepstone protested against the decision, which, however, Sir Henry Bulwer upheld; while Sir Bartle Frere finally decides that "Sir H. Bulwer and I, approaching the question by somewhat different roads, agree in the conclusion that we must accept the Commissioners' verdict." Their report was made on June 20th, 1878, but it was not until November 16th that Sir H. Bulwer sent to Cetshwayo to say that "the Lieut.-Governor is now in a position to inform Cetshwayo that His Excellency the High Commissioner has pronounced his award, etc.," and to fix twenty days from the date of the departure of the messengers carrying this message from Pietermaritzburg, as a convenient time for a meeting on the borders of the two countries at the Lower Tugela Drift, at which the decision should be delivered to the king's *indunas* by officers of the Government appointed for the purpose.

But before this conclusion was arrived at another attempt had been made to bring accusations against Cetshwayo, who said himself at the time (June 27th, 1878): "The name of Cetshwayo is always used amongst the Boers as being the first to wish to quarrel." Alarming accounts reached the Natal Government of a fresh military *kraal* having been built by the king, and notices to quit being served by him upon Boers within the disputed territory, in spite of his engagement to await the decision of the Commissioners. The farmers complained of being obliged to fly, "leaving homes, homesteads, and improvements to be destroyed by a savage, unbridled, revengeful nation."[27] Sir T. Shepstone re-echoed their complaint,[28] and Sir Bartle Frere comments severely upon the alleged Zulu aggressions.

The matter, however, when sifted, sinks into insignificance. Some squabbles had taken place between individual Boers and

27. The homestead specially spoken of in this case does not appear to have been destroyed or injured till March, 1879, in the midst of the war, nor was any human being, white or black, belonging to these farms, killed by this "savage, unbridled, revengeful nation," before the war began.
28. 2220, p. 27.

Zulus, such as were only natural in the unsettled state of things; and Cetshwayo's explanation of the so-called "notices to quit" placed them in a very different light.

Sir Henry Bulwer writes to Sir Bartle Frere as follows on this point (July 16th):

> The Zulu king says that all the message he sent was a request that the Boers should be warned not to return to the disputed country, as he was informed they were doing since the meeting of the Commission. We know that some of the Boers did return to the disputed territory after the Commission broke up;[29] and this, no doubt, was looked upon by the Zulus as an attempt on the part of the Boers to anticipate the result of the inquiry, and led to the giving those notices. . . . The fault has been, no doubt, on both sides.

The military *kraal*, also, turned out to be no more of the nature ascribed to it than was its predecessor: "An ordinary private Zulu *kraal*" —see report of Mr. Rudolph[30]—"built simply to have a *kraal* in that locality, where many of Cetshwayo's people are residing without a head or *kraal* representing the king . . . . the king having given instructions that neither the white nor the native subjects of the Transvaal were in any way to be molested or disturbed by the Zulus;" and having sent a small force to do the work, because the large one he had sent on a previous occasion had frightened the white people.

Colonel Pearson, commanding the troops in Natal and the Transvaal, writes, June 8th, 1878:[31]

> The Landrost of Utrecht I know to be somewhat of an alarmist, and the border farmers have all along been in a great fright, and much given to false reports. I allude more particularly to the Boers. I enclose Lieut.-Colonel Durn-

---

29. Apparently by Sir T. Shepstone's orders, as the following phrase appears in one of the Boer protests against arbitration, April 25th, 1873: "The majority of the people have, by order of your Excellency, trekked into *laager* on December 14th last, and after having remained in *laager* for nearly five months, we are to go and live on our farms again."
30. 2144, p. 186.
31. 2144, p. 236.

ford's views of the *kraal* question. He is an officer who knows South Africa intimately, and his opinion I consider always sound and intelligent.

And the following is the statement of Lieut.-Colonel Durnford, K.E., June 8th, 1878:[32]

I know the district referred to, in which are many Zulu *kraals*, and believe that, if such a military *kraal* is in course of erection on the farm of one Kohrs, believed to be a field-cornet in the Wakkerstroom district, residing about fifteen miles from the mission station of the Rev. Mr. Meyer, it is being constructed that order may be kept amongst the Zulus here residing who owe allegiance to the Zulu king alone and in the interests of peace. . . . I further believe that, if the German or other residents at or near Luneburg have been ordered to leave, it is not by orders of the King of Zululand, who is far too wise a man to make a false move at present, when the boundary between himself and the Transvaal is under consideration.

The excitement concerning the "notices to quit," and the second "military *kraal*," appears to have been as unnecessary as any other imaginary Zulu scare; and there are no proofs to be extracted from the official papers at this period of the slightest signs of aggressive temper on the part of the Zulu king.

On the contrary; if we turn to the "Message from Cetywayo, King of the Zulus, to His Excellency the Lieut.-Governor of Natal," dated November 10th, 1878, we find the concluding paragraph runs:

Cetywayo hereby swears, in presence of Oham, Mnya-mana, Tshingwayo, and all his other chiefs, that he has no intention or wish to quarrel with the English.[33]

32. 2144, p. 237.
33. P. P. (C. 2308) p. 16

CHAPTER 11

Sihayo, Umbilini and the Missionaries in Zululand

Much has been said of late years concerning the duty imposed by our superior civilisation upon us English, in our dealings with the South African races, of checking amongst the latter such cruel and savage practices as are abhorrent to Christian ideas and practices. We will proceed to show how this duty has been performed by the Government of Natal.

One of the commonest accusations brought against the Zulus, and perhaps the most effectual in rousing English indignation and disgust, is that of buying and selling women as wives, and the cruel treatment of young girls who refuse to be thus purchased.

Without entering into the subject upon its merits, or inquiring how many French and English girls yearly are, to all intents and purposes, sold in marriage, and what amount of moral pressure is brought to bear upon the reluctant or rebellious amongst them; or whether they suffer more or less under the infliction than their wild sisters in Zululand do under physical correction; we may observe that the terrors of the Zulu system have been very much exaggerated. That cruel and tyrannical things have occasionally been done under it no one will deny, still less that every effort should have been made by us to introduce a better one. Amongst the Zulus, both in their own country and in Natal, marriages are commonly arranged by the parents, and the young people are expected to submit, as they would be in civilised France. But the instance which came most directly under the present writer's own observation, is one rather tending to prove that the custom is one which, although occasionally bearing hardly upon individuals, has been too long the practice of the people, and to which they have always been brought up, to be looked upon by them as a crying evil, calling for armed intervention on the part of England. In the early days of missionary work at Bishopstowe (between 1860-70), five girls took refuge at the station within a few days of each other, in order to avoid marriages arranged for them by their parents, and objected to by them. They dreaded pretty forcible coercion, although of course, in Natal, they could not actually be put to death. They were, of course, received and protected at Bishopstowe, clothed, and put to school, and there they: might have remained in safety for any length of time, or until they could return home on their own terms. But the restraint of the civilised habits imposed on them, however gently, and the obligation of learning to read, sew, and sweep, etc., was too much for these wild young damsels, accustomed at home to a free and idle life.[1] Within a few weeks they all elected to return home and marry the very men on whose account they had fled; and the conclusion finally arrived at concerning them was, that their escapade was rather for the sake of attaching a little additional importance to the surrender of their freedom, than from any real objection to the marriages proposed for them.

Now let us see what means had been taken by the English to institute a better state of things and greater liberty for the women. In Natal itself, of course, any serious act of violence committed to induce a girl to marry would be punished by law, and girls in fear of such violence could usually appeal for protection to the magistrates or missionaries. Let us suppose that a girl, making such an appeal, receives protection, and is married to the man of her own choice by English law and with Christian rites. What is the consequence to her? She has no rights as a wife, in fact she is not lawfully a wife at all, nor have her children

---

1. The married women work in the *mealie*-gardens, etc., and the *little* girls carry the babies; but the marriageable young women seem to have an interval of happy freedom from all labour and care.

any legal claims upon their father; the law of the colony protects the rights of native women married by native custom, which it virtually encourages by giving no protection at all to those who contract marriages by the English, or civilised system.[2]

So much for our dealings with the Zulus of Natal; and even less can be said for us concerning those over the border.

Until quite lately the practice existed in the colony of surrendering to Zulu demands refugee women, as well as cattle, as "property," under an order from the Natal Government, which was in force at the time of Sir H. Bulwer's arrival, but was at some time after rescinded.[3]

It was well known that, by the laws of Zululand, the offence of a woman's escaping from her husband with another man was punishable by death, therefore unhappy creatures thus situated were delivered up by the Natal Government to certain death, and this practice had been continued through a course of many years.

The law being altered in this respect, and cattle only returned, Sir H. Bulwer writes, on February 3rd, 1877:

> Some few weeks ago I had occasion to send a message to Cetywayo on account of the forcible removal from Natal territory of a Zulu girl, who had lately taken refuge in it from the Zulu country. A party of Zulus had crossed the Tugela River in pursuit, and taken the girl by force back to Zululand. I therefore sent to inform Cetywayo of this lawless act on the part of some of his subjects.[4]

Cetshwayo replies with thanks, saying that he knew nothing previously of what had happened, and that "should anything of the same kind take place to-morrow he (the Governor of Natal) must still open my ears with what is done by my people."

This is apparently all. There is no attempt to make a serious

---

2. This was comprehensible during the attempt, which proved so signal a failure, on the part of Sir T. Shepstone, to impose a marriage tax upon the natives. The tax was so extremely unpopular that it was thought advisable to relinquish it, and to make the desired increase in the revenue of the colony by doubling the hut-tax.
3. Sir T. Shepstone, when he says (1137, p. p. 18) "Natal gives up the cattle of Zulu refugees. . . . The refugees themselves are not given up," plainly includes–women amongst the cattle or "property" of the Zulus.
4. 1776, pp. 86, 87.

national matter of it; no demand for the surrender of the offenders, nor for the payment of a fine. Nor is there even a warning that any future occurrence of the same description will be viewed in a more severe light. Sir Henry "informs" Cetshwayo of what has taken place, and Cetshwayo politely acknowledges the information, and that the action taken by his people deserves censure. "I do not send and take by force," he says; "why should my people do so? It is not right."

Eighteen months later, on July 28th, 1878, a similar case was reported. A wife of the chief Sihayo had left him and escaped into Natal. She was followed by a party of Zulus, under Mehlokazulu, the chief son of Sihayo, and his brother, seized at the *kraal* where she had taken refuge, and carried back to Zululand, where she was put to death, in accordance with Zulu law.

The Zulus who seized her did no harm to Natal people or property; in fact their only fault towards England was that of following and seizing her on Natal soil, an act which for many years, and until quite lately, they would have been permitted to do, and assisted in doing, by the border Government officials. A week later the same young men, with two other brothers and an uncle, captured in like manner another refugee wife of Sihayo, in the company of the young man with whom she had fled. This woman was also carried back, and is supposed to have been put to death likewise; the young man with her, although guilty in Zulu eyes of a most heinous crime, punishable with death, was safe from them on English soil they did not touch him. But by our own practice for years past, of surrendering *female* refugees as *property*, we had taught the Zulus that we regarded women as cattle.

While fully acknowledging the savagery of the young men's actions, and the necessity of putting a stop to such for the future, it must be conceded that, having so long countenanced the like, we should have given fair notice that, for the future, it would be an act of aggression on us for a refugee of either sex to be followed into our territory, before proceeding to stronger measures.

Sir Henry Bulwer, indeed, though taking a decided view of

the young men's offence, plainly understood that it was an individual fault, and not a political action for the performance of which the king was responsible. He says:

> There is no reason whatsoever as yet to believe that these acts have been committed with the consent or knowledge of the king.[5/6]

His message to Cetshwayo merely requests that he will send in the ringleaders of the party to be tried by the law of the colony.

On a previous occasion the king had, of his own accord, sent a Zulu named Jolwana to the Natal Government to be punished by it for the murder of a white man in the Zulu country. Jolwana was returned upon his hands with the message that he could not be tried in Natal as he was a Zulu subject. Under these circumstances it was not unnatural that Cetshwayo should have taken the opportunity, apparently offered him by the use of the word *request*, of substituting some other method of apology for the offence committed than that of delivering up the young men, who, as he afterwards said, he was afraid would be *sjambokked* (flogged).

Cetshwayo's first answer is merely one acknowledging the message, and regretting the truth of the accusation brought by it. He allows that the young men deserve punishment, and he engages to send *indunas* of his own to the Natal Government on the subject; but he deprecates the matter being looked upon in a more serious light than as the "act of rash boys," who in their zeal for their father's house (? honour) did not think what they were doing.

About this date, August, 1878, when all sorts of wild reports were flying about, in and out of official documents, relative to Cetshwayo's supposed warlike preparations, he had ordered *that none of his people should carry arms on pain of death.*

This was in consequence of a circumstance which had oc-

---

5. 2220, p. 125.

6. And later, Nov. 18, 1878 (2222, p. 173), he says: "I do not hold the King responsible for the commission of the act, because there is nothing to show that it had his previous concurrence or even cognizance. But he becomes responsible for the act after its commission, and for such reparation as we may consider is due for it."

curred some months before (January, 1878), when during the Umkosi, or feast of first-fruits, a great Zulu gathering which annually takes place at the king's *kraal*, two of the regiments fell out and finally came to blows, resulting in the death of some men on either side. Sir B. Frere says, in his correspondence with the Bishop (p. 4), that many hundred men were killed on this occasion; but Mr. F. Colenso, who happened to be there a few days after the fight, heard from a white man, who had helped to remove the dead, that about fifty were killed. In consequence of this—

.... an order had gone forth, forbidding native Zulus, when travelling, to carry arms, nothing but switches being allowed. A fire took place, which burned the grass over Panda's grave,[7] and the doctors declared that the spirits of Dingane and Chaka had stated that they view with surprise and disgust the conduct of the Zulus at the present day in fighting when called before their king; that this was the reason Panda's grave was burned; and such things would continue until they learned to be peaceful among themselves, and wait until they are attacked by other natives before spilling blood.

Cetshwayo's next message, September 9th,[8] after he had inquired into the matter of Sihayo's sons, acknowledges again that they had done wrong, but observes that he was glad to find that they had hurt no one belonging to the English. "What they had done was done without his knowledge. The request of the Natal Government concerning the surrender of the offenders, he said, should be laid before the great men of the Zulu people, to be decided upon by them; he could not do it alone,

He finally, with full and courteous apologies in the same tone, begs that the Natal Government will accept, instead of the persons of the young men, a fine of fifty pounds, which he sent down by his messengers, but which was promptly refused. Sir Henry Bulwer appears to have been inclined to allow of the substitution of a larger fine for the surrender of the culprits;[9] but Sir B. Frere insists on severer measures, saying: "I think it

7. Since rifled by our troops, and the bones of the old king brought over to England.
8. 2260, p. 32.
9. 2222, p. 173.

quite necessary that the delivery up to justice of the offenders in this case should have been demanded[10] and should now be peremptorily insisted on, together with a fine for the delay in complying with the reiterated demand.

John Dunn, who is supposed to have advised the king to send money as an atonement, affirms that the invasion had been mutual, fugitives from justice having been fetched out of Zululand by Natal officers; and he (Dunn) asks whether outraged husbands, even amongst civilised people, are prone to pay much respect to the rights of nations when upon the track of their unfaithful spouses. Plainly, neither he nor the king looked upon the matter in so serious a light as Sir Bartle Frere chose to do when he said, September 30th, 1878,[11]—

> .... and, unless apologised and atoned for by compliance with the Lieut.-Governor's demands (?) that the leader of the murderous gangs shall be given up to justice, it will be necessary to send to the Zulu king *an ultimatum, which must put an end to pacific relations with our neighbours.*[12]

Sir M. Hicks-Beach, in reply to Sir B. Frere's last-quoted despatch, writes, November 21st:

> The abduction and murder of the Zulu woman who had taken refuge in Natal is undoubtedly a serious matter, and no sufficient reparation for it has yet been made. But I observe that Cetshwayo has expressed his regret for this occurrence; and although the compensation offered by him was inadequate, there would seem to have been nothing in his conduct with regard to it which would preclude the hope of a satisfactory arrangement.[13]

But the whole of Sir Bartle Frere's statements at this pe-

---

10. No "demand" was made until it appeared in Sir B. Frere's ultimatum.

11. 2220, p. 280.

12. On perusing the above italicised words, one learns for the first time that the ultimatum, which Sir Bartle Frere sent to the Zulu king a few months later, was actually sent for the express purpose of putting "an end to pacific relations with our neighbours." This is hardly the light in which the British public has been taught to look upon the matter.

13. P. P. (C. 2220), p. 320.

riod concerning Cetshwayo are one-sided, exaggerated, or entirely imaginary accusations, which come in the first instance with force from a man of his importance, but for which not the slightest grounds can be traced in any reliable or official source. He brings grave charges against the king, which are absolutely contradicted by the official reports from which he draws his information; he places before the public as actual fact what, on investigation, is plainly nothing more than his own opinion of what Cetshwayo thinks, wishes, or intends, and what his thoughts, wishes, and intentions may be at a future period. Every circumstance is twisted into a proof of his inimical intentions towards Natal, the worst motives are taken for granted in all he does. When the king's messages were sent through the ordinary native messengers between him and the Government of Natal, they are termed mere "verbal" messages (as what else should they be?), not "satisfactory or binding;" when they were sent through Mr. John Dunn they were called "unofficial," although Mr. Dunn had been repeatedly recognised, and by Sir B. Frere himself, as an official means of communication with Cetshwayo on matters of grave importance; and, when Mr. Dunn writes, on his own account, his opinion that the "boys" will not be given up, Sir B. Frere calls his letter "a similar informal message (i.e. from the king), couched in insolent and defiant terms." In nothing that passed between the king and the Government of Natal during this whole period is there one single word, on Cetshwayo's part, which could possibly be thus described. There are, indeed, many apologies and entreaties to the Government to be satisfied with some other atonement for the fault committed than the surrender of the culprits, and there is a great deal from various sources, official and otherwise, about cattle collected, even beyond the demands of the Government, as a propitiation; but of Sir B. Frere's "semi-sarcastic, insolent, and defiant" messages not one word.

It would take many pages to point out how utterly misleading is every word spoken by the High Commissioner on this subject, but to those who are curious in the matter, and in proof of the truth of our present statements, we can only recommend the South African *Blue-Books* of 1878-79. We cannot, however, better illustrate our meaning than by a quotation from Lord Blachford:[14]

> What did Sir B. Frere say to all this? He was really ashamed to answer that he did not know. He had studied the series of despatches in which Sir B. Frere defended his conduct, and he willingly acknowledged the exuberance of literary skill which they exhibited. But when he tried to grapple with them he felt like a man who was defending himself with a stick against a cloud of locusts.
>
> He might knock down one, and knock down another, but 'the cry is still they come.' His only consolation was, that they did not appear to have convinced Her Majesty's Government, whose replies were from beginning to end a series of cautions, qualifications, and protests.

On turning to the subject of the robber chief, Umbilini, and his raids, we are at once confronted by the fact that he was not a Zulu at all, but a Swazi, and a claimant to the Swazi throne. His claim had not been approved by the majority of the Swazi nation, and his brother Umbandeni, the present king, was appointed instead. Umbilini, however, was not a man to quietly sink into an inferior position, and having taken possession, with his followers, of some rocky caves in the borderland, forming an almost impregnable fortress, he lived for many years, much in the fashion of the border freebooters of whose doings we read in Scottish history, making raids upon his neighbours on all sides, and carrying off cattle, women, and children. His expeditions were most frequently directed towards the party against him in his own country, but neither his Boer nor Zulu neighbours escaped entirely. On first leaving Swaziland he went to offer homage to the Zulu king, and was given land to settle upon in Zululand. No doubt Cetshwayo looked upon a warrior of Umbilini's known prowess as rather an important vassal, especially in the event of a war between him and his ancient enemies the Swazis, in which case Umbilini's adherence would probably

---

14. *Daily News*, March 26th, 1872.

divide the enemy amongst themselves. But he appears to have been in perpetual trouble on account of his turbulent vassal, and to have given him up altogether at one time. After a raid committed by him upon the Dutch, the latter applied to Cetshwayo to have him delivered up to them. "I could not do this," says Cetshwayo; "I should have got a bad name if I had done so, and people would have said it was not good to *konza* (pay homage) to Cetshwayo. I therefore refused, but paid one hundred head of cattle for the offence he had committed;[15] and Cetshwayo's own account to Mr. Fynney is as follows:[16]

> Umbilini came to me for refuge from his own people, the Ama-Swazis, and I afforded him shelter; what would the world have said had I denied it to him? But, while allowing him to settle in the land as my subject, I have always been particularly careful to warn my people not to afford him any assistance or become mixed up in any quarrel between him and the Boers; and although I do not deny that he is my subject, still I will not endorse his misdeeds. When Mr. Rudolph complained to me of the trouble Umbilini was giving, I told Mr. Rudolph to kill him I should not shield him; this the Boers tried to do, but, as usual, made a mess of it.

In fact, on a repetition of Umbilini's offence against the Boers, Cetshwayo refused to be longer responsible for his acts, and gave the Dutch permission to kill him. They fought him, and were beaten by him with his small band of only nineteen men. On a subsequent occasion, after a raid committed by Umbilini upon the Swazis, Cetshwayo was so incensed that he sent out a party to take and kill him; but he got notice beforehand, and escaped.

Sir Bartle Frere chooses to consider the king responsible for all Umbilini's doings, and even Sir H. Bulwer says:

> The king disowned Umbilini's acts. . . . But there is nothing to show that he has in any way punished him, and, on the con-

---

15. Mr. H. Shepstone (Secretary for Native Affairs in the Transvaal) acknowledges that this fine was paid (2222, p. 99).
16. 1961.

trary, it is quite certain (of which *certainty* however, no proofs are forthcoming) that even if Umbilini did not act with the express orders of Cetshwayo, he did so with the knowledge that what he was doing would be agreeable to the king.[17]

This accusation was made in January, 1879, and refers to raids of the previous year, by which time, as the Swazis were our allies and the Boers our subjects, Umbilini's raids in all directions except those on the Zulu side had become offences to us for which Cetshwayo was held responsible. In point of fact, it was no such simple matter to "punish" Umbilini, whose natural fortress could be held by a couple of men against anything short of the cannon which Cetshwayo did not possess. Nor was it singular that, at a time when the king had already strong suspicions that his country was about to be attacked, he should not have wasted his strength in subduing one who, in the event of war, would be most useful to himself.

That, when the evil day came and his country was invaded, Cetshwayo should have made common cause with all who would or could assist him is a mere matter of course, and it was but natural that so bold and skilful a leader as Umbilini has proved himself to be should then have been promoted and favoured by the unfortunate king.

We need scarcely say more upon this point, beyond calling our readers' attention to the fact that the expressions *"Zulu raids" "indiscriminate massacres" "violation by the Zulus of Transvaal territory" "horrible cruelties"*,[18] so freely scattered through the despatches written to prove the criminality of the Zulu king, *all, without exception*, apply to acts committed either by Umbilini and his (chiefly) *Swazi* followers, or by Manyonyoba, a small but independent native chief, living north of the Pongolo.[19]

The "case of Messrs. Smith and Deighton" is the only charge against the Zulu king, in connection with Natal, which we have

---

17. 2260, p. 46.
18. 2308, p. 62, and elsewhere.
19. Manyonyoba owed allegiance to Cetshwayo (as did Umbilini). He lived north of the Pongolo, in a part of the country over which Sir Bartle Frere and Sir Henry Bulwer altogether deny Cetshwayo's supremacy, and was claimed as a subject of the Transvaal Government.

now to consider, and it is one in which, as we shall see, a great deal was made of a very small matter.

Mr. Smith, a surveyor in the Colonial Engineer's department, was on duty inspecting the road down to the Tugela, near Fort Buckingham. The Zulu mind being in a very excited state at the time owing to the obvious preparation for war, of which they heard reports from Natal, troops stationed at Grey town, and war-ships seen close to the Zulu shore, as though looking for a landing-place—Mr. Smith was specially instructed to proceed upon his errand alone, and with great discretion. By way of carrying out these directions he took with him only a trader—Deighton by name—and their discretion was shown by "taking no notice" when, having arrived at the drift into Zululand, they were questioned by Zulus, who were on guard there in consequence of rumours that our troops were about to cross.[20]

Mr. Wheelwright (a Government official), to whom the matter was reported a week after it occurred, not by Mr. Smith, the principal person concerned, but by Mr. Deighton, says:

> The fact that the two white men took no notice of ' lots of Zulus shouting out' from their own bank, 'What do you want there?' but 'walked quietly along'[21] as if they had not heard, or as if they were deaf, very naturally confirmed the suspicion that they were about no good.

The consequence was, that when the white men reached an islet in the middle of the river (or rather one which is generally in the middle of the stream when it is full it was low at the time), they were seized by the Zulus, and detained by them for about an hour and a half, whilst all sorts of questions were asked:

"What are you doing there?"

"What had the soldiers come to Grey town for?"

20. Sir H. Bulwer says "they have suspected, quite wrongly, that we had some design against them in making it" (the new road to the drift). It is to be questioned how far their suspicion was a wrongful one, seeing that it was understood from the first that the drift was intended especially for military purposes, and was undoubtedly inspected by Mr. Smith for the same.

21. Quotations from Mr. Deighton's report to Mr. Wheelwright.

"What did the white men want coming down there? There were two down not long ago, then other two only a few days since, and now there is other two; you must come for some reason."

However, after a time, they were allowed to depart, an attempt made to take their horses from them being prevented by the *induna* of the Zulus.

Sir Bartle Frere does not seem to have thought very much of the matter at first, for Sir M. Hicks-Beach, when acknowledging his despatch reporting it, says:[22]

> I concur with you in attributing no special importance to the seizure and temporary arrest of the surveyors, which was partly due to their own indiscretion, and was evidently in no way sanctioned by the Zulu authorities.

But a little later although with no fresh facts before him Sir B. Frere takes a very different tone.[23]

> I cannot at all agree with the lenient view taken by the. Lieut.-Governor of this case. Had it stood quite alone, a prompt apology and punishment of the offenders might have been sufficient. As the case stands, it was only one of many instances of insult and threatening, such as cannot possibly be passed over without severe notice being taken of them. What occurred, whether done by the king's order, or only by his border-guards, and subsequently only tacitly approved by his not punishing the offenders, seems to me a most serious insult and outrage, and should be severely noticed.

There is no sign that it was ever brought to the king's knowledge, and when Sir B. Frere speaks of its being "only one of many instances of insult and threatening," he is drawing largely on his imagination, as there is no other recorded at all, unless he means to refer to the "notices to quit" in the disputed territory of which we have already treated.

We must now consider the points connected with the internal management of the Zulu country, which have generally been looked upon as a partial excuse for our invasion. Foremost

22. 2220, p. 320.
23. 2222, p. 176.

amongst these is the infraction of the so-called "coronation promises," of which we have spoken in a previous chapter. Frequent rumours were current in Natal that the king, in defiance of the said promises, was in the habit of shedding the blood of his people upon the smallest provocation, and without any form of trial. Such stories of his inhuman atrocities were circulated in the colony that many kind-hearted and gentle people were ready to think that war would be a lesser evil. Yet, whenever one of these stories was examined into or traced to its source, it turned out either to be purely imaginary, or to have for its foundation some small act of more or less arbitrary authority, the justice of which we might possibly question, but to which no one would apply the words "barbarities," "savage murders," etc.

An instance of the manner in which the Zulu king has obtained his character of "a treacherous and bloodthirsty sovereign,"[24] came under the notice of the present writer about December of last year (1878). Happening to be on a visit to some friends in Pietermaritzburg, and hearing them mention Cetshwayo's cruelties, I observed that I did not much credit them, as I had never yet met anyone who knew of them from any trustworthy source. I was met with the assurance that their "kitchen-Kafir," Tom, from whom they had received their accounts, was a personal witness, having himself escaped from a massacre, and they vouched for the truthfulness of the man's character. I asked and obtained permission to question the man in his own language, being myself anxious to find any real evidence on the subject, especially as, at that time with military preparations going on on every side it was apparent to all that "we" intended war, and one would have been glad to discover that there was any justification for it on our side. The same evening I took an opportunity of interrogating "Tom," saying, "So I hear that you know all about this wicked Zulu king. Tell me all about it." Whereupon the man launched out into a long account of the slaughter of his people, from which not even infants were spared, and from which he was one of the few who had escaped. He had

---

24. Words applied to him by Mr. Brownlee, late Secretary for Native Affairs of the Cape Government.

plainly been accustomed to tell the tale (doubtless a true one), and there were touches in it concerning the killing of the children which showed that he had been in the habit of recounting it to tender-hearted and horror-struck English mothers. When he had finished his tale I asked him when all the horrors which he had described had taken place. "Oh!" he replied, "it was at the time of the fight between Cetshwayo and Umbulazi (1856); that was when I left Zululand."

"And you have never been there since? "

"No; I should be afraid to go, for Cetshwayo kills always."

"How do you know that?" I inquired, for he had started upon a fresh account of horrors relating to the time at which he was speaking.

"Oh! I know it is true," was the ready and confident reply, "because the white people here in 'Maritzburg tell me so out of the papers."

In point of fact the man, on whose word to my own knowledge rested the belief of a considerable circle of the citizens, could only give personal evidence concerning what happened at the time of the great civil war, when Zululand was in such confusion that it would not be easy to distribute responsibility, and when Cetshwayo himself was a young man in the hands of his warriors. All he could tell of a later date he had himself learnt from "white people" in the town, who, again, had gathered their information from the newspapers; and Bishop Schreuder, long resident in Zululand, says:

> I had not with my own eyes seen any corpse, and personally only knew of them said to have been killed. . . . I myself had my information principally from the same sources as people in Natal, and often from Natal newspapers.

The king's own reply to these accusations may be taken entire from Mr. Fynney's report on July 4th, 1877,[25] with the portions of the message delivered by the latter to which it refers:

> You have repeatedly acknowledged the house of England to be a great and powerful house, and have expressed your-

25. 1961.

self as relying entirely upon the goodwill and power of that house for your own strength and the strength of the country over which you are king; in fact you have always looked towards the English Government.

Which way is your face turned to-day? Do you look, and still desire to look, in the same direction? Do you rely on the good-will and support of the British Government as much as you formerly did?

The Government of Natal has repeatedly heard that you have not regarded the agreements you entered into with that Government, through its representative, Sir Theophilus Shepstone, on the occasion of your coronation. These agreements you entered into with the sun shining around you, but since that time you have practised great cruelties upon your people, putting great numbers of them to death. What do you say?

In reply to the above, Cetshwayo said:

I have not changed; I still look upon the English as my friends, as they have not yet done or said anything to make me feel otherwise. They have not in any way turned my heart, therefore I feel that we have still hold of each other's hands. But you must know that from the first the Zulu nation grew up alone, separate and distinct from all others, and has never been subject to any other nation; Tyaka (Chaka) was the first to find out the English and make friends with them; he saved the lives of seven Englishmen from shipwreck at the mouth of the Umfolosi, he took care of them, and from that day even until now the English and Zulu nations have held each other's hands. The English nation is a just one, and we are united. I admit that people have been killed. There are three classes of wrongdoers that I kill (1) the *abatakati* witches, poisoners, etc.; (2) those who take the women of the great house, those belonging to the royal household; and (3) those who kill, hide, or make away with the king's cattle. I mentioned these three classes of wrong-doers to Somtseu (Sir T. Shepstone), when he came to place me as king over the Zulu nation, as those who had always been killed. I told him that it was our law, and that three classes of wrong-doers I would kill, and he replied: 'Well, I cannot put aside a standing law of the land.' I always give a wrongdoer three chances, and kill him if he passes the last. Evil-doers would go over my head if I did not punish them, and that is our mode of punishing. . . . I do not see that I have in any way departed from, or broken in anything, the compact I made with the Natal Government through Somtseu.

The next subject to be considered is that of the treatment of the missionaries and their converts in Zululand.

Sir T. Shepstone, in his account of what passed at the installation of Cetshwayo, writes as follows:[26]

The fourth point was the position of Christian missionaries and their converts. Cetywayo evidently regretted that they had ever been admitted at all, and had made up his mind to reduce their numbers by some means or other. . . . He said they had committed no actual wrong, but they did no good, and that the tendency of their teaching was mischievous; he added converts, or even retaining those around them, were for the present at an end. . . . I find there were all sorts of wild (?) rumours going about from station to station—one that the British Government intended to annex Zululand at once. I am afraid that this and the like rumours have done harm. Several of the missionaries have been frequently to the king of late, and, as he told me, have worried him to such an extent that he does not want to see them any more.[27]

In August of the same year Lord Carnarvon requests Sir Henry Bulwer to make a special point of causing "the missionaries to understand distinctly that Her Majesty's Government cannot undertake to compel the king to permit the maintenance of the mission stations in Zululand," and to recommend them, if they cannot carry on their work without armed support, to leave it for the present.

---

26. C. 1137, p. 19.
27. On one of these visits a missionary is reported to have said to the king coarsely in Zulu, "You are a liar!" (*unamanga!*) upon which Cetshwayo turned his back to him, and spoke with him no more.

Sir Henry Bulwer writes:[28]

> The action taken by some of the missionaries in leaving
> that country has apparently proved not only unnecessary, but
> ill-advised for their own interests. The king was not sorry that
> they should go, but he was angry with them for going.[29]

On January 26th, 1878, a message arrived from Cetshwayo,
concerning those that remained, to this effect:[30]

> Cetshwayo states that he wishes His Excellency to know
> that he is not pleased with the missionaries in the Zulu
> country, as he finds out that they are the cause of much
> harm, and are always spreading false reports about the Zulu
> country, and (he) would wish His Excellency to advise them
> to remove, as they do no good.

Shortly after the Rev. Mr. Oftebro and Dr. Oftebro, Norwegian missionaries from Zululand, were granted an interview by
the Lieut.-Governor of Natal for the purpose of laying their case
before His Excellency. The king, they said, had informed them
that he was now quite persuaded that they had communicated
to the governors of Natal and the Transvaal, and to the editors
of the public papers in Natal, all important matters that occurred
in the Zulu country—that the accounts they sent were not even
truthful and that he had believed these missionaries were "men,"
but that he now found them to be his enemies.

They believed that amongst the "white men," from whom he
had obtained his information, were Mr. John Mullins, a trader,
and Mr. F. E. Colenso, a son of the Bishop of Natal, who had
been at the king's *kraal* for some six days and who, they said,
"*had translated, for the king's information, accounts of doings in the
Zulu country*, from several newspapers of the colony." This last, as
it happens, was pure fiction. Sir Henry Bulwer, indeed, believed
it at the time, and wrote upon it as follows:[31]

---

28. 2000, p. 33.
29. Or rather he was angry with them for the rudeness which they committed in
going *without taking leave*. He said they had never received anything but kindness
from him, and might as well have paid him the compliment of a farewell salutation.
30. 2100, p. 61.
31. 2100, p. 89.

I notice in Messrs. Smith and Colenso's letter to the Earl of Carnarvon, a statement to the effect that the disposition and dealings of Cetshwayo had been sedulously misrepresented by the missionaries and by the Press. And this statement tends, I am afraid, to confirm the belief that Mr. F. E. Colenso, when he lately visited the Zulu country, . . . made certain representations regarding the missionaries in Zululand, which were greatly calculated to prejudice the king's mind against them, or against some of them.

But Mr. Colenso, on seeing for the first time the above statements in the *Blue-Book*, wrote to Sir M. Hicks-Beach as follows:[32]

The suspicions expressed by the missionaries as to my proceedings are entirely without foundation in fact. So far from attempting to prejudice the king's mind against them, I confined myself, in the little I did say to Cetshwayo on the subject, to supporting their cause with him. The king had received, through some of his various channels of information, an account of the numerous contributions made by missionaries and others living under his protection in Zululand, to the colonial newspapers, and in particular, of an exaggerated and sensational report, written by the Zululand correspondent of *The Natal Mercury*, of the catastrophe which occurred at the annual Feast of First-fruits some ten days before my last conversation with the king, which report he attributed to the Rev. Mr. Robertson, from the fact that his wagon-driver was the only white man present on the occasion, except Dr. Oftebro, Mr. Mullins, and Mr. Dunn. Cetshwayo expressed himself as indignant at the conduct of Mr. Robertson, who, he said, had never, during his long residence in Zululand, received anything but good treatment at the hands of his (Cetshwayo's) father and himself, and, he added, 'I have borne with him too long.' To this I replied that, if he had any distinct ground of complaint against Mr. Robertson, he (the king) should get it set down in writing, and send it to His Excellency the Lieut.-Governor of Natal; and I wished him to understand that any different course would be productive of no good effect. I

32. 2220, p. 318.

then told Cetshwayo, omitting further reference to Mr. Robertson, that in my opinion the presence of the missionaries as a body in his country was a great advantage to him, and that they merited his protection. He disclaimed having ever treated them with anything but great consideration.

The particular statement of the two missionaries Oftebro, concerning the translation of newspapers, also Mr. Colenso specially and distinctly contradicts, saying that he had no newspapers with him nor extracts of newspapers, nor were any such read to Cetshwayo in his presence.

Sir H. Bulwer states, at the request of the Messrs. Oftebro,[33] that no member of the Norwegian mission had supplied this Government with information as above. But it does not follow that no such communications had been made to Sir B. Frere and Lord Carnarvon. Missionaries had written anonymously to the colonial papers, and the account in *The Natal Mercury* of the fight at the Umkosi was attributed by Cetshwayo, not without reason, to the Rev. R Robertson. The tone of this letter, and its accuracy, may be gathered from the following extract, referring to the land which, in the opinion of the Commissioners, "was by right belonging to the Zulus."

> Never was a more preposterous demand made upon any Government than that which Cetshwayo is now making upon the English Government of the Transvaal. . . . For be it remembered that, until very lately, the Zulus have never occupied any portion of it, (!) and even now very partially. It is most earnestly to be hoped that Sir T. Shepstone, while doing all in his power to keep the peace, *will be equally firm in resisting the unjust pretensions of the Zulus.*"[33]

How far the Zulu king was justified in his opinion that the missionaries were not his friends may be gathered from the above, and from the replies to Sir B. Frere's appeal to the "missionaries of all denominations" for their opinions on native politics, as published in the *Blue-Books*, of which the following examples may be given:[34]

---

33. Author's italics.
34. 2316.

From letter of the Rev. P. D. Hepburn, December 17th, 1878:

All in these parts are quiet, and are likely to remain quiet, if His Excellency overthrows the Zulu chief, and disarms the remaining Zulus. The Zulus are very warlike; will attack in front, flank, and rear. They are, and have been, the terror of the neighbouring tribes since the days of Chaka.[35] Only the utter destruction of the Zulus can secure future peace in South Africa. May His Excellency not allow himself to be deceived by the Zulu chief Cetywayo.

On full inquiry it will be found that our late war, (Kaffraria) here was to a great extent attributable to Zulu influence.[36] If our forces suffer defeat at Natal, all native tribes in South Africa will rise against us. I am a man of peace; I hate war; but if war, let there be no dawdling and sentimental nonsense.

True and faithful to God, our Queen, and the interests of the empire, we have the approbation of God, our Queen, and our own conscience. I would have much liked had there been a regiment of British cavalry at Natal. Sword in hand, the British are irresistible over all natives. The battle at the Gwanga in 1846, under Sir Henry Darrell, lasted only about fifteen minutes; about four hundred Kafirs were cut down. . . .

God, our God, put it into the minds of our rulers that all tribes in south-east and east Africa must submit to British power, and that it is the interest of all Africans to do so. Heathenism must perish; God wills it so.[37]

These remarks are from a missionary in Kaffraria, but the tone of these in Zululand is the same, or even worse. Compare the following statement made to the Natal Government by two native converts from the Etshowe mission station Mr. Oftebro's:[38]

We know that as many a hundred (Zulus) in one day see

---

35. "Our Correspondent" of The Daily News speaks, in to-day's issue (November 17th, 1879), of the "tranquillising fear" of Cetshwayo having been removed from "our own native population."
36. A mere assertion, often made, but never supported by the slightest proof.
37. And so the Rev. Mr. Glockner, speaking of the late war, says that they (the missionaries) had often warned the native chiefs of what would befall them, if they refused to become Christians. Vide The Scotsman, February 5th, 1880.
38. 1883, p. 2.

the sun rise, but don't see it go down. . . . The people, great and small, are tired of the rule of Cetshwayo, by which he is finishing his people. The Zulu army is not what it was, there are only six full regiments. Cetshwayo had by his rule made himself so disliked, that they knew of no one, and especially of the headmen, who would raise a hand to save him from ruin, no matter from what cause.

Mr. John Shepstone adds, April 27th, 1877:[39]

The above was confirmed only yesterday by reliable authority, who added that a power such as the English, stepping in now, would be most welcome to the Zulus generally, through the unpopularity of the king, by his cruel and reckless treatment of his subjects.

And Mr. Fynney, in the report already quoted from, says:

The king appeared to have a very exaggerated idea both of his power, the number of his warriors, and their ability as such. . . . While speaking of the king as having exaggerated ideas as to the number of his fighting-men, I would not wish to be understood as underrating the power of the Zulu nation. . . . I am of opinion that King Cetywayo could bring six thousand men into the field at a short notice, great numbers armed with guns; but the question is, would they fight? . . . I am of opinion that it would greatly depend against whom they were called to fight. . . . While the Zulu nation, to a man, would have willingly turned out to fight either the Boers or the Ama-Swazi, the case would be very different, I believe, in the event of a misunderstanding arising between the British Government and the Zulu nation. . . . I further believe, from what I heard, that a quarrel with the British Government would be the signal for a general split up amongst the Zulus, and the king would find himself deserted by the majority of those upon whom he would at present appear to rely.

While Sir T. Shepstone says, November 30th, 1878:[40]

---

39. 1883, p. 4.
40. 2222, p. 175.

I will, however, add my belief that the Zulu power is likely to fall to pieces when touched.

Such were the opinions given by men supposed to be intimately acquainted with Zulu character and feeling, one of them being *the* great authority on all native matters; and on such statements did Sir Bartle Frere rely when he laid his scheme for the Zulu War. How absolutely ignorant, how foolishly mistaken, were these "blind leaders of the blind" has been amply proved by the events of 1879.

We need not enter very fully into the accusations brought by the missionaries against the Zulu king of indiscriminate slaughter of native converts for their religion's sake. They were thoroughly believed in Natal at the time; but, upon investigation, they dwindled down to three separate cases of the execution of men (one in each case) who happened to be converts, but of whom two were put to death for causes which had nothing whatsoever to do with their faith (one of them being indeed a relapsed convert); and the third, an old man, Maqamsela, whose name certainly deserves to be handed down to fame in the list of martyrs for religion's sake, was killed without the sanction or even knowledge of the king, by the order of his prime minister Gaozi.[41] That the latter received no punishment, although the king disapproved of this action, is not a fact of any importance. It is not always convenient to punish prime ministers and high commissioners, or powerful *indunas*.

Sir Bartle Frere of course takes the strongest possible view of the matter against the king, and speaks of his having killed Zulu converts[42]—

> . . . . at first rarely, as if with reluctance, and a desire to conceal what he had ordered, and to shift the responsibility to other shoulders, latterly more frequently, openly, and as an

---

41. Story of Maqamsela, from *The Natal Colonist* of May 4th, 1877: "Another case referred to in our previous article was that of a man named Maqamsela, particulars of which, derived from eye-witnesses, we have received from different sources. On Friday, March 9th, he attended morning service at Etshowe mission station as usual, went home to his *kraal*, and at noon started to go over to the *kraal* of Minyegana, but was seized on the road and killed because he was a Christian!"
42. 2220, p. 270.

avowed part of a general policy for re-establishing the system of Chaka and Dingane.

This little phrase is of a slightly imaginative nature, resting on no (produced) evidence. It is, in fact, a "statement."[43]

Sir Henry Bulwer's reply—November 18th, 1878[44]—which forms an able refutation of various statements of Sir B. Frere, contains the following sentence: "I took some pains to find out how the case really stood, and ascertained that the number of natives, either converts or living on mission stations, who had been killed, was three. I have never heard since that time of any other mission natives being killed. . . . I was, therefore, surprised, on reading your Excellency's despatch, to see what Messrs. Oftebro and Staven had said. I have since made particular inquiries on that point, but have failed to obtain any information showing that more than three mission natives have been killed. Among others to whom I have spoken is the Rev. Mr. Robertson, of Zululand, who was in 'Maritzburg a few weeks ago. He told me that he had not heard of any other than the three cases."

Sir Bartle Frere replies, December 6th, 1878:[45/46]

I have since made further inquiry (he does not say what), and have *no doubt* that though His Excellency *may possibly* be right as to the number regarding which there is *judicial evidence* (Sir H. Bulwer plainly decides that there was *no evidence at all*); the missionaries had *every reason to believe* that the number slain *on account of their inclination to Christianity* was considerably greater than three. One gentleman, who had better means of obtaining the truth than anyone else, told me *he had no doubt* the number of converts killed was considerable.

This gentleman, Sir Bartle Frere assures us—

---

43. This indiscriminate killing is disproved and denied by Cetshwayo himself and his principal chiefs (*vide* "A Visit to King Ketshwayo," *Macmillan's Magazine*, March, 1878.
44. 2222, p. 171.
45. 2222, p. 175.
46. Author's italics throughout.

.... knows the Zulus probably better than *any living European*; he is himself an old resident in Zululand, and a man *above all suspicion of exaggeration or misrepresentation* (!). He gave me this information, under stipulation that his name should not be mentioned, otherwise it would, I am sure, at once be accepted as a guarantee for the accuracy of his statements.

With such phrases, "I have no doubt," "every reason to believe," "I feel sure," etc. etc,, has Sir Bartle Frere continually maligned the character of the Zulu king, called since the war by Mr. John Dunn, "the most injured man in South Africa."

One is rather puzzled who the man may be to whom Sir Bartle Frere gives so high a character, his opinion of which he evidently expects will quite satisfy his readers. We should much like to have the gentleman's name. The number of gentlemen "long resident in Zululand" are not so many as to leave a wide field for conjecture. Besides the missionaries, the only names that occur to us to which the phrase can apply are those of Mr. John Shepstone, Mr. John Dunn, and Mr. Robertson.

The only point in the indictment against Cetshwayo which we have now to consider, is that of the killing of girls under the Zulu marriage law, and the reply to Sir Henry Bulwer's remonstrance on the point, which Sir Bartle Frere speaks of in his final memorandum as expressed "in terms of unprecedented insolence and defiance;" while *The Times of Natal* (generally recognised as the Government organ) went still further, and has twice charged the Zulu king with sending *repeatedly*, insolent messages to the Natal Government. As to the *repetition* of the offence, it need only be said that there is no foundation in the *Blue-Books* for the assertion. And as to this particular offence it is enough to say that no notice had been taken of it to Cetshwayo himself, till two years afterwards it was unearthed, and charged upon him, as above, by the High Commissioner, notwithstanding that, whatever it may have been, it had been subsequently condoned by friendly messages from this Government.

The marriage law of Zululand is thus described by Sir T. Shepstone:[47]

---

47. 1137, p. 21.

The Zulu country is but sparsely inhabited when compared with Natal, and the increase of its population is checked more by its peculiar marriage regulations than by the exodus of refugees to surrounding governments. Both boys and girls are formed into regiments, and are not allowed to marry without special leave from the king, or until the regiments to which they belong are fortunate enough to receive his dispensation. Caprice or state reasons occasionally delay this permission, and it sometimes happens that years pass before it is given. Contravention of these regulations is visited by the severest penalties.[48]

The history of the case which we are now considering may be given in the following extracts. On September 22nd, 1876, Mr. Osborn, resident magistrate of Newcastle, writes:

> The Zulu king lately granted permission to two regiments of middle-aged men to marry. These were, however, rejected by the girls, on the ground that the men were too old; upon which the king ordered that those girls who refused to marry the soldiers were to be put to death. Several girls were killed in consequence, some fled into the colony, others into the Transvaal Republic, and on October 9th, Government messengers report:[49]

> We heard that the king was causing some of the Zulus to be killed on account of disobeying his orders respecting the marriage of girls, and we saw large numbers of cattle which had been taken as fines. Otherwise the land was quiet.

---

48. Two Zulu prisoners, captured while on a peaceful errand, just before the commencement of hostilities, and who were permitted to reside at Bishopstowe when released from gaol, until they could safely return home, were questioned concerning these regulations, and said that they applied only to those who voluntarily joined the regiments, concerning which there was no compulsion at all, beyond the moral effect produced by the fact that it was looked upon, by the young people themselves, as rather a poor thing to do to decline joining. Once joined, however, they were obliged to obey orders unhesitatingly. These young men said that in the coast, and outlying districts, there were large numbers of people who had retained their liberty and married as they pleased, but that strict loyalty was the *fashion* nearer the *court*. It was in these very coast districts that the Zulus surrendered during the late war, the loyal inhabitants proving their loyalty to the *bitter end*.
49. 1748, p. 198.

As far as the most careful investigations could discover, the number killed was not more than four or five, while the two Zulus already quoted said that, although they had *heard* of the matter, they did not *know* of a single instance; and as these young men themselves belonged to one of the regiments, it can hardly be supposed that any great slaughter could have taken place unknown to them.

At the time, however, reports, as usual, greatly exaggerated the circumstances, and Sir Henry Bulwer speaks[50] of *"numbers of girls and young men"* and *"large numbers of girls and others connected with them"* as having been killed.

He sent a message to Cetshwayo on the subject, which in itself was a temperate and very proper one for an English governor to send, in the hope of checking such cruelty in future, and was not unnaturally somewhat surprised at receiving an answer from the usually courteous and respectful king, which showed plainly enough that he was highly irritated and resented the interference with his management of his people. Sir Henry had reminded him of what had passed at his coronation, and Cetshwayo replies that if Somtseu (Sir T. Shepstone) had told the white people that he (the king) had promised never to kill, Somtseu had deceived them. "I have yet to kill," he says. He objects to being dictated to about his laws, and says that while wishing to be friends with the English, he does not intend to govern his people by laws sent to him by them. He remarks, in a somewhat threatening way, that in future he shall act on his own account, and that if the English interfere with him, he will go away and become a wanderer, but not without first showing what he can do if he chooses. Finally he points out that he and the Governor of Natal are in like positions,[51] one being governor of Natal, the other of Zululand.

It is plain that this reply, as reported by the Government messengers, produced a strong effect on Sir H. Bulwer's mind, and considerably affected his feeling towards the king, though,

---

50. 1748, p. 198.
51. "We are equal," said the interpreter; but the expression used is more correctly translated as above.

as already stated, he never brought it, at the time or afterwards, to the notice of Cetshwayo, and has since exchanged friendly messages with him. And no doubt the reply was petulant and wanting in due respect, though a dash of arrogance was added to it by the interpreter's use of the expression "we are equal," instead of "we are in like positions"—each towards our own people. But that the formidable words "I have yet to kill," "I shall now act on my own account," meant nothing more than the mere irritation of the moment is plain from the fact that he never made the slightest attempt to carry them out, though recent events have taught us what he might have done had he chosen to "act on his own account."

The tone of the reply would probably have been very different had it been brought by Cetshwayo's own messengers. By an unfortunate mistake on the part of the Natal Government, one of the messengers sent was a *Zulu refugee* of the party of Umbulazi and Umkungo, between whom and the king there was deadly hostility, which had lately been intensified by the insulting manner in which Umkungo's people had received Cetshwayo's messengers, sent in a friendly spirit to inform them of King Umpande's death. The very presence of this man, bringing a reproof from the Government of Natal, would naturally be resented by the Zulu king, who had already declined communications from the Transvaal sent through refugee subjects of his own;[52] and was now obliged to receive with courtesy, and listen to words of remonstrance from, one of these very refugees who had fled to Natal, and, under Zulu law, was liable to be put to death as a traitor, when he made his appearance in Zululand. The king's words, exhibiting the irritation of the moment, whatever they may have been, would lose nothing of their fierceness and bitterness by being conveyed through such a medium.

We do not wish to defend such practices as those of forcing girls into distasteful marriages, or putting them to death for disobedience in that respect. But we must remember that, after all, the king, in ordering these executions, was enforcing, not a

---

52. Sir Henry Bulwer 1748, p. 10.

new law laid down by himself, but "an old custom."[53] From his point of view the exercise of such severity was as necessary to maintaining his authority as the decimation of a regiment for mutiny might appear to a commander, or the slaughter of hundreds of Langalibalele's people, hiding in caves or running away, which we have already described, appeared to Sir B. Pine and Sir T. Shepstone in 1873-74.

The king himself gave an illustration of his difficulties in a message sent to Sir H. Bulwer early in 1878.[54] He reported to His Excellency that two of his regiments had had a fight, and many of his men had been killed, at which he was much annoyed. He reports this to show His Excellency that, although he warned them that he would severely punish any regiment that caused any disturbance at the Umkosi, he cannot rule them without sometimes killing them, especially as they know they can run to Natal.

We have now considered in turn every accusation brought against the Zulu king up to the end of 1878, when Sir Bartle Frere delivered his ultimatum, which he had said beforehand would put an end to our peaceful relations with our neighbours. We venture to assert that, with the exception of the last, every one of these accusations is distinctly refuted on evidence gathered from official sources. Of that last, we would observe, that, although it cannot be entirely denied, the fault has been greatly exaggerated; while that part of it which referred to the sole instance of a hasty reply to the Natal Government, has been condoned by two years' friendly relations since the offence, before it was raked up by Sir Bartle Frere as an additional pretext for the war. And, at all events, had Cetshwayo's severity to his people been a hundred times greater than it ever was, he could not in a lifetime have produced the misery which this one year's campaign has wrought.

Yet these accusations were the sole pretexts for the war, except that fear of the proximity of a nation strong enough and warlike enough to injure us, *if it wished to do so*, which Sir Bartle

53. 1748, p. 198.
54. 2079, p. 96.

Frere declared made it impossible for peaceful subjects of Her Majesty to feel security for life or property within fifty miles of the border, and made the existence of a peaceful English community in the neighbourhood impossible.[55] He speaks in the same despatch[56] of the king as "an irresponsible, bloodthirsty, and treacherous despot," which terms, and others like them, do duty again and again for solid facts, but of the justice of which he gives no proof whatever. We cannot do better than give, in conclusion, and as a comment upon the above fear, a quotation from Lord Blachford's speech in the House of Lords, March 26th, 1879, which runs:

> Some people assumed that the growth of the Zulu power in the neighbourhood of a British colony constituted such a danger that, in a common phrase, it had to be got rid of, and that, when a thing had to be done, it was idle and inconvenient to examine too closely into the pretexts which were set up. And this was summed up in a phrase which is used more than once by the High Commissioner, and had obtained currency in what he might call the light literature of politics. We might be told to obey our 'instincts of self-preservation.' No doubt the instinct of self-preservation was one of the most necessary of our instincts. But it was one of those which we had in common with the lowest brute—one of those which we are most frequently called on to keep in order. It was in obedience to the 'instinct of self-preservation' that a coward ran away in battle, that a burglar murdered a policeman, or, what was more to our present purpose, that a nervous woman jumped out of a carriage lest she should be upset; or that one man in a fright fired at another who, he thought, meant to do him an injury, though he had not yet shown any sign of an intention of doing so. The soldiers who went down in the *Birkenhead* what should we have thought of them if, instead of standing in their ranks to be drowned,

---

55. The natives of Natal, "peaceful subjects of Her Majesty," were living in perfect security on one side of the border, and the Zulus on the other, the two populations intermarrying and mingling in the most friendly manner, without the smallest apprehension of injury to life or property, when Sir B. Frere landed at Durban.
56. 2269, pp. 1, 2.

they had pushed the women and children into the hold and saved themselves? A reasonable determination to do that which our safety requires, so far as it is consistent with our duty to others, is the duty and interest of every man. To evade an appeal to the claims of reason and justice, by a clamorous allegation of our animal instinct, is to abdicate our privileges as men, and to revert to brutality.

CHAPTER 12

Commencement of the Campaign

On December 11th the boundary award was delivered to the Zulus by four gentlemen selected for the purpose, who, by previous arrangement, met the king's envoys at the Lower Tugela Drift. The award itself, as we already know, was in favour of the Zulus; nevertheless it is impossible to read the terms in which it was given without feeling that it was reluctantly done. It is fenced in with warnings to the Zulus against transgressing the limits assigned to them, without a word assuring them that *their* rights also shall in future be respected; and, while touching on *Zulu* aggressions on *Boers* in the late disputed territory, it says nothing of those committed *by* Boers.

But perhaps the most remarkable phrase in the whole award is that in which Sir Bartle Frere gives the Zulus to understand that *they* will have to pay the compensation due to the ejected Transvaal farmers, while he entirely ignores all that can be said on the other side of injuries to property and person inflicted on Zulus in the disputed territory,[1] not to speak of the rights and advantages so long withheld from them, and now decided to be their due.

Sir Henry Bulwer plainly took a very different view on this point when he summed up the judgment of the Commissioners[2], and added as follows:

I would venture to suggest that it is a fair matter for consideration if those Transvaal subjects, who have been induced

---

1. Of which, the *Blue-Books* contain ample proof.
2. 2220, p. 388.

... under the sanction, expressed or tacit, of the Government of the Republic, to settle and remain in that portion of the country, have not a claim for compensation from their Government for the individual losses they may sustain.

Sir Bartle Frere, starting with phrases which might be supposed to agree with the above, gradually and ingeniously shifts his ground through propositions for compensation to be paid to farmers "*required or obliged* to leave" (omitting the detail of *who is to pay*), and then for compensation to be paid to farmers *wishing* to remove, until he finally arrives, by a process peculiarly his own, at a measure intended to "secure private rights of property," which eventually blossomed out into a scheme for maintaining, in spite of the award, the Boer farmers on the land claimed by them, which we shall presently relate in full. Although nothing appeared in the award itself on this point, the whole tone of it was calculated to take the edge off the pleasure which the justice done them at last would naturally give the Zulus, and it was promptly followed up by an "ultimatum" from the High Commissioner calculated to absorb their whole attention.

This "ultimatum" contained the following thirteen demands, and was delivered on the same day with the award, an hour later:

1. Surrender of Sihayo's three sons and brother to be tried by the Natal courts.
2. Payment of a fine of five hundred head of cattle for the outrages committed by the above, and for Ketshwayo's delay in complying with the request[3] of the Natal Government for the surrender of the offenders.
3. Payment of a hundred head of cattle for the offence committed against Messrs. Smith and Deighton.[4]
4. Surrender of the Swazi chief Umbilini, and others to be named hereafter, to be tried by the Transvaal courts.[5/6]
5. Observance of the coronation "promises."

3. Not *demand.*
4. Twenty days were allowed for compliance with 1 & 2, *i.e.* until December 31st, inclusive.
5. No time was fixed for compliance with this demand.
6. Ten days more were allowed for compliance with demands (4-13).

6. That the Zulu army be disbanded, and the men allowed to go home.

7. That the Zulu military system be discontinued, and other military regulations adopted, to be decided upon after consultation with the Great Council and British Representatives.

8. That every man, when he comes to man's estate, shall be free to marry.

9. All missionaries and their converts, who until 1877 lived in Zululand, shall be allowed to return and reoccupy their stations.

10. All such missionaries shall be allowed to teach, and any Zulu, if he chooses, shall be free to listen to their teaching.[7]

11. A British Agent shall be allowed to reside in Zululand, who will see that the above provisions are carried out.

12. All disputes in which a missionary or European (*e.g.* trader or traveller) is concerned, shall be heard by the king in public, and in presence of the Resident.

13. No sentence of expulsion from Zululand shall be carried out until it has been approved by the Resident.

The Natal Colonist, August 21st, 1879, condenses the opinions of Sir B. Pine upon the ultimatum—from his article in *The Contemporary Review,* June, 1879—thus:

> He thinks the depriving Messrs. Smith and Deighton of their handkerchiefs and pipes hardly a matter deserving of a place in such a document; that the Sihayo and Umbilini affairs were more serious, but that 'full reparation . . . . might have been obtained by friendly negotiations.' He does not attach to the promises alleged to have been made by Cetshwayo 'the force of a treaty which we were bound to see executed.' And while approving of a British Resident being placed in the Zulu country, he frankly recalls the fact that 'Cetshwayo has himself, on more than one occasion,

---

7. Compare with 9 and 10 the distinct instructions on this point given by Lord Carnarvon during the previous year (1961, p. GO): "I request, therefore, that you will cause the missionaries to understand distinctly that Her Majesty's Government cannot undertake to compel the king to permit the maintenance of the mission stations in Zululand." Yet here the clause is made one of the conditions of an ultimatum, the alternative of which is war.

requested such an arrangement. At the same time,' he adds, 'I think that the powers proposed to be invested in this officer are more than are necessary or expedient, and I would especially refer to those relating to the protection of missionaries. Christianity ought not to be enforced at the point of the sword.' In reference to Cetshwayo's alleged coronation promises, we may note in passing that Sir B. Pine is careful to point out that one chief reason for his sanctioning that expedition was 'out of deference to Mr. Shepstone's judgment;' and that it was expressly stipulated by the High Commissioner that no British troops should accompany Mr. Shepstone, 'so that Her Majesty's Government might not be compromised in the matter.' With such a stipulation it is amazing that anyone should still contend that Cetshwayo entered into engagements so solemn as to call for invasion of his country to punish the breach of them.

And the Special Correspondent of *The Cape Argus* writes:

As regards the alleged coronation engagements, Dunn affirms that no undertaking was made by, or even asked from, Cetshwayo. In the act of coronation, Mr. (now Sir T.) Shepstone gave to the king a piece of paternal counsel, and the conditions were in reality nothing more than recommendations urged upon his acceptance by the Special Commissioner.

Lord Kimberley, who was Secretary of State for the Colonies at the time of Sir T. Shepstone's installation of Cetshwayo, spoke upon this subject in the House of Lords.

The Daily News, March 26th, 1879, reports this as follows:

With respect to the so-called coronation promises, nothing had more astonished him in these papers than to learn that these promises were supposed to constitute an engagement between us and the Zulu nation. He happened to have had some concern in that matter; and if he had supposed that Sir T. Shepstone, in asking for these promises from Cetshwayo, had rendered us responsible to the Zulu nation to see that they were enforced, he would not have lost a mail in disavowing any such responsibility. He was supported in the view which he took by the late Colonial Secretary (Lord

Carnarvon). The fact was that these were friendly assurances, given in response to friendly advice, and constituted no engagement. But Sir B. Frere put these 'coronation promises' in the foreground.

Sir M. Hicks-Beach, also, says:[8]

> It is obvious that the position of Sir T. Shepstone in this matter was that of a friendly counsellor, giving advice to the king as to the good government of the country.

The demands which we have recorded were delivered to the Zulu envoys, who were not allowed to discuss or comment upon them, on the ground that the Commission had no authority for that purpose. The envoys, indeed, appeared seriously concerned by their import. They denied that the coronation stipulations had ever been disregarded, and said that they could not understand why the Zulu army should be disbanded; the army was a national custom with them as with the English. They also asked for an extension of time, and considered that on such important matters no specified time should have been fixed; the reply to which request was that the time was considered ample.

Sir B. Frere, in his covering despatch to the Secretary of State, remarks that the "enclosed extracts from demi-official letters," from the Hon. Mr. Brownlee and the Hon. Mr. Littleton—

> .... give an outline of the proceedings, and show that the messages were *carefully delivered*, *well explained*, and *thoroughly understood*, copies of the English text with Zulu translations being given to the Zulu envoys.

On turning to "the enclosed extracts," however, we do not find in them a single word of the sort from either gentleman, while the extract from Mr. Littleton's letter consists of not a dozen lines describing the spot where the meeting took place, and in which the writer's opinions are limited to these: "they (the Zulus) seemed to take the award very quietly," but "were evidently disturbed" by the ultimatum, and "Mr. Shepstone seemed to me to manage very well." The young gentleman could not

---

8. 2144, p. 1.

well say any more, as he did not know a word of Zulu; but one is puzzled to know how Sir B. Frere draws his deductions from either extract. How far the opinions of the other honourable gentleman are to be depended upon, may be gathered from the following assertion made by him some months after the Boundary Commissioners had deliberately decided that the Boers had no claim whatever to the disputed territory, but that it would be expedient to allow them to retain the Utrecht district. Mr. Brownlee says:

> The falsehood of the Zulu king with regard to the Utrecht land question is quite on a par with his other actions. After misleading the Natal Government upon the merits of the case, it is now discovered on the clearest and most incontrovertible proof[9] that a formal cession was made of this disputed land to the Transvaal Republic.

The special correspondent of *The Cape Argus*, however, writes about this time as follows:

> Dunn states that Cetshwayo does not, even now, know fully the contents of the ultimatum, and still less of the subsequent memorandum.[10] The document was read over once, and its length was such[11]—six pages of the *Blue-Book*—that the messengers could not possibly fix the whole of it in their memory.

True, a copy was given to Dunn himself; but, for sufficient reasons of his own, he did not make known the contents of the document in person, but sent word to the king by his own messengers, between whom and the *indunas* there was a considerable discrepancy. According to Dunn, Cetshwayo was in a great fury upon hearing the word of the High Commissioner.[12] He re-

---

9. Sir T. Shepstone's incontrovertible, overwhelming, and clear evidence, sifted and proved worthless by the Commissioners.

10. Sir Bartle Frere declares (Correspondence, p. 57) that Cetshwayo "could have known nothing of the memorandum," although (ibid. p. 6) he himself asserts that "it was intended to explain for Cetshwayo's benefit what was the nature of the cession to him," and it was plainly very generally known, and therefore naturally by the king.

11. 2222, pp. 203-9.

12. Probably as to the maintenance of Boer "private rights" over his land.

proached his adviser with having thwarted his purpose to exact satisfaction at the hands of the Dutch, and doubly blamed him for having represented the English as just in their intercourse and friendly in their intentions. Until this time he had thought, as Dunn himself had, that the congregation of troops upon his borders represented nothing but an idle scare. But he saw at length that the English had thrown the bullock's skin over his head, while they had been devouring the tid-bits of the carcass.

The three causes alleged in the ultimatum for war—the raid of Sihayo's sons, the assault on Messrs. Smith and Deighton, and the proceedings of Umbilini—occurred long after Sir B. Frere had been preparing for war, in the full expectation that the Border Commission would decide against the Zulu claims, and that Cetshwayo would not acquiesce peacefully in such a decision. It would seem, indeed, from his remarks on the subject,[13] that he would have even set aside the decision of the Commissioners, if he had found it possible to do so. Although, he failed in doing this, he sought to attain practically the same end by means of a remarkable "memorandum," prepared and signed by himself not submitted to Sir Henry Bulwer, but *"prematurely"* published in the Natal newspapers.

The memorandum in question was on the appointment of a Resident in Zululand, and, as Sir Bartle Frere himself says:

.... it was intended to explain for Cetshwayo's benefit what was the nature of the cession to him of the ceded territory. . . .

It contained the following clause:

It is intended that in that district (the late disputed territory) individual rights of property, which were obtained under the Transvaal Government, shall be respected and maintained, so that any Transvaal farmers, who obtained rights from the Government of the Republic, and who may now elect to remain on the territory, may possess under British guarantee the same rights they would have possessed had they been grantees holding from the Zulu king under the guarantee of the great Zulu council.

---

13. *Correspondence*, Letters II and IV.

The *whole* of the disputed territory had been apportioned in farms to Transvaal subjects, and without doubt every one of these farms would immediately be claimed, since their value would be immensely raised by the fact that in future they would be held "under British guarantee." Therefore, to thus maintain the farmers upon them without regard to the wishes of the Zulu king and nation was simply to take away piecemeal with one hand what had just been given as a whole with the other.

This "memorandum" was hailed with triumph by some of the colonial papers, and the news that, after all, the Zulus were to get no solid satisfaction from the award, soon circulated amongst all classes, not excluding the Zulus themselves.

It was upon this subject that the "correspondence" between Sir Bartle Frere and the Bishop of Natal, already referred to, commenced. In December, 1878, the High Commissioner was good enough to invite the Bishop, both by message and personally, to "criticise" his policy towards the Zulus. The invitation, indeed, came far too late for any arguments or information, which the Bishop might be able to afford, to be of the very slightest use. However, the High Commissioner desired criticism, and received it in a series of letters, which—except the last two, withheld for some reason best known to himself—were published, with Sir B. Frere's replies, in the *Blue-Books*.

The Bishop pointed out that, under the interpretation of this memorandum, "the award gives back the land in name only to the Zulus, whereas in reality Ketshwayo will have no control over it; he will not be able to exercise authority over his own people living on it, without coming into collision immediately with their Boer masters, who would fiercely resent any intrusion on his part on their farms; he will not be able to send any of his people to live on it, or any of his cattle to graze on it, or even to assign places in it to such of his people as may elect to move from the Boer to the Zulu side of the new boundary.[14] To which Sir Bartle replies, that he had "a strong impression[15] that, if Cetshwayo were simply told the disputed land was assigned to

14. Correspondence, p. 3.
15. *ibid.* p. 6.

him, he would at once conclude that it was his in full Zulu sovereignty;" which he assumed to be impossible with regard to any land which had once been under the British flag, while to eject a settler who had bought the land from the Transvaal Government, in the belief that it could maintain him upon it, he regarded as an "unjust and immoral act." In point of fact, the land in question could only have been looked upon as "under the British flag," in trust for the rightful possessors, and the farmers had settled upon it in the full knowledge that the title to it was in dispute; while, even had it been otherwise as to the latter point, the only just claim that could be raised would be against the Boer Government, or its representative, and certainly not against the right of the Zulu people to be restored to actual occupation of the land.

But that from the first, and long before he left Cape Town for Natal, the High Commissioner was preparing for war with the Zulus, is evident from his despatch and telegram of January 26th, 1878 already quoted from, in the former of which he speaks of the delay caused by the border inquiry being no disadvantage, as, besides other reasons, it "will increase our means of defending whatever we may find to be our unquestionable rights;" and in the latter he says again:

> I hope the delay caused will not be great, and whatever there is will have compensating advantages, for I have some hopes of being able to strengthen your hands.

These phrases, indeed, might merely refer to Sir Bartle Frere's desire to be "ready to defend ourselves against further aggressions;" but certain statements made by Commodore Sullivan show that he had already in view the invasion of Zululand.

Extracts from these statements run as follows:

> I am informed by the Governor (Sir B. Frere) that there is every chance of hostility in the debateable land between the Transvaal, Zululand, and Natal.[16]

> His Excellency (Sir B. Frere) pointed out to me that, as it appeared almost certain that serious complications must shortly arise with the Zulu tribe of Kafirs on the borders of

16. December 16th, 1877 (2000, p. 45).

Natal and the Transvaal, which will necessitate active operations, he considered it better that the *Active* should remain here, in order to render such assistance by sea and land as may be practicable.[17]

The object of my visit here was . . . .to make myself acquainted with such points on the (Zulu) coast as might be available for cooperating with Her Majesty's land forces by landing troops or stores.[18]

It had been my intention (abandoned by Sir H. Bulwer's desire) to have examined the north of the Tugela River both by land and sea, also a reported landing-place situated almost thirty miles eastward of the Tugela by sea.

The High Commissioner was plainly determined not to allow the Zulus the slightest *law*, which, indeed, was wise in the interests of war, as there was considerable fear that, in spite of all grievances and vexations, Cetshwayo, knowing full well, as he certainly did, that collision with the English must eventually result in his destruction, might prefer half a loaf to no bread, and submit to our exactions with what grace he could. And so probably he would; for, from all accounts, every effort was made by the king to collect the fines of cattle, to propitiate the Government.

Sir Bartle Frere, accordingly, was very particular in requesting Sir Henry Bulwer to give Cetshwayo notice[19] that *"rigid punctuality with regard to time will be insisted on, and, unless observed, such steps as may appear necessary will be immediately taken to ensure compliance,"* which Sir H. Bulwer notifies to the Zulu king upon the same day, December 16th.[20]

Two days later Mr. John Dunn wrote to say that he had received a message from the king[21], requesting him—

. . . . to write and say that he agrees to the demands of giv-

---

17. April 12th, 1878 (2144, p. 32).
18. Compare with Sir Bartle Frere's suggestion to Sir Henry Bulwer that the latter should persuade the Zulu king that the *Active* and her fellows were mostly merchant vessels, but that the English war vessels would be sufficient to *protect his coast!*
19. C. 2222, p. 222.
20. C. 2308, p. 31.
21. C. 2222, p. 227

ing up Sihayo's sons and brother, and the fines of cattle; but begs that, should the number of days (twenty) have expired before the arrival of the cattle, His Excellency will take no immediate action, as, owing to the many heavy rains[22] we have had since the meeting of His Excellency's Commissioners and his *indunas*, they have not been able to reach him yet; and Sihayo's sons being at their *kraals*, which are some way from him, it will take some days to send for them.

On the other demands he will give his answer on consulting his *indunas*.

Yet Sir Bartle Frere declares[23] that Cetshwayo "was resolved on war rather than on compliance with any demand of ours."

Bishop Schreuder's opinion, reported through Mr. Fannin on December 22nd[24], was that all the demands would be agreed to except that of the disbandment of the army and the abolition of the military system. Mr. Fannin says:

> The king and nation will consider it a humiliation, and a descent from their proud position as independent Zulus to the lower and degrading position of Natal Kafirs, to agree to this demand. I asked if the announcement that the restriction on marriage would be removed would not reconcile the young men to the change. He (Bishop Schreuder) thinks not; they will stand by their king, and fight for the old institutions of their country.

The king's request for some indulgence as to time was peremptorily refused, and was looked upon as "a pitiful evasion," on the grounds that he had already had four months to consider the question of Sihayo's sons. In point of fact, however, the first "demand" had only been made a week before, and, until then, the word "request" having been used, the king was at liberty to offer atonement for the offence other than the surrender of the offenders, as Sir Henry Bulwer himself suggested[25], by paying a fine of five thousand head of cattle from the Zulu nation.

---

22. Our own troops' experience showed that this was no idle excuse.
23. P. P. (C. 2454) p. 136.
24. 2308, p. 31.
25. 2222, p. 173.

Sir B. Frere's answer to Cetshwayo through Mr. Dunn[26] was:

That the word of Government as already given, cannot now be altered.

Unless the prisoners and cattle are given up within the term specified, Her Majesty's troops will advance. But in consideration of the disposition expressed in Mr. Dunn's letter to comply with the demands of Government, the troops will be halted at convenient posts within the Zulu border, and will there await the expiration of the term of thirty days without, in the meantime, taking any hostile action unless it is provoked by the Zulus.

And John Dunn adds on his own account[27], that the king evidently does not attach sufficient importance to the time stipulated. The cattle, he said, "are still being collected, and it will be impossible now for them to be up in time." John Dunn in the same letter put in a petition on behalf of his own cattle and people, saying that the latter would be willing to join in with any force should they be required.

Meanwhile, from accounts given by Mr. Fannin,[28] by Mr. Robson,[29] by Mr. Fynney,[30] and from other sources, it is plain that Cetshwayo was doing his utmost to collect the required cattle in time, though hampered in doing so by the extreme difficulty of complying in a hurry with the other demands implying such radical changes in the administration of the country, and exceedingly distressed at the turn affairs were taking. Every report shows plainly enough that, far from desiring war, and looking out for an opportunity to try their strength with the English, the Zulu king and people, or the major part of it, were thrown into utmost consternation by the menacing appearance of their hitherto friendly neighbours. But all explanations were disregarded, all requests for time treated as impudent pretexts, preparations on our part for an invasion of Zululand were hur-

---

26. 2222, p. 227.
27. 2308, p. 34.
28. 2308, pp. 35 and 37.
29. 2242, pp. 11, 12; 2308, p. 35.
30. 2308, p. 36.

ried on, while every sign of agitation (the natural consequences of our own attitude) on the other side of the border was construed into an intention on the part of the Zulu king to attack Natal, and urged as an added reason for our beginning hostilities. There were, at that time, no grounds whatsoever for this supposition. It is plain enough that, when it became apparent that war would be forced upon him by us, the Zulu king contemplated nothing but self-defence, and that, during these preliminaries to the unhappy campaign of 1879, there were numerous occasions on which, by the exercise of a little patience, justice, and moderation, any ruler less bent on conquering Zululand than was Sir Bartle Frere could have brought matters to a peaceful issue, without the loss of honour, men, and money which England has since sustained.

Lord Chelmsford (then Lieut.-General the Hon. F. Thesiger) arrived in Natal in August, 1878, and at once began his preparations for the expected campaign. One of the measures upon which great stress was laid was that of forming a native contingent to act with the British troops. The original scheme for the organisation of this contingent in case of necessity had been prepared and carefully worked out by Colonel Durnford, R.E., and was based on his thorough knowledge of the natives. During the eight years of his life in South Africa he had had ample opportunity of learning, by experience, how utterly and mischievously useless was the plan, hitherto invariably followed, of employing disorganised, untrained bodies of natives as troops under their own leaders, without any proper discipline or control. The bravest men in the world would be apt to fail under such circumstances; while mere bands of untaught savages, unaccustomed to fighting and half-armed, had repeatedly proved themselves in former campaigns excellent for running away, but otherwise useless except as messengers, servants, and camp-followers. Added to which there was no possibility of preventing such "troops" as these committing every sort of lawless violence upon the wounded or captured enemy.

Colonel Durnford's scheme was intended to meet both difficulties, and, when laid before the General on his arrival in Natal, met with his unqualified approval. So much was he struck with it that he was at first disposed to entrust the organisation and chief command of the entire contingent to one who, by the ability and completeness with which he had worked out the scheme, proved himself the fittest person to carry it out, and take command of the whole force. But the General changed his mind, and decided to divide the native contingent amongst the various columns, the details of its distribution being as follows:

The 1st Regiment Natal Native Contingent of three battalions (Commandant Montgomery, Major Bengough, and Captain Cherry), and five troops mounted natives formed No. 2 Column, commanded by Lieut.-Colonel Durnford.

The 2nd Regiment Natal Native Contingent (two battalions, under Major Graves) was attached to No. 1 Column, commanded by Colonel Pearson.

The 3rd Regiment Natal Native Contingent (two battalions, under Commandant Lonsdale) was attached to No. 3 Column, commanded by Colonel Glyn, and about two hundred Natal Native Contingent were attached to No. 4 Column, commanded by Colonel Wood.

Each battalion of Native Contingent was to consist of 5 staff and 90 officers and non-commissioned officers (white), and 110 officers and non-commissioned officers and 900 privates (natives); the native non-commissioned officer being armed with a gun, and being a section-leader of 9 men armed with *assegai* and shield.

Lord Chelmsford speaks in various despatches of this Native Contingent in the following terms:

The Lieut.-Governor, I am happy to say, has acceded to the request I made some little time ago for the services of six thousand Natal natives. I hope to be in a position to equip and officer them very shortly.[31]

At the time of my arrival in the colony, three months ago, these natives possessed no military organisation, nor had any arms provided for them by Government.

31. C. 2234, p. 25.

The Natal Government have within the last fourteen days allowed me to raise and organise seven thousand natives for service within or without the border.[32].

The arrival of these officers (special service officers from England) has also enabled me to place Imperial officers in command of some of the battalions of native levies. . . .

The Natal Contingent consists of three regiments, two of two battalions and one of three.[33]

There are in addition five troops of mounted natives and three companies of pioneers. . . .

The pioneers have been raised, officered, and equipped under the orders of the Natal Government, and are now placed at my disposal. The remainder of the Contingent have been raised at the cost and under the orders of the Imperial authorities.[34]

In none of his despatches is there mention of any special officer in connection with this native force, but the following officers were responsible for the organisation of the various regiments:

No. 1 Regiment and mounted contingent, Lieut.-Colonel Durnford, R.E.

No. 2 Regiment, Major Graves.

No. 3 Regiment, Commandant Lonsdale.

Great difficulties appear to have been thrown in the way of the proper equipment, etc. of the native levies; but by untiring effort and personal determination, better arrangements for pay, clothing, and discipline were made for (at all events, a portion of) the levy than had been known amongst South African troops. The indiscriminate appointment of officers caused considerable trouble, illustrative of which we may mention an anecdote. Men were repeatedly sent to Lieut.-Colonel Durnford with orders from the military secretary that they were to receive commissions, some of these unfitted by disposition and education for the duties required of them. A friend has lately furnished an instance very much to the point.

---

32. C. 2234, p. 26.
33. C. 2234, p. 39.
34. C. 2234, p. 40.

A young fellow came one day to Colonel Durnford from Colonel Crealock, who said he had served in the old colony, and boasted that *he* knew how to make Kafirs fight.

'How is that?' was the inquiry made.

'Oh!' replied the youth, 'just to get behind them with a *sjambok* (i.e. whip) that's the way to do it!'

'All right,' replied the Colonel quietly; 'I have just one piece of advice to give you though—*make your will* before you start! If you're not stabbed by your own men, you will deserve it.'

How successful was the training of the men of the 2nd Column may be judged by the behaviour of the "Natal Native Horse," a body of mounted men (Basuto, Edendale, and Zikali natives) who fought at Isandhlwana; and did right good service throughout the campaign.[35] Lieut.-Colonel Durnford also raised, equipped, and trained the three companies of Native Pioneers, organising two field-parks, and providing complete bridge equipment for crossing the Tugela; besides preparing, mainly from his own personal observations (having been at Ulundi in 1873, and in Zululand on many occasions), the map of Zululand in universal use during the campaign, and mentioned in despatches as "Durnford's map."

In reply to Sir Bartle Frere's inquiries as to proposed movements of troops up to Natal, Sir H. Bulwer writes, July 18th, 1878, that in his opinion—

> . . . . it is desirable under the present circumstances, and pending the final decision in the matter of the boundary dispute, to avoid as much as possible any military demonstration, as liable to be misunderstood and to be interpreted as showing our intention to settle the question by force. The delay, too, that has occurred since the sitting of the Commission might be attributed by the Zulu king to our desire to make preparations, and it might be thought that we were playing false.[36]

---

35. One of Colonel Durnford's officers writes, January 26th, "that he (the Colonel) had worked so hard at equipping this Native Contingent, against much opposition, and took special pride in his mounted men, three hundred men, that he called 'The Natal Native Horse.'"

36. P. P. (C. 2220) p. 395.

And here we may appropriately refer to the opinion expressed by the Home Government at a later date. Sir M. Hicks-Beach writes to Sir B. Frere, 21st November, 1878:

> I trust that . . .. Cetywayo may have been informed that a decision regarding the disputed boundary would speedily be communicated to him. His complaint that the Lieut.-Governor of Natal 'is hiding from him the answer that has come from across the sea, about the land boundary question, and is only making an excuse for taking time, so as to surprise him,' is not altogether an unnatural one for a native chief situated in his circumstances, who is necessarily ignorant of much that has passed on this subject, and of many of the causes to which the delay is attributable. But it is a misunderstanding which it should be the earnest endeavour of the Government to remove, and I am confident that there is no need to impress upon you the importance of losing no time in dealing with this question or the beneficial effect which its satisfactory settlement may be expected to have upon the strained relations which you describe as now existing between the colony of Natal and the Zulu nation.[37]

We must now briefly run through the principal points in despatches bearing on the question of increasing the military strength in Natal. Sir B. Frere, writing from Cape Town on September 10th, says:

> I have consulted General Thesiger on the subject. He is very unwilling to ask for reinforcements on the Natal border without the full concurrence of the Government of that colony, and I understand that His Excellency Sir H. Bulwer is specially anxious that nothing should be done in Natal which could possibly justify to the Zulu chief the belief that we were preparing for active hostilities against him. I confess that, as at present informed, I very imperfectly comprehend the grounds on which the objections of His Excellency the Lieut. Governor, as I understand them, to strengthening the Natal frontier are based.[38] They will doubtless be more fully

---

37. P. P. (C. 2220) p. 322.
38. These words deserve special remark.

explained when I have the advantage of personal communication with him. In the meantime I feel quite certain that the preservation or speedy restoration of peace will be rendered much more certain if General Thesiger had two more battalions of Her Majesty's Army within his reach.[39]

On September 14th, referring to the above despatch, Sir B. Frere says he has "since received a telegraphic communication from General Thesiger, in which he expresses his views in regard to his military requirements in the event of hostilities breaking out with the Zulus." The General asks for six more special duty officers, and fifteen captains or subalterns for transport duties.

General Thesiger considers that an addition of two regiments would be essential, and that the presence of a cavalry regiment would be of enormous advantage.[40]

From Durban, Sir B. Frere telegraphs on September 23rd to Sir M. Hicks-Beach:

I find that the urgency of supporting General Thesiger's request is much greater even than I supposed. I trust there will be no delay in complying with his request to its fullest extent.[41]

There had been serious and disturbing reports of a Zulu force being assembled on the Tugela River, for the ostensible purpose of hunting, with reference to which Sir H. Bulwer writes to Sir M. Hicks-Beach, 14th September:

.... on the subject of the gathering of a Zulu force within a short distance of our border across the Tugela. You will learn from these papers that the gathering has broken up, and the Zulus returned home.[42]

Sir M. Hicks-Beach, on October 17th, replies to Sir B. Frere's despatches of 14th and 23rd September, that—

.... arrangements will be made for the early despatch of some additional officers for special duty. Her Majesty's

---

39. P. P. (C. 2220) pp. 282, 283.
40. *Ibid.* p. 254.
41. *Ibid.* p. 255.
42. *Ibid.* p. 270.

Government are, however, not prepared to comply with the request for a reinforcement of troops. All the information that has hitherto reached them with respect to the position of affairs in Zululand appears to them to justify a confident hope that, by the exercise of prudence, and by meeting the Zulus in a spirit of forbearance and reasonable compromise, it will be possible to avert the very serious evil of a war with Cetywayo; and they cannot but think that the forces now at your disposal in South Africa, together with the additional officers about to be sent, should suffice to meet any other emergency that may arise, without a further increase to the Imperial troops.[43]

On September 30th, Sir B. Frere writes from Pietermaritzburg:

I regret that I find the position of affairs in this colony far more critical even than I expected.[44]

And, after a very exaggerated description of the state of affairs, he says:

An attempt of native tribes to combine to resist the white man and drive him back has been long foreseen. There can be no doubt that this design is now in process of attempted execution "(ibid. pp. 278-82).[44]

Of the truth of this startling assertion, let Sir H. Bulwer's despatches, as well as after-events, speak.

Enclosed in this despatch of Sir B. Frere is General Thesiger's memorandum on the military requirements, and his sketch for a defensive scheme for Natal, for which he requires "6000 natives, 600 mounted men, 6 guns, and 3 battalions of British infantry;" but he remarks:

I cannot, however, conceal from myself that security from invasion depends almost entirely upon the forbearance of Cetywayo; for defensive purposes alone, therefore, Natal and Transvaal colonies require 3 battalions of infantry in addition to what they have already got.[45]

---

43. *Ibid.* p. 273.
44. *Ibid.* p. 278-82.
45. *Ibid.* pp. 285, 286.

In reply, Sir M. Hicks–Beach writes, 21st November:

The several circumstances which you have reported as tending to cause an open rupture do not appear, in themselves, to present any difficulties which are not capable of a peaceful solution. . . . On a full review, therefore, of all the circumstances reported by you, and influenced by the strong representations made by Lord Chelmsford as to the insufficiency of his present force to ensure the safety of the European residents in Natal and the Transvaal, Her Majesty's Government have felt themselves justified in directing that further reinforcements of troops, as well as the additional officers recently placed under orders for special service, should be sent out to Natal, and the necessary steps will at once be taken for this purpose. But in conveying to you the decision at which, in compliance with your urgent representations, Her Majesty's Government have arrived, it is my duty to impress upon you that in supplying these reinforcements it is the desire of Her Majesty's Government not to furnish means for a campaign of invasion and conquest, but to afford such protection as may be necessary at this juncture to the lives and property of the colonists. Though the present aspect of affairs is menacing in a high degree, I can by no means arrive at the conclusion that war with the Zulus should be unavoidable, and I am confident that you, in concert with Sir H. Bulwer, will use every effort to overcome the existing difficulties by judgment and forbearance, and to avoid an evil so much to be deprecated as a Zulu war.[46]

On November 11th, the Lieut.-General says that he has just been permitted by the Natal Government to raise and organise 7000 natives, and ventures—

. . . . to express an opinion that the demand for two extra battalions cannot be considered unreasonable even for purely defensive purposes; "but he goes on to say: "a defensive plan, however, cannot be considered as satisfactory unless there is the possibility of taking the offensive at the right moment.

---

46. *Ibid.* pp. 320, 321.

This I am doing my best to prepare for; and, so soon as my native contingent is mobilised, I shall be ready, so far as my limited means will allow, to enter Zululand, should such a measure become necessary.[47]

On December 18th, Sir M. Hicks-Beach says:

I take this occasion, however, of reminding you that it is the desire of Her Majesty's Government, in sending these reinforcements, to assist the local Government as far as possible in providing for the protection of the settlers in the present emergency, and not to furnish the means for any aggressive operations not directly connected with the defence of Her Majesty's possessions and subjects.[48]

On December 2nd, Sir B. Frere forwards copies of memoranda by Sir T. Shepstone and Mr. Brownlee, in which the former proposes measures which—

.... involve the extinction of the Zulu power as it now is, and the attempt to adopt them must, if decided upon, be made with the knowledge that the Zulu chief will oppose them, whatever course the headmen and common people may adopt.[49]

Mr. Brownlee says plainly:

The time has arrived for decisive action; we will never again have so favourable an opportunity as the present; if it is lost, sooner or later we will be taken at a disadvantage.[50]

On December 10th, Sir B. Frere writes to Sir M. Hicks-Beach:

The chance of avoiding war under such circumstances by any exercise of prudence, or by meeting the Zulus in a spirit of forbearance or reasonable compromise, may depend upon ourselves or upon the Zulus, or upon the nature of the issues pending between us. . . . Can we then rest on an armed truce? . . . After the most anxious consideration, I can arrive

47. P. P. (C. 2222) p. 19.
48. *Ibid.* p. 21.
49. *Ibid.* p. 134.
50. *Ibid.* p. 138.

at no other conclusion than that it is impossible to evade the necessity for now settling this Zulu question thoroughly and finally . . . . there is clearly no possibility of now evading bringing matters to an issue with the Zulus.[51]

On the 23rd January, 1879, Sir M. Hicks-Beach acknowledges the receipt of Sir B. Frere's despatches containing—

> . . . . the demands with which Cetywayo has been called upon to comply, together with your own descriptions of the situation with which you have to deal, as well as other very important memoranda by Sir H. Bulwer, Sir T. Shepstone, and Mr. Brownlee. I may observe that the communications which had previously been received from you had not entirely prepared them[52] for the course which you have deemed it necessary to take. The representations made by Lord Chelmsford and yourself last autumn as to the urgent need of strengthening Her Majesty's forces in South Africa were based upon the imminent danger of an invasion of Natal by the Zulus, and the inadequate means at that time at your disposal for meeting it. In order to afford protection to the lives and property of the colonists, the reinforcements asked for were supplied, and, in informing you of the decision of Her Majesty's Government, I took the opportunity of impressing upon you the importance of using every effort to avoid war. But the terms which you have dictated to the Zulu king, however necessary to relieve the colony in future from an impending and increasing danger, are evidently such as he may not improbably refuse, even at the risk of war; and I regret that the necessity for immediate action should have appeared to you so imperative as to preclude you from incurring the delay which would have been involved in consulting Her Majesty's Government upon a subject of so much importance as the terms which Cetywayo should be required to accept before those terms were actually presented to the Zulu king.[53]

---

51. *Ibid.* pp. 183-85.
52. Her Majesty's Government.
53. *Ibid.* pp. 187, 188.

The preliminary arrangements for the campaign were the formation of four columns, with sufficient transport, etc. to enter Zululand at different points, and concentrate on Ulundi.

No. 1 Column, Colonel Pearson, to assemble on the Lower Tugela, garrison Fort Pearson, and cross and encamp on the Zulu side, under the protection of the guns of the fort.

This Column at first was composed of 2 guns Royal Artillery, 1 company Royal Engineers, 2nd Battalion "The Buffs," 99th Regiment, Naval Brigade (2 guns and 1 Gatling), 1 squadron Mounted Infantry, about 200 Natal Volunteers, 2nd Regiment Natal Native Contingent (2 battalions), and 1 company Natal Native Pioneers.

No. 2 Column, Lieut.-Colonel Durnford, R.E., to cover the Tugela, and co-operate with Colonel Pearson, was almost entirely composed of natives. Its strength, a rocket battery, 1st Regiment (3 battalions) Natal Native Contingent, 315 Natal Native Horse, and 1 company Natal Native Pioneers.

No. 3 Column, Colonel Glyn, C.B., to cross at Rorke's Drift, when the time granted the Zulu king had expired. "On the advance being ordered," it would "require two days for this column to reach a good military position; "and it was to keep up communications "with the columns on the left and right." Strength of column, 6 guns Royal Artillery, 1 squadron Mounted Infantry, 1-24th Regiment, 2-24th Regiment, about 200 Natal Volunteers, 150 Mounted Police, and 3rd Regiment (2nd Battalion) Natal Native Contingent, also one company Natal Native Pioneers. A company of Royal Engineers was ordered to join this column.

No. 4 Column, Colonel Wood, V.C., C.B., to advance to the Blood River. Strength, 6 guns Royal Artillery, 1-13th Regiment, 90th Regiment, Frontier Light Horse, some 200 Native Contingent; and a small Dutch force was expected to join this column.

A 5th Column (which had been operating against Sekukuni) was under the command of Colonel Rowlands, V.C., C.B., composed of the 80th Regiment, three guns, and mounted irregulars.

The strength of the columns is given as:

	Imperial & Colonial Troops	Native Contingent	Conductors & Drivers	Wagons & Carts
No 1 Column	1872	2256	238	266 (144 hired)
No 2 Column	5	3488	84	30
No 3 Column	1747	2566	293	233 (82 hired)
No 4 Column	1843	387	162	102 (21 hired)
No 5 Column	1202	338	25	62 (50 hired)
Grand Totals	6669	9035	802	693 (297 hired)

with about 1200 horses belonging to cavalry, etc., and 691 horses, 361 mules, and 5231 oxen. In addition, there were the conductors, drivers, etc., and 4572 oxen of the hired wagons.

The columns to operate on the following bases and lines, Ulundi being the objective point of the force:

No. 1   Durban—Lower Tugela
No. 2   Pietermaritzburg, Greytown—Middle Drift
No. 3   Ladysmith—Rorke's Drift (Buffalo River)
No. 4   Newcastle—Utrecht—Blood River
No. 5   Middleburg—Derby—Pongolo River

In place of any urgent necessity for commencing the war, putting political questions on one side, there were strong military reasons for postponing it.

Sir Bartle Frere, in his despatch of 30th June, 1879[54], seeks to prove that the time of moving across the border was "well chosen," and accorded with information received, yet the fact remains that advice was given that the most favourable time for military operations in Zululand was between the periods of summer rains and winter grass-fires—*i.e.* the months of March, April, and May. In spite of Sir Bartle Frere's pleas, we must hold that no competent "military critic" would recommend invading an enemy's country during the rainy season, when rivers are in flood, plains in many cases marshes, and roads almost impassable; especially if the invading forces were required to move with a ponderous wagon-train.

---

54. P. P. (C. 2454) p. 137.

Lord Chelmsford himself proves the case: he writes (January 12th) on the day after crossing the border:

> The country is in a terrible state from the rain, and I do not know how we shall manage to get our wagons across the valley near Sirayo's *kraals*.[55]

And again on January 14th, from the headquarter camp, Zululand, near Rorke's Drift, he writes:

> Between this camp and Greytown alone, a distance of some seventy miles, three rivers are now impassable, and wagons have to cross by ferries, a laborious operation requiring more skilled labour than we at present have available.
>
> The road at various points requires the most constant supervision, and in some parts the heavy rain frequently dislodges huge boulders from the hillsides overhanging the roadway, and in many places watercourses become torrents after an hour's rain.
>
> Beyond this camp towards the Izipezi Hill (my first objective point) the road will require great labour to make it passable; but strong working-parties have already been at work. The transport difficulties are augmented by the great mortality in oxen; this is inevitable, but it will probably decrease in a few weeks' time.[56]

It is believed that the first project of operations was to advance in three lines on Ulundi from the Lower Tugela, Rorke's Drift, and Blood River the columns to move forward by short marches, entrenching strongly at each halting-place, doing no injury to the Zulu people, and thus inducing them to submit quietly. This wise and consistent idea was unfortunately never even attempted. On the 8th January, 1879, Lord Chelmsford writes:

> All the reports which reach me tend to show that the Zulus intend, if possible, to make raids into Natal[57] when the several columns move forward. . . . The strength of the three

---

55. P. P. (C. 2242) p. 43.
56. *ibid.* p. 47.
57. After-events proved the fallacy of these "reports." Even when the Zulus could have swept Natal with fatal effect, they refrained.

columns, Nos. 1, 3, and 4, is only just sufficient to enable them to advance.[58]

The directions for the various columns were, briefly—

No. 1. To cross the Tugela at Fort Pearson and encamp on the Zulu side; when ordered to advance, to move on Etshowe, and there, or in its neighbourhood, to form a depot, well entrenched.

No. 2. To form a portion of No. 1 Column, but act separately, reporting to Colonel Pearson; to remain on the Middle Tugela frontier till an advance is ordered, and Colonel Pearson has reached Etshowe.

The defence of the frontier was to rest with the Colonial Government; but on the 8th January the General altered the instructions for No. 2 Column, and directed two-thirds of it to move up to the Sand Spruit Valley for the protection of the Umsinga border, and to operate in conjunction with No. 3 Column. The third battalion to remain at Middle Drift.

No. 3 Column to cross at Rorke's Drift when the thirty days expired; to move forward and form an advanced depot, strongly entrenched, as found advisable from the nature of the country, etc. To assist in clearing the border south-east of Rorke's Drift, and to keep up communication with the columns on left and right.

No. 4 Column to advance to the Blood River.

> The civil authorities on the border will take every care to warn the Zulus that our first advance need not be deemed hostile, but that no collection of armed natives in the vicinity of our forces can be permitted; no act on our part to unnecessarily bring on hostilities should be permitted.[59]

In the event of a further advance, the advanced depot of this column to be near the intersection of the roads from Utrecht to Ulundi, and Rorke's Drift to Swaziland; but—

> .... to delay its advance toward the Umvolosi River until the border is cleared, and to move in a southerly direction towards Colonel Glyn's column to assist it against Sirayo.[60]

---

58. P. P. (C. 2242) p. 26.
59. P. P. (C. 2222) p. 223.
60. P. P. (C. 2242) pp. 27, 28.

On January 11th, the General met Colonel Wood, and arranged with him that he should—

. . . . occupy himself with the tribes in his front and left flank, until ready to advance to Izipezi Hill.[61]

By this unfortunate change of plan, the left of No. 3 Column was exposed, of which the Zulus took fatal advantage.

We must now return to Sir Bartle Frere, who, considering that he had—

. . . . exhausted all peaceable means for obtaining redress for the past, and security for the future. . . . by a notification dated the 4th of January, 1879, placed in the hands of Lieut.-General Lord Chelmsford, K.C.B., commanding Her Majesty's forces in South Africa, the further enforcement of all demands. . . . it only remains for us to await the issue with perfect confidence in the justice of our cause. The contest has not been provoked by the British Government. That Government has done its best to avoid war by every means consistent with honour.

An absolute truth as regards the Home Government. *That* Government, as Sir B. Frere cleverly remarks, *had done its best to avoid war*, and did not see the necessity, or, at all events, the immediate necessity, of that war into which its servant, contrary to its instructions, plunged it.

The period allowed to Cetshwayo having expired, on the 11th January, 1879, the following notification was published in both English and Zulu:

January 11th, 1879

The British forces are crossing into Zululand to exact from Cetywayo reparation for violations of British territory committed by the sons of Sirayo and others; and to enforce compliance with the promises, made by Cetywayo at his coronation, for the better government of his people.

The British Government has no quarrel with the Zulu people. All Zulus who come in unarmed, or who lay down

---

61. *ibid.* p. 42.

their arms, will be provided for till the troubles of their country are over; and will then, if they please, be allowed to return to their own land; but all who do not so submit will be dealt with as enemies.

When the war is finished, the British Government will make the best arrangements in its power for the future good government of the Zulus in their own country, in peace and quietness, and will not permit the killing and oppression they have suffered from Cetywayo to continue.

H. B. E. Frere
High Commissioner.

This is a message to the Zulu population which the General will make as widely known as possible.[62]

On December 29th, Mr. Fynney, Border Agent, writes at the request of the Lieut.-General Commanding to the Lieut.-Governor of Natal that the General—

.... has taken the opportunity offered by the return of Sintwangu and Umpepa to send the following message to the Zulu king:

1. That, in the event of the cattle demanded as a fine, together with Sirayo's sons and brother, not being delivered before the expiration of the time allowed, Her Majesty's troops will occupy Zulu territory without delay.
2. That no forward movement into Zululand will be made till the expiration of the thirty days; but at the end of that time, if all the demands are not complied with, the troops will advance.
3. That such advance will not be directed against the Zulu nation, but against the king, who has broken the promises he made at his coronation. So that in the event of hostilities, all Zulu subjects willing to lay down their arms, and wishing to take refuge in British territory, will be fed and protected till such time as peace is restored, when they will be at liberty to return

---

62. Sir B. Frere. P. P. (C. 2242) p. 24.

to their homes; but that all who remain in Zululand will be considered as enemies.

4. That these are His Excellency's instructions, which he intends to carry out to the best of his ability.[63]

On the 11th January, Lord Chelmsford, with No. 3 Column, crossed the Buffalo River at Rorke's Drift, the infantry crossing on a barrel-raft, a punt, and a small boat; the cavalry and natives by a ford lower down the river. The force encamped in the Zulu country where it crossed.

The General, with the cavalry, rode to the left to meet Colonel Wood commanding No. 4 Column, which was at Bemba's Kop—about thirty-five miles off. They met about halfway. Colonel Wood, on his return, commenced operations against the Zulus by seizing some 2000 cattle belonging to Inkomi and Sihayo, the Zulus only making "a show of resistance." In addition to this, Colonel Wood reports, on the 13th January, that he had also captured 2000 or 3000 head of cattle from the Sondolosi tribe, and on the same day an attack was made on a petty chief, Mbuna, whose men refused to disarm, and seven Zulus were killed.[64]

Colonel Wood crossed the Blood River on the 6th January, and here we must leave No. 4 Column for the present.

No. 1 Column had some difficulty in effecting the passage of the Tugela, the river being in flood. The fortunes of this column will be followed in a future chapter.

Colonel Durnford, No. 2 Column, reported to the General (on his return to camp on the 11th) that the country in his front was quite quiet. He then returned to his command with further instructions as to its disposition, when "he and the mounted men and rocket battery were to join me with No. 3 Column," writes the General on January 14th.[65]

On the 11th, the General writes:

Both Colonel Wood and Major Russell took a good number of Sirayo's cattle this morning, which we found qui-

---

63. P. P. (C. 2308) p. 39.
64. P. P. (C. 2242) p. 45.
65. P. P. (C. 2242) p. 47.

etly grazing along our line of advance. . . . Several hundred head of cattle, etc. were taken by Nos. 3 and 4 Columns on the 11th. This I considered desirable on political grounds, as they all belonged to Usirayo, as well as from military necessities.[66]

It is rather difficult to reconcile this commencement of operations with the words—"The British Government has no quarrel with the Zulu people;" or with the General's message to the Zulu king (through Mr. Fynney, Border Agent, and the Zulu messengers Sintwangu and Umpepa, December 29th, 1878)—

.... if all the demands are not complied with the troops will advance. That such advance will not be directed against the Zulu nation, but against the King. ...[67]

On the 12th January, No. 3 Column first came into contact with the Zulus. The General made a reconnaissance in the Bashi Valley and towards Izipezi Hill. Sihayo's people were seen driving the cattle to the shelter of the hills, the General says:

.... as, however, it is well known that we had made a distinct demand for the punishment of the sons of this chief, and that his clan was one of the bravest and most warlike of the Zulu nation, I considered it very desirable to punish them at once by capturing their cattle.

The Ingqutu Mountain was occupied by infantry, when "a fire was opened upon them by the Zulus, who were occupying very strong positions in the caves and rocks above." An officer present states that the actual first shot was from the side of the British, but this is not of great importance, as it is impossible to imagine the Zulus could have been expected to look calmly on, whilst their cattle were being captured. After about half-an-hour's fight the cattle and horses were taken. The mounted force was likewise engaged higher up the mountain. Our loss, 2 Native Contingent killed and 12 wounded. The loss inflicted on the enemy, 30 killed, 4

66. *ibid.* pp. 43–46.
67. P. P. (C. 2308) p. 39.
68. P. P. (C. 2242) pp. 47, 48.

wounded, and 10 prisoners; the cattle, etc. taken, 13 horses, 413 cattle, 332 goats, and 235 sheep.[68]

These first steps in Zululand have been given in considerable detail, as they afford much food for reflection on the contrast between *words* and *deeds*.

CHAPTER 13

Isandhlwana

Having crossed into Zululand, the "difficulties . . . . in the way of those who are endeavouring to move forward into an enemy's country, over tracts which have never been traversed, except by a very few traders' wagons,"[1] began to declare themselves; and Lord Chelmsford remarks, January 16th:

> No. 3 Column at Rorke's Drift cannot possibly move forward even eight miles until two swamps, into which our wagons sank up to the body, have been made passable. This work will occupy us for at least four days, and we shall find similar obstacles in front of us in every march we are anxious to make.

We find Lord Chelmsford, on January 27th, stating:

> The country is far more difficult than I had been led to expect, and the labour of advancing with a long train of wagons is enormous. It took seven days hard work, by one half of No. 3 Column, to make the ten miles of road between Rorke's Drift and Insalwana Hill practicable, and even then had it rained hard I feel sure that the convoy could not have gone on. The line of communication is very much exposed, and would require a party of mounted men always patrolling, and fixed entrenched posts of infantry at intervals of about ten miles.[2]

Under these circumstances we can only wonder that the advance with cumbersome trains of wagons was undertaken, and

1. Lord Chelmsford, January 16th, 1879. P. P. (C. 2252) p. 63.
2. P. P. C. 2252.

the apparent want of knowledge of the invaded country is al-most equally surprising. All previous experience goes to prove that a general moving in an enemy's country *with* his *impedimenta* should form a defensible camp at every halt; and this Lord Chelmsford apparently recognised when he promulgated the *Regulations for Field Forces in South Africa*; but we shall find how fatally he neglected the most ordinary precautions.

A hint for the advance might well have been taken from Sir Garnet Wolseley's campaign in Ashantee, and the various columns moved on Ulundi about eighty miles in the lightest possible or-der, and without a ponderous wagon train. Rapid movement was the more imperatively necessary, the enemy being in force, and able to make most rapid concentrations. Guns (7-pounders) could have been moved over very difficult ground with com-parative ease, and even carried along piecemeal if necessary.

The strangeness of the situation is shown plainly in Lord Chelmsford's despatch of the 16th January, written at Rorke's Drift on the very borders of Zululand at the very outset of the war. Having spoken of "difficulties "(as already quoted), he says:

Accepting the situation, therefore, it remains for me to determine what modification of the plan of campaign at first laid down will be necessary.

His idea still is to drive—

. . . . as far as possible, all the Zulus forward towards the north-east part of their country. . . . and with Nos. 1, 2, and 3 Columns, to thoroughly clear or subjugate the country. . . . by means of expeditions made by those columns from cer-tain fixed positions. . . .

This, he hopes, will—

. . . . have the effect of removing any dangerously large body from the Natal borders.

Colonel Wood, with No. 4 Column, to act independently; he continues:

By these movements I hope to be able to clear that por-tion of Zululand which is situated south of the Umhlatoosi

River. . . . Cetywayo will be obliged to keep his army mobilised, and it is certain that his troops will have difficulty,
in finding sufficient food. If kept inactive, they will become
dangerous to himself; if ordered to attack us, they will be
playing our game.

How these plans answered, one week sufficed to show.

The first step in advance from Rorke's Drift was to push
forward four companies of the 2-24th Regiment, a battalion
of Natal Native Contingent, and a detachment of Natal Native
Pioneers into the Bashi Valley on the 14th January, for the purpose of repairing the road. This detachment remained encamped
there until the 20th, five miles from the remainder of the column at Rorke's Drift, and with no attempt at *laager* or other
defence, Lord Chelmsford did not see the need of precaution,
and his instructions to the officer in command were, "Use the
bayonet" if a night attack took place.

On the 17th the General made a reconnaissance as far as
Isandhlwana; and on January 20th No. 3 Column moved from
Rorke's Drift and Bashi Valley, to the spot selected for the camp
to the east of Isandhlwana Hill. The post at Rorke's Drift (where
the Buffalo was crossed) of vital importance to the safety of the
column was left with a garrison of one company of 1-24th Regiment, but without any attempt whatever at entrenchment: nor
were any defensive precautions taken at Helpmakaar, the store
depot in Natal, twelve miles from Rorke's Drift. The march to
Isandhlwana was accomplished "without much difficulty," but
"half a battalion 2-24th was obliged to halt short of this camp
owing to the oxen being fatigued." They bivouacked for the
night in the open.

The position of the camp is thus described:

> At the spot where our road crossed. . . . we had a small
> *kopje* on the right, and then about fifty yards to our left ris-
> es abruptly the Isandhlwana Mountain. . . . entirely unap-
> proachable from the three sides nearest us, but on the farther,
> *viz.* that to the north, it slopes more gradually down, and it is
> there connected with the large range of hills on our left with
> another broad neck of land. We just crossed over the bend,

then turned sharp to the left, and placed our camp facing the valley, with the eastern precipitous side of the mountain behind us, leaving about a mile of open country between our left flank and the hills on our left, the right of the camp extending across the neck of land we had just come over, and resting on the base of the small *kopje* described beforehand.

The camp was formed in the following order from left to right: 2-3rd Natal Native Contingent, 1-3rd Natal Native Contingent, 2-2 4th Regiment, Royal Artillery, mounted troops, and 1-24th Regiment.

> The wagons were all placed between the camp and the hill at the back, and behind them, immediately against its base, the headquarters' tents were pitched with their wagons beside them. . . . Not a single step was taken in any way to defend our new position in case of a night or day attack from the enemy.[3]

On the same day (20th) the General reconnoitred on the "wagon-track, which skirts Inhlazatye Mountain, as far as a place called Matyana's Stronghold," at a distance of about twelve miles, but saw nothing of the enemy. "Not having time to properly examine the country round this peculiar stronghold," the General ordered that next day two separate parties should move out from the camp at an early hour; one of mounted men under Major Dartnell to reconnoitre on the road he had taken, whilst two battalions of Native Contingent under Commandant Lonsdale worked round the Malakata Mountain: the orders being that these officers were to effect a communication on the Inhlazatye range, and then return to camp.[4]

At about ten o'clock the Zulus were found in force by the mounted men; the contingent being on a range of hills distant about five miles. The enemy appeared anxious to fight, but Major Dartnell did not think it prudent to engage without supports. The Zulus occupied a large *kloof*, and whenever the mounted men approached they came out in large numbers. A small body were sent up close, under Mr. Mansel, to try and make the Zulus

---

3. Captain N. Newman.
4. P. P. (C. 2252) pp. 74, 75.

show their force, when they advanced throwing out the "horns" and tried to surround the party, following them down into the open, where Major Dartnell and the remainder of the mounted troops were. The whole then retired and joined the contingent, about three miles from the *kloof*.

In the evening, says Major Clery, "a message arrived from Major Dartnell that the enemy was in considerable force in his neighbourhood, and that he and Commandant Lonsdale would bivouac out the night," which they were permitted to do.[5]

The wisdom of this may be doubted, as the Native Contingent seemed particularly liable to alarm; twice, writes an officer, they—

.... were seized with panic, rushing about everywhere, the night being very dark. They knocked us down and stampeded our horses, causing the greatest confusion. If the Zulus had come on we should all have been cut to pieces.

That night Major Dartnell sent off messengers to Lord Chelmsford that he had marked the Zulus down in a *kloof*, and asked for two companies of infantry to be sent out as a support, and that he would attack the Zulus in the morning.

Major Clery says:[6]

About 1.30 a.m. on the 22nd, a messenger brought me a note from Major Dartnell to say that the enemy was in greater numbers than when he last reported, and that he did not think it prudent to attack unless reinforced by two or three companies of the 24th Regiment. The General ordered the 2nd Battalion 24th Regiment, the Mounted Infantry, and four guns, to be under arms at once to march.

The Natal Native Pioneers, about 50 strong, accompanied the force, which "marched out from the camp as soon as there was light enough to see the road." Lieut. Colonel Pulleine, l-24th Regiment, was instructed to take "command of the camp during the absence of Colonel Glyn"—the force left with

5. Some Zulus (a chief named Gandama, and others) came into the camp on the 21st, saw the General, and were allowed to depart. P. P. (C. 2454) p. 182.
6. P. P. (C. 2260) p. 81.

him consisting of 5 companies 1-24th and 1 company 2-24th Regiment; 2 guns Royal Artillery; about 20 Mounted Infantry and Volunteers; 30 Natal Carbineers, 31 Mounted Police, and 4 companies Natal Native Contingent. An order was also despatched to Colonel Durnford (at Rorke's Drift) to move up to Isandhlwana. Lieut.-Colonel Pulleine's instructions for the defence of the camp were, briefly, to draw in his "line of defence" and "infantry outposts," but to keep his cavalry vedettes "still far advanced."[7] We may here note that the only country searched was that direct to the front and right front the direction of the wagon-track although it is stated—

.... the Lieut.-General had himself noticed mounted men in one direction (our left front) on the 21st, and in this direction he had intended to make a reconnaissance.[8]

After the departure of the advance column nothing unusual occurred in camp until between seven and eight o'clock, when it was reported from the advanced picquet (on the Ingqutu range of hills, about 1500 yards to the north) that a body of the enemy could be seen approaching from the north-east: and various small bodies were afterwards seen. Lieut.-Colonel Pulleine got his men under arms, and sent a written message off to headquarters that a Zulu force had appeared on the hills on his left front. This was received "between 9.30 and 10 a.m."

Colonel Durnford received the General's order when on an expedition into Natal to obtain wagons, but at once returned to Rorke's Drift, and marched for Isandhlwana. Lieutenant Chard, R.E., who had ridden to camp for orders, "met Colonel Durnford about a quarter of a mile from the camp at the head of his mounted men" about 10.30 a.m., and told him the troops were in column outside the camp, and Zulus showing "on the crest of the distant hills," "several parties" working round so far to the left that he "was afraid they might be going to make a dash at the Drift." He took orders to Major Russell to hurry up with the rocket battery, to detach a company of Sikali men to protect the baggage, and for all to "look out to the left."

7. Major Clery.
8. P. P. (C. 2260) p. 99.

Colonel Durnford reached the camp, and received all the information Lieut.-Colonel Pulleine could afford, finding the situation to be: Lonsdale's natives on outpost duty on the hills to the left, the guns in position on the left of the camp, and the infantry under arms. The oxen were driven into camp and—Mr. Brickhill says—tied to the yokes, but not inspanned. Constant reports were coming in from the hills to the left—"The enemy are in force behind the hills." "The enemy are in three columns." "One column is moving to the left rear, and one towards the General." "The enemy are retiring in every direction."

The enemy's force was given at 400 to 600.

On hearing these reports, Colonel Durnford sent one troop Natal Native Horse to reinforce his baggage guard; two troops to the hills to the left (under Captains G. Shepstone and Barton) one to move along the crest of the range, one to search the valley beyond—and determined himself to go out to the front—

> .... and prevent the one column joining the *impi*, which was supposed at that time to be engaged with the troops under the General. ...

He asked Lieut.-Colonel Pulleine for two companies of the 24th, to which Colonel Pulleine replied—

> .... that two companies could ill be spared, but that if Colonel Durnford ordered them, of course they should go.

On consideration, Colonel Durnford decided only to take his own men,[9] and moved out with his remaining two troops Natal Native Horse, followed by Major Russell's rocket battery, with its escort of a company of Native Contingent, under Captain Nourse.

A company 1-24th, under Lieutenant Cavaye, was sent out as a picquet to the hills about 1200 yards north of the camp, and

---

9. "There were no high words," Lieutenant Cochrane says, of any kind between the colonels, as some would lead the public to suppose. The above remarks are taken from Lieutenant Cochrane's account of what passed; and he says: "I think no one lives who was present during the conversation but myself; so that anything said contradictory to my statement is invented."

the remainder of the troops dismissed to their private parades, where the men were to lie down in readiness to turn out if required. At this time there was no expectation of an attack during the day, and no idea had been formed regarding the probable strength of the enemy.[10]

The two troops sent on the hills to the left "to ascertain the enemy's movements," had proceeded "about five miles from the camp," when "the Zulu army came forward, advancing straight on towards the camp." Captain Shepstone ordered a retreat on the camp, and himself rode in with the warning that the "whole Zulu army was advancing to attack it."[11] Captain Shepstone met Captain Gardner on reaching the camp, and both officers then went to Colonel Pulleine, but, says Captain Gardner, the enemy were "already on the hill on our left in large numbers."

Colonel Durnford, having despatched his two troops to the left, had moved out to the front at a canter, followed at a foot's pace by the rocket battery, etc. About five miles out, a trooper rode down from the hills on the left, and reported an immense *impi* behind the hills, and almost immediately the Zulus appeared in force in front and on the left, in skirmishing order, ten or twelve deep, with supports close behind. They opened fire at about 800 yards, and advanced very rapidly. Colonel Durnford retired a little way—to a *donga*—and extended his men, then fell back, keeping up a steady fire, for about two miles,[12] when he came upon the remains of the rocket battery, which (it appeared) had turned to the left on hearing firing on the hills, been cut off, and broken up. Fighting was still going on here, but the Zulus were speedily driven back.

Colonel Durnford retired slowly on the camp, disputing every yard of ground, until he reached a *donga* about 800 yards in front of the right of the camp; there, prolonging the line of the camp troops, and the right being reinforced by between thirty

---

10. Captain Essex, 75th Regiment.
11. Lieutenant Raw, Natal Native Horse.
12. Lieutenant Cochrane, 32nd Regiment.

and forty mounted men, under Captain Bradstreet, a stand was made. Mr. Brickhill, interpreter to No. 3 Column, says:

> This gully the mounted force held most tenaciously, every shot appearing to take effect. . . . a thousand Zulu dead must have laid between the conical hill and the gully. They lay just like peppercorns upon the plain.

The two troops of native horse sent to reconnoitre the Ingqutu Hills, retired fighting before the enemy in good order—

> . . . . to a crest in the neck which joins Sandhlwana to Ingqutu. Leaving their horses well sheltered here, they held this crest splendidly, keeping up a steady galling fire.[13]

They were eventually compelled to retire, with the loss of Captain G. Shepstone.[14]

We must now consider what had taken place at the camp. All was quiet till about twelve o'clock, when firing was heard on the hill where the company on picquet was stationed; the troops were immediately turned out and formed on the left front of the camp. About this time Captain Gardner, 14th Hussars, arrived with an order from the General, addressed to Lieut.-Colonel Pulleine, "to send on the camp equipage and supplies of the troops camping out, and to remain himself at his present camp and entrench it."[15] Captain G. Shepstone reached the camp with his warning about the same time. Colonel Pulleine decided it was impossible to carry out the General's order, as the enemy were already in great force on the hills to the left. Captain Gardner sent off a message to headquarters, saying that "our left was attacked by about ten thousand of the enemy." A message was also sent by Colonel Pulleine.

One company (Captain Mostyn's) was moved up to support the picquet; the enemy distant about 800 yards, moving "towards our left." Orders to retire were received almost immediately, and the whole retired to the foot of the slope, the enemy

---

13. Mr. Brickhill.

14. Having disengaged his men, Captain G. Shepstone said: "I must go and see where my Chief is," and rode in again. His devotion cost him his life.

15. Captain Gardner.

rushing forward to the crest of the hill as our men disappeared. Captain Younghusband's company was at this time in echelon on the left.[16]

The guns came into action about 400 yards on the left front of the camp, "where they were able to throw shells into a large mass of the enemy that remained almost stationary about 3400 yards off."[17]

The three advanced companies of the 24th retired on the main body, when the situation was this: the two guns and the whole of the 24th in line, about 300 yards from the left front of the camp; the natives took post on the right of the 24th; then came Durnford's Basutos; and the extreme right was formed by about forty mounted Europeans[18]—the force holding the only position that afforded any shelter, *viz.* broken ground and a *donga* in front of the camp; the infantry "in good position among the stones and boulders to the left and left centre of the camp, and who stood their ground most gallantly."[19] The enemy approached to within about 400 yards, the two guns firing case. The heavy fire from the line told so upon the Zulus that they wavered and lay down; they are said to have covered the valley in detached groups to the depth of about three-quarters of a mile.[20]

The enemy now began to work round the rear (which they could do with impunity owing to the formation of the ground), and Captain Essex says:

> I rode up to Lieut.-Colonel Durnford, who was near the right, and pointed this out to him. He requested me to take men to that part of the field, and endeavour to hold the enemy in check. . . . those of the Native Contingent who had remained in action, rushed past us in the utmost disorder, thus laying open the right and rear of the 24th, the enemy dashing forward in the most rapid manner.

---

16. Captain Essex.
17. Lieutenant Curling, R.A.
18. Captain Essex.
19. Lieutenant Cochrane.
20. Mr. Brickhill.

The ammunition of the mounted troops failing (supplies had been repeatedly sent for, but none came), Colonel Durnford retired them towards the right of the camp (where the wagons and ammunition of the Native Horse were), and himself galloped off to the 24th, having previously told Captain Gardner that the position was too extended, and he desired to concentrate the force. Colonel Durnford's intention undoubtedly was to withdraw all the troops to the rising ground on the right of the camp, to which point he had retired his Native Horse.

The Zulus rushed on the left in overwhelming numbers, completely surrounding the 24th. The guns limbered up, and made for the Rorke's Drift Road, but found it blocked by the enemy; they therefore "followed a crowd of natives and camp-followers, who were running down a ravine; the Zulus were all among them, stabbing men as they ran." Down this ravine the fugitives hastened, the enemy round and among them, the *assegai* doing its deadly work.

Lieut.-Colonel Pulleine was said by Lieutenant Coghill to have been killed,[21] and during the flight Major Stuart Smith, E.A. (who had been wounded), Surgeon-Major Shepherd, and many a man, mounted and on foot, were killed. The Buffalo was gained at a point about five miles below Rorke's Drift, and numbers of the fugitives were either shot, or carried away by the stream and drowned. Lieutenants Melville and Coghill rode from the camp, on its being carried by the Zulus, the former with the Queen's colours of his regiment. These he bore into the river, but lost his horse, and was left struggling in the swift current; Lieutenant Coghill, who had safely crossed, rode in to his assistance, when his horse was shot. These brave young officers succeeded in gaining the Natal shore, but were soon overtaken by the enemy, and died fighting to the last. The Natal Native Horse escaped with little loss; they assisted many in the retreat, which they covered as well as they could, especially under Captain Barton on the banks of the Buffalo. Captain Essex puts the time of the retreat from the camp at "about 1.30 p.m."

---

21. Lieutenant Curling.

After this period no one living escaped from Isandhlwana, and it was supposed that the troops had broken, and, falling into confusion, that all had perished after a brief struggle.

Nothing was known of the after-events of that fatal day for months, till, on the 21st May, the scene of the disaster was revisited, and the truth of the gallant stand made was established. This will be treated of in another chapter.

We must now turn to the movements of the column under Colonel Glyn, with the General; and it will be most convenient to take the occurrences of the day as described by Lord Chelmsford and his military secretary Lieut.-Colonel Crealock.

Leaving camp at daybreak,[22] the General—

> .... reached Major Dartnell about 6.30 a.m., and at once ordered him to send out his mounted men to gain intelligence of the enemy, whose whereabouts did not appear to be very certain.[23]

The enemy shortly after showed in considerable strength at some distance, but retired without firing as the troops advanced. Lieut.-Colonel Crealock says:

> Between 9.30 and 10 a.m. we were off-saddled some twelve miles from camp. During the three previous hours we had been advancing with Colonel Glyn's column against a Zulu force that fell back from hill to hill as we advanced, giving up, without a shot, most commanding positions.[24]

It was at this time—"about 9 a.m.," the General says—that the message was received from Lieut.-Colonel Pulleine, that a Zulu force had appeared on the hills on his left front. The General says he at once sent his aide-de-camp, Lieutenant Milne, R.N., to the top of a high hill, from which the camp could be seen. He had "a very powerful telescope, but could detect nothing unusual."[25] Lieut.-Colonel Crealock says that all the news

---

22. Three mounted Zulu scouts were seen on the hills on the right from the rear guard, by an officer, who pointed them out to one of the staff.
23. P. P. (C. 2252) p. 75.
24. P. P. (C. 2260) p. 99.
25. Some remarks made by Lieutenant Milne, R.N. (aide-de-camp), are worthy of notice: January 21st. We then rode up to the (continued on next page)

he gave "was that the cattle had been driven into camp," and he acknowledges "our own attention was chiefly bent on the enemy's force retiring from the hills in our front, and a party being pursued by Lieut.-Colonel Russell three miles off."

The *kloof* where the enemy had been was found deserted, but a large body of Zulus were seen beyond it, and a portion of the mounted force sent after them, Major Dartnell and the rest of his men moving off to the right in the direction of another body of Zulus. These turned out to be Matshana's people, with the chief himself present: they were engaged, their retreat cut off, and then driven back on the Native Contingent. Of this party Matshana and one or two of his people alone escaped.

"Having no cause, therefore, to feel any anxiety about the safety of the camp," the General ordered the mounted infantry to sweep round "to the main wagon track, whilst a portion of the infantry went over the hilltop to the same point, and the guns, with an escort, retraced their steps," with instructions to join Colonel Glyn near the Mangane Valley, where the General proceeded with Colonel Glyn to fix upon a site for a new camp. Captain Gardner, 14th Hussars, was sent back to camp "with the order to Lieut.-Colonel Pulleine to send on the camp equipage and supplies of the troops camping out, and to remain at his present camp, and entrench it."[26]

The 1st Battalion Native Contingent was ordered to march back to camp across country, and examine *dongas*, etc. en route. Colonel Crealock says:

---

high land to the left of our camp, the ascent very steep, but possible for horses. On reaching the summit of the highest hill, I counted fourteen Zulu horsemen watching us at the distance of about four miles; they ultimately disappeared over a slight rise. Two vedettes were stationed at the spot from where I saw these horsemen; they said they had seen these men several times during the day, and had reported the fact. . . . We then returned to camp, the General having determined to send out a patrol in this direction the next day. (P. P. (C. 2454) p. 183). On January 22nd Lieutenant Milne was sent to the top of a hill to see what was doing in camp, and says: On reaching the summit I could see the camp; all the cattle had been driven in close around the tents. I could see nothing of the enemy on the left. (ibid. p. 184) We are not quite certain about the time. But it is just possible that what I took to be the cattle having been driven into camp may possibly have been the Zulu impi. (ibid. p. 187).
26. P. P. (C. 2260) p. 101.

Not a sign of the enemy was now seen near us. Not a suspicion had crossed my mind that the camp was in any danger, neither did anything occur to make me think of such a thing until about 1.15. . . .

When it was fancied firing was heard (the natives were certain of it).

We were then moving back to choose a camp for the night about twelve miles from Isandula.

About 1.45 p.m., a native reported:

. . . . heavy firing had been going on round the camp. We galloped up to a high spot, whence we could see the camp, perhaps 10 or 11 miles distant. None of us could detect anything amiss; all looked quiet. This must have been 2 p.m. The General, however, probably thought it would be well to ascertain what had happened himself, but not thinking anything was wrong, ordered Colonel Glyn to bivouac for the night where we stood; and taking with him some 40 mounted volunteers, proceeded to ride into camp. Lieut.-Colonel Cecil Russell, 12th Lancers, now joined us, and informed me that an officer of the Natal Native Contingent had come to him (about 12 noon, I think) when he was off-saddled, and asked where the General was, as he had instructions to tell him that heavy firing had been going on close to the camp. . . . This officer, however, did not come to us.

This information from Colonel Russell was immediately followed by a message from Commandant Brown, commanding the 1st Battalion Natal Native Contingent, which had been ordered back to camp at 9.30 a.m.—(the battalion was halted a mile from us, and probably eight miles from camp)—to the effect that large bodies of Zulus were between him and the camp, and that his men could not advance without support. The General ordered an immediate advance of the battalion, the mounted volunteers and mounted infantry supporting it.

I am not aware what messages had been sent from[27] the camp and received by Colonel Glyn or his staff; but I know that neither the General nor myself had up to this time received any information but that I have mentioned.

225

At 3.15 the General appeared to think that he would be able to brush through any parties of Zulus that might be in his road to the camp without any force further than that referred to, *viz.* 1st Battalion Native Contingent and some eighty mounted white men.

At 4 p.m.,[28] however, the native battalion again halted, about six miles from the camp, and shortly after—the General says—Commandant Lonsdale rode up to report that he had ridden into camp and found it in possession of the Zulus.

The General at once sent word to Colonel Glyn to bring back all the troops, and advanced about two miles, sending Lieut.-Colonel Russell forward to reconnoitre; he fully confirmed Commandant Lonsdale's report. Colonel Glyn rejoined the General about 6 p.m., when the troops were formed in "fighting order," and advanced across the plain; "but could not reach the neighbourhood of our camp until after dark."

It may properly be here remarked that from the outskirts of the force firing had been seen at the camp as late as nearly four o'clock; and about six, large bodies of the enemy were seen retiring from the camp, through openings in the Ingqutu range.

When a move was first made by the General in the direction of the camp, an officer who was in advance narrates what he saw when he came to a rising ground from which the camp was first seen:

> There certainly were some tents standing then, but seemed very few, and away to the left front of the camp there was some smoke, though not much, and it was high up, just as if there had been musketry fire and the smoke had floated away; but there was certainly no musketry fire going on then. A few seconds afterwards a sergeant. . . . said:
> 'There go the guns, sir.'
> I could see the smoke, but we could hear nothing. In a

---

27. (see previous page) One message only is mentioned by the General or his military secretary as having been received from the camp. But an officer of rank *who had seen them*, says that five or six messages were received from the camp during the day by the General or his staff; and he says distinctly that the messages were in the possession of Lieut.-Colonel Crealock.
28. About this hour the tents in camp suddenly disappeared.

few seconds we distinctly saw the guns fired again, one after the other, sharp. This was done several times—a pause, and then a *flash—flash!* The sun was shining on the camp at the time, and then the camp looked dark, just as if a shadow was passing over it. The guns did not fire after that, and in a few minutes all the tents had disappeared. The sergeant said:

'It's all over now, sir.'

I said, 'Yes, and I hope it is the right way.'

We could see there was fighting going on, but of course did not know which way it had gone. The men all thought the Zulus had retired, but I felt doubtful in my own mind, but had no idea really of the catastrophe that had taken place. . . . This must have been about 3 p.m.

Lieutenant Milne says:

Within two miles of camp, four men were seen slowly advancing in front of us; a few mounted men were sent out; the men in front previously seen then took cover behind some rocks, but were fired upon by our men; one fell, the remainder ran out in the open, throwing up their hands to show they were unarmed. On being taken prisoners, they were found to be Native Contingent, escaped from the massacre.[29]

On nearing the camp it was nearly dark, but it was observed that wagons were drawn up across the neck; the guns were therefore brought into action and shelled them. Then, no sound being heard, Major Black, with a wing of his regiment, moved forward to occupy the small hill close to Isandhlwana. No enemy was seen, and the camp was found tenanted by those who were taking their last long sleep.

A halt was made for the night amidst the debris of (the proper right of) the camp, on the "neck;" the infantry covering the west, and the mounted troops and guns the east side. During the night there were one or two false alarms, and the whole force, at early dawn, moved off towards Rorke's Drift, as the General was anxious about the safety of that important post; also the troops had no spare ammunition,[30] but little food, and "it was certain

---

29. P. P. (C. 2454) p. 185.

30. No spare ammunition was taken by the force with the General.

that daylight would reveal a sight which could not but have a demoralising effect upon the whole force."[31]

In Lord Chelmsford's despatch of 27th January, he gives a narrative of the attack on the camp, but remarks "the absolute accuracy of which, however, I cannot vouch for."[32]

On comparing his "narrative" with the *facts*, it will be found to be *absolutely inaccurate*. But Lord Chelmsford makes some remarks which cannot be passed, over in silence. He says: "Had the force in question but taken up a defensive position in the camp itself, and utilised there the materials for a hasty entrenchment;" but he does not point out how the "force in question" was to know of the near approach of the Zulu army, he himself having neglected to search the country where that army lay. He had prepared no "defensive position;" but he had selected a fatal spot for his camp, which, covering a front of about half a mile, was utterly indefensible as it stood; and he had "pooh-poohed" the suggestion of taking defensive precautions when made by Colonel Glyn; and, further, it does not appear that there was any time whatever for the "force in question" to do anything but fight.

Lord Chelmsford then says:

> It appears that the oxen were yoked to the wagons three hours before the attack took place, so that there was ample time to construct that wagon-*laager* which the Dutch in former days understood so well.

This remark comes with peculiar ill grace from Lord Chelmsford, who not only had not taken any precautions, but had not permitted any *laager* or other defence to be made; and whose reply to a suggestion of a *laager* at Isandhlwana was, "It would take a week to make." Also it must not be forgotten that the attack on Isandhlwana was *without warning*. He next says:

> Had, however, the tents been struck, and the British troops placed with their backs to the precipitous Isalwana Hill, I feel sure that they could have made a successful resistance.

---

31. P. P. (C. 2252) p. 76.
32. pp. 76, 77.

Here again he would blame the dead to cover the faults of the living! But even had the troops been thus placed (as some eventually appear to have been), how long could they keep at bay, when ammunition failed[33] an enemy armed with weapons they could use with fatal effect out of reach of the bayonet?

And lastly, Lord Chelmsford speaks of rumours "that the troops were deceived by a simulated retreat," and thus "drawn away from the line of defence." The *facts* prove the exact contrary. The only person deceived by a "simulated retreat" was Lord Chelmsford himself, whose troops *during three hours* had advanced "against a Zulu force that fell back from hill to hill. . . . giving up without a shot most commanding positions." And where was *their "line of defence?"* We do not find one word of Lord Chelmsford's own want of the most ordinary precautions his want of *intelligence*, and neglect to obtain it— of his seeing the enemy's mounted scouts on the left front, and intending (but not making) a reconnaissance in that direction—his fixed belief that the enemy *could* only be in force in his front—the transparent way in which he was drawn off farther from the camp—the absence of any attention to the signs that something was wrong at the camp—the prevention of assistance reaching the beleaguered camp when one of his officers *had* recognised the emergency, etc.; to which must be added that we do not find one word of regret for the untimely fate of the gallant men who fell doing *their* duty. In justice to Colonel Glyn, commanding No. 3 Column, it must be remarked that the General himself gave the orders for the various movements, etc. And in justice to Lord Chelmsford also, we note it is asserted that the shock he experienced told severely upon him at the time; and he may not have very carefully studied the despatch, which was the work of his military secretary.

Before finally leaving the events of the 22nd January, we must fully notice an important episode that occurred, and which had a serious bearing on the disaster we have to lament.

---

33. The reserve ammunition is said to have been packed in wagons, which were then filled up with stores.

We have seen that "the guns with an escort" were ordered to retrace their steps. . . . to join Colonel Glyn at the rendezvous near the Mangane Valley. We will now follow their movements.

When Lord Chelmsford discovered that the enemy he had come in search of had disappeared, 4 guns Royal Artillery, 2 companies 2-24th Regiment (Captains Church and Harvey), and about 50 Natal Native Pioneers, the whole under the command of Lieut.-Colonel Harness, R.A., were ordered to march to a rendezvous in advance by a different route to that taken by the remainder of the column; this was necessary, as the guns could not go over the ground taken by the latter. To carry out the order, they had to retrace for over two miles the route by which they had come in the morning, and then bear to the left. This was done (a short halt having first been made, to let men and horses have a rest), and about twelve o'clock they reached some rising ground, when they again halted, not being certain of the direction of the rendezvous, to await Major Black, 2-24th, Assistant Quartermaster-General, who had gone on to find it. Almost immediately after this halt the firing of cannon was heard, and looking towards the camp, about eight miles off, they saw shells bursting against the hills to the left of it. Soon afterwards a body of about 1000 natives suddenly appeared in the plain below, between them and the camp; the Native Pioneers thought they were' Zulus. Captain Church told Colonel Harness if he would let him have a horse he would go and find out. Colonel Harness at once gave him one, and sent a mounted sergeant with him. As they galloped towards the natives, a European officer rode out, and when they met said:

"The troops behind me are Commandant Browne's contingent, and I am sent to give you this message: *'Come in every man, for God's sake! The camp is surrounded, and will be taken unless helped at once.'*"

Captain Church rode back as fast as he could, and found Colonel Harness in conversation with Major Gosset (aide-decamp) and Major Black, both of whom had come up during his absence. Colonel Harness promptly said:

"We will march back;" but Major Gosset ridiculed the idea,

and advised him to carry out his orders. Colonel Harness then asked Major Black and Captain Church their opinions. They both agreed with him without hesitation. Colonel Harness gave the order to return, and started without a moment's delay; Major Gosset riding off in the direction of the General. About 1.30 p.m. Lieut.-Colonel Harness was on his way to the camp, and had got over about two miles of ground when he was overtaken by Major Gosset with orders from the General to march back to the rendezvous. The order was obeyed.

Now the startling reflection comes home that to this most important fact, bearing on the events of the day (for even if too late to save life, Colonel Harness would have saved the camp), there is not a hint even in the despatches of Lord Chelmsford, or the official statement of his military secretary.[34] The latter goes so far as to say, in paragraph 17 of his statement:[35]

I am not aware what messages had been sent from the camp and received by Colonel Glyn or his staff; but I know that neither the General nor myself had up to this time received any information but that I have mentioned.

This statement refers to a time *after* the General had arrived at a spot about a mile from where Commandant Browne's battalion of natives were halted, *after* he had received the message, "Come in, every man, for God's sake," etc., and *after* he had met Colonel Harness on his return march to the rendezvous; and not only that, but apparently *after* the receipt of a most important message from Lieut.-Colonel Pulleine, described as follows by the special correspondent of *The Times of Natal*—Captain Norris-Newman:

We did halt there, and found the staff there as well, looking on through the field-glasses at some large bodies of Kafirs (Zulus), who were in close proximity to our camp about ten miles off. The Mounted Police were ordered to halt and off-saddle; but Captain T. Shepstone and his volunteers had orders

---

34. The first official mention of this appears in a *Blue-Book* of August, 1879, where Lieutenant Milne, R.N. (aide-de-camp), says: *In the meantime, news came that Colonel Harness had heard the firing, and was proceeding with his guns and companies of infantry escorting them to camp. Orders were immediately sent to him to return and rejoin Colonel Glyn.* P. P. (C. 2454) p. 184.
35. P. P. (C. 2260) p. 100.

to proceed back to camp to see what was up. I joined them, and we had not gone far on the road when a mounted messenger came up with a note from Colonel Pulleine to the General, saying that the camp was attacked by large numbers of Kafirs, and asked him to return with all the help at his command. With this we halted, and awaited the up-coming of the General, who came along at once, and proceeded up the valley to reconnoitre. About three miles had been got over, during which we passed the four guns under Colonel Harness, and some of the 24th. . . . on their way to encamp at the new ground. A mounted man was then seen approaching, and was recognised as Commandant Lonsdale. He brought the dreadful news that, having chased a Zulu on horseback, he got separated from his men, and had ridden quietly back to camp; but on arrival there, within about three hundred yards of it (at about 2 p.m.), he found large bodies of the enemy surrounding it and fighting with our men. He had just time to discover his mistake, turn, and fly for his life, when several bullets were fired at him, and many Zulus started in chase.[36]

The above message is undoubtedly that mentioned by Captain Gardner as having been despatched from the camp at or soon after twelve o'clock.[37] And there still remains the fact that, not only as regards Colonel Harness, does there appear to be an unaccountable omission in the "statement"[38] alluded to, but also we find mention of only *one* message from the camp; whereas other messages are known to have been received, and to have been in the possession of the Assistant Military Secretary.

Here also we must allude to Sir Bartle Frere's despatches of January 27th, and February 3rd and 12th. In the first he says:

> In disregard of Lord Chelmsford's instructions, the troops left to protect the camp were taken away from the defensive position they were in at the camp, with the shelter which the wagons, parked, would have afforded. . . .

---

36. *Natal Colonist*, January 30th, 1879.
37. P. P. (C. 2260) p. 81.
38. By the General's directions this statement was to be "of the facts which came under his cognizance on the day in question." P. P. (C. 2260) p. 80.

We know that the troops did the best they could, left as they were by their general in an open camp we know they had no "defensive position" and we know that the wagons were not "parked," but drawn up in rear of their own camps. Sir Bartle says, February 3rd:

> It is only justice to the General to note that his orders were clearly not obeyed on that terrible day at Isandhlwana camp.

And on February 12th, he says (a little qualifying his sweeping assertion of February 3rd):

> It is impossible to shut one's eyes to the fact that it was, in all human probability, mainly due to disregard of the General's orders that so great a disaster occurred.

But yet again Sir Bartle returns to the charge, and says, June 30th:

> It is difficult to over-estimate the effect of such a disaster as that at Isandhlwana on both armies, but it was clearly due to breach of the General's order, and to disregard of well-known maxims of military science.

On what grounds Sir Bartle Frere bases those assertions we know not—no known orders were disobeyed and, in spite of the special pleading in these despatches, we must come to the conclusion that Sir Bartle Frere's remarks were penned in utter ignorance of facts, and that the accusations concerning "disregard of well-known maxims of military science" should have been applied, not to the soldiers who fell at Isandhlwana, but to those who placed them in that fatal position.

---

39. P. P. (C. 2454) p. 138.

Rorke's Drift

The garrison of the Rorke's Drift post consisted of B Company 2-24th Regiment (Lieutenant Bromhead), and—with officers and casuals—was of a total strength of 139. It was encamped on the Natal side of the Buffalo, where there was a mission station, one building of which was used as a hospital and one as a commissariat store. The crossing of the river was effected by what are called *ponts*—boats used as a kind of *flying bridge*—and there were drifts, or fords, in the vicinity. Major Spalding, Deputy-Assistant-Adjutant-General, and Lieutenant Chard, R.E., were stationed here. The former rode off to Helpmakaar at 2 p.m., 22nd January, "to bring up Captain Rainforth's company, 1st Battalion 24th Regiment, to protect the *pont,*" leaving Lieutenant Chard in command of the post.

About 3.15 p.m., Lieutenant Chard was at the *ponts*, when two men came riding from Zululand at a gallop, and shouted to be taken across the river. They were Lieutenant Adendorff, Natal Native Contingent, and a carbineer, who brought tidings of the disaster at Isandhlwana and the advance of the Zulus towards Rorke's Drift. Lieutenant Adendorff remained to assist in the defence of the post, and the carbineer rode on to take the news to Helpmakaar.

Lieutenant Chard at once gave orders to secure the stores at the *ponts*, and rode up to the commissariat store, when he found a note had been received from the 3rd Column, saying the enemy were advancing, and directing them to strengthen and hold the post at all cost. Lieutenant Bromhead was actively at work preparing for defence, ably assisted by Mr. Dalton, of the Commissariat Department, loopholing the buildings and connecting them by walls of *mealie*-bags and two wagons that were there. Lieutenant Chard then rode down to the *pont*, and brought up the guard and stores.

An officer, with about a hundred of "Durnford's Horse," now arrived, and asked for orders. He was instructed to throw out men to watch the drifts and *ponts*, to check the enemy's advance, and fall back on the post when forced to retire. These men had, however, been in the saddle since daylight, and had gone through a heavy engagement: they were quite exhausted (besides being dispirited by the loss of their beloved leader), and, after remaining a short time, retired to Helpmakaar. A detachment of Natal Native Contingent also left the post.

Lieutenant Chard now commenced an inner work—"a retrenchment of biscuit-boxes." This was two boxes high when, about 4.30 p.m., 500 or 600 of the enemy came in sight, and advanced at a run against the south wall. They were met with a well-sustained fire, but, in spite of their loss, approached to within about fifty yards.

Here they were checked by the cross-fire from the attacked front and the store-house. Some got under cover and kept up a heavy fire, but the greater number, without stopping, moved to the left, round the hospital, and made a rush at the wall of *mealie*-bags. After a short but desperate struggle the enemy were driven back with heavy loss into the bush around the post. The main body of the enemy coming up, lined the ledge of rock, caves, etc., overlooking the work, at a distance of about 400 yards to the south, and from whence a constant fire was kept up, and they also occupied in great force the garden, hollow road, and bush.

The bush not having been cleared away enabled the enemy to advance under cover close to the wall, and a series of desperate assaults were made, extending from the hospital along the wall as far as the bush reached; each assault was brilliantly met and repulsed with the bayonet, Corporal Scheiss, Natal Native Contingent, distinguishing himself greatly. The fire from the rocks took the work completely in reverse, and was so heavy that about 6 p.m. the garrison was obliged to retire behind the entrenchment of biscuit-boxes.

During this period the enemy had been storming the hospital, and at last succeeded in setting fire to the roof. The garrison defended it most gallantly, bringing out all the sick that could be moved; Privates Williams, Hook, K. Jones, and W. Jones, 2-24th Regiment, being the last men to leave, and holding the doorway with the bayonet when their ammunition was expended. The want of communication and the burning of the house rendered it impossible to save all the sick.

It was now found necessary to make another entrenchment, which was done with two heaps of *mealie*-bags, Assistant-Commissary Dunne working hard at this, though much exposed. As darkness came on the little garrison was completely surrounded, but gallantly repulsed several serious assaults; it was, however, eventually forced to retire to the inner entrenchment, which it held throughout the night. The attack continued vigorously till midnight, the men firing on the assailants with the greatest coolness, aided by the light afforded by the burning hospital. A desultory fire was kept up by the enemy throughout the night, but this ceased about 4 a.m. on the 23rd, and at daybreak the enemy was out of sight. Lieutenant Chard at once set about patrolling round the post, collecting the Zulu arms, and strengthening the defences.

About 7 a.m., a large body of the enemy appeared on the hills to the south-west, and Lieutenant Chard sent off a note to Helpmakaar asking for assistance. About 8 a.m., No. 3 Column appeared in sight, the enemy falling back on its approach. Thus ended a most gallant defence, reflecting the utmost credit on all concerned.

The loss of the garrison was 15 non-commissioned officers and men killed, and 12 wounded (of whom two died almost immediately). The attacking force was estimated at 3000 men, of whom upwards of 350 were killed.

Lord Chelmsford, with the remains of No. 3 Column, had moved off from Isandhlwana, as we have already described, at daybreak that morning. It had been thought necessary to insist upon absolute inaction through the night; no attempt was allowed at identifying the dead, or even at making sure that no life remained in the camp; and men lay down to rest, ignorant whether a careless hand might not fall on the lifeless form of a dead comrade or, mayhap, a brother. The remainder of the Natal Carbineers, as they afterwards discovered, bivouacked that night on the right of the camp, upon the very neck of land where so gallant a stand was made; their captain recognising the body of Lieutenant Scott, and therefore being able afterwards to identify the spot. That life might exist without its being known to the returning column is proved by the fact that a native groom lay for dead, although unwounded, in the camp throughout the night. The man had feigned death when the camp was taken, and did not dare to move on the return of the General's party, lest he should be taken by them for a Zulu, and should share the fate of the few actual Zulus found intoxicated beneath the wagons, and bayoneted by our soldiers. He crept out in the morning, and followed the retreating column to Rorke's Drift at a distance, meeting on the way with narrow escapes of losing his life from both friend and foe.

On coming within sight of Rorke's Drift, heavy smoke was seen rising from it, and Zulus retiring; this caused the liveliest apprehensions for the safety of the post. However, to the intense relief of all, on nearing the Buffalo River the waving of hats was seen from a hastily-erected entrenchment, and the safety of the little garrison was known.

Lieut.-Colonel Russell was sent with a mounted escort to Helpmakaar, to see if the road was open and all safe there; but some officers of Major Bengough's battalion Natal Native Contingent rode in and reported the road open, Helpmakaar *laagered*, and no attack made on it. Some men of the Buffalo Border Guard also rode in from Fort Pine and reported all well there.

The General and staff hurried down to Pietermaritzburg *via* Helpmakaar, while the garrison at Rorke's Drift was left in utter confusion,[1] as testified by many of those present at the time. No one appeared responsible for anything that might happen,

---

1. "The panic and confusion were fearful," says one of themselves.

and the result was one disgraceful to our English name, and to all concerned. A few Zulu prisoners had been taken by our troops—some the day before, others previous to the disaster at Isandhlwana, and these prisoners were put to death in cold blood at Rorke's Drift. It was intended to set them free, and they were told to run for their lives, but they were shot down and killed, within sight and sound of the whole force. An eye-witness—an officer—described the affair to the present writer, saying that the men whom *he* saw killed numbered "not more than seven, nor less than five." He said that he was standing with others in the camp, and hearing shots close behind him, he turned, and saw the prisoners in question in the act of falling beneath the shots and stabs of a party of our men.[2] The latter, indeed, were men belonging to the Native Contingent, but they were supposed to be under white control, and should not have been able to obtain possession of the prisoners under any circumstances. Scenes like these were not likely to impress the savages with whom we were dealing with our merciful and Christian qualities, nor to improve the chances of European prisoners who might fall into their hands during the campaign.

As soon as order was a little restored, the cover round the post of Koike's Drift was cleared away, barricades built, the thatched roof taken off the house, and the four guns placed in position within the enclosure.

The General and staff reached Pietermaritzburg early on January 26th. There, as everywhere else, panic reigned, and gloom spread over all. From the city especially many a son and brother had gone out to fall upon that fatal day, and grief was mingled there with terror for what might come next. It was long before any accurate information could be gained as to what had happened, and who had fallen; and, owing to the hurried retreat of No. 3 Column from Isandhlwana before daybreak on the 23rd, the great burden of uncertainty was laid upon many heavy hearts both upon the spot and at home in England.

At first all who had had friends at the camp hoped they might be amongst the saved, since it was known that some had escaped

---

2. The number of prisoners thus killed is said to have been about twenty.

by "The Fugitives' Drift," a spot some five miles from Rorke's Drift, where those flying from Isandhlwana crossed the river; and day by day the lists of killed and missing appeared with the names gradually removed from the latter to the former. Well had an hour's daylight been spent that morning to spare the uncertainty that hung over many an English and South African home for days and weeks, and even months.

No time was now lost in making such preparations for defence as the principal towns afforded. An invasion of the colony by the victorious Zulu army was hourly expected, and with some reason, since retaliation for our invasion might naturally be feared. Sir Bartle Frere himself remarks, on February 12th:[3]

> It has become painfully evident that the Zulu king has an army at his command which could almost any day unexpectedly invade Natal; and owing to the great extent of frontier, and utter helplessness of the undisciplined hordes of Natal natives to offer effectual resistance, the Zulus might march at will through the country, devastating and murdering, without a chance of being checked, as long as they abstained from attacking the entrenched posts of Her Majesty's troops, which are from 50 to 100 miles apart. The capital and all the principal towns are at this moment in *laager* prepared for attack, which even if successfully resisted, would leave two-thirds of them in ashes, and the country around utterly desolated.[4]

Whatever reasonable fears of retaliation were entertained by the people of Natal, they soon rose to panic height in consequence of the great alarm displayed by the chief authorities, both military and civil. By their orders, the central part of 'Maritzburg, including the Court House, was barricaded with loopholed boarding, as a refuge for the citizens in case of attack, wells

---

3. C. 2269.
4. Yet Sir B. Frere, on the 30th June, writes: "The position of Wood's and Pearson's columns effectually checked the execution of an attempt at invasion." These two columns, being some ninety miles apart and secure in their own positions only, would have been of little avail had the Zulu king desired to make "an attempt at invasion." It needed no better strategists than Cetshwayo and his chiefs to have masked each of the posts at Kambula and Etshowe with some 5000 men, and then "the Zulus might march at will through the country."

were dug inside the Court House, and notice given that the usual guns, announcing the arrival of the English mails, would be discontinued for the present, but that three guns would be fired as a signal for the citizens to go into the *laager* within three hours, while four guns would signify that the danger was urgent, and they must fly into it at once, taking stores of food, which they were to have ready beforehand, beside what the borough council had provided, and they must then comply with an elaborate series of rules, which was published in the Government *Gazette*. So great, indeed, was the scare that some of the citizens of 'Maritzburg did actually take refuge one night in the *laager*, and others hurriedly left the colony, while many natives, living near the city, slept out, with their wives and children, some nights in the open field. On that night, when terror was at its height, it is said that the bedding of the Governors and their staff, together with the official records of Government House, was removed to the neighbouring gaol, a strong stone building, just under the guns of Fort Napier, which was chosen as a place of refuge for their Excellencies. It is also said that Lord Chelmsford's horse was kept saddled and bridled all night; and a stretcher was placed, by express order, outside the window of a lady in delicate health, without her knowledge, so as to be ready in case of emergency—as if a Zulu *impi* could drop suddenly, at a moment's notice, into the middle of the city, the frontier, at the nearest point, being sixty miles off.

Whether or no the High Commissioner was really in such a state of alarm as he appeared to be, the existence of such a scare in Natal would, no doubt, help to support his policy in the eyes of those at home, as an actual inroad of Zulus at that time would have still more effectually justified the charges he had made against Cetshwayo, and the strong measures he had taken in invading Zululand, for the good of the Zulus themselves and the safety of the colony. After the disaster at Isandhlwana, Sir B. Frere of course reiterates his charges against the king of intending to invade the colony.[5]   But these charges are sufficiently answered by the mere fact that although, as Sir B. Frere himself

5. C. 2269.

points out, Natal lay at his mercy for some months after the disaster, he made no attack whatever either upon Swazis, Boers, or English. After Isandhlwana, if ever, such invasion was to be dreaded, yet not only was none attempted, but even the Zulus who, in the flush of victory crossed into Natal at Rorke's Drift on the 22nd, were called back by their officers with the words, "Against the orders of your king!"

In startling contrast to the panic which reigned after the 22nd January was the ignorance and carelessness shown by the authorities beforehand. At the very time of the disaster to No. 3 Column there was a train of fifteen wagons, with sixty-five boxes of ammunition each, moving unguarded up to Helpmakaar, upon a road eight miles from and parallel to the Zulu border!

With the exception of Rorke's Drift, no military station was at this time more open to attack than Helpmakaar, distant from it about twelve miles. The fugitives from Isandhlwana, Captains Essex and Gardner, Lieutenants Cochrane, Curling, and Smith-Dorrien, with about thirty others, reached this place between 5 and 6 p.m., and at once set about forming a wagon-*laager* round the stores. The garrison of two companies of the 1-24th Regiment had marched towards Rorke's Drift during the day; but Major Spalding says:

> On reaching the summit of a hill from which the mission-house is visible it was observed to be in flames; this confirmed the statement of the fugitives that the post had been captured. This being the case, it was determined to save, if possible, Helpmakaar and its depot of stores. . . .

The column reached Helpmakaar by 9 p.m.[6] Captain Gardner, soon after reaching Helpmakaar, left for Utrecht, it having occurred to him to carry the news of the disaster himself to Colonel Wood. Our loss at Isandhlwana is given as 689 officers and men Imperial troops, and 133 officers and men of Colonial Volunteers, Mounted Police, and Natal Native Contingents Europeans;[7] but the actual loss was slightly in excess of those numbers.

---

6. P. P. (C. 2260) p. 88.
7. P. P. (C. 2260) pp. 93-98.

The Zulu army appears to have consisted of the following regiments: 'Kandampemvu (or Umcityu), 'Ngobamakosi, Uve, Nokenke, Umbonambi, Udhloko, Nodwengu, and Undi (which comprises the Tulwana, 'Ndhlondhlo, and Indhlnyengwe), whose full nominal strength reaches a total of 30,900 men; but the actual numbers are estimated at from 20,000 to 25,000.

The Zulus acknowledge to having suffered heavily, and their loss is estimated at 3000.

Cetshwayo's youngest brother, Nugwende, who surrendered on 27th April, said he was present at Isandhlwana. That the front and left flank attack was beaten, and fell back with great loss until the fire of the white troops slackened; the right flank entering the camp, the attack was renewed, the English being unable to prevent their onset from want of ammunition. The Zulu army, he says, numbered 20,000 of the king's best troops.

A court of inquiry, composed of Colonel Hassard, C.B., R.E., Lieut.-Colonel Law, R.A., and Lieut.-Colonel Harness, R.A., assembled at Helpmakaar on the 27th January, when the following officers gave evidence: Major Clery; Colonel Glyn, C.B.; Captain Gardner, 14th Hussars; Captain Essex, 75th Regiment; Lieutenant Cochrane, 32nd Regiment; Lieutenant Smith-Dorrien, 95th Regiment; Captain Nourse, Natal Native Contingent; and Lieutenant Curling, R.A.

The evidence taken consisted of statements made by the above officers, not one of whom appears to have been questioned. The (so-called) inquiry seems to have been strictly limited to the occurrences at the camp, as we find Major Clery's evidence finish abruptly, "I saw the column out of camp and accompanied it." Colonel Glyn merely corroborated Major Clery 's statement; and the other officers gave their respective versions of the occurrences at the camp; Captain Essex giving a very clear and detailed account of the movements of the 24th Regiment.

The proceedings were forwarded on the 29th, with these remarks:

> The court has examined and recorded the statements of the chief witnesses.

The copy of proceedings forwarded was made by a confidential clerk of the Royal Engineers.

The court has refrained from giving an opinion, as instructions on this point were not given to it.

The proceedings were forwarded from Durban to the Secretary of State for War on February 8th by Lord Chelmsford, who said:

The court has very properly abstained from giving an opinion, and I myself refrain also from making any observations, or from drawing any conclusions from the evidence therein recorded.

He regrets that more evidence has not been taken, and has directed his military secretary "to append a statement of the facts which came under his cognizance on the day in question."[8]

On this officer's *statement* some remarks have been made in the previous chapter; and we must now quote one or two passages from the public prints, which appeared when Colonel Harness's share in the proceedings of the 22nd January first came to light. *The Daily News* of April 8th, referring to this episode and the court of inquiry, says:

Lord Chelmsford seems to have been as unfortunate in the selection of his staff-officers as he was in everything else.

Lieut.-Colonel Crealock's *statement* is stigmatised as "palpably written to establish a preconceived theory;" and *The Daily News* says most justly that—

Colonel Harness should not have sat as member of the court of inquiry. How it could have been supposed that an officer who had taken so prominent a part in the doings of the 22nd January was a fit and suitable member of a court assembled even to take evidence merely, is more than we can understand. Besides, the very fact of his being a member, we are told, precluded Colonel Harness from giving his own valuable evidence.

The Natal Witness of May 29th, 1879, makes some reflections on the same subject, which are very pertinent. We need not repeat its criticisms on the court of inquiry, etc. but it says:

---

8. P. P. (C. 2260) p. 80.

It is notorious that certain members of Lord Chelmsford's staff—there is no need to mention any name or names—came down to 'Maritzburg after the disaster, prepared to make Colonel Durnford bear the whole responsibility, and that it was upon their representations that the High Commissioner's telegram about 'poor Durnford's misfortune' was sent.

How a court of inquiry, assembled without the power, apparently, of asking a single question, was to throw much light on the causes of the disaster, does not appear. Its scope was limited to the doings at the camp; and under any circumstances it could not well criticise the faults of the General. The proceedings of this court of inquiry can therefore only be considered as eminently unsatisfactory,

We might here leave this painful subject, were it not for the undisguised attempts that have been made to throw the blame on the dead.

In considering the question of blame, we must first put before us the circumstances in which the camp defenders found themselves when they were required "to defend the camp."

Now the orders given to Lieut.-Colonel Pulleine are stated by Major Clery, senior staff-officer of No. 3 Column, thus:

> Before leaving the camp I sent written instructions to Colonel Pulleine, 24th Regiment, to the following effect: 'You will be in command of the camp during the absence of Colonel Glyn; draw in (I speak from memory) your camp, or your line of defence'—I am not certain which—'while the force is out; also draw in the line of your infantry outposts accordingly, but keep your cavalry vedettes still far advanced.' told him to have a wagon ready loaded with ammunition ready to follow the force going out at a moment's notice, if required. I went to Colonel Pulleine' s tent just before leaving camp to ascertain that he had got these instructions, and again repeated them verbally to him.[9]

As regards the force left to defend the camp, there were no instructions to form a defensive post; the General did not think

---

9. P. P. (C. 2260) p. 81.

it necessary, though to him was the almost prescient remark made: "We should be all right if we only had a *laager*." He saw no danger; he was about to move his camp on, and a *laager* would be useless work, so he put the suggestion on one side with the remark: "It would take a week to make." Thus Lieut.-Colonel Pulleine was left, and he had no reason to anticipate danger, till, almost without a moment's warning, he found the camp threatened by an overwhelming force; he then, after trying in vain to check the enemy's right, endeavoured to hold the *donga* and broken ground close in front of the camp, where his men found some cover; the camp itself being absolutely indefensible.[10] Colonel Durnford, as we have seen, reached the camp about 10.30 a.m., before which time Major Chard says: "The troops were in column. . . . out of camp," and he saw Zulus "on the crest of the distant hills," and several parties moving to the left towards Rorke's Drift. Colonel Durnford takes out his mounted men to (as he thinks) assist his General, and to see what the enemy is about.[11]

Again, some assert that the action was brought about by Colonel Durnford's Native Horse in the Ingqutu Hills. Even had it been so, yet this officer's duty distinctly was to feel and reconnoitre the enemy.[11] When the Zulu army moved forward to the attack, he, with his handful of men, fell slowly back, gaining all the time possible for the camp defenders.

Taking the whole of the circumstances of the day, we may conclude that, had the enemy remained hidden on the 22nd, we should probably have lost the entire column instead of part; but the account given by an English Officer with one of the troops that first saw the enemy, and other accounts from Zulus, seem to make it clear that the Zulus were moving on the camp

---

10. Some officers who were with the advance column, and who afterwards visited Isandhlwana, say that they appear to have "tried to get the wagons together to form a *laager*," but there was not time.

11. With respect to this, Lord Chelmsford lays down a principle (relative to the border raids, but even more strongly applicable here) that if a force remains "on the passive defensive, without endeavouring by means of scouting in small bodies or by raiding in large ones, to discover what the enemy is doing in its immediate front, it deserves to be surprised and overpowered." P. P. (C. 2318) p. 80.

when they came in contact with the horsemen. That they had no intention of remaining hidden is shown by their unconcealed movements on the hills throughout the morning.[12]

Now, whether these defenders did or did not take the best measures "to defend the camp" when it was attacked, the primary causes of the disaster were undoubtedly these:

1. The fatal position selected for the camp, and the total absence of any defensive precautions.

2. The absence of systematic scouting, whereby an army of upwards of 20,000 Zulus was enabled to approach Isandhlwana on the 21st, and remained unobserved till the 22nd, although their mounted scouts were actually seen by the General and staff on the 21st, watching *them.*

3. The subdivision of the force, and the absence of proper communications by signalling or otherwise.

4. The neglect of warnings given by the events of the day, and messages from the camp; also the withdrawal of a force actually on the march to the relief of the camp.

For these principal causes of the disaster, none of those who fell were responsible.

That Lord Chelmsford was shaken by the tragic events of January is evident from his letter to the Secretary of State for War:

---

12. It is stated that on the previous evening there was no intention on the part of the Zulus to attack the camp upon the 22nd, which was not thought by them a propitious day, being that of the new moon. It is also said that the Zulu army came with pacific intentions, in order to give up Sihayo's sons, and the cattle for the fine. In all probability they left the king with such orders that is to say, to make terms if possible, but to fight if forced to it, and if the English intentions were plainly hostile. This hostility was thoroughly proved before the morning of the 22nd, when the departure of Lord Chelmsford's force from the camp must have been a strong temptation to the Zulus to attack the latter. Warning of the Zulu army moving against Nos. 1 and 3 Columns was received on the border, and communicated to Mr. Fannin, Border Agent, on January 20th. The warning stated that the whole Zulu army, over 35,000 strong (except about 4000 who remained with the king), was marched in two columns, the strongest against Colonel Glyn's column, the other against Colonel Pearson; this was to take up its position on the 20th or 21st January at the royal *kraal* near Inyezane, and the first to approach Rorke's Drift. The writer complains of the little and inadequate use made of the information, which might have been communicated from Fort Pearson to Rorke's Drift in time to have averted the fearful disaster of the 22nd January. P. P. (C. 2308) pp. 69, 70.

Durban

Natal

February 9th, 1879

I consider it my duty to lay before you my opinion that it is very desirable, in view of future contingencies, that an officer of the rank of major-general shall be sent out to South Africa without delay. In June last I mentioned privately to His Royal Highness the Field-Marshal Commanding-in-Chief that the strain of prolonged anxiety and exertion, physical and mental, was even then telling on me. What I felt then, I feel still more now. His Excellency Sir Bartle Frere concurs in this representation, and pointed out to me that the officer selected should be fitted to succeed him in his position of High Commissioner. In making this representation, I need not assure you that it will be my earnest desire to carry on my duties for Her Majesty's service up to the fullest extent of my powers.[13]

The exact meaning of this letter has never been made clear. No doubt Lord Chelmsford was feeling "the strain of prolonged anxiety and exertion, physical and mental," but His Royal Highness the Commander-in-Chief said that he had no previous knowledge of it. Students of Greek history will note the striking parallelism of this case with that of Nicias, who, when commanding before Syracuse in the year 414 B.C., applied to be superseded.

> Such was the esteem which the Athenians felt for this union of good qualities, purely personal and negative, with eminent station, that they presumed the higher aptitudes of command. . . the general vote was one not simply imputing no blame, but even pronouncing continued and unabated confidence.[14]

But of all the strange and incomprehensible circumstances connected with that sad time, the one which struck Natal as the strangest was the utter desertion of the battle-field and the long neglect of the dead who lay there. On the 4th February Major Black, 2-24th Regiment, with a small party, found the bodies

---

13. P. P. (C. 2260) p. 79.
14. Grote's *History of Greece*

of Lieutenants Melville and Coghill about 300 yards from the river on the Natal side, near the Fugitives' Drift, and they were buried on the spot, the colours which they had striven to save being found in the river, and returned next day to the regiment at Helpmakaar.

The fatal field of Isandhlwana was not again seen till the 14th March, when Major Black, 2-24th, with a small mounted party, paid a flying visit to the spot, a few shots only being fired at them from a distance. No attempt was made to bury the dead, and until the 21st of May that ghastly field remained as it was left on the 23rd of January, although there does not appear to have been any period since the disaster when a moderate force might not with perfect safety have done all that was necessary.

On the morning after the return of Colonel Glyn's Column to Rorke's Drift—

> Commandant Lonsdale mustered the Contingent and called out the *indunas*, and told them in the hearing of all that he wanted to find out the men who were courageous and would stand by their officers and die with them if necessary, and that those who were willing to do this were to come forward. At this time the mounted infantry and volunteers were moving off to Helpmakaar. The general reply of the Contingent was that they were willing to go over to fight along with the white people, their shield against Cetywayo; but that now that they saw their shield going away they would not go over by themselves, and that no one could say he was not afraid.[15]
>
> They were then dismissed, but in the afternoon they were all disarmed (of their guns), and their belts and *puggaries* and blankets taken from them by their officers. Each company had a flag, which they asked to take home with them; some were allowed to do so, but others were not. They were then all told to go home, and to keep together till they reached the Umsinga, and then to divide each for his own home.

On January 24th, Colonel Glyn wrote to Lord Chelmsford:

---

15. P. P. (C. 2318) p. 12.

The whole of the Native Contingent walked off this morning. Their rifles were taken from them; all the hospital-bearers then went, and now the Native Pioneers are going. I am now left without any natives.

The General immediately forwarded Colonel Glyn's letter to Sir Henry Bulwer, with the remark:

Unless these men are at once ordered back to their regiments, or punished for refusing to go, the most serious consequences will ensue.[16]

Sir Henry Bulwer very properly abstained from taking any strong measures as to punishing the men until he had inquired into the causes which led to their desertion. Eventually, indeed, he discovered that most of them had not deserted at all, but had been disbanded by their leader, Commandant Lonsdale. But meanwhile there was a great deal to be said, and on January 29th Sir Henry writes, pointing out that—

. . . . the great disaster which happened to our force at Isandhlwana Camp on the 22nd inst., the circumstances under which these men passed the night of the 22nd, and the retirement of the remainder of the column on Rorke's Drift and back into Natal, were all calculated to have their effect on the natives who belonged to this column. . . . I am told, too, that whilst the European force at Rorke's Drift on the night of the 23rd were entrenched, the Native Contingent was not entrenched; and further I am told that, on an alarm being given that night, the European officers and non-commissioned officers who were with the Native Contingent left their men and took refuge within the entrenchments. On the following morning, the 24th, the General and his staff left the camp; and this circumstance, those acquainted with the native character tell me, may very probably have had a further depressing effect upon the natives.[17]

On February 7th, Sir Henry Bulwer writes again that he has received answers from the magistrates whom he had directed

16. *ibid.* p. 3.
17. P. P. (C. 2318) p, 4.

to make inquiries into the causes of the dispersion of the men. These reports speak of the cheerful spirit and loyal tone of the chiefs, and of very many of the men having reported themselves to their magistrates on their return from the front. The accounts given by the different magistrates are unanimous as to the causes of the dispersion. Some of the men declared that officers of the Contingent told them to return home and await further orders, as provisions were short; others, to use their own words, said: "We saw that the Government was driven out of Zululand, and the wind blew us back also."

They thought also that the Commander-in-Chief's hasty departure from Rorke's Drift was a flight from the enemy. Another reason for their retreat, and to them a very strong one, was the necessity of going home and performing the rights of purifying after shedding blood.[18] It was also stated that some of them were led by their officers in their retreat. Others saw their officers killed, were left without control, and fled. Their friends were now laughing at them, and they were eager to return to the front under proper guidance.

These, indeed, were ample explanations for the fact of the dispersion of the 3rd Regiment Natal Native Contingent, but they were followed by many and serious complaints, made by the men and reported by the magistrates, of the manner in which the former had been treated since the campaign began. These complaints comprised insufficiency of food, floggings for disobedience to orders which they had either never heard, or had not understood, and bad officers.[19] These were the most important items, the rest referring to their preference for their own methods of fighting, to which, as we have already shown, there were the strongest objections.

These reports referred solely to the contingent attached to Colonel Glyn's column, with the exception of one, which was concerning the remnant of the Zikali men, escaped from Isandhlwana.

---

18. Had Lord Chelmsford been acquainted with this peculiarity of the Zulus, he might not have thought it necessary to hurry away from Isandhlwana on the 23rd. There was no fear of the same force attacking again for some days to come.
19. P. P. (C. 2318) pp. 11-17.

It was finally decided that the men of the contingents belonging to No. 1 Column might—

> .... be allowed to leave in batches, but they must be made to understand that they are required for the defence of Natal.[20]

The contingent forming No. 2 Column remained steadily serving throughout the war. Major Bengough's battalion had a narrow escape of sharing in the disaster of Isandhlwana, and the men were somewhat shaken and disheartened at seeing the contingent of No. 3 Column dispersing; but this ill-effect soon passed away.

Colonel Pearson's remarks on the company of Native Pioneers belonging to his column are concise and valuable. He says:

> The men worked cheerfully. They had eyes like hawks, and they did all their scouting to perfection. It convinced me that the Natal Zulus, under proper management, would make excellent troops.

---

20. P. P. (C. 2260) p. 22.

CHAPTER 15

The Campaign Against Sikukuni

We have already, in a previous chapter, explained the circumstances which led to the war between the Transvaal Boers and Sikukuni, independent chief of a mixed race of natives commonly called the *Makatisi*, more properly the *Bapedi*, tribe. The immediate cause of the war was a border dispute between some of the gradually encroaching Boer farmers and the natives whom they had displaced, which ended in the latter taking possession of some cattle belonging to the former.

This affair took place during a temporary absence of Mr. Burgers (then President of the Republic), who, on his return, demanded the cattle at the hands of Sikukuni, and the restraint of his people within the limits assigned to them by their Boer neighbours. Sikukuni expressed his willingness to make the required restitution, but took the opportunity of reminding the President that he laid claim to a considerable piece of territory already occupied by Boers, to whom he denied having ever willingly relinquished it. This reply was the signal for a declaration of war against Sikukuni on the part of the President and Volksraad, and a large *commando* or volunteer force, was called out to attack him early in July, 1876.

This force, consisting of some 3000 Boers and over 4000 of their Swazi allies, made its way through the country, ravaging and destroying as it went, until it reached the famous stronghold known as Sikukuni's Town, upon which it made an unsuccessful night attack, on August 2nd.

A single reverse was sufficient to dishearten the gallant Boers, who immediately discovered various reasons which made their return to their homes absolutely necessary. The commando dispersed, leaving a force of volunteers composed of stray Englishmen, Germans, and half-bred natives to occupy a couple of posts—Fort Burgers and Fort Weber—which they built for the purpose. From these posts they carried on a system of raiding expeditions upon Sikukuni's people, which effectually prevented the cultivation of their land, and finally produced a scarcity of food amongst them. This state of things was too harassing to last, and Sikukuni sued for peace, which was granted him early in 1877, conditionally upon his paying a heavy fine in cattle.

A month later, and before the fine had been paid, Sir T. Shepstone had annexed the Transvaal, and, as we have already described, took over, with the country, its quarrels and demands. He tried to enforce the fine imposed by the late Boer Government upon Sikukuni, while remitting the war-tax levied upon the whites. After having been subjected to so long a course of marauding on the part of the Dutch, it is not impossible that the chief really had some difficulty in procuring, at a moment's notice, the 2000 head of cattle demanded by Sir T. Shepstone.[1] At all events, the fine was not paid so promptly as the administrator expected; and the whole country being in an unsettled condition, perpetual disturbances still took place between Sikukuni's people and the border farmers, and also between the former and petty chiefs who had placed themselves under British protection.

The most restless of the independent native rulers seems to have been a woman, Legolwana, a sister of Sikukuni's, who had her own clan, and whose headquarters was a mountain stronghold, called Masellaroon. In February, 1878, her people had a quarrel (nor was it for the first time) with a neighbouring native chief under our rule, from whom they took some cattle. Whether or no there were two sides to the question, the despoiled chief was our subject, and it so happened that Legolwana's people were met in the act of driving off the cattle by a patrol of Transvaal volun-

1. Who, it is said, insisted upon the animals being fine and in good condition, returning some which were sent in below the required mark.

teers, who promptly interfered. This occurrence led to a general outbreak of hostilities. Legolwana's men attacked the two forts simultaneously, and the officers in command, Captain Clarke and Lieutenant Eckersley, with their men, escaped from them, and retired to Lydenburg. From thence Captain Clarke sent embassies to the Swazi king and another independent chief, asking for assistance against Sikukuni. His invitations, however, were politely declined, the chiefs in question not caring to interfere, although wishing to remain upon friendly terms with the English.

Having obtained reinforcements from the gold-fields and Pretoria, Captain Clarke marched back to Fort Weber, and re-occupied it with a force consisting of 40 mounted volunteers under Captains Van Deventer and Ferreira, 150 Natal Zulus under Lieutenants Lloyd and Dacomb, and 300 Bechuanas under Mr. Tainton.

Captain Clarke's first intentions were to attack Legolwana and reduce her to submission. Captain Lacon Hervey, 71st Regiment, gives the following description of her stronghold in his account of the Secocoeni War:

> The town, or *kraal*, of Legolani consisted of a number of straw and wattle-and-daub huts, beehive-shaped, situated at the base and on the terraces of a mountain of rocks and huge boulders 700 feet high, covered over with thick clumps of bush. The huts at the base of the mountain were surrounded by an impenetrable hedge of prickly pear; a single entrance, barricaded with timber, led through an avenue of prickly pear and cactus into the group of huts surrounded by palisading, wattle screens, and stone walls. Each group of huts was commanded by the rocks above; from behind these a direct, flanking, and enfilade fire could be poured on the attacking party, which, on account of the intricacy of the ground, would be compelled to advance in single file along the tortuous goat-paths leading up to the mountain. In addition to the cover afforded by the caves and fissures in the rocks, *schanzes*, or low stone walls, were built up wherever favourable positions with safe means of retreat presented themselves. The paths leading from one rock entrenchment,

or terrace, to the one above it, were so concealed by rock and bush as to be difficult to find. Finally, the Kafirs' most valued treasure, the cattle, was placed on the summit of the mountain, on a level plot of ground, surrounded by a stone wall.

This stronghold was attacked by Captain Clarke's orders on the 5th April, and, "after about two hours' sharp work, the north of the hill was carried."[2] The fighting force, not being sufficient to complete its work, was ordered to withdraw, after having swept all the cattle from that side of the hill (277 head of cattle and 211 sheep and goats). A considerable number of Legolwana's people are supposed to have fallen in this assault, the loss on our side being 10 killed and 12 wounded, amongst the latter Captain Van Deventer slightly, and Lieutenant Lloyd severely. These two officers are reported as having led the attack with great gallantry.

The partial success gained by the storming of Masellaroon (with the loss of life on our side—considerable under the circumstances) was not such as to encourage Captain Clarke in the tactics with which he had commenced his operations. He therefore abandoned all idea of seizing the native strongholds, and "established a cordon of forts, about twelve miles from each other. . . . with a view of harassing the Kafirs by preventing them from cultivating the Indian corn."

> Legolwana had sued for peace, but Captain Clarke would not listen to anything except unconditional surrender, with the guarantee that all life should be spared.[3]

Thus, with the usual notion that "no terms can be made with savages," which has again and again produced such disastrous consequences for them and for us, a system of petty warfare was kept up, tedious, unnecessary, and by which no good could be done nor honour gained. To the volunteers, many of whom, says Captain Harvey, were "gentlemen by birth and education," there may have been some amusement in what that officer speaks of as "actions of daring individual enterprise," and which he describes as follows:

---

2. Captain Clarke's report (C. 2144), p. 37.
3. Sir T. Shepstone to Sir H. Bulwer, April 16th, 1878 (C. 2144).

Volunteers went out and lay ambuscades at night, to surprise and cut off Kafirs proceeding from *kraal* to *kraal*, or to cultivate their fields, and 'cattle-lifting' expeditions were planned and boldly carried out.

But the life must have become monotonous in the extreme before July, when the native auxiliaries became so discontented with it that some of them were allowed to return to their homes, while a troop of mounted infantry was summoned from Pretoria to keep order amongst those who remained.

It was about this time that Colonel Rowlands, V.C., came upon the scene. This excellent officer, of whose services in 1878-79 so little mention has been made, was sent out on "special service," and was for a short time attached to the staff of Lord Chelmsford (then General Thesiger) during the Kaffrarian war. He was subsequently sent by the High Commissioner to Pretoria, which he reached on May 6th. He employed the two following months in an inspection of the northern and eastern frontiers of the Transvaal,[4] and by dint of considerable personal exertion was enabled to supply valuable information to headquarters. Towards the end of July, Colonel Rowlands was appointed Commandant of the Transvaal. At this time the regular forces in the Transvaal consisted only of the 13th Light Infantry, a few engineers, and departmental staff quite inadequate for the work required of them; but the Commander-in-Chief, in signifying his approval of the manner in which Colonel Rowlands proposed to distribute the troops already under his command, informed him that he was about to reinforce the Transvaal with the 80th Regiment and Frontier Light Horse, with a view to active operations against Sikukuni.

The promised reinforcements arrived by degrees from Natal, and meanwhile there were Pretoria, Middleburg, Lydenburg, and Standerton, where considerable stores of ammunition, etc. were collected, to be garrisoned, as well as the cordon of forts, already mentioned, along the Leolu Mountains, which left no large proportion of the troops—about 800 of the 13th and under 300 volunteers and Zulu police—for service in the field.

---

4. Upon the Zulu border.

However, by the 29th August Colonel Rowlands found himself in a position to leave Pretoria for the confines of the Transvaal, and reached Fort Weber on the 13th September. From thence to Fort Burgers was a long and tedious march through a difficult and trackless country. The column was forced to make its own road as it went, and had several skirmishes with Sikukuni's people *en route*. Reinforced by the Frontier Light Horse under Major Buller, and a party under Major Russell from Pretoria, Colonel Rowlands at last reached Fort Burgers, and, after a few days' halt for repairs, patrolling, and scouting the country, recommenced his march towards Sikukuni's Town, distant about twenty-five miles.

On the 3rd October he advanced with 338 mounted men (Mounted Infantry, Frontier Light Horse, and Transvaal Volunteers), 130 infantry, and 2 7-pounder mountain guns; his intention being to establish himself before Sikukuni's town, thoroughly reconnoitre it, and, should he find that there was a chance of success, and that the position could be afterwards held, to attack it when he had brought up reinforcements.

The position was one of extreme difficulty, greatly increased by the singular drought which was experienced at the time, both in the Transvaal and Natal.

From Fort Burgers to Sikukuni's Town, the approach lay chiefly through a defile commanded by *kopjes* (piles of rock and boulders, often some hundred feet in height), of which the enemy did not fail to take advantage. The weather was intensely hot, the thermometer standing daily at over 100 in the shade, and the unusual drought had dried up the springs and small watercourses to an extent previously unknown.

The camp was fired into on the night before the force sighted Sikukuni's Town, but from a considerable distance, causing no damage beyond one horse wounded, and a general stampede of the slaughter cattle; a determined advance of the piquets, reinforced by their supports, quickly driving back the enemy, who did not advance again.

The stronghold was sighted upon the following day, but it soon became apparent to Colonel Rowlands that, while to attempt its capture with the small force at his disposal would be a mere reckless sacrifice of the troops under his command, it was equally impossible to carry out his original intention of establishing himself before it, under the existing circumstances of absolute want of water and forage. Deeply disappointing as was this discovery, Colonel Rowlands was convinced that his only course under the circumstances was to retire, and, his opinion being confirmed by the senior officers present, he reluctantly commenced his return march on the 6th October.

Encouraged by the retreat of the force, the enemy, now in large numbers, followed and harassed it, almost until it reached the bivouac, eight miles from Fort Burgers. Thirteen thousand rounds of ammunition were expended in keeping off the foe during the march, and both man and beast suffered severely from want of water and the intense heat of the sun. The force reached Fort Burgers the following day, with the loss of 1 man wounded; 5 horses were killed, 10 died of horse sickness, and 4 horses and 1 mule were wounded. Here they remained for several weeks, in hopes that the summer rains, which it was natural to expect should fall at this time of year, would enable them to make a second advance upon Sikukuni's Town. Meanwhile mounted patrols, under Major Buller, Major Russell, Captain Clarke, and Lieutenant Eckersley (in command of Swazi levies), swept the country in every direction, harrying the natives and capturing their cattle, but without meeting with any armed opposition. Horse sickness now set in—that South African scourge, from which the force had hitherto suffered but slightly, and in single cases, but which at this time became an epidemic, deaths occurring daily, sometimes but a few hours after the animal was attacked by the disease. This unfortunate circumstance added greatly to the difficulties of the situation.

After the retreat of the force from before Sikukuni's Town, the enemy made several determined attacks upon the forts in the Mamalubi Valley, especially upon Fort Faugh-a-Ballagh; and although these attacks were in every case successfully resisted, they necessitated the strengthening of the garrisons of the forts along this line.

Lord Chelmsford (then General Thesiger) had previously given notice to Colonel Rowlands that a column from the Transvaal, under the command of the latter, would be required to cooperate with the Ama-Swazi in the invasion of Zululand. The 13th Regiment, Frontier Light Horse, and Lieutenant Nicholson's guns, were all to be available for that purpose as soon as the Sikukuni affair (which was then lightly considered) should be settled. By this arrangement, the 80th Regiment and volunteers alone were reserved for the defence of the Transvaal. As the season was now far advanced, Colonel Rowlands was obliged to make the best arrangements he could for the defence of the border with the force—an absurdly small one, considering the disturbed state of the country—which would be left after the withdrawal of those intended by the General for the Zulu invasion. His chief adviser, Captain Clarke, was of opinion that a precipitate retirement from the valleys of the Steelport and Speckboom rivers would be unadvisable. These valleys contained large numbers of Kafir gardens, and, by holding them a little later, the natives would be prevented from sowing their crops for another season, and starvation would ensue. With this object in view, Fort Burgers was garrisoned with 100 of the 13th Regiment, and some 50 mounted volunteers, while Colonel Rowlands himself retired to Speckboom Drift, about thirteen miles from Fort Burgers, where he constructed another fort in such a position as to cover the junction of four important roadways. Having completed this work, he determined to attack some native strongholds in the Steelport Valley, into which he marched, with 3 guns, 140 mounted men, 340 infantry, and 250 natives, on the 26th October. Moving before daybreak the following morning, he commenced the attack, at 7 a.m., upon a large *kraal*, built upon a mountain spur. Here there was some sharp work, difficult positions seized, and the valley finally cleared. Several *kraals* were burnt, about 12,000 lb. of grain destroyed, and 100 head of cattle taken. Sixteen of the enemy were *accounted for*, the loss on the side of the attacking party being 1 killed and 10 wounded. At 10 o'clock the same morning the Commandant returned to his camp on the Steelport, and, a few days later, to the new fort at Speckboom Drift. Despatches from headquarters awaited him here, instructing him to withdraw altogether, and as speedily as possible, from the enemy's country.

Arrangements were immediately made for the evacuation of Fort Burgers, which was the advanced post on the direct road to Sikukuni's Town, the withdrawal of troops and stores being masked by a strong patrol under Captain Carrington, composed of mounted volunteers and native foot levies, who were sent, *via* Fort Burgers and Origstaadt Valley, to the Oliphant River. The headquarters of the 13th Regiment (340), Russell's Mounted Infantry (63), and Lieutenant Nicholson's two mountain guns, left camp for Lydenburg the whole under the command of Lieut.-Colonel Gilbert, 13th Light Infantry—immediately; and in a few days' time Fort Burgers was emptied and demolished. Captain Carrington's patrol having returned, after capturing 345 head of cattle, and meeting no enemy except a small guard and the cattle-herds, Colonel Rowlands marched from Speckboom about the 7th November, leaving at that fort a sufficient force to guard the ammunition and stores which remained there. About thirteen miles from Lydenburg he halted and constructed a small fort, to cover the principal road leading to that town, and which he purposed to garrison with a detachment of volunteers.

Considerable difficulty was now experienced by Colonel Rowlands in arranging the small force to be left at his disposal, so as to efficiently protect the great length of frontier, extending from Fort Mamalubi (under the west side of the Leolu range, and about twenty-five miles from Oliphant's River) to Kruger's Post on the east, besides garrisoning Pretoria, Middleburg, and Lydenburg, in which were large quantities of supplies and war *matériel*. His plans were laid with due consideration for the nature of the country and the enemy, and after careful consultation with those officers who were supposed to be most fully acquainted with both. Nevertheless they did not meet with full approval from headquarters, from whence Colonel Rowlands finally received orders to remain where he was, and be responsible for the arrangements he had made, instead of proceeding at the head of No. 5 Column to the eastern border for the invasion of Zululand, as originally intended. Shortly afterwards Lieut.-Colonel Gilbert was directed to proceed with the 13th Light Infantry and Lieutenant Nicholson's guns to Derby, Lieut.-Colonel Buller having preceded him to that place, which was now removed from under Colonel Rowlands' command and placed under that of Colonel Wood.

The attention of the former officer was now turned to the disposition of the force that remained to him, and to the raising of new corps of volunteers and strengthening those already formed, which he deemed necessary for the security of the Transvaal. To this work he set himself with great energy and considerable success, stifling thereby the disappointment which it was but natural that he should feel at being excluded from the Zulu campaign. Towards the close of the month, however, he received a letter from the General, asking him to spare two companies of the 80th Regiment to take the place of the force under Colonel Gilbert, which had been moved to Luneburg, and which shortly after joined Colonel Wood's column. Somewhat to his surprise, he was reminded that Derby was in his command, and was told that the General commanding would be glad if he would proceed there in person to reassure the Swazis. That same day the two companies of the 80th, under Major Creagh, were put in orders to march as directed, and Colonel Rowlands followed a week later, leaving the forces defending the northern border under the able command of Major Carrington, who, however, took such instructions from Captain Clarke as he considered necessary to give as Commissioner of that district under His Excellency the Administrator of the Transvaal.

At Derby there was, not unnaturally, some slight confusion owing to this double appointment of officers in command; but having overcome this difficulty, Colonel Rowlands set himself seriously to consider the situation, which was by no means a promising one. A force composed of two companies of Europeans and 250 natives, collected from the neighbouring country, was clearly useless for any aggressive purposes, while the Swazis, though ready and willing to cooperate with an English force large enough to support them, were evidently far from satisfied with the number collected at Derby. That town, or hamlet rather, consisting of but two houses in point of fact, is situated from twenty to five-and-twenty miles from the Zulu border of a part of Zululand peopled by some of the most warlike tribes of that nation, and so small a garrison as the above did but invite attack and disaster. Upon these considerations Colonel Rowlands determined to reinforce himself from. Pretoria and Lydenburg. He sent instructions to Major Tyler, 80th Regiment, to send him three companies of the 80th, two Armstrong guns, and a troop of Weatherley's Border Horse, but directing him to consult the colonial authorities as to whether the troops could be safely spared, before complying with the order.

At this time, about the middle of January, the Zulus throughout this northern and thickly-populated part of the country were perfectly quiet and even friendly. There was still a possibility that the difficulty between their king and the English might be settled without bloodshed, and the people were evidently anxious to avoid giving cause of offence. Colonel Rowlands, who employed his time while waiting for his reinforcements (which would take some weeks to arrive) in reconnoitring the country, found the roads open and the inhabitants inoffensive. At this period he also attempted to organise a frontier force of farmers—Englishmen, Boers, and Germans—whom he summoned to a meeting for consideration of the question. From fifty to sixty attended, and, after hearing his address, their spokesman responded to the effect that they were willing to take service for the defensive object proposed, but that it was to be clearly understood that by uniting themselves to a common protective cause, they did not thereby acknowledge allegiance to the British crown. But a committee, subsequently formed to consider details connected with the proposed force, fell out amongst themselves, and the scheme was abandoned.

On the 26th January, Colonel Rowlands received from Sir T. Shepstone the news of the disaster at Isandhlwana; and from this time nothing but contradictory orders and impossible commands seem to have reached him at his distant post. He heard of the troops he had intended for special purposes being ordered elsewhere; he was directed by Lord Chelmsford to take orders from his junior, Colonel Wood; he received different instructions, entirely opposed to each other, concerning the calling out of the Swazi allies; nevertheless, in spite of the confusion which reigned at that unhappy epoch, he kept his head, and went steadily on with the plans he had formed. By the second week in February he had, with some difficulty, collected a force of something under a thousand Europeans and natives, and was prepared to operate. It seemed, however, impossible to get any distinct orders or definite instructions from those in command, either military or civil; and representations having been made to him by the border Boers that a Zulu *impi* was about to attack them from the Tolaka Mountains, he marched out with a portion of his force in that direction, leaving Major Tucker (80th) in command of the rest. While halted at the Assegai River upon this expedition, he received a despatch from Colonel Wood, requesting him to march his force from Derby to Luneburg to his support. Sending a note to Major Tucker, directing him to start for Luneburg next morning, he continued his march, attacked and took the Tolaka Mountain, and then proceeded towards Luneburg with his own force. He was now about eighteen miles from where his head-quarters camp under Major Tucker would be, with a broken and hilly country to pass through, over which he had great difficulty in conveying his wounded (fortunately but few), and the captured women and children. These captives were, on this account, offered their freedom, but refused to accept it, which, perhaps, was not unnatural, seeing that their homes and crops were destroyed, and they had no longer any means of livelihood.

The force passed through the Intombi Valley, laying the country waste for miles on either side of the road as it went, and met on its way messengers from Colonel Wood, requesting the immediate presence of the mounted corps. But upon the 23rd February, Colonel Rowlands received a memorandum to the effect that the Lieut.-General, by desire of the High Commissioner, wished him to proceed at once back to Pretoria, to prepare some defence against the Boers, who had assumed a threatening attitude. Upon the receipt of this order he quitted the Luneburg district, and arrived on the 6th of March at the capital of the Transvaal. Here there were but 200 infantry and some few mounted volunteers; but by Colonel Rowlands' exertions the number was soon swelled to 600 or 700, by the addition of city corps and other volunteers.

A considerable number of Boers who had never willingly accepted the annexation of their country by the English, had taken the opportunity, offered by the general confusion which reigned after the disaster of the 22nd January, of endeavouring to regain the independence of their state. Mass meetings were held to discuss the subject, and finally a large body of armed men formed a camp at no great distance from Pretoria. The situation appeared a very serious one; and the High Commissioner himself travelled to Pretoria to endeavour by his honeyed words to calm an agitation which might prove so singularly inconvenient should the angry feelings of the indignant Boers find vent in blows. On the 12th of April, just two years from the day of the annexation, Sir B. Frere met a deputation of the Transvaal farmers at Erasmus Spruit, about six miles from Pretoria, and held a long discussion with them upon the subject of their rights and wrongs. They repeatedly and plainly asserted that Sir T. Shepstone had coerced the people into submission by threatening them with the Zulus, and declared unanimously that nothing would satisfy them but the recovery of their liberties. Sir Bartle Frere gave them to understand in return that this was the only thing for which they might not hope. He assured them that he looked upon the *voortrekkers* as an honour to their race, and that he felt proud to belong to the same stock. The Queen, he told them, felt for them "as for her own children;"[5] and he hoped to tell her that she had "no better subjects in her empire," than amongst them. The committee, however, retired in complete dissatisfaction, and addressed a petition to Her Majesty, in which they remark, "unwilling subjects but faithful neighbours we will be;" and more than hint that they are prepared to "draw the sword" to prove how much they are in earnest. The excitement, however, calmed down for the time being, and Sir Bartle Frere departed.

---

5. C. 2367, p. 90.

During his stay in Pretoria, he desired Colonel Rowlands to make preparations to resume hostilities against Sikukuni, and accordingly, by the end of May, that officer had increased the number of his mounted volunteers by 450. He then made a vain attempt to induce Lord Chelmsford to spare him another regiment of regular troops; but finding that this was decidedly refused, and that no operations were likely to take place in the Transvaal for some time, he accepted the General's offer of a brigade in the lower column.

On the arrival of Sir Garnet Wolseley at Port Durnford, he applied to that general for the command in case operations should be resumed in the Transvaal. To this he had a strong claim, both on account of his experience and of his laborious services there; but the request was refused.

Intombi—Indhlobane—Kambula

On January 6th, No. 4 Column, under Colonel Wood, V.C., C.B. strength previously detailed crossed the Blood River (the Zulu boundary according to the award of the Commission) and advanced to Bemba's Kop.

On the 11th, Colonel Wood met the General halfway to Rorke's Drift, and received instructions "to occupy himself with the tribes on his front and left flank, notably Seketwayo," until No. 3 Column was ready to advance to Isipezi Hill, when he was to proceed to Ingwe, both columns to establish advanced depots, bring up supplies, and then move forward. Colonel Wood induced the Zulu chief Bemba to give up his arms and come in, which he did on the 10th, bringing with him about eighty of his people and 1000 head of cattle, sheep, and goats; they were sent to Utrecht.

On the 11th, Colonel Wood, who had advanced with a portion of the force from Bemba's Kop towards Rorke's Drift to meet the General on his return march, seized about 2000 head of cattle, the owners of which were quietly tending them as usual (these were supposed to be Sihayo's), and next day attacked a petty chief, who was said to have "given considerable trouble" to the Transvaal farmers, with the result of seven Zulus killed and upwards of 500 head of cattle captured.

Some 2000 to 3000 head of cattle were also taken from the Sondolosi tribe,[1] a slight resistance being offered by the Zulus,

---

1. Sondolosi, deceased brother of Seketwayo.

of whom one was killed. Colonel Wood thus endeavoured to induce Seketwayo's people to be pacified, and was "therefore most anxious to refrain from taking any steps which might discourage these men from coming in!"

The General, on entering Zululand, finding the difficulties greater than he had anticipated, instructed Colonel Wood "to act altogether independently, about the head waters of the White Umveloosi River" (16th January, 1879), and when Seketwayo had either surrendered or been defeated, to "take up a position covering Utrecht and the adjacent Transvaal border, wherever he considers his force can be most usefully employed," and not to "attempt to advance towards the Inhlazatye Mountain until an advance by the other three columns across the Umhlatoozi River has become possible."[2] Colonel Wood, from Bemba's Kop, communicated with Uhamo a brother of Cetshwayo who had asked for a way to be pointed out by which he might escape.

No. 4 Column now moved towards Intemgeni River, and encamped there on 18th January, Colonel Wood reporting "many of the natives are giving themselves up to me; I have captured about 4000 head of cattle." On the previous day a party of Wood's *irregulars* attacked some Zulus, killing 9, wounding about 20, and taking 5 prisoners and 100 sheep; with a loss to themselves of 2 wounded.[3] On the 19th and 20th there were skirmishes with some of Tinta's people, of whom about 12 were killed. A prisoner was brought in by the Native Contingent on the 19th, whom they gravely asked permission to kill in the evening, "thinking they had done their whole duty in obeying orders and bringing the man in."

The column encamped at Tinta's *kraal*, on the left bank of the Umvolosi River, and a stone fort was commenced. A reconnaissance across the Umvolosi to Zinguni Mountain met the Zulus in force, and was compelled to retire with a loss of two wounded, the enemy not being checked until the river was recrossed. January 22nd, the Zinguni Mountain was patrolled by a strong force, the enemy retiring hastily, and leaving about 600 head of cattle.

---

2. P. P. (C. 2252) p. 63.
3. *ibid.* p. 66.

In the distance a large force, estimated at 4000, was seen, and it apparently ascended the Indhlobane Mountain. The column had a smart engagement with the enemy on the 24th, and drove them off with a loss of about fifty killed; but on receiving intelligence of the disaster to No. 3 Column, retired to Fort Tinta.

At Luneburg a *laager* was formed by the Dutch farmers, under Commandant Schermbrucker, and Colonel Wood moved his force to Kambula Hill, to cover Utrecht and the neighbouring border, and there firmly entrenched himself. The situation chosen was a commanding and central position between the Umvolosi and Pevana rivers on the *Jagt-pad* (Hunter's path), covering the country northward to Luneburg, eastward to the Amaqulusi, southward to the Umvolosi, and westward to Balte's Spruit and Utrecht.

The Zulus abandoned the open, and remained in the mountains and broken country, where rocks and caves afforded them secure positions.

On February 1st, Lieut.-Colonel Buller, with 140 irregular cavalry, made a dash at the Amaqulisini (or Amaqulusi) *kraal*, thirty miles distant. This was a military stronghold, deemed by the Boers to be impregnable. It was situated in a basin at a distance of nearly two miles from the summit of the rugged heights by which it was surrounded, and almost hidden from view, although about 300 yards in diameter and containing at least 250 huts.

Leaving thirty men as a covering party, Colonel Buller moved with the remainder down the almost precipitous slopes, the horsemen frequently obliged to dismount and lead their horses. However, the *kraal* was not occupied in force, and, after a few shots, the inmates fled. Six Zulus were killed, 270 head of cattle taken, and the *kraal* burnt, the force returning from this daring exploit without casualty, after a hard day's work of twenty hours.

A small fort was finished and armed on February 3rd, and, on the 10th, Lieut.-Colonel Buller, with 400 irregular cavalry, reconnoitred the Indhlobane Mountain, and, after a slight skirmish, captured 490 head of cattle.

A new fort was commenced at Kambula, about two miles higher up the spur, and the camp moved to this spot on the 13th, the fort being garrisoned by two companies of infantry and two guns.

It was reported that Manyonyoba (an independent native chief) had been killing and plundering in the Intombi Valley, so Colonel Buller was sent with a force to the spot. The Swazi chief Umbilini was also reported by Commandant Schumbrucker to have raided, in combination with Manyonyoba, and done much mischief to life and property; however, a force sent from Luneburg had a successful skirmish with them.

The king's brother, Uhamo, came in to Captain McLeod from the Swazi border with 300 of his people and 1000 cattle, and reached Derby on February 4th, his following increased to about 600, and was moved down to Luneburg, where he arrived on March 7th.

A sad disaster occurred on the Intombi River to a detachment of the 80th Regiment on the 12th March. Captain Moriarty, with 104 men of the 80th, was escorting a convoy from Derby to Luneburg. On reaching the Intombi Drift (about four miles from Luneburg) the river was found to be rising, and by the time the advanced guard (thirty-five men, under Lieutenant Harward) had crossed, it was impossible to take the wagons over. They were therefore *laagered* on the river-bank in the shape of a triangle; and there they remained next day. About 4 a.m. on the 12th a shot was fired, and the troops turned out, remaining under arms for half an hour, when, all being quiet, they returned to their tents (it transpired afterwards that the outlying sentries had been surprised and killed by the enemy). Suddenly the fog lifted, and a large body of Zulus without any warning rushed on and took the *laager*, driving the troops into the river. The party under Lieutenant Harward, which was encamped on the opposite bank, opened a brisk fire, but were soon broken, and obliged to fly towards Luneburg; Lieutenant Harward, galloping in, gave the alarm. Only forty-four men of this detachment survived.

Major Tucker sallied out from Luneburg, when the enemy slowly retreated. The wagons were saved, and the bodies of Captain Moriarty and his unfortunate men buried.

The comparatively quiet time at Kambula was passed thus: Colonel Wood was up with the first in the early morning, and often out with the patrols who daily scouted the country round for miles; his force securely entrenched; himself a very strict but kind commander, who had the full confidence and goodwill of his troops. Sports were got up for the amusement and occupation of the men. A band played in the evening, and the singing and laughter in camp showed that all were in excellent spirits. The daily business was cutting wood from the mountain-side some three miles distant, escorts, patrols, and piquet duty. One of the night piquets (eight men) posted at some distance from camp was termed *the forlorn hope*; its special duty was to give early warning of an enemy's approach. But the most unpleasant feature in this camp life was the absence of comfort at night. The troops necessarily *turned in* dressed, armed, and ready for instant work, with the personal discomfort illustrated by this soldier's joke that it was "Cetshwayo outside—and Catch-away-o! inside."

Lieut.-Colonel Buller, having returned to Kambula, patrolled Uhamo's district, and in the direction of the Indhlobane range; and on the 16th brought into camp 958 of Uhamo's people.

On March 28th, a reconnaissance by the whole cavalry force was made towards Indhlobane. The Zulus were in possession of the mountain, which was ascended in skirmishing order as rapidly as possible, the enemy keeping up a heavy fire from caves and from behind huge rocks. The summit was reached with the loss of one officer—Lieutenant Williams—and serious fighting was kept up for some time in the endeavour to dislodge the Zulus from their secure positions. Captain the Hon. E. Campbell was killed, also Lieutenant von Sticenstron, and Colonel Wood himself had a very narrow escape.

Whilst engaged in this struggle a Zulu army was moving up to seize the approaches to the mountain, and cut off the force from the camp. Immediately on this being observed a retreat was made in rapid but good order, until a very steep and stony *krantz* was reached, where the men could only move in single file; here the enemy got in amongst the troopers, causing utter confusion. The officers did their best to steady their men, but it became a case of *sauve qui peut*.

Captain Barton's troop was sent down the mountain to recover the body of Lieutenant Williams, and returned, having been joined by Mr. Uys. On the flats they came up with Colonel Weatherley's troop, and found the enemy in front and on the right and left. Retreating a short distance they were surrounded, so, opening out, they charged through the enemy and over the neck, which was lined with Zulus. But few were enabled to win their way through this perilous pass, and of those who did many were overtaken and killed on the plain. Of Captain Barton's troop but eight men returned to camp that night.

The broken force fought its way to the camp, followed by the enemy for several miles. Many a man's life was saved by a comrade halting and taking him up on his own horse, a personal instance of which Captain D'Arcy gives. His horse had been killed under him in the descent of the mountain, and he ran for his life for some 300 yards, when a man named Francis caught a horse for him, which, however, he shortly relinquished to a wounded comrade, running on himself on foot. Colonel Buller picked him up when nearly exhausted, but when he recovered his breath he dismounted; he was a second time in difficulties, and assisted by Lieutenant Elaine, and again, a third time, by Major Tremlett, R.A. Indeed, most of the men got into camp with comrades mounted behind them. The loss was 12 officers and 84 non-commissioned officers and men killed, and also Colonel Wood's staff-officer, Captain the Hon. E. Campbell; Captain Barton, Coldstream Guards; and Mr. Lloyd, Political Assistant. Colonel Wood's horse was shot under him.

Mr. Piet Uys, the leader of the Burgher force, was likewise amongst those killed in action this day.

Small patrols were sent out next morning to endeavour to find any men who might have escaped.

Warning of an intended attack on Kambula was brought in by a native—one of Uhamo's men—and, about 11 a.m., dense masses of the enemy were seen in the distance, when all the force was assembled and the cattle driven into their *laager*. At 1.30 p.m. the action commenced by mounted troops, under Colonels Buller and Russell, engaging the enemy on the north of the camp. They were speedily forced to return into the *laager*, followed by the Zulus until they were within 300 yards, when a heavy fire from the 90th Regiment checked their advance, and they opened out round the camp.

At 2.15 the right front and rear of the camp were attacked by heavy masses of the enemy, who, apparently well supplied with Martini-Henry rifles, occupied a hill commanding the *laager*, enfilading it so that the company of the 13th posted at the right rear of the enclosure had to be withdrawn. The front of the cattle-*laager* was, however, stoutly held by a company of the 13th; but the Zulus coming boldly on, Major Hackett, with two companies of the 90th, was directed to clear the slope. They sallied out into the open, driving the Zulus back in a gallant manner under a heavy fire, until ordered to retire by Colonel Wood.

While bringing his men in, Major Hackett was dangerously wounded.

The two guns in the redoubt were admirably worked by Lieutenant Nicholson, R. A., until he was mortally wounded; when Major Vaughan, R.A., replaced him.

Major Tremlett, R.A., with four guns, remained in the open during the engagement.

The attack began to slacken about 5.30 p.m., enabling Colonel Wood to assume the offensive; the Zulus were driven from the cattle *kraal* into which they penetrated, and from the immediate vicinity of the camp, the infantry doing great execution among the retreating masses.

The pursuit was taken up by the mounted men under Colonel Buller, and continued for seven miles, "killing great numbers, the enemy being too exhausted to fire in their own defence" (*vide* Colonel Wood's despatch of March 30th). All agreed in admiring the pluck of the Zulus, who, "under tremendous fire, never wavered, but came straight at us."

The loss of No. 4 Column was 2 officers killed, 5 wounded, and 80 men killed and wounded. The strength of the enemy was thought to be about 20,000, of whom 1000 are supposed to have been killed. Colonel Wood's operations at Indhlobane were for the purpose of "making demonstrations against the enemy," as directed by the General, who had reason to believe at that time, that he should find the whole Zulu army between his force and Etshowe.[4] One trooper, a Frenchman named Grandier, had a very remarkable escape from Indhlobane, of which the following is his account:

On coming down the mountain we were met by a large Zulu force, and fell back across the neck assailed on all sides. I was about the last, having put a comrade on my horse whilst I ran alongside, when a Kafir caught me by the legs, and I was made prisoner. I was taken to Umbilini's *kraal* and questioned; after which, I passed the night tied to a tree. Next day I was taken into the middle of a large *impi*, where I was threatened with death, but the leader said he would send me to Cetywayo. Next day I started for Ulundi, in charge of four men, who were riding, but I had all my clothes taken from me, and had to walk, carrying their food. On the evening of the fourth day we reached Ulundi, and I was kept tied in the open till about noon next day, when Cetywayo sent for me, and questioned me about what the English wanted, where Shepstone was, etc. A Dutchman acted as interpreter, and I saw a Portuguese, and an English-speaking Zulu, who could read.[5] Cetywayo had a personal guard of about one hundred men, but I did not see any large numbers of men at his *kraal*, but there were two small cannons there. During my stay I was fed on *mealies*, and frequently beaten. At last messengers arrived reporting the death of Umbilini, and Cetywayo said he would send me to his Kafirs to kill. On 13th April I started in charge of two Kafirs, one armed with a gun and both with *assegais*. About midday we were lying down, the Kafirs being sleepy, when I seized an *assegai* and killed the man with the gun, the other running away. I walked all night guided by the stars; next day I saw an *impi* driving cattle towards Ulundi, so had to lie still. After this I saw no Kafirs, and walked on at night. On the morning of the 16th I met some of our own people and was brought into camp.

---

4. P. P. (C. 2367) p. 35.
5. Trooper Grandier's story of ill-treatment has since been contradicted by this Dutchman.

Trooper Grandier, when brought in, was dressed in an old corduroy coat, cut with *assegai* stabs, and a pair of regimental trousers cut off at the knee; these he had picked up on the Veldt. He had strips of cloth round his feet.

The independent chief Umbilini, who was such a thorn in the side of the Transvaal, was killed early in April. Small parties had raided into the Pongolo Valley from Indhlobane, opposite Luneburg, until they were said to number some hundreds, when they came upon two companies of the 2-24th on the march; these at once *laagered*, and the enemy moved on; Umbilini, Assegai's son, and four horsemen, going back with twenty horses. They were pursued by Captain Prior, 80th Regiment, with seven mounted men (80th), and another European, when Assegai's son was killed, and Umbilini mortally wounded.

The raiders were attacked by some parties of natives, but went off to the *Assegai* River with several beasts and sheep.[6]

Meanwhile, many attempts were made by the Zulu king to arrest the tide of invasion, and to bring about a more peaceable solution of the difficulties between him and the English Government.

When Lord Chelmsford first crossed into Zululand, messengers were sent by the king to the column on the Lower Tugela asking for an explanation of the invasion, suggesting that hostilities should be suspended, that the British troops should re-cross the Tugela, and that talking should commence.[7] These men did not return to the king, but remained at the Lower Tugela, Sir Bartle Frere says by their own desire, since they dared not return with an unsatisfactory answer.

Bishop Schreuder narrates on March 3rd that—

> Two Zulus arrived here yesterday with a message from the king. . . . The king says:
>
> > Look here, I have taken care of the deserted mission-stations, and not allowed them to be destroyed, thinking that the missionaries in time would return to them, such as Mr. Robertson's at Kwamagwaza, and Ofti-

---

6. P. P. (C. 2374) p. 51.
7. C. 2374, p. 109.

bro's at Ekhowe, but we now see what use the missionaries make of the station-houses; Robertson has come with an *impi* (army) to the Ekhowe mission-station, and there has made a fort of it, the houses being turned to advantage for our enemies. Seeing this, my people have of their own accord destroyed the other mission-stations; and although I have not ordered this destruction, still I cannot complain of it, seeing that the houses on the stations will serve as a shelter for our present invading enemy. I am in a fix what to do with your station Entumeni, for it is reported. . . . that the column at Miltongambill is to. . . . march to Entumeni, turn the station into a fort, like Robertson has had the Ekhowe turned into a fort. In that case I will, much against my wish, be obliged to destroy the house at Entumeni, as a matter of self-protection, the last thing I ever thought of doing, as I have no grudge against you or your station.

This is the substance of the king's message to me with respect to my station, Entumeni; it, therefore, now will entirely depend on the decision of the General Lord Chelmsford, whether the Entumeni station-houses are to be destroyed or not.

The messengers also report that the king has sent, through a certain Ikolwa Klass; (not known to me), that copy of Sir T. Shepstone's report which I, on behalf of the Natal Government, handed over to him from Her Majesty Queen Victoria, August, 1875.

Already Umavumendaba had requested the king to send that book with the deputation that met at Tugela, 11th December, 1878, in order that there might be proved from that book wherein the king had sinned, since the English had put forth such warlike demonstrations; but Umavumendaba's request was not then acceded to. The king now sends this book that from the contents of it may be proved wherein he has broken the compact made at his installation, 1st September, 1875 (1873).[8]

---

8. P. P. (C. 2318) pp. 35–37.

Bishop Schreuder requested Mr. Fannin, the border agent, "to receive the message from the messenger's own lips, and communicate it to His Excellency." He reported that Cetshwayo wished to explain to the Government that he had never desired war. He had not, he said, refused the terms proposed at the Lower Tugela; he had collected 1000 head of cattle to pay the demand made on him, and would even have delivered up Sihayo's sons to the General, but "any Zulu that showed himself was immediately, fired upon." The attack upon Sandhlwana, he protested, was not made by his orders, and his *induna* was in disgrace for having made it. As regards Inyezane, the king contended that Colonel Pearson provoked the attack made on him by burning *kraals*, and committing other acts of hostility. He asked that both sides should put aside their arms, and resume negotiations with a view to a permanent settlement of all questions between himself and the Government. He would, he said, have sent in a message some time since, but was afraid, because the last time, when he sent eight messengers to the Lower Tugela, they were detained, whom he now begged might be sent back to him.

Mr. Fannin, on the 22nd March, reports the arrival of the messengers with the book, and says:

> Cetywayo sends by the messengers the book containing the laws promulgated at the time of his coronation, and presented to him by Her Majesty the Queen.
>
> It will be remembered that this book was handed to the Zulu king by Bishop Schreuder at the request of the Natal Government some time after the coronation took place. The king now returns it, and asks him to cast his eye over its contents, and say in what way he has transgressed its provisions.[10]

On March 28th Mr. Fannin reports that—

> .... three messengers have arrived with a message from Cetywayo. Their names are Johannes (a native of Entumeni), Nkisimana, and Umfunzi. On approaching the ferry they were fired on by the Native Contingent. ... The message is

9. *ibid.* pp. 40, 41.
10. *ibid.* p. 47.

very short; it is simply to say, Cetywayo sees no reason for the war which is being waged against him, and he asks the Government to appoint a place at which a conference could be held with a view to the conclusion of peace.

They further brought a message from Dabulamanzi, that—

.... a few days ago he sent a white flag with two messengers to Ekhowe, to ask for a suspension of hostilities, until the result of this mission was known, but the men have not returned. He asks that the men may be released.

Mr. Fannin says: "Four other Entumeni men have arrived with these messengers," and he suggests, "that the Entumeni men should not be allowed to return to Zululand"[11]
On June 17th Sir B. Frere says:

Owing to some misunderstanding between the various civil and military authorities, these messengers also were detained for several weeks, and have only lately been sent back. I do not for a moment suppose that either the civil or military authorities were aware of this, or could have prevented it by bringing their detention to notice at an earlier period, but it shows the difficulties of intercourse on such subjects with the Zulus, where such things could occur without the slightest ground for suspicion of bad faith on the part of either the civil or military authorities."[12]

It is not easy to discover what unusual and mysterious difficulties the civil and military authorities can have found in communicating with the Zulu messengers (men who had been employed for many years in carrying the *words* of Government and the Zulu king to each other), and it is still more inexplicable to whose notice the said authorities could have brought their detention. The whole matter is about as comprehensible as the statement which appeared at the time in the Natal pa-

---

11. *ibid.* pp. 44, 45.
12. Nevertheless, during the end of March and beginning of April communications took place between the Lieut.-Governor and the General commanding, on this subject (C. 2318, p. 45); therefore both the military and civil authorities were aware of it.

277

pers, that when these same messengers—a small party—approached our camp, bearing a white flag, *"we fired upon it* (i.e. the flag) *to test its sincerity."*

The detention of these messengers as prisoners at Kranz Kop came to the knowledge of the Bishop of Natal about the middle of April, and he at once brought the fact to the notice of the civil and military authorities. On the 20th April he saw Lord Chelmsford in Pietermaritzburg, and spoke to him on the subject. The General informed him that he had already ordered them to go back to Cetshwayo, and to say that he must send *indunas* to meet him (Lord Chelmsford) at General Wood's camp, to which he was then bound. Nevertheless the General's message, which would take but two days on the road, had not reached Kranz Kop on the 29th, nor were the men actually released until the 9th of May. When finally set at liberty they carried with them a message calculated to discourage any further attempts on the Zulu king's part at bringing about a peaceful issue to the war, being merely that if "Cetywayo sends any more messengers he must send them to the Upper Column (Dundee)."

Nevertheless on the 12th of June the same two old men appeared again, brought down, bearing a white flag, to 'Maritzburg by policemen from Mr. Fynn, resident magistrate at the Umsinga. Apparently they had been afraid to cross at Kranz Kop, where the *sincerity* of their white flag had been *tested* before, and were sent, not to the military authorities, but to the civil magistrate, who sent them down to Sir Henry Bulwer. He would have nothing to say to them, and transferred them to General Clifford, who examined them on the 13th, and sent them off on the following day to Lord Chelmsford. They had already walked one hundred and fifty miles from Ulundi to 'Maritzburg with their message of peace, and had then still further to go in order to reach the General, before they could get any kind of answer. Meanwhile the campaign was prosecuted without a pause.

General Clifford's account of this is as follows:

> I began by informing them that I was only going to ask them such questions as would enable me to judge whether I should be justified in sending them on to my Chief, Lord

Chelmsford, now in Zululand carrying on the war. The head man, Umfundi, then made the following statement:

We are Umfundi and Umkismana, Zulu messengers from Cetywayo. I am sent here by Cetywayo to ask for time to arrange a meeting of Chiefs with a view to arranging peace. We did not go to the head white Chief, because Fynn at Rorke's Drift, whom I knew, told me the Great White Chief was in Zululand, and we had better see Shepstone and the second White Chief, who were at Pietermaritzburg, so we came on here advised by Fynn. I have been here about twice a year for the last six years as King's messenger, but not as Chief. I am nothing but a messenger, and I have no authority from the King to treat for peace, or to do anything besides delivering my message, asking if time will be given to assemble a meeting of Chiefs. I know Mr. Shepstone, Mr. Gallway, and Bishop Colenso, and I have seen Bishop Colenso in this town, and also at his place in the country, but I do not wish to see him now, and I have not asked to see him.[13] I want to see the Great Chief, as the King ordered me to do. I only came here to deliver my message and because Fynn told me. This is the seventeenth day since I left the King's *kraal*. I am an old man and cannot go so fast as I could when I was young, and heavy rain detained me three days. The King told me to hurry on and return quickly. It will take us seven days to get from here to Ibabamango Mountain if we go by Rorke's Drift. We only know of two other messengers sent by the King; one is Sintwango, the name of the other we do not know. They have been sent to the lower column be-cause Cetywayo thinks there are two Chiefs of equal power, one with the upper column and the other with the lower column. They are sent like us to ask for time to get out by the door. The King does not know the name of your big Chief, and we do not either. We are the same messengers the King sent to Fort Bucking-

---

13. This, according to their custom, merely implied that they had no message for him.

ham with the same message we have now. Only then our orders were not to go to your Chief as now, but to go to Fort Buckingham and wait for the answer there. We delivered our message to the military Chief there, and he sent the message on. The Chief was at Etshowe fighting, and the answer did not come for two months; when it came it was that the great Chief was surprised we were still there. He thought we had gone back to the King long ago. The officer at Fort Buckingham advised us to go to the great white Chief, but we said: "No, those are not the King's orders; our orders are to come here, and now we will return and tell the King;" and it was half of the third month when we got back to him. We told him what had taken place. He consulted his great Chiefs, and then sent us with the orders we now have to go and see the great white Chief, and that is now what we are trying to do. I have no power given me but to ask for time. The King sends his messengers first, because it is the custom of the country to do so, and not to send a great Chief till arrangements have been made where the Chiefs are to assemble to talk about peace. We have no power to talk about terms of peace. None but messengers have yet been sent. The messengers sent to the lower column went before the fighting began; they were detained and did not return to the King's *kraal* till we did.

I said I was satisfied they ought to be sent on at once to Lord Chelmsford. I would give a letter, written by me to Lord Chelmsford, to Umfunzi, to be given by him with his own hand to Lord Chelmsford, and outside the letter I would say that no one but Lord Chelmsford was to open it. This appeared to please them much. I said I would write to the commanding officers along the road they were going to look after them, and to the officer at Rorke's Drift to see them safe to Ibabamango. 'Would a white man be safe going with them?' 'Yes,' they said, 'quite,' and they wished one could be sent with them; but still more, the King would be pleased if a white man was sent to him. I said I would not send a white man alone into Zululand with them, because my Chief did not approve, still less could I send one to the King, because I was only under the big Chief. Anything they wished to say about peace or anything else they must say to the big Chief when they saw him.[14]

At no time during the war, indeed, did we encourage the Zulu king in his persistent efforts to get peace; but more of this hereafter. Here we will only add one further instance, namely, that of two messengers sent to Colonel Pearson at Etshowe, who, although brought blindfold into the camp, were kept as prisoners in irons until the garrison was relieved. The pretext for this detention was that they were *supposed* to be spies; but officers present were satisfied that there were no grounds for the supposition, or for the treatment which they received.

Sir Bartle Frere of course inclines to the opinion that *all* Cetshwayo's messengers were spies, his entreaties for peace but treacherous pretexts to cover his evil intentions. Some of the men sent were old accredited messengers to the Government, whose names are frequently mentioned in earlier *Blue-Books*, yet Sir Bartle Frere says of them: "In no case could they give any satisfactory proof that they really came from the king."[15]

But the High Commissioner's habit of finding evil motives for every act of the Zulu king, made the case of the latter hopeless from the first.

Meanwhile the despatches received from Sir Michael Hicks-Beach contained comments amounting to censure upon the High Commissioner's proceedings in forcing on a war with the Zulus. He is plainly told that he should have waited to consult Her Majesty's Government upon the terms that Cetshwayo should be called upon to accept, and that (says the Secretary of State)—

.... they have been unable to find in the documents you have placed before them that evidence of urgent necessity for immediate action which alone could justify you in taking,

---

14. P. P. (C. 2374)) p. 111.

15. John Dunn is understood to have come back from his interview with the last peace messengers, and to have reported that the message was *bona fide*, and that Cetshwayo "means to have peace if possible."

without their full knowledge and sanction, a course almost certain to result in a war, which, as I had previously impressed upon you, every effort should have been used to avoid.

The communication which had passed between us as to the objects for which the reinforcements were requested and sent, and as to the nature of the questions in dispute with the Zulu king, were such as to render it especially needful that Her Majesty's Government should understand and approve any important step, not already suggested to them, before you were committed to it; and if that step was likely to increase the probability of war, an opportunity should certainly have been afforded to them of considering as well the time as the manner of coming to issue should it be necessary to come to issue with the Zulu king. And though the further correspondence necessary for this purpose might have involved the loss of a favourable season for the operations of the British troops, and might have afforded to Cetywayo the means of further arming and provisioning his forces, the circumstances rendered it imperative that, even at the risk of this disadvantage, full explanations should be exchanged.

The despatch from which the above is quoted was written on the 19th March, and another, dated the following day, expresses the writer's "general approval of the principles on which the boundary award was based," as intimated in a previous despatch, but gives a very qualified assent to Sir B. Frere's emendations by which he seeks to secure the "private rights" of settlers on the wrongfully appropriated land, and remarks that he is disposed to think that the recognition of these said private rights of European settlers in the district declared to be Zulu territory should have been restricted as far as possible to those cases in which *bona fide* purchasers had improved their farms by building, planting, or otherwise, which restriction would have limited them to a very small number indeed. Sir M. Hicks-Beach also reminds Sir B. Frere that Her Majesty's Government had distinctly said beforehand that "they could not undertake the obligation of protecting" the missionaries in Zululand. His comments upon the terms of the ultimatum, he says, are intended for Sir B. Frere's guidance when the time for once more proposing terms should arrive, and he concludes:

It is my wish that, as far as possible, you should avoid taking any decided step, or committing yourself to any positive conclusion respecting any of them until you have received instructions from Her Majesty's Government.[16]

Again, upon April 10th, after receiving Sir Bartle Frere's explanations, Sir M. Hicks-Beach writes as follows:

Since I addressed to you my despatches of the 19th and 20th March, I have received your two despatches of February 12th and March 1st, further explaining the considerations which induced you to decide that the demands made upon Ketshwayo must be communicated to him without delay. The definite expression of the views and policy of Her Majesty's Government contained in my despatches already referred to, which will have reached you before you receive this, makes it unnecessary that I should enter into any examination of the arguments or opinions expressed in your present despatches. It is sufficient to say that Her Majesty's Government do not find in the reasons now put forward by you any grounds to modify the tenor of the instructions already addressed to you on the subject of affairs in South Africa, and it is their desire that you should regulate your future action according to these instructions.

But there is one point alluded to in your despatch of March 1st which I feel it necessary at once to notice, in order to prevent any misunderstanding. You refer, in the thirty-second paragraph of that despatch, to 'much that will remain to be done on the northern Swazi border and in Sekukuni's country' and to the probability that 'the Transvaal, the Diamond Fields, Basutoland, and other parts now threatened with disturbance, will not settle down without at least an exhibition of force.' I entertain much hope that in each of these cases, including that of Sekukuni, the troubles now existing or anticipated may disappear, either independently of or as a consequence of that complete settlement of the Zulu

---

16 P. P. (C. 2260) pp. 108-111.

difficulty which I join with you in trusting to see speedily effected. But, if this expectation should unfortunately not be fulfilled, you will be careful to bear in mind that Her Majesty's Government are not prepared to sanction any further extension, without their specific authority, of our responsibilities in South Africa; that their desire is that the military operations now proceeding should be directed to the termination, at the earliest moment consistent with the safety of our colonies and the honour of our arms, of the Zulu question; and that any wider or larger action of the kind apparently suggested in your despatch, should be submitted to them for consideration and approval, before any steps are taken to carry it into effect.[17]

17. P. P. (C. 2316) p. 36.

CHAPTER 17

Etshowe

The first step taken towards preparing for the campaign and advance of a column on Ulundi by the coast road was the landing of a Naval Brigade from H.M.S. *Active*, in November, 1878, under the command of Commander Campbell, E.N. The "Actives" at once marched up to Lower Tugela Drift, and commenced preparations for the crossing of the river. A *pont* was established, and boats collected preparatory to the passage of the troops. Fifty men from the *Tenedos*, under Lieutenant Kingscote, R.N., joined the Naval Brigade on January 7th, 1879, but remained at Fort Pearson and took charge of the *pont*, etc., when the "Actives "moved up with No. 1 Column.

The passage of the Tugela was a difficult and rather hazardous undertaking, the river being nearly 300 yards wide, with a strong current flowing. The preparations, including taking across a wire hawser for the working of the *pont*, were conducted in a very business-like and satisfactory manner by Commander Campbell and the Naval Brigade.

The Navy had received early notice of impending hostilities, and, as early as April, 1878, Sir Bartle Frere had requested Commodore Sullivan, C.B. (the naval chief), to remain in Natal, "in order to render such assistance by sea and land as may be practicable. . . . as it appeared almost certain that serious complications must shortly arise with the Zulu tribe . . . . which will necessitate active operations."[1]

---

1. P. P. 2144, p. 32.

The coast was explored by the Commodore as far as St. Lucia Bay, and every possible assistance willingly rendered by him and the force under his command before and throughout the campaign. Valuable assistance was also given by Captain Baynton, commodore of the Union Steamship Company's fleet. The force detailed for Colonel Pearson's command styled No. 1 Column concentrated on Fort Pearson, on the Lower Tugela; its detail has been previously given.

It was directed that this column should cross the river and encamp on the Zulu bank, under the guns of the fort, there to await further orders; but, from the flooded state of the river and other causes, the passage was not effected till the 12th January, when the principal part of the force crossed and encamped in Zululand.

The 2nd (Captain Wynne's) Company Royal Engineers arrived at Fort Pearson on the 12th, and crossed on the 13th. It immediately set about the construction of Fort Tenedos on the left bank, about 600 yards from the river, to cover the crossing, protect stores, etc.

The Naval Brigade were constantly at work, day and night, working the boats and pontoon across the river, with the exception of the night of the 14th, when a heavy flood swept away the wharves. Twice the pontoon was upset, and one of the Actives men was drowned.

Reconnaissances were made in the Zulu country, and a few prisoners taken, but there were no signs of any large body of the enemy. One of John Dunn's men reported on the 17th that "the whole of his neighbourhood" was "now deserted and the cattle driven into the interior."

Everything being carefully prepared, the advance was made on the 18th, a strong advanced guard and the Natal Native Pioneers[2] preceding the column. Every precaution was taken to

---

2. This company of Native Pioneers (one of those organised by Colonel Durnford, R.E., before the war) was raised from the employees of the Colonial Engineer Department, and commanded by Captain Beddoes of the same department; this officer being highly commended by his chief. The company worked under the supervision of Lieutenant Main, R.E., and rendered excellent service. Colonel Pearson remarked: "The men worked cheerfully. They had eyes like hawks, and they did their scouting to perfection."

prevent a surprise, extra vigilance being necessary on account of the long wagon-train carrying tents, rations for fifteen days, and a large quantity of food and ammunition destined for an advanced depot to be formed at or near Etshowe.

We may here say a few words on the extreme difficulties of South African transport difficulties so serious and full of danger that they should have been eliminated from the plan of the campaign.

The wagons used were, as a rule, the ordinary South African ox-wagons, clumsy and heavy to move, each drawn by a team of fourteen to eighteen oxen. The Zulu oxen are superior to the up-country oxen, as they stand more work, and will swim rivers; they even swam the Tugela, whilst the remainder had to be ferried over.

The pace of the ox-wagon is about a mile and a half an hour, and drifts and hills cause frequent delays. Take for instance the train of No. 1 Column: it accomplished the march to Etshowe, a distance of thirty-seven miles, in between five and six days from daylight on the 18th to 10 a.m. 23rd having only been detained by the enemy at Inyezane for about two hours: the train was necessarily some six miles in length, an element of the utmost danger had the swift-footed Zulus been a little more enterprising. Two or three thousand Zulus might easily have prevented Colonel Pearson reaching Etshowe with his train, in spite of all the precautions he might and did take. The commanding officers of the various columns had no option in the matter of wagon-train, and as far as they were concerned the transport under their control worked well.

The difficulty of moving with a long train of wagons during the summer, or rainy season, can scarcely be exaggerated. Double spanning over drifts and soft places, making bad places good with brushwood, oxen getting tired owing to the length of time they were yoked, rather than from the distance travelled, all gave endless trouble and anxiety, and entirely upset all calculations as to distances to be traversed. The transport duties of No. 1 Column were admirably carried out by Captain Pelly Clarke and Assistant-Commissary Kevill Davis.[3]

---

3. One of the hardest workers in this department was Commissary J. W. Elmes, who distinguished himself by his untiring zeal and energy.

The force advanced from the Tugela in two columns the first crossed the Inyoni and encamped weather very wet and trying. The second column started on the following day (19th) and joined its leader at Umsundusi. At this camp the troops remained during the 20th. The reconnoitring parties had reported the Amatikulu impassable, and Colonel Pearson pushed forward engineers (native pioneers), with a strong working-party and guard, to render the drift practicable, which, after a day's hard work, was done. On the 21st the column again advanced, and, crossing the Amatikulu, encamped in the evening at Kwasamabela, four miles from Inyezane; during the day a reconnoitring party burnt a military *kraal* near Ngingindhlovu. Up to this time only a few of the enemy's scouts had been seen, and nothing had occurred beyond an occasional nocturnal alarm.

On the 22nd the column marched at 5 a.m., crossed the Inyezane River, and halted for breakfast, and to outspan the oxen for a couple of hours, in a fairly open spot, though the country round was a good deal covered with bush. The halt here was unavoidable, as there was no water for some distance beyond, but the country had been previously carefully scouted by the mounted troops under Major Barrow.

At eight o'clock piquets were being placed, and the wagons parked, when a company of the Native Contingent who were scouting in front, under the direction of Captain Hart, staff officer attached to the regiment discovered the enemy advancing rapidly over the ridges, and making for the adjacent clumps of bush. The Zulus now opened a heavy fire upon this company, and almost immediately inflicted a loss upon it of 1 officer, 4 non-commissioned officers, and 3 men killed.

The Naval Brigade (with rockets), under Captain Campbell, the guns of the Royal Artillery, two companies of "The Buffs," and the Native Pioneers were at once posted on a knoll close by the road, from whence 3 whole of the Zulu advance was commanded. From knoll the bush near was well searched with shell rockets, and musketry.

The wagons continuing to close up and park, two companies of "The Buffs," who moved up with them, were ordered to clear the enemy out of the bush, guided by Macgregor, Deputy-Assistant-Quartermaster-General. This they did in excellent style, driving the Zulus into the open, which again exposed them to a heavy fire from the knoll.

The engineers and mounted troops were now enabled to move up from the drift, and, supported by a half company of "Buffs" and a half company of the 99th, sent on by Lieut.-Colonel Welman (99th) from the rear of the column, cleared the Zulus out of the bush on the right flank, where they were seriously threatening the convoy. The Gatling gun also moved up from the rear, and came into action on the knoll. The enemy now endeavoured to outflank the left, and got possession of a *kraal* about 400 yards from the knoll, which assisted their turning movement. This *kraal* was carried by Captain Campbell with his Naval Brigade, supported by a party of officers and non-commissioned officers of the Natave Contingent under Captain Hart, who were posted on high ground on the left of the road. Lieut.-Colonel Parnell with a company of "Buffs," and Captain Campbell with the Naval Brigade, now attacked some heights beyond the *kraal*, upon which a considerable body of the enemy was still posted. This action was completely successful, and the Zulus fled in all directions. About half-past nine the last shot was fired, and the column was re-formed, and resumed its march at noon.

The loss sustained in this action was 2 privates ("The Buffs") killed, 2 officers, 4 non-commissioned officers, and 4 natives killed, and 1 officer and 15 men wounded. Colonels Pearson and Parnell had their horses shot under them.

The enemy's force was estimated at 4000 the Umxapu, Udhlambedhlu, and Ingulubi Regiments, and some 650 men of the district—and their loss upwards of 300 killed. The wounded appear to have been either carried away or hidden.

Four miles beyond the scene of this engagement the column bivouacked for the night; and, moving off at 5 a.m. next day, reached Etshowe at 10 a.m.; the rear guard not getting in till the afternoon.

Etshowe was a mission station, abandoned some months before, but now selected for an entrenched post, in preference to

more open and commanding ground to the north, in consequence of the necessity of utilising the buildings for the storage
of supplies. The station consisted of a dwelling-house, school,
and workshop, with storerooms—three buildings of sun-dried
brick, thatched; there was also a small church, made of the same
materials, but with a corrugated iron roof; and a stream of good
water ran close by the station. Here the column encamped, and
preparations for clearing the ground and establishing a fortified
post for a garrison of 400 men were made.

Two companies of "Buffs," two companies Native Contingent, and some mounted men, were sent back to reinforce
Lieut.-Colonel Ely, 99th Regiment, who, with three companies
of his regiment, was on the march to Etshowe with a convoy of
sixty wagons.

On the 25th, Major Coates was sent down to the Tugela with
a strong escort and forty-eight empty wagons, for a further supply of stores; and next day a "runner" arrived with news that a
disaster had occurred on the 22nd. On the 28th a telegram was
received from Lord Chelmsford, hinting at disaster—that he had
been compelled to retire to the frontier—that former instructions were cancelled, and Colonel Pearson was to hold Etshowe
or withdraw to the Tugela, also that he must be prepared to bear
the brunt of an attack from the whole Zulu army.

Colonel Pearson at once assembled his staff and commanding
officers, when it was finally decided to hold the post, sending
back to the Tugela the mounted troops and Native Contingent.
These marched, unencumbered with baggage, and reached the
Tugela in ten hours—a contrast with the upward march! The
various buildings were loopholed, and the church prepared for
use as a hospital, all tents struck, and the entrenchments supplemented by an inner line of wagons. In the evening Colonel Ely's
convoy arrived safely.

The mounted men were sent back from Etshowe, because a
large proportion of the horse forage consisted of *mealies*, which
it was thought might be required for the use of the garrison, as
eventually was the case.

To replace the mounted men, a small vedette corps was formed under Lieutenant Rowden, 99th Regiment, and Captain Sherrington, of the Native Contingent, and did excellent service.

These vedettes were constantly under fire. One was killed at his post. Another was attacked by some dozen Zulus, who crept upon him through the long grass; he lost two fingers of his right hand, had a bullet through each leg and one in his right arm; his horse was *assegaied*; yet he managed to get back to the fort, retaining his rifle.

The vedettes being much annoyed in the early morning by the fire of some Zulus from a high hill, Captain Sherrington and six of the men went out one night and lay in wait for them, behind some rocks near the top of the hill, wounding three and putting an end to the annoyance.

Colonel Pearson felt it to be necessary to reduce the bread and grocery rations of the troops, but was enabled to increase the meat ration by a quarter of a pound, as a large number of cattle had been brought up with Colonel Ely's convoy. The wagons of the troops sent back to the Tugela were officially searched, and a quantity of food, medicines, and medical comforts thus added to the stock, the two latter subsequently proving of the utmost value. All articles of luxury were eventually sold by auction, and fetched almost fabulous prices: matches were sold for 4s. a box, bottles of pickles 15s. each, and tobacco 30s. a pound!

The water supply was excellent, both in quality and quantity; and in the lower part of the stream bathing places for both officers and men were constructed; and all sanitary arrangements most carefully attended to.

A wagon-*laager* was formed for the cattle, and every effort made to provide for the security of the fort, as we may now call it deepening ditches, strengthening parapets, erecting stockades all most energetically carried on under the direction of Captain Wynne, R.E.

So things went on, till, on February 9th, Zulus were observed to be collecting; but nothing occurred beyond an occasional alarm.

On the 11th two "runners" arrived from the Lower Tugela with a despatch[4] from the General, almost requiring Colonel Pearson

---

4. P. P. (C. 2260) p. 104.

to retire with half his force to the Tugela, leaving the remainder to garrison the fort. This, after a council of war, was decided not to be practicable, the country being occupied by the Zulus in force. A flying column, however, was organised, in case it became necessary to carry out what the General seemed to desire.

Having questioned the messengers, and ascertained that they were willing to return on the following Saturday, Colonel Pearson sent a despatch, asking for further instructions, and saying he would be prepared to start on Sunday night at twelve o'clock if necessary.

This message was twice repeated on different days, but no reply received.

Alterations and improvements in the defences, to enable the fort to be held by a smaller garrison, went steadily on in spite of bad weather; ranges from 600 to 700 yards were marked round the fort, and *trous-de-loups* and wire entanglements formed on the north, south, and east faces.

On March 1st an expedition was led out by Colonel Pearson to attack a military *kraal* (Dabulamanzi's) six miles distant; this was done and the *kraal* burnt, a smart skirmish being kept up with the Zulus during the homeward march.

On the 2nd it was noticed that heliograph signals were being flashed from the Lower Tugela, but no message was made out.

Next day further signalling, though vague, was taken to mean that a convoy was to be expected on the 13th instant with 1000 men, and that on its approach Colonel Pearson was to sally out and meet it. A heliograph was improvised by Captain Macgregor, Deputy Assistant-Quartermaster-General, by means of a small looking-glass, and efforts made to flash back signals, but bad weather ensued, preventing further communication till the 10th.

A new road to Inyezane, shortening the distance by about three miles, and avoiding much of the bush, was commenced, and reported fit for use on the 13th, though the work had been hindered by very bad weather, and by the working-parties being constantly under fire. Fortunately no one was hit, except Lieutenant Lewis, of "The Buffs."

On March 23rd two Zulus came up with a white flag, and

were brought in to the fort each with a *mealie*-bag over his head; they are said to have come with a message from the king to the effect that if our force would return to Natal he would order the officers commanding his large armies not to touch it. These men were detained as prisoners in irons, and interviewed by Lord Chelmsford on his arrival at Etshowe; but of their subsequent disposal nothing appears known.

At first the health of the troops was extremely good, but before the end of February the percentage of sick had largely increased, there being 9 officers and upwards of 100 men on the sick-list when it was relieved. The principal disorders were diarrhoea, dysentery, and fevers, aggravated by the want of proper medicines and medical comforts, which had been soon exhausted. The church was used as the hospital, and both officers and men lived under the wagons, over which the wagon-sails were spread, propped up with tent-poles; thus the troops actually lived at their alarm-posts.

The relief took place none too soon, there being then but six days' further supply of reduced rations available for the garrison.

> From first to last, the men showed an excellent spirit, the highest discipline was maintained, and the reduction of the food was never grumbled at or regarded in any other light than a necessity and a privation to be borne, and which they were determined to bear cheerfully.[5]

5. P. P. (C. 2367) p. 39.

CHAPTER 18

Relief of Etshowe

Lord Chelmsford, having moved down to Durban, reports (February 8th) that No. 1 Column is secure at Etshowe; that he is about to forward troops to the Lower Tugela; and that Durban, Stanger, Pietermaritzburg, and Greytown are prepared for defence, "with garrisons which should prevent panic among those living around;" the frontier quiet, and the road from Greytown quite open.

The first reinforcement for Natal was brought by H.M.S. *Shah*, which chanced to be at St. Helena (on her voyage home from the Pacific), when the news of the disaster in Zululand arrived. Captain Bradshaw, R.N., immediately decided to proceed to Natal with his ship; the Governor, after consultation with the officer commanding the troops, Colonel Philips, R.E., arranging to send in her all the available force that could be spared from the island. Accordingly she sailed on February 12th, with 3 officers and 52 men of the Royal Artillery, and 2 officers and 109 men of the 88th Regiment.

H.M.S. *Boadicea* also arrived on the station, bringing Commodore Richards, who relieved Rear-Admiral Sullivan, C.B.

Communications had been established with Etshowe by means of flashing signals, which were conducted by Lieutenant Haynes, R.E., who, after some failure and, discouragement at first, persevered until complete success was attained.

Previous to this there had been no communications with Colonel Pearson for a considerable time, but on March 11th a cipher message from him (dated 9th) said that the flashing signals had been understood, and that as officers and men were generally sickly, it would be desirable to relieve the whole of the garrison, and that any relieving force should bring a convoy and be prepared to fight.[1]

On March 16th the signals from Etshowe were first made out, and one of the messages received was:

> Short rations until 3rd April. Breadstuff's until 4th April. Plenty of trek oxen. Captain Williams, "The Buffs," died at Ekowe on 13th March.[2]

Reinforcements arriving from England, Lord Chelmsford determined to effect the relief of Etshowe, and assembled a strong force on the Lower Tugela for that purpose. The column to be in two divisions: the first, under the command of Lieut.-Colonel Law, R.A., composed of the Naval Brigade of *Shah* and *Tenedos*, 57th Regiment, 2 companies "Buffs," 5 companies 99th Regiment, mounted infantry, volunteers, and natives, and 5th Battalion Natal Native Contingent; artillery—2 9-pounders, 2 24-pounder rocket-tubes, and 1 Gatling gun; also 150 of John Dunn's people as scouts. The second division Lieut.-Colonel Pemberton, 60th Rifles, commanding Naval Brigade of H.M.S. *Boadicea*, Royal Marines of *Shah* and *Boadicea*, 60th Rifles, 91st Highlanders, and 4th Battalion Natal Native Contingent; artillery—2 24-pounder rocket-tubes and 1 Gatling gun; making a total fighting strength of 3390 white troops and 2280 natives. The Lieut.-General decided to take command of the column himself, and directed that it should advance by the coast road, so as to avoid the bush country; to advance without tents, and with only a blanket and waterproof-sheet for each man. The convoy, taking one month's provisions for the garrison and ten days' supplies for the column, consisted of about 100 wagons and 44 carts.[3]

The assembling of this column and preparation for an advance occupied some weeks, and on the 23rd March Lord

---

1. P. P. (C. 2316) p. 81.
2. *ibid.* p. 83.
3. P. P. (C. 231 8) pp. 74,75.

Chelmsford assumed the personal command, the force being assembled on the left bank of the Tugela and organised in two brigades, as already detailed, by the 28th. Next day, at 6 a.m., the column marched from the Tugela and encamped at Inyone, reaching next day the Amatakulu River. Now, profiting by bitter experience, every precaution was taken, and an entrenched wagon-*laager* formed before nightfall at each halting-place.

The crossing of the Amatakulu River took nine hours, and the column encamped a mile and a half beyond it. Nothing had been seen of the enemy until the 31st, when the scouts noticed small bodies of Zulus near the Amatakulu bush. Captain Barrow, with a mounted force, reconnoitred towards the Engoya Forest, and burnt the *kraal* of one of the king's brothers.

On April 1st, the column marched to Ngingindhlovu, and about a mile from the Inyezane River a *laager* was formed in a favourable position. From this point to Etshowe, the track, after crossing swampy ground, winds through a bushy and difficult country for about fifteen miles, the country covered with high grass, and thus affording easy cover.

Etshowe could be plainly seen from the *laager*, and flash signalling was at once established.

As this *laager* was destined to be the scene of an important engagement, we will describe the disposition of the troops: Front face (north), 60th Rifles; right flank, 57th Regiment; left flank, 99th Regiment and "Buffs;" rear face, 91st Regiment; the angles manned by blue-jackets and marines, and armed with the guns, Gatlings, and rocket-tubes. The night passed without alarm, and the troops stood to arms at 4 a.m., the mounted men being sent out scouting as usual at earliest dawn. From scouts and piquets came reports, at 5.45 a.m., that the enemy was advancing, and at six the attack commenced on the north front. The Zulus advanced with great rapidity and courage, taking advantage of every bit of cover; they even pushed forward to within twenty or thirty yards of the entrenchments, but were checked by the steady fire of the 60th and the Gatling gun. Lieut.-Colonel Northey, 3-60th Rifles, received a dangerous wound, but cheered on his men to the end of the engagement.

The attack, checked here, rolled round to the left face; and, whilst this was being developed, a fresh force came up against the rear, probably anticipating that all the faces of the *laager* could not be defended at the same time. Here they obstinately held their ground, finding cover in the long grass and undulations.

The mounted troops were now sent out, the mounted infantry and volunteers to clear the front face, and Captain Barrow to attack the enemy's right flank. On their appearance the Zulus commenced to retreat. It was now 7.30 a.m.; and the Natal Native Contingent, clearing the ditch of the rear face, dashed out in pursuit, which, led by Captain Barrow's horsemen, was carried on for several miles.

The loss of the enemy in this engagement is estimated at 1000: 671 bodies were actually counted. The attacking force is said to have numbered about 11,000 men.

Colonel Pearson, who had watched the fight through a glass, telegraphed his congratulations to the General.

The loss of the column was 2 officers and 9 men killed (including Lieut.-Colonel Northey, 60th Rifles), 5 officers and 57 men wounded.

On the 3rd April, leaving a garrison in the *laager*, Lord Chelmsford pushed on to Etshowe with a convoy of fifty-eight carts with stores. The advance was unopposed, but the difficulties of the country were such that it was nearly midnight before the rear-guard had traversed the fifteen miles and entered Etshowe.

The garrison had suffered severely from sickness during the preceding month, losing by disease 4 officers and 20 non-commissioned officers and men; and when relieved there were sick in hospital, 8 officers and 44 non-commissioned officers and men, and attending hospital, 1 officer and 78 non-commissioned officers and men—out of a total force of 53 officers, 1289 non-commissioned officers and men, and 121 natives.

The constant wet weather and close quarters in the fort, with little or no shelter, the want of medicines, and insufficient food, might well have caused even heavier loss.

The General determined to evacuate Etshowe, as he found it so difficult of approach: future operations being planned to be carried on by the coast road. On the 4th Colonel Pearson evacuated the fort he had so tenaciously held, taking with him his wagons and all his stores that were of any use; unserviceable tools and metal-work were buried, but the fort was not destroyed.

Colonel Pearson's march to the Tugela was performed without any interruption from the enemy.

On the 4th a *kraal* of Dabulamanzi's on the Entumeni Hill was destroyed by a patrol from Etshowe, and on the 5th the relieving column left, and bivouacked near the Infuchini mission station. Early next morning an unfortunate alarm occurred, causing the death of three men. A sentry fired at what he thought was a body of the enemy, and the piquet on the opposite side of the entrenchment retired into shelter, together with native scouts who were out in front. Although it was a bright moonlight night, and no mistakes should have been made, fire was opened from the entrenchment, and five of the 60th were wounded and nine natives bayoneted as they attempted to gain the shelter of the *laager*.

On reaching Ngingindhlovu a new *laager* was formed, about a mile from the old one; this was garrisoned on the 7th, the column moving on to the Tugela.

The small mounted force under Captain Barrow, 19th Hussars, rendered excellent service, both during the engagement at Ngingindhlovu, and by the manner in which the scouting duties were carried out.

A party of Mr. John Dunn's people (natives), 150 in number, were also of the greatest utility in scouting and outpost duties. Mr. Dunn himself accompanied the General; his knowledge of the country and sound advice being of much use.[4]

John Dunn was an Englishman, resident in Zululand, where he had lived for many years and adopted many Zulu customs. He amassed a considerable property, and had an extensive following. He invariably received the greatest kindness and consideration from the Zulu king, and was frequently employed by him in various communications with the English Government. When the danger of war between English and Zulus appeared

---

4. *ibid.* p. 122.

imminent, John Dunn appealed to the English for protection for himself, his property, and people, who were ready, he said, to fight on the English side. At the same time Cetshwayo sent him a message to the effect that he saw the English were going to attack him, and therefore Dunn had better leave his country, with his people and cattle, and go to a place of safety. This John Dunn did, crossing the Tugela about the 3rd of January, and settling near Fort Pearson.

At the time the General determined to move to the relief of Etshowe he—

> .... sent secret instructions to the different commanders along the border, from the Lower Tugela up to Kambula Hill, requesting them to make strong demonstrations all along the line, and, if possible, to raid into Zululand in order to make a diversion in favour of the relieving column. . . . (thinking he). . . . might possibly have to meet the full strength of the Zulu army.[5]

On the 2nd of April a small force of Native Contingent crossed the Tugela and burnt two large *kraals*, no resistance being made. On the next day a force crossed again and burnt an unoccupied *kraal*, exchanging a few shots with Zulus, of whom a considerable number were seen at a distance. On the following day the natives refused to cross, and the Border Agent, Mr. Fannin, remarks:[6]

> I think it is fortunate it was not attempted, as the Zulus had assembled a considerable body of men to resist.

The reserve native force had co-operated in these movements by being assembled and placed in position along the Tugela, but the colonial commander declined to proceed over the border, or send any of his force into Zululand, without the sanction of the Lieut.-Governor.

The Government of Natal had placed at Lord Chelmsford's disposal a number of natives (over 8000) for service in the Zulu country. Some of these were intended for fighting purposes, and formed what we have already described as the Natal Native Con-

---

5. P. P. (G 2318) p. 56.
6. P. P. (C. 2367) p. 104.

tingent. The rest were supplied for transport, pioneer, and hospital-corps services, and all were expected to cross the border.

But besides these men, native levies were called out, when the war began, for service *in the colony*—that is to say, for the defence of the border under colonial district commanders. These levies were to be used solely as a border-guard, and were not intended to cross into Zululand at all. Sir Henry Bulwer, in permitting them to be raised, had been careful to protect as far as possible the interests of both the white and the native population of Natal, and had made very proper stipulations as to the services for which he placed these levies at the disposal of the General. The latter, indeed, expressed it as his opinion that every available fighting native in the colony should be called out; but Sir Henry, with a greater comprehension of consequences, demurred to this rash proposal, and a personal interview between the two resulted in the above-mentioned arrangement.

Consequently the Lieut.-Governor was not a little surprised to learn on the 8th April that the native levies had been ordered, in conjunction with the other troops, to make raids across the border into Zululand. To this he objected, writing to the High Commissioner on April 9th in the following terms:

> I venture to suggest for your Excellency's consideration the question of the policy of raids of this kind. The burning of empty *kraals* will neither inflict much damage upon the Zulus, nor be attended with much advantage to us; whilst acts of this nature are, so it seems to me, not only calculated to invite retaliation, but to alienate from us the whole of the Zulu nation, men, women, and children, including those who are well disposed to us. We started on this war on the ground that it was a war against the king and the Zulu Government, and not against the nation. . . .[7]

A correspondence ensued between the Lieut.-Governor and the Lieut.-General, in which the two differed in a very decided manner. Lord Chelmsford complained that the action taken by the Lieut.-Governor, "in refusing to allow the orders" issued by him to the native forces to be carried out, appeared to him

7. P. P. (C. 2367) p. 103.

"fraught with such dangerous consequences" that he considered it necessary to refer the question to the Home Government.[8] He implied that this interference had (in conjunction with the state of the Tugela River) prevented a general raid being made, which might have proved an important diversion in favour of the column relieving Etshowe, and he declared, in behalf of the raiding system, that "it would be madness to refrain from inflicting as much damage as possible upon our enemy."[9]

It was a well-known fact that the fighting men of the Zulu nation were with their army, and that the only occupants of the *kraals* to be raided were the women, children, and the infirm and other non-combatants; therefore the General's following remark, "I am satisfied that the more the Zulu nation at large feels the strain brought upon them by the war, the more anxious will they be to see it brought to an end," was of a highly Christian, wise, and soldierly nature, hardly to be matched by anything attributed to the Zulu monarch himself.

Sir Henry Bulwer's replies were temperate but decided. He pointed out that the statement contained in Lord Chelmsford's despatch to the Secretary of State for War, implying that the Governor's interference had (or might have) seriously interfered with the relief of Etshowe, was erroneous; Etshowe having been relieved on the 3rd of April, five days before Sir Henry even heard of the order for the Natal natives to make raids. To the General himself he observes that his interference had been limited to approval of the action of the district commander, who declined to employ his force in a manner contrary to the express stipulations under which they were raised, and concludes:

> The views of this Government are very strongly against the employment, under the present circumstances, of the native levies or native population along the border in making raids into the Zulu country, as being, in the opinion of the Government, calculated to invite retaliation, and also as being demoralising to the natives engaged in raiding.[10]

8. P. P. (C. 2318) p. 56.
9. *ibid.* p. 56.
10. *ibid.* p. 55.

The Lieut.-Governor's views were that these native levies "were called out expressly and solely for service in the colony, and for the defence of the colony, and were placed under the colonial district commanders for that purpose only," and that no authority had been given to employ these native levies "on any service in the Zulu country."

And it seems that raids along the border had been ordered *after* the relief of Etshowe was effected.

Sir H. Bulwer writes, 16th April, that he had received, on the 7th, a copy of a military telegram written after the relief of Etshowe, showing that the General had "ordered raids to be made across the border wherever feasible," and, on the following day, a copy of a memorandum, written from Etshowe by Colonel Crealock, the Assistant Military Secretary, and addressed to the officer commanding at the Lower Tugela, and, among other things, it contained the following instruction: "Send word up to the frontier to raid across the river wherever the river permits." And the same evening he heard of the native levies having been required to cross.[12]

The question of the employment of the native levies in making raids across the border was referred by the Lieut.-Governor to the Executive Council of Natal, which, on the 23rd April, expressed itself as—

> .... strongly opposed to the employment, in making raids into the Zulu country, of the native levies, who.... have been called out for the *defence* of the colony only.[13]

But, in view of the Lieut.-General's strongly-expressed opinions, the Council felt there was no alternative but that the General—

> .... should have the power of so employing the native levies on the border. At the same time, the Council desires .... to record emphatically its objections to the course proposed, and to such employment of the levies.[13]

---

11. *ibid*. p. 54.
12. *ibid*. p. 53.
13. P. P. (C. 2367) p. 132.

This decision of the Executive Council was communicated to the General on April 25th by the Lieut. Governor, with the remark:

> Your Excellency will therefore have the power to employ the native levies across the border in the way named by you, should you think it imperatively necessary for military reasons. Your Excellency will not fail to perceive, however, that such employment of the native levies is against the decided opinion of this colony as to its inexpediency.[14]

On the 20th May raids were again made into Zululand from three different points, under Major Twentyman's command. One party crossed at the Elibomvu Drift, and burnt fifteen *kraals* and large quantities of grain; another burnt three *kraals* and captured a large herd of cattle; and the third burnt two *kraals*, and then, seeing the Zulus assembling in force, beat a hurried retreat across the Tugela.[15]

Sir Henry Bulwer, on the 24th May, writes to the High Commissioner:

> Major-General the Hon. H. H. Clifford, commanding the base of operations . . .. was wholly unaware that any such raid was being organised by Major Twentyman, who, I believe, acted under general instructions received from headquarters. . . . The views of the Government of Natal on the subject of these raids, your Excellency is already acquainted with. The material advantage to be gained by the work of destruction or of plunder of Zulu property can be at the best but trifling and insignificant, and on every other account I fear our action will prove positively injurious to us, to our interests, and to our cause. We are absolutely provoking retaliation. Already, I am informed, since the raid reported in these papers took place, some native huts on the Natal side of the Tugela have been burned by Zulus; and to what extent this work of revenge and retaliation may be carried, with what losses of property, and even of life, inflicted on our border natives, it is impossible to say. . .

14. *ibid.* p. 133.
15. P. P. (C. 2374) p. 91.

.What result we have gained to justify even the risk of such retaliation against us, and of such a sacrifice to our own native population, I know not.[16]

The fears of the Lieutenant-Governor were in some measure realised on the 25th June, when he writes:

> A raid was made by two bodies of Zulus, numbering, it is estimated, about 1000, into the Tugela Valley, below the Krans Kop in this colony. The Zulus destroyed several *kraals*, and carried off a number of cattle. I regret to say also that several of our Natal natives, including women, were killed, and some women and children carried off.
>
> There can be little doubt that this raid has been made in retaliation for the one that was made into the Zulu country opposite the Krans Kop by a force under Major Twentyman, of Her Majesty's 4th Regiment, on the 20th May, and which was reported to you in my despatch of the 31st of that month.[17]

Thus the opinions expressed in Sir H. Bulwer's despatch of 24th May were to some extent justified, with the probability of a blood-feud being set up between the two border populations, and widening the breach between ourselves and the Zulu people; and with it the increased difficulty of obtaining a satisfactory settlement for the future.

16. *ibid.* pp. 89, 90.
17. P. P. (C. 2454) p. 150.

CHAPTER 19

Isandhlwana Revisited

During the latter part of March and April reinforcements kept steadily pouring into Natal, and with them four general officers Major-General the Hon. H. H. Clifford, V.C., C.B., who was stationed at Pietermaritzburg, to command at the base of operations; Major-General Crealock, C.B., to command No. 1 Division, concentrating on the Lower Tugela; Major-General Newdigate, to command No. 2 Division, headquarters Dundee; and Major-General Marshall, to command the Cavalry Brigade attached to No. 2 Division; Brigadier-General Wood, V.C., C.B., retaining his previous command to be styled the Flying Column.

By the middle of March the available force consisted of an effective strength of non-commissioned officers and men—Imperial troops, 7520; volunteer cavalry, etc., 1367; Europeans, attached to native contingents, 495; making a total of 9382 Europeans, with 5769 natives.[1]

No operations of any consequence took place beyond concentrating troops and forwarding supplies. On the 20th April, Lord Chelmsford reported that Major-General Crealock had taken up his command and, if transport arrangements permitted, would shortly commence operations. Major-General Newdigate was on his way to his command.

The reinforcements alone considerably exceeded the strength of the force with which the war was so rashly undertaken. They consisted of the 1st Dragoon Guards, 17th Lancers; 21st, 57th,

1. P. P. (C. 2316) p. 85.

58th, 60th, 88th (one company), 91st, 94th Foot; two batteries Royal Artillery, and detachments from St. Helena and Mauritius; one company and half C troop Royal Engineers; drafts for various regiments; detachments of Army Service and Army Hospital Corps; etc. etc.—a total (including the staff embarked in February from England) of 387 officers and 8901 men.

But even after the arrival of this enormous accession of strength, further reinforcements of three battalions were demanded "for reserve and garrison purposes."[2]

At the end of April the effective force was:

First Division, Major-General Crealock	
Imperial and irregular troops	6508
Native Contingent (151 mounted)	2707
Second Division, Major-General Newdigate	
Imperial and irregular troops	6867
Natives (243 mounted)	3371
Flying Column, Brigadier-General Wood	
Imperial and irregular troops	2285
Natives (75 mounted)	807

Making a total strength of 22,545 men available for the conquest of Zululand.

On the 14th May, Lord Chelmsford reported: "The troops are in position, and are only waiting for sufficient supplies and transport to advance."[3]

The transport difficulties naturally increased with the increasing force. The colony did not eagerly press forward to the rescue, and although transport for service in the colony could be obtained, that for trans-frontier work was not procurable in any quantity on any terms.

The colonial view somewhat appeared to be, "No government has power, either legally or morally, to force any man to perform acts detrimental to his own interest." No doubt the colony felt itself more secure whilst the troops remained within its borders, and naturally was not anxious to assist in their departure; and it may have thought the war "was an Imperial con-

2. P. P. (C. 2367) p. 162.
3. P. P. (C. 2374) p. 97.

cern, brought about by an Imperial functionary;" and therefore the Empire should be left "to worry out the affair for itself;" as remarked by a colonial paper at the time.

On the other hand, it must be acknowledged that the necessities of the troops, during this campaign, taxed the resources of the colonists to the utmost. If some profited in a mercantile point of view, and were unpatriotic enough to try to make every penny they could out of the army intended for their protection, there were others who acted in a very different spirit. The sacrifice and loss of both life and property through the Zulu war has been as great, in proportion, to Natal as to the mother country; and if the former was weak—and wicked or perhaps only *thoughtless*—enough to wish for war, she has now received a lesson which will prevent her ever making so great a mistake again. While upon the one side we hear stories of transport riders and others who lost no opportunity of fleecing at every turn both Government and military in their necessity, on the other hand we have equally well-authenticated accounts of strict honesty, and even generosity, on the part of other Natalians. One story is told of a transport rider who had earned the sum of £1500, which was to be paid by instalments of £500 each: after he had received two of these the officer who paid him was removed, and his successor, unaware of previous payments, handed over to the transport rider's messenger the whole £1500. The honest fellow at once returned the £1000 overpaid.

It is also a well-known fact that many of the principal tradesmen permitted their shopmen to join the volunteer corps to which they belonged, still continuing to pay them their respective salaries during their absence.

The colony was not revelling in a shower of gold, as some at home imagine: a few individuals, doubtless, thought to "make hay while the sun shines," but to the population at large the war was certainly not advantageous. For some months fresh provisions were almost at famine prices, or even unattainable by private persons.

Many farmers were with the army, either as volunteers or with the transport train; others again had sold their wagons and oxen, and thus had no means of bringing in their produce. The market supply was consequently very small, and generally at once bought up for the garrisons.

Transport difficulties, we have said, increased with the increasing force. The 9000 Imperial troops sent as reinforcements had to be fed, and their food conveyed to where they were stationed. Three or four thousand horses and mules also had to be fed in a country from which grass was disappearing, and in which supplies of forage were small. The larger part of the troops and horses were sent up-country—some two hundred miles from the coast where winter grass fires might be expected, and nature's stores were certain soon to be exhausted; and thus arose the terrible strain in the transport resources of the country.

But much more was required than was necessary. In place of the ponderous train accompanying each column—a fruitful source of difficulty and danger on the inarch by day, if a protection when halted at night—the advance should have been made from entrenched depots in the lightest possible order. A rapid advance on the king's *kraal* in compact formation, and, wherever the enemy might stand, a decisive battle fought—the result of which, with the most ordinary care, could not be doubtful—and the war would be virtually over. There need have been no weary inactivity, with its following of disease and death, and the saving to the country would have been enormous.

Supplies were pushed forward from the Lower Tugela to the Inyezane, where a fort was constructed (Fort Chelmsford); and from the base up to Conference Hill the supplies required by Lord Chelmsford before an advance could be made being two months' with the depots.[4]

But little further was done through this period of indecision and vacillation, in which plans were made only to be changed, and orders given one day to be countermanded the next. Sickness laid its heavy hand on many a man—exposure and inaction in the first place, then want of proper care and nursing, gradually swelling the death-roll. Before the war, and throughout its

4. P. P. (C. 2374) p. 115.

course, a body of ladies of Natal were most anxious to place themselves under the orders of the medical staff as nurses for the sick and wounded; but their offers, though repeatedly pressed upon the authorities, were declined.

It was at this period that the following message was telegraphed by Lord Chelmsford to the High Commissioner:

> May 16th, 1879—General Crealock telegraphs:
>
> Messengers from king are at his advanced post. King sues for peace. John Dunn sent to see them. Message as follows:
>
>> White man has made me king, and I am their son. Do they kill the man in the afternoon whom they have made king in the morning? What have I done? I want peace; I ask for peace.
>
> King asks for a black man or white man to return with his messengers to say message delivered rightly. Undwana, one of the messengers, states that he has sent to Dabulamunzi to order him to go to the king. Message had been delivered to him by Undwana, and he ought to have reached king yesterday. All principal chiefs have been sent for to the king. He says army is dispersed. Chiefs have been urging peace on king.
>
> General C. has only informed Clifford and Lieutenant-Governor of the above. I have telegraphed back to Crealock:
>
>> Tell messengers I informed king's messenger at Etshowe that any message must be sent to me at Colonel Wood's camp. I am ready to receive any messenger under flag of truce. Tell them something more than words will be required. Supply them with flag of truce; relax no preparations or precautions.
>
> I shall be glad to receive your Excellency's early instructions. I consider the king should not be allowed to remain on the throne, and that the terms of peace should be signed at Ulundi in presence of British force. I shall not make any change in my arrangements in the meantime.[5]

---

5. P. P. (C. 2374) pp. 100, 101.

To Major-General Marshall belongs the credit of performing the long-neglected duty of revisiting the fatal battle-field of Isandhlwana, and burying as many as possible of those that fell there. With General Newdigate's permission, the Cavalry Brigade under General Marshall made a reconnaissance of the Bashi Valley and Isandhlwana, having moved down to Rorke's Drift for that purpose.

The left column of the brigade proceeded up the Bashi Valley, and moving round the Ingqutu range, joined the right column at Isandhlwana.

The reconnaissance was proposed to include burying the dead, bringing away the wagons, etc.; but an order was received prohibiting touching the 24th, who were to be interred by their own comrades.

The battlefield was a fearful sight—though softened much by the kindly hand of nature. There plainly lay revealed the widely-spread camp (or rather line of camps), the hopeless position in which it was placed; the absolute impossibility, circumstanced as it was, of any result but the sad one we have already chronicled. And there, too, were the evidences of a gallant resistance, and a stand made by men "faithful unto death."

It was well said:

> The field of Isandhlwana is beginning to give up its secrets; the mists of fiction are being dispersed by the dry light of fact. It has not been through mere idle curiosity that there has been a desire to know what passed during the final moments of that fatal struggle. There were difficulties to be explained, reputations to be cleared, allegations to be contradicted. There was the desire to know how those who were lost had died. To be sure that they died with their faces to the foe; to be satisfied that their death was not attended with any excess of cruelty or suffering. And there can be little doubt that it is the very anxiety to be assured of all this that stands responsible for the numerous fictions as we must now hold them to be which have been circulated with regard to what passed on that memorable day.[6]

---

6. *Natal Witness*, 29th May, 1879.

A short description of the spot, taken from that written by Mr. Archibald Forbes, may be of interest:

At the top of the ascent beyond the Bashi we saw, on our left front, rising above the surrounding country, the steep, isolated, and almost inaccessible hill, or rather crag, of Isandhlwana; the contour of its rugged crest strangely resembling a side view of a couchant lion. On the lower neck of the high ground on its right were clearly visible up against the sky-line the abandoned wagons of the destroyed column. Now we crossed the rocky bed of the little stream and were cantering up the slope leading to the crest on which were the wagons, and already tokens of the combat and bootless flight were apparent. The line of retreat towards Fugitives' Drift, along which, through a gap in the Zulu environment, our unfortunate comrades who thus far survived tried to escape, lay athwart a rocky slope to our right front, with a precipitous ravine at its base. In this ravine dead men lay thick. All the way up the slope could be traced the fitful line of flight. Most of the dead here were 24th men; single bodies and groups where they seemed to have gathered to make a hopeless gallant stand and die. On the edge of a gully was a gun-limber jammed, its horses hanging in their harness down the steep face of the ravine; a little farther on a broken ambulance wagon, with its team of mules dead in their harness, and around were the bodies of the poor fellows who had been dragged from the intercepted vehicle. Following the trail of bodies through long grass and scattered stores, the crest was reached. Here the dead lay thick, many in the uniform of the Natal Mounted Police. On the bare ground on the crest itself, among the wagons, the dead were less thick; but on the slope beyond, on which from the crest we looked down, the scene was the saddest and more full of weird desolation than any I had yet gazed upon. There was none of the horror of a recent battlefield; nothing of all that makes the scene of yesterday's battle so rampantly ghastly shocked the senses. A strange dead calm reigned in this solitude; grain had grown luxuriantly round the wagons, sprouting from the seed that dropped from the loads, falling on soil fertilised by the life-blood of gallant men. So long in most places had grown the grass that it mercifully shrouded the dead, whom four long months to-morrow we have left unburied. In a patch of long grass, near the right flank of the camp, lay Colonel Durnford's body, a central figure of a knot of brave men who had fought it out around their chief to the bitter end. A stalwart Zulu, covered by his shield, lay at the Colonel's feet. Around him lay fourteen Natal Carbineers and their officer, Lieutenant Scott, with a few Mounted Police[7] (twenty). Clearly they had rallied round Colonel Durnford in a last despairing attempt to cover the flank of the camp, and had stood fast from choice, when they might have essayed to fly for their horses, who were close by their side at the piquet-line. With this group were about thirty gallant fellows of the 24th. In other places the 24th men were found as if fallen in rallying square, and there were bodies scattered all along the front of the camp.

The fallen were roughly buried, except those of the men of the 24th Regiment. These were ordered to be left untouched. General Marshall had nourished a natural and seemly wish to give interment to all the dead who so long had lain at Isandhl-wana, but it appeared that the 24th desired to perform the ceremony themselves in presence of both battalions. One has much sympathy with the regiment, but General Marshall offered to convey a burial-party with tools from Rorke's Drift in wagons, and it seemed scarcely right to postpone longer than absolutely necessary what respect for our honoured dead required. Thus, the Zulus, who have carefully buried their own dead, will return to find we visited the place, not to bury our dead, but to remove a batch of wagons!

In the desolate camp were many sad relics, and the ground was strewn with them and the spoil of the plundered wag-

7. Mr. Mansel, the officer commanding this troop of Natal Mounted Police, says: "When we went out the morning before the fight we left thirty-one men behind, men whose horses had sore backs, etc. These men were in charge of only a corporal. Seven men escaped, and we buried all of the twenty-four that were killed. Twenty were killed just around Colonel Durnford. Three about two hundred yards away, and one at the Fugitives' Drift.

ons. Scarcely any arms were found, and no ammunition a few stray rusted bayonets and *assegais* only were to be seen.

Teams of horses were hitched on to the soundest of the wagons, till forty fit to travel were collected on the crest, and sent under escort to Rorke's Drift, and meantime scouting-parties had fired the *kraals* around, but found no Zulus.

I shall offer few comments on the Isandhlwana position. Had the world been searched for a position offering the easiest facilities for being surprised, none could have been well found to surpass it. The position seems to offer a premium on disaster, and asks to be attacked. In the rear *laagered* wagons would have discounted its defects; but the camp was more defenceless than an English village. Systematic scouting could alone have justified such a position, and this too clearly cannot have been carried out.[8]

On the 20th, 23rd, and 26th June the burial of the remainder of those who fell at Isandhlwana was completed by a force under the command of Lieut.-Colonel Black, 24th Regiment. He carefully noted the signs of the fight, and reported that the bodies of the slain lay thickest in the 1-24th camp, in which 130 dead lay (in two distinct spots), with their officers, Captain Wardell, Lieutenant Dyer, and a captain and a subaltern not recognisable; close to the place where the bodies of Colonel Durnford, Lieutenant Scott, and other Carbineers, and men of the Natal Mounted Police were found. This is described as being a "centre of resistance," as the bodies of men of all arms were found converging as it were to the spot. About sixty bodies, with those of Captain Younghusband and two other officers, lay in a group under the southern precipice of Isandhlwana, as if they had held the crags and fought till ammunition failed. The proofs of hand-to-hand fighting were frequent. The fugitives' track, too, told its tale:

> Here and there around a wagon, here and there around a tree, a group had formed and stood at bay; shoulder to shoulder they fired their last cartridge, and shoulder to shoulder they plied the steel; side by side their bones are lying and tell the tale.

8. *Daily News*, 20th June, 1879.

Eight hundred yards from the road the guns had come upon ground no wheels could pass, and from here the bodies were more and more apart till, about two miles from camp, the last one lies and marks the limit reached by white men on foot.

The fatal trail again began near the river's bank, where Major Smith, R.A., and others rest, a river's breadth from Natal; across the river it runs until the graves of Melville and Coghill nearly mark its end.

The Standard and Mail of September 16th says:

> It is a noticeable fact that Cetywayo declares that his men were completely disheartened by Isandula, and that as a matter of fact he was never able to get them thoroughly together again after that event. He says that a large part of the forces engaged on that occasion were actually retreating when another part made the fatal rush. . . . Of course these statements are of interest as showing what Cetywayo said, but they must be accepted with reservation, as he has throughout taken up the theory that he and his men had no intention of inflicting so much injury upon us as they did.

Bishop Schreuder, on the 3rd March, says:

> The Zulus' version of the Isanlwana story tells us some most remarkable things with respect to the battle and the effect of it on the Zulus. The Zulus, after having ransacked the camp, bolted off with the booty as fast as they could when the English army was seen returning to the camp, even at a great distance. The detachment of the Zulu army seen by Glyn's column on its way, the 23rd January, back to Rorke's Drift, was a part of the Undi corps and Utako (Udhloko) retreating from the unsuccessful attack on the Commissariat stores at Rorke's Drift. Among the horsemen was Udabulamanzi, who says that they were so tired, and glad that Glyn's column did not attack them, for if attacked they would have bolted every one. Comparatively few and inferior oxen were brought to the king, as the izinduna appropriated to themselves the best and most of the captured oxen; Udabulamanzi, for instance, took home twenty good oxen. The Zulus say that the affair at Isan'lwana commenced with a victory

and ended with a flight, for, as it is the case after a defeat, the whole army did not return to the king, but the soldiers dispersed, making the best of their way with what booty they had got to their respective homes, and to this day they have not reassembled to the king, who is very much displeased with his two generals, Umnkingwayo (Tsingwayo) and Umavumengwane (Mavumengwana), and other izinduna.[9]

Some of the Zulu and native accounts of Isandhlwana are worth noticing. One says the engagement "lasted till late in the afternoon."[10] Another speaks of the fighting when the 24th retired on the tents, and of their ammunition failing. Another (Nugwende, a brother of Cetshwayo) says that the main, or front and the left flank attack of the Zulu army were beaten and fell back with great loss until the fire of the white troops slackened. The right flank entering the camp, the main body was ordered to renew the attack, which the English were unable to prevent from want of ammunition.

The following "Statement of a Zulu Deserter regarding the Isandlwana Battle "was taken by Mr. Drummond, headquarters staff:

> The Zulu army, consisting of the Ulundi corps, about 3000 strong; the Nokenke Regiment, 2000 strong; the Ngobamakosi Regiment, including the Uve, about 5000 strong; the Umcityu, about 4000 strong; the Nodwengu, 2000 strong; the Umbonambi, 3000 strong; and the Udhloko, about 1000 strong, or a total of about 20,000 men in all, left the military *kraal* of Nodwengu on the afternoon of the 17th of January. It was first addressed by the King, who said:
>
> "I am sending you out against the whites, who have invaded Zululand and driven away our cattle. You are to go against the column at Rorke's Drift, and drive it back into Natal; and, if the state of the river will allow, follow it up through Natal, right up to the Draakensburg. You will attack by daylight, as there are enough of you to 'eat it up,' and you will march slowly, so as not to tire yourselves."

---

9. P. P. (C. 231 8) p. 37.
10. P. P. (C. 2374) p. 24.

We accordingly left Nodwengu late in the afternoon, and marched in column to the west bank of the White Umfolosi, about six miles distant, where we bivouacked for the night. Next day we marched to the Isipezi military *kraal*, about nine miles off, where we slept and on the 19th we ascended to the table-land near the Isihlungu hills, a march of about equal duration with that of the day previous. On this day the army, which had hitherto been marching in single column, divided into two, marching parallel to and within sight of each other, that on the left consisting of the Nokenke, Umcityu, and Nodwengu Regiments, under the command of Tyingwayo, the other commanded by Mavumingwana. There were a few mounted men belonging to the chief Usirayo, who were made use of as scouts. On the 20th we moved across the open country and slept by the Isipezi hill. We saw a body of mounted white men on this day to our left (a strong reconnaissance was made on the 20th, to the west of the Isipezi hill, which was probably the force here indicated). On the 21st, keeping away to the eastward, we occupied a valley running north and south under the spurs of the Ngutu hill, which concealed the Isandlana hill, distant from us about four miles, and nearly due west of our encampment. We had been well fed during our whole inarch, our scouts driving in cattle and goats, and on that evening we lit our camp-fires as usual. Our scouts also reported to us that they had seen the vedettes of the English force at sunset on some hills west-south-west of us (Lord Chelmsford with some of his staff rode up in this direction, and about this time, and saw some of the mounted enemy). Our order of encampment on the 21st of January was as follows: on the extreme right were the Nodwengu, Nokenke, and Umcityu; the centre was formed by the Ngobamakosi and Mbonambi; and the left, of the Undi Corps and the Udhloko Regiment. On the morning of the 22nd of January there was no intention whatever of making any attack, on account of a superstition regarding the state of the moon, and we were sitting resting, when firing was heard on our right (the narrator was in the Nokenke Regiment), which we at first imagined was the Ngobamakosi engaged, and we armed and ran forward in the direction of the sound. We were, however, soon told it was the white troops fighting with Matyana's people some ten miles away to our left front, and returned to our original position. Just after we had sat down again, a small herd of cattle came past our line from our right, being driven down by some of our scouts, and just when they were opposite to the Umcityu Regiment, a body of mounted men, on the hill to the west, were seen galloping, evidently trying to cut them off. When several hundred yards off, they perceived the Umcityu, and, dismounting, fired one volley at them and then retired. The Umcityu at once jumped up and charged, an example which was taken up by the Nokenke and Nodwengu on their right, and the Ngobamakosi and Mbonambi on the left, while the Undi Corps and the Udhloko formed a circle (as is customary in Zulu warfare when a force is about to be engaged) and remained where they were. With the latter were the two commanding officers, Mavumingwana and Tyingwayo, and several of the king's brothers, who with these two corps bore away to the north-west, after a short pause, and keeping on the northern side of the Isandlana, performed a turning movement on the right without any opposition from the whites, who, from the nature of the ground, could not see them. Thus the original Zulu left became their extreme right, while their right became their centre, and the centre the left. The two regiments which formed the latter, the Ngobama-kosi and Mbonambi, made a turning along the front of the camp towards the English right, but became engaged long before they could accomplish it; and the Uve Regiment, a battalion of the Ngobamakosi, was repulsed and had to retire until reinforced by the other battalion, while the Mbonambi suffered very severely from the artillery fire. Meanwhile, the centre, consisting of the Umcityu on the left centre, and the Nbkenke and Nodwengu higher up on the right, under the hill, were making a direct attack on the left of the camp. The Umcityu suffered very severely, both from artillery and mus-ketry fire; the Nokenke from musketry fire alone; while the Nodwengu lost least. When we at last carried the camp, our regiments became mixed up; a portion pursued the fugitives down to the Buffalo River, and the remainder plundered the camp; while the Undi and Udhloko Regiments made the best of their way to Rorke's Drift to plunder the post there in which they failed, and lost very heavily, after fighting all the afternoon and night. We stripped the dead of all their clothes. To my knowledge no one was made prisoner, and I saw no dead body carried away or mutilated. If the doctors carried away any dead bodies for the purpose of afterwards doctoring the army, it was done without my knowing of it; nor did I see any prisoner taken and afterwards killed. I was, however, one of the men who followed the refugees down to the Buffalo River, and only returned to the English camp late in the afternoon. (This portion of the prisoner's statement was made very reluctantly.) The portion of the army which had remained to plunder the camp did so thoroughly, carrying off the maize, breadstuff's (sic), and stores of all kinds, and drinking such spirits as were in camp. Many were drunk, and all laden with their booty; and towards sunset the whole force moved back to the encampment of the previous night, hastened by having seen another English force approaching from the south. Next morning the greater part of the men dispersed to their homes with their plunder, a few accompanying the principal officers to the king, and they have not reassembled since.[11]

Another account, taken by the interpreter of one of the column commanding officers (a version of which has appeared in the columns of *The Army and Navy Gazette*, of 11th October 1879, and is described as a "full and accurate account "), is selected as being corroborated in all main points by survivors of the British force, and by the battle-field itself. It is the story of Uguku, a Zulu belonging to the Kandampenvu (or Umcityu) Regiment, who says:

> We arrived at Ingqutu eight regiments strong (20,000 to 25,000 men) and slept in the valley of a small stream which runs into the Nondweni river to the eastward of

11. *The Times*, March 22nd, 1879.

Sandhlwana. The regiments were Kandampenvu (or Umci-tyu), Ngobamakosi, Uve, Nokenke, Umbonambi, Udhloko, Nodwengu (name of military *kraal* of the Inkulutyane Regiment), and Undi (which comprises the Tulwana, Ndhlondhlo, and Indhluyengwe). The army was under the joint command of Mavumengwana, Tsingwayo, and Sihayo. It was intended that Matshana ka Mondisa was to be in chief command, but he having been a Natal Kafir, the other three were jealous of him, and did not like him to be put over them; they therefore devised a plan of getting him out of the way on the day of the battle. They accomplished this plan by getting him to go forward with Undwandwe to the Upindo to reconnoitre, and promised to follow. As soon as he had gone they took another road, viz. north of Baba-nango, while Matshana and Undwandwe went south of it, being accompanied by six *mavigo* (companies). It was our intention to have rested for a day in the valley where we ar-rived the night before the battle, but having on the morn-ing of the battle heard firing of the English advance guard who had engaged Matshana's men, and it being reported that the Ngobamakosi were engaged, we went up from the valley to the top of Ingqutu, which was between us and the camp; we then found that the Ngobamakosi were not engaged, but were quietly encamped lower down the val-ley. We saw a body of horse coming up the hill towards us from the Sandhlwana side. We opened fire on them, and then the whole of our army rose and came up the hill. The enemy returned our fire, but retired down the hill, leaving one dead man (a black) and a horse on the field. The Uve and Ngobamakosi then became engaged on our left with the enemy's skirmishers, and soon afterwards we were all engaged with the skirmishers of the enemy. We were not checked (stopped) by them but continued our march on the camp until the artillery opened upon us. The first shell took effect in the ranks of my regiment, just above the *kraal* of Baza. The Nokenke then ran out in the shape of a horn towards the *kraal* of Nyenzani on the road between Isandhl-wana and Rorke's Drift (the continuation of the road, to the eastward of the camp). The engagement now became very hot between the Mangwane (mounted natives) and us, the Mangwane being supported by the infantry, who were some distance in their rear. We were now falling very fast. The Mangwane had put their horses in a *donga*, and were firing away at us on foot. We shouted 'Izulu!' (The heavens!)[12] and made for the *donga*, driving out the Mangwane towards the camp. The infantry then opened fire on us, and their fire was so hot, that those of us who were not in the *donga* retired back over the hill. It was then that the Nokenke and Nodwengu regiments ran out towards Nyenzani's *kraal*. We then shouted ' Izulu! ' again, and got up out of the *dongas*. The soldiers opened fire on us again, and we laid down. We then got up again, and the whole of my regiment charged the infantry, who formed into two separate parties one party standing four deep with their backs towards Sandhlwana, the other standing about fifty yards from the camp in like formation. We were checked by the fire of the soldiers standing near Sandhlwana, but charged on towards those standing in front of the camp, in spite of a very heavy fire on our right flank from those by Sandhlwana. As we got nearer we saw the soldiers were beginning to fall from the effects of our fire. On our left we were supported by the Umbonambi, half the Undi, Ngobamakosi, and Uve. Behind us were the other half of the Undi and Udhloko, who never came into action at Sandhlwana, but formed the reserve (which passed on and attacked Rorke's Drift). As we rushed on the soldiers retired on the camp, fighting all the way, and as they got into the camp we were intermingled with them. It was a disputed point as to which of the following regiments was the first in the English camp, *viz.*: Undi, Kandampenvu, Ngobamakosi, and Umbonambi; but it was eventually decided that the Umbonambi was the first, followed by Undi.

One party of soldiers came out from among the tents and formed up a little above the ammunition-wagons. They held their ground there until their ammunition failed them, when

12. Properly Uzulu the Zulu nation.

they were nearly all *assegai* ed. Those that were not killed at this place formed again in a solid square in the neck of Sandhlwana. They were completely surrounded on all sides, and stood back to back, and surrounding some men who were in the centre. Their ammunition was now done, except that they had some revolvers which they fired at us at close quarters. We were quite unable to break their square until we had killed a great many of them, by throwing our *assegais* at short distances. We eventually overcame them in this way.[13]

When all we have narrated was known in Natal, the question was asked in the public prints:

> Who, in the light of these recently discovered facts, were the real heroes of that day? Surely the two officers who commanded in that narrow pass at the rear of the camp.... Surely, too, no smaller heroism was that of the fourteen carbineers....who, mere boys as they were, gave their lives away in order to afford their comrades-in-arms a chance of retreat....Any one of these men might have had a chance for his life, had he chosen to follow the example set by so many. They remained, however, and they died, and only after four months of doubt, contradiction, and despatch writing, is it made known to the world who they were who have most deserved the coveted decoration 'For Valour.'

---

13. The above is corroborated on all main points by Mehlokazulu, son of Sihayo, who states that he was sent with three other *indunas* (mounted), on the morning of the 22nd, to see what the English were doing. On reporting to Tshingwayo, he said, "All right, we will see what they are going to do." "Presently," says Mehlokazulu, "I heard Tshingwayo give orders for the Tulwana and Ngyaza regiments to assemble. When they had done so, he gave orders for the others to assemble and advance in the direction of the English camp. We were fired on first by the mounted men, who checked our advance for some little time." He says the soldiers were at first "in loose order," but afterwards he saw them "massing together," when "they fired at a fearful rate." When the Zulus broke the infantry and closed in, they "came on to a mixed party of mounted men and infantrymen," about one hundred, who "made a desperate resistance, some firing with pistols and others using swords, and I repeatedly heard the word 'Fire!' given by someone. But we proved too many for them, and killed them all where they stood. When all was over I had a look at these men, and saw a dead officer, with his arm in a sling and a big moustache (Colonel Durnford, R.E.), surrounded by dead carbineers, soldiers, and other men whom I did not know. *R. E. Journal*, Feb. 1880.

The dead shall live, the living die! Never was this well-known line of Dryden's more strikingly illustrated than by the events of the past fortnight.

The dead shall live, the mists of doubt, over-clouding many a reputation, have been cleared up by a visit to the now sacred field of Isandhlwana.

The living die: the hopes of a large party in a European nation have been extinguished by the *assegais* of a mere handful of savages. (Alluding to the death of the Prince Imperial of France.) The two events stand side by side in startling contrast, and suggest thoughts which even the wisest might with advantage ponder. Turn, for instance, to the story of the field of Isandhlwana, as now told in plain though interrupted and awful characters by the remains found resting near the 'neck.' Could it have been guessed that, while human recollection and human intelligence failed so utterly to convey to the world a history of the events of that too memorable day, Nature herself would have taken the matter in hand, and told us such a story as no one who hears it will ever forget? Four months, all but a day, had elapsed since the defenders of the field stood facing the Zulu myriads four months of rain and sun, of the hovering of slow-sailing birds of prey, and of the predatory visits, as it might well be deemed, of unregarding enemies. Four months! and during all that time, while the world was ringing from one end to the other with the news of a terrible disaster, while reinforcements were crowding on to our shores, and special correspondents were flooding the telegraph-wires with the last new thing, all through those four months the dead slept quietly on, waiting almost consciously, as one might think, for the revelation which was to establish their fame, and, where necessary, relieve their unjustly sullied reputation. For four months was there a sleep of honour slept upon that bitter field a sleep unbroken by any of the noise of the war that rolled both to southward and to northward. The defeat of Indlobane had been suffered; the victory of Kambula had been gained; the defenders of Rorke's Drift had been rewarded, at least with a nation's praise; the imprisoned column had been released from Etshowe; all the roads in Natal had rung to the tread of men and the rolling of wagon wheels, as the force which was to "wipe out" the disaster of Isandhlwana moved up to the front. Yet still the honoured dead slept in silence. Only the grasses that waved round them in the autumn breeze murmured to them of their coming resurrection; only the stars that looked down on them, when the night wind even had ceased, and the hills loomed black and silent in the morning hours, bade them be patient and wait. There were many and varied fates entwined in that quiet group: there was the trained officer, there was the private soldier, there was the man who had come to find employment in a colonial service, there were the lads from the colony itself; all these were there, waiting till the moment should come when their heroism should be recognised, when the vague slanders of interest or of cowardice should be dispelled, and the wreath of undying fame hung round each name in the historic temple. And the moment, long waited for long promised, as it might almost seem, by the beneficent hand of Nature herself, who held firmly to some unmistakable tokens of recognition the moment at last arrived. There could be no mistake about it. Those lying here were those who had often been called by name by those who found them. If one means of recognition was absent, another took its place. If the features were past identification, there was the letter from a sister, the ornament so well known to companions, the marks of rank, the insignia of office. Ghastly tokens, it will be said, making up the foreground of a ghastly scene. Yes, ghastly tokens, but glorious tokens also—tokens enabling many a family to name those that died with a regret no longer mingled with doubt or with pain; tokens that will long be cherished, and which will be shown to children as preserving the memory of lives that are to be imitated. A black cloud has, by these revelations, been lifted from the rocks of Isandhlwana, and many whom we deemed dead are living again—living as examples, never to be defaced, of the honour which tradition has so fondly attached to a British soldier's name.[14]

---

14. *The Natal Witness* of June 7th, 1879

CHAPTER 20

The Prince Imperial

Early in April the South African community was greatly impressed and interested by the arrival of the young Prince Imperial, who came out to Natal to take his share in the fortunes of war, and to see something of active service against the Zulus. The colonists were not a little gratified by the fact of this young hope of an illustrious house having come to fight for and with them against their dreaded foes; yet amongst them all there was hardly one, great or small, gentle or simple, whose second thought was not one of sincere regret that he, who, besides being of such importance in the future of Europe, was also his widowed mother's only son and sole comfort, should be allowed to risk his life in a savage warfare. Many a thought of kindly sympathy was directed from Natal towards that royal mother for whom English men and women have always had so sincere a feeling, whether in prosperity or adversity; and many a warm-hearted woman's eyes filled with tears at the sight of the gallant youth, and at the very thought of what his loss would be to her who remained to pray for him at home, the home which she had found amongst our countrymen in England. On every side anxious hopes were expressed that the Prince would be carefully guarded from danger, and not allowed needlessly to throw away his precious young life; all these hopes and anxieties were redoubled when he arrived, and, by his winning ways and gallant bearing, won the hearts of all who came in contact with him. Had Natal been asked, he would have been sent straight home again instead of across the borders, and yet it would have been hard to resist and thwart the eager wish to be of use, to work, and to see service which characterised him throughout his short campaign, and which, combined with gentleness and humanity as it was, proved him to be a true soldier to the heart's core.

Since he had come to Natal he could not, of course, be kept away from the front, and the day he left 'Maritzburg good wishes from all classes attended him along the road. It was thought, indeed, that in all human probability he was safe, except in the event of some such battle as would make the chances equal for all, from general to drummer-boy. "At all events," it was said, "Lord Chelmsford will keep him by his side." Others, again, opined that the General would find it no easy task to restrain the eager young spirit that scorned to be treated with more care than others of his age. But this doubt was answered by one who knew the Prince, and who said that he was too good a soldier ever to disobey an order. Throw himself in the way of difficulty and danger he might wherever possible, but any distinct *order* would be promptly and fully obeyed.

For some little time the Prince acted as extra aide-de-camp to Lord Chelmsford, and accompanied him in that capacity to Colonel Wood's camp at Kambula, and back to Utrecht. Colonel Harrison, B.E., was also of the party, and during the journey very friendly relations were established between him and the Prince, which lasted to the end, and were drawn closer by the former's careful attendance during an indisposition which befell the latter.

Whilst at Kambula the General reconnoitred the Indhlobane Mountain on May 4th, and on return to camp was joined by the Prince Imperial, when, to show him the defence of a *laager*, the alarm was sounded. In three minutes every man was at his allotted post, and an inspection of the camp, with its double tier of rifles ready for work, was made by the General and staff. Next day the camp was broken up, and the column moved to about a mile from the White Umvolosi, near the Zinguin range—Lord Chelmsford and staff, with the Prince, proceeding to Utrecht.

On May 8th, the General, having appointed Colonel Harrison, R.E., Assistant-Quartermaster-General of the army, and

Lieutenant Carey, 98th Regiment, Deputy Assistant-Quarter-master-General, requested the former "to give some work to the Prince Imperial, as he was anxious for it, and did not find enough to do in the duties of an extra aide-de-camp." This request was a verbal one, and the words used may not be letter for letter, but of the purport there is no doubt; and such a request from the Commander-in-Chief was, of course, an order which was immediately carried out. The Prince was directed to collect and record information respecting the distribution of troops, location of depots, and the like, and he worked hard at this for some days. Lord Chelmsford shortly afterwards left for Newcastle, but before his departure Colonel Harrison suggested that it would be advisable, during his lordship's absence, to make a reconnaissance into Zululand, on the borders of which they had been hovering so long, so as to determine the exact line of route which the columns ought to take in the impending invasion.

Lord Chelmsford accepted the suggestion, asking Colonel Harrison to take the Prince with him on the expedition, and appointing an intelligent officer to accompany them. The reconnoitring party started with a strong escort, and reached Conference Hill on May 13th. Here they were joined by Colonel Buller and 200 horsemen, and were engaged on their reconnaissance till May 17th, bivouacking at night with horses saddled and bridled, and marching at dawn, scouring the country, and sweeping Zulu scouts before them. The Prince was delighted with the life, the simple fare of the officers—his comrades—cooked by themselves at their camp-fire, the strange country, the sight of the enemy, the exhilarating gallops over the grass up hill and down dale after fleet Zulu spies, the bivouac under the star-lit heavens. All this pleased him immensely; as he told Colonel Harrison: "Made him feel that he was really doing soldiers' work such as he had never done before." Always anxious to be of use, he made most careful and copious notes and observations on all they saw or did.

On the 17th the party returned to Conference Hill, Colonel Harrison and Colonel Buller having arranged for a combined and further reconnaissance of the country from that place and Brigadier-General Wood's camp; but as the special duty to which the Prince and the intelligence officer had been assigned was over, Colonel Harrison would not allow them to accompany him farther, but directed them to return to Utrecht. They obeyed; but, on the 18th, after Colonel Harrison had started on his expedition and was already in Zululand, he was surprised by the appearance of the Prince Imperial, who had galloped all the way from Balte Spruit by himself to overtake him, bringing with him the permission, for which he had sent a messenger to Lord Chelmsford, to go on the new reconnaissance. The party now consisted of Colonel Harrison, the Prince, Lieutenant Carey, one officer and five men Bettington's Horse, and one officer and twenty men Natal Native Horse (Basutu). The escort would have been stronger, but that the junction with Colonel Buller from Wood's camp was looked for to add to it. The first day was occupied in searching the country as before, and in looking out for Buller; and the party bivouacked at night with vedettes and sentries posted all round, as Zulus had been seen on the hills, although they did not molest the reconnoitring party.

On the following day (the 19th), whilst exploring a deep rough valley, the party was suddenly confronted by a number of Zulus, who came down the hill at one side of the *donga*, and spread out in the usual way in two wings or horns, in order to overlap or outflank it, firing as they advanced. The officer in command of the advance at once put spurs to his horse and rode straight up the hill at the weak centre of the Zulu detachment, followed by the rest of the party. They pushed right through the centre of the Zulus, and the horns at once broke away, and escaped among the rocks with some loss. Smaller bodies of Zulus were met with subsequently, but did not attempt to try conclusions with the horsemen, who were obliged to keep on the move the greater part of the night, as the enemy was all around them.

Next morning they reached Conference Hill, without meeting Colonel Buller; Colonel Harrison and the Prince proceeding to Utrecht to report to Lord Chelmsford.

Lord Chelmsford now informed Colonel Harrison that "He was to consider the Prince Imperial as attached to the Quartermaster-General's staff for duty, but it was not put in orders, in consequence of the Prince not being in the army." The Prince lived, as before, with the General's personal staff, and Colonel Harrison, therefore, only saw him when he came for work or orders, which was very frequently.

On May 25th the headquarters having been established at Landman's Drift—the Prince, having called for work as usual, was directed to prepare a plan of a divisional camp. That evening Colonel Harrison was spoken to by Lord Chelmsford, because the Prince Imperial had gone outside the lines without an escort, but replied "That the work he had given the Prince to do referred to the camp inside the outpost lines." The General then told Colonel Harrison "To take care that the Prince was not to go out without an escort when working for him, and in the matter of escort to treat him, not as a royal person, but the same as any other officer, taking all due precautions."

Colonel Harrison then said that "He would see the Prince, and tell him he was never to leave the camp without a suitable escort, and that he was to apply to him for one when it was wanted;" and Lord Chelmsford replied that "That would do."

The same day Colonel Harrison saw the Prince, and told him this, and to make the matter quite sure, he then and there gave him the instructions in writing.

He next directed him to make a map of the country, from the reconnaissance sketches of Lieutenant Carey and others. This work the Prince executed very well, and so eager was he for employment, so desirous to be always up and doing, that he went, not once or twice, but often every day to Colonel Harrison's tent asking for more.

On the 28th of May, headquarters were at *Kopje* Allein, and on that and the two following days reconnaissances were pushed far into the enemy's country, but no enemy was seen. Small parties, even single officers, rode about unmolested all over the district round, and went beyond the spot where so sad a scene was shortly afterwards enacted.

On the 31st of May the Prince went to Colonel Harrison's tent with a report which he had written, and, as usual, asked for some more work. He was told that the army was to march next day, and that he might go out and report on the roads and camps for the day following; with which instructions the Prince was greatly pleased. Next day the 2nd Division (with which were Lord Chelmsford and the headquarters' staff) were ordered to march towards Ulundi; Wood's column being in advance some miles, on the other side of the Blood River, on a road which would take it out eventually on the line of march of the headquarters' column. Lieutenant Carey, whilst conversing on duty matters with Colonel Harrison, expressed a wish to go out with the Prince, as he desired to verify a sketch he had made on the previous day; and, although Colonel Harrison had intended to ask one of the General's personal staff to accompany the Prince, he said, when Lieutenant Carey volunteered to go: "All right; you can look after the Prince!" At the same time he told Lieutenant Carey to let the Prince do the work for which he was going out, namely, a detailed report on the road and the selection of a site for the camp. Lieutenant Carey was known to Colonel Harrison as a cautious and experienced officer, who had been frequently out on patrol duties with Colonel Buller and others, who was acquainted with the nature of the work he had to do, the precautions to be taken, and the actual ground to be gone over; and there was every reason to believe that he thoroughly understood his position, and would make, as he had done before, the proper arrangements for an escort.

On the morning of the 1st, Colonel Harrison, hearing that no escort had arrived at the hour fixed for the departure of the reconnoitring party, went over to General Marshall's tent, and obtained from him the order for the number of men he thought sufficient "six Europeans and six Basutos;" and, having informed Lieutenant Carey of this, he rode off to attend to his own duties superintending the march of the army, inspecting the fords, and moving on in advance (in company with Major Grenfell) to select the site for watering-places and the next camp. On a ridge in front of the column Colonel Harrison and his companion presently found the Prince and Lieutenant Carey halted with the European troopers only, and heard from them that they were waiting for the Basutos, who had not joined them in camp; but some were now in sight on the hillside flanking the line of march, and moving in a direction which would bring them upon it a little in advance of the spot where the party was waiting.

As Lieutenant Carey had been already over the country, he was asked by Colonel Harrison to point out the place where the water supply for the next camp was, and the whole party rode slowly along a *donga* towards the supposed stream or ponds. Colonel Harrison did not think the water sufficient for their purpose, and rode back to the high ground, where he was re-joined by Major Grenfell, who told him that the Prince's party had just discovered a better supply a little farther on. There was a ridge in front of them which they considered marked the end of the day's march, and the officers dispersed to attend to their own duties, not imagining for an instant that the reconnoitring party would go on without the Basutos, who, from their wonderful power of sight and hearing, and quickness at detecting the approach of danger, were always regarded as essential to an escort.

Unhappily, however, such was the case. The party rode on until they came to a deserted *kraal*, situated some 200 yards from the river, and consisting of five huts, one with the usual small cattle enclosure. Between the *kraal* and the river stretched a luxuriant growth of *tambookie* grass, five or six feet in height, with *mealies* and Kafir corn interspersed. This dense covert, however, did not completely surround the *kraal*, for in front there was an open space, apparently used by the Zulus, judging from the ashes and broken earthenware strewn about, as a common cooking-ground.

Here the party halted, and the Prince, having first sent a native guide to make sure that the huts were all uninhabited, gave the order that the horses should be off-saddled and turned out to graze. Some of them lit a fire and made coffee, while the Prince and Lieutenant Carey, after the latter had taken a look round with his glass, proceeded to make sketches of the surrounding country. It is said that the Prince's talent with pen and pencil, combined with his remarkable proficiency in military surveying—that great gift of recognising at once the strategic capabilities of any spot which distinguished the First Napoleon—made his contributions to our knowledge of the country to be traversed of great value; and he never lost an opportunity of making himself of use in this and every other way.

It was about 3 p.m. when the party halted at this deserted *kraal*, the Prince deciding that they should leave again in an hour's time. That the Zulus had been upon the spot not long before was apparent from signs of freshly-chewed *imfi* (native sugar-cane) upon the ground, while a few dogs lingering about might have suggested that their masters were not far off. Before the hour was over, however, the native guide came in to report that he had seen a Zulu coming over the hill, and it was now thought prudent to retire, the Prince giving directions to collect and up-saddle the horses, followed by the order to "Mount."

Some of the men were already in the saddle, others in the act of mounting, when a sudden volley fired upon them from amongst the tall stalks of the *mealies* (Indian corn) which grew on every side, betrayed the presence of a numerous armed foe, who had returned unseen to those who were in temporary occupation of their *kraals*. The distance was not twenty yards, and the long grass swayed to the sudden rush of the Zulus, as with a tremendous shout, they charged towards the Prince and his companions. The horses all swerved at the suddenness of the tumult, and one broke away, its rider being shot before he could recover it and mount. The young Prince was riding a fine grey charger, a grey of sixteen hands, always difficult to mount, and on this occasion, frightened by the firing, it became restive and could not be controlled. Lieutenant Carey, apparently, had at this moment been carried by his horse in a direction which brought one of the huts between him and the Prince, of whose difficulties he was therefore unaware. From the moment of the attack no man seems to have known much of what the rest were doing; to gallop away was the only chance for life, and all hurried off, the Prince in vain endeavouring to mount his restive steed unaided. He was passed by Trooper Letocq: *"Depechez vous, s'il vous plait, Monsieur!"* he cried, as he dashed past, himself only lying across his saddle, but the Prince made no answer; he was already doing his utmost, and in another minute he was alone. He was seen endeavouring to mount his rearing charger, as it followed the retreat, while he ran beside it, the enemy close at hand. He made one desperate attempt to leap into the saddle by the help of the holster-flap; that gave way, and then he fell. The charger dashed riderless past some of the mounted men, who, looking back, saw the Prince running after them on foot, with the Zulus but a few paces behind him. Alas! not a man turned back, they galloped wildly on, and carried back to camp the news that the gallant young Prince, for or with whom each of them should have died that day, lay slain upon the hillside where he had made his last brave stand alone. Two troopers fell besides—one was struck down by a bullet as he rode away; the other was the man who had lost his horse, Trooper Rogers, and who was last seen in the act of levelling his carbine at the enemy. The native guide was killed as well, after a hard fight with the foe, witnessed to by the blood-stained and broken weapons found. by his side next day. The fugitives rode on for some distance, when they met General Wood and Colonel Buller, to whom they made their report. From the brow of an adjacent hill these officers, looking through their glasses, could see the Zulus leading away the horses they had taken the trophies of their successful attack.

That evening Colonel Harrison was in his tent, engaged in writing orders for the next day's march, when Lord Chelmsford came in to tell him "The Prince is killed!" and Lieutenant Carey soon after confirmed the dreadful, well-nigh incredible news. He said they were off-saddled at a *kraal*, when they were surrounded and fired into, and that the Prince must have been killed, for no one had seen him afterwards.

Colonel Harrison asked the General to let him take a few men to the *kraal*, and see if, by any chance, the Prince were only wounded, or were hidden near at hand, but his request was not granted, and the testimony of the survivors extinguished all hope.

Next day General Marshall, with a cavalry patrol, went out to search for the Prince, being assisted by scouts of the Flying Column. The bodies of the troopers were soon found, and shortly afterwards that of His Imperial Highness was found by Captain

Cochrane, lying in a *donga* about 200 yards from the *kraal* where the party had halted. The body was stripped with the exception of a gold chain with medallions attached, which was still round his neck. Sword, revolver, helmet, and clothes were gone; but in the grass were found the Prince's spurs and one sock.

The body had eighteen *assegai* wounds, all in front, and the marks on the ground and on the spurs indicated a desperate resistance.

The two white troopers were laid together beside a cairn of stones, which was erected to mark the exact spot where the Prince was found, and later in the day they were buried there, the chaplain on duty with the column performing the funeral service.

But for the Prince himself a true soldiers' bier was formed of lances lashed together and horse blankets, and, borne thus, the body of the noble lad was carried up the hill towards the camp which he had left the previous day so full of energy and life.

The melancholy news was telegraphed throughout the colony, causing universal grief and consternation. Every heart was wrung with sympathy for *the mother*; and even those to whose homes and hearts the war had already brought desolation, felt their own grief hushed for awhile in the presence of a bereavement which seemed to surpass all others in bitterness and depth.

What citizen of 'Maritzburg will ever forget the melancholy Sunday afternoon, cold and storm-laden, when, at the first distant sound of the sad approaching funeral music, all left their homes and lined the streets through which the violet-adorned coffin passed on its way to its temporary resting-place.

In Durban, too, the solemn scene was repeated; the whole colony being deeply moved at the sad and untimely death of the gallant Prince. H.M.S. *Boadicea*, flag-ship of Commodore Richards, had the honour of conveying the body to Simon's Bay, when it was transferred to H.M.S. *Orontes* with every possible mark of respect for conveyance to England.

A court of inquiry was at once assembled by Lord Chelmsford, and reported that Lieutenant Carey had not understood the position in which he stood towards the Prince, and, as a consequence, failed to estimate aright the responsibility which fell to his lot; also that he was much to blame for having proceeded on the duty in question with a portion only of the escort; and that the selection of the *kraal* where the halt was made, surrounded as it was by cover for the enemy, and adjacent to difficult ground, showed a lamentable want of military prudence. And, finally, the court deeply regretted that no effort was made after the attack to rally the escort and to show a front to the enemy, whereby the possibility of aiding those who had failed to make good their retreat might have been ascertained.

Lieutenant Carey was then tried by court-martial and found guilty. The home authorities decided, however, that the conviction and sentence could not be maintained, and consequently ordered this officer to be released from arrest and to return to his duty.

In justice to Lieutenant Carey it must be said that the Prince appears to have been actually in command of the party; Lieutenant Carey accompanied it, by permission, for the purpose of completing some of his own work, taking advantage of the protection of the escort to enable him to do so; he received no order about the command of the escort, or other instructions beyond the words, "You can look after the Prince," which were evidently interpreted as *advise him*, but could scarcely warrant controlling his movements.

The Prince's written instructions from Colonel Harrison were lost with him.

On dangerous duties pertaining to the Quartermaster-General's Department in an enemy's country the Prince Imperial should never have been employed; as long as he remained with the British forces he should have been retained on the personal staff of the General commanding.

CHAPTER 21

Ulundi

Before entering on the history of the advance of the main column on Ulundi, we will glance at the doings of No. 1 Division, which was to operate against Ulundi from the eastward.

During May entrenched posts had been established—Fort Crealock, on the left bank of the Amatikulu River and close to John Dunn's Road, about fourteen miles from Fort Pearson, on the Tugela; Fort Chelmsford, on the right bank of the Inyezane, also on John Dunn's Road, and eight miles from Fort Crealock; and, in June, Fort Napoleon, on the left bank of the Umlalazi River, between Fort Chelmsford and Port Durnford, where a landing-place was established—a brief account of which may be interesting. The spot is described as a straight sandy coast near the mouth of the Umlalazi River, always having a boiling surf rolling in on the beach. The landing operations were carried out by means of large decked surf-boats of about forty tons burden each.

The mode of working them was as follows: One end of a long hawser was made fast to an anchor dropped some distance outside the surf, and the other end taken on shore by a small line, hauled taut, and secured to shore moorings.

By means of this "warp" the surf-boat travels to and from the beach. Having picked up the warp by the buoy-rope, it is placed in grooves in the bow and stern of the boat, and there retained by pins. The roll of the surf takes the boat in, large rope-stoppers being used to check her should she be going too fast.

In this way some 3000 tons of stores were landed, at a very great saving of expense over land transport. The landing operations were at all times difficult, sometimes impossible; they were conducted by Commander Caffin, R.N., and to him and the Naval Brigade there stationed is due the entire credit of the excellent work done.

Forwarding supplies and bridging the Tugela was the work of the 1st Division through May and well into June; everything military, except convoy duty, appeared at a standstill. There was a great deal of sickness amongst the troops, but General Crealock did much in providing proper hospital accommodation and improving sanitary arrangements.

Fort Pearson was converted into an extensive hospital, where there were as many as 400 patients at times, and whose garrison, after the advance of the division, was composed of the convalescents. At this hospital some wily patients managed to appropriate £5000 of the public moneys; but this fortunately was all recovered, except about £33.

Telegraphic communication was established by the Royal Engineers between Fort Chelmsford and the Lower Tugela; and Colonel Walker, C.B., Scots Guards, was appointed to the command of this portion of the base, and stationed at Fort Pearson.

On the 18th June the long-expected move was made by No. 1 Division, and General Crealock, with the advanced portion of the force, left Fort Pearson and the Lower Tugela. Moving by Fort Chelmsford, he reached the Umlalazi River on the 22nd. The river was bridged by the train under Captain Blood, K.E., and a work commenced on the left bank called Fort Napoleon.

The General was engaged reconnoitring on the 23rd and following days, capturing a few cattle, one of which appeared to resent its capture, charging the General, and severely injuring his horse. On the 28th the force encamped near Port Durnford.

But little interest attaches to this division, which had great opportunities before it. An earlier advance and a little dash would have given the laurels of the second campaign to the 1st Division, which at the beginning of May consisted of upwards of 9000 men 6500 being Europeans a sufficient force to have accomplished the destruction of Ulundi with ease; but it was not to be.

Many absurd stories are told as to causes of delays, one being the want of so many rations of *pepper*, and the whole ending in the well-known telegram, "Where is Crealock?"

We may here devote a few remarks to the Naval Brigade, which rendered such good service throughout the campaign; and, had opportunity offered, would have largely added to the laurels it won.

After the relief of Etshowe, the Naval Brigade was divided between Lower Tugela and Fort Chelmsford, Commander Brackenbury in command at the latter post, Captain Campbell in chief command. The main force advanced with General Crealock 545 officers and men of *Active, Boadicea,* and *Shah,* with 3 9-pounder guns, 6 rocket-troughs, and 5 Gatling guns. At Port Durnford they remained disembarking stores till July 21st, when, after being reviewed by Sir Garnet Wolseley, the *Active's* and *Shah's* men embarked, leaving the *Boadicea's* to continue temporarily the duties of the landing station.

Captain Bradshaw of the *Shah,* and Captain Adeane of the *Tenedos,* rendered good service at Durban and Simon's Bay respectively.

The Royal Marines of the squadron served with the Naval Brigade. Lieutenant Dowding, R.M.L.I., was at first the senior officer, and advanced with Colonel Pearson's column to Etshowe, remaining there until its relief. Captain Phillips, R.M.L.I., and Captain Burrowes, R.M.A., were landed from H.M.S. *Shah,* the former senior officer, and in command of the Marines at the battle of Ngingindhlovu.

We must now return to the 2nd Division and Flying Column, which at last began to move in the right direction. Zululand had been carefully reconnoitred to the Babanango Mountain by Colonel Buller, and the advance of the 2nd Division, with the headquarters, in this direction was covered by the flying column, which was always within striking distance.

The troops now were carefully protected at night by *laagers*; the ordinary form being a rectangle in three compartments, with a shelter trench two yards outside the wagons, so that there might be a second line of fire from the top of the wagons, without risk to the defenders of the shelter trench.

The flying column bore the brunt of work in the advances, scouting the country in every direction, the most reliable "eyes and ears" of the force the Natal Native Horse, then commanded by Captain Cochrane. These men (Edendale men and Basutu) in small numbers crowned the summit of every hill right and left of the route, and miles in front they were pushed to feel the way. On the 4th June the scouts reported a considerable number of the enemy, these, after the exchange of a few shots, Colonel Buller tried to draw towards the camp, but in vain, and the patrol, not being strong enough to risk an engagement, returned to camp. There three messengers from Cetshwayo were being received by Lord Chelmsford.

They were sent back on June 6th with the following message:

> He must at once give proof of being earnest in desiring peace, proof to be—1st. Two 7-pounder guns, and the oxen now with him taken from us to be sent in with the ambassadors. 2nd. A promise from Ketchwayo that all the arms taken during war, etc., when collected shall be given up. 3rd. One regiment to come to my camp and lay down its arms as a sign of submission. Pending Cetywayo's answer, there will be no military operations on our part; when he has complied with them, I will order cessation of hostilities pending discussion of final terms of peace.[1]

On the previous day (5th June), Colonel Buller took a force of about 300 men to reconnoitre the proposed route. The Zulus seen the day before came out from their *kraals*, and formed as if for an attack. The ground in their rear was broken and covered with thorny bush, the *kraals* large, apparently belonging to a chief; and beside one of them were four wagons, evidently taken from Isandhlwana. Colonel Buller determined to burn the *kraals*, but as he approached the enemy broke and retired into the cover, opening a heavy fire. A portion of the force engaged the Zulus from the edge of the bush whilst the remainder set fire to the *kraals*, which was accomplished with the loss of two men wounded.

---

1. P. P. (C. 2374) p. 107.

Major-General Marshall came up with a portion of the Cavalry Brigade, and, with a view to ensuring the safety of Colonel Buller's retreat, advanced three troops of the 17th Lancers under Colonel Drury-Lowe to hold the enemy in check.

The enemy was found to be very strongly posted in the thorns, and the ground being impracticable for cavalry, the Lancers were ordered to retire. Their Adjutant, Lieutenant Frith, was in this fruitless skirmish shot through the heart.

During this affair an incident occurred (told by an officer present at the time), showing the individual bravery of the Zulus: A single warrior, chased by several Lancers, found himself run down and escape impossible. He turned and faced his enemies; spreading his arms abroad he presented his bare breast unflinchingly to the steel, and fell, face to the foe, as a brave soldier should.

On the 6th a post called Fort Newdigate was established, and on this evening the warmth of the double line of fire from the *laager* of the 2nd Division was unpleasantly experienced by the 5th Company Royal Engineers. This company had marched up that afternoon in advance of the Flying Column (which was going down-country for supplies), and had camped close to one of the unfinished redoubts outside the *laager*, an alarm was given in the *laager*, and a heavy fire opened therefrom. The Engineers coolly lay down flat on the ground, and waited till the excitement was over. It was due entirely to their own steadiness that the causalities were not greater; as it was, one sergeant was wounded and two horses killed,

On the 7th, the division advanced, clearing the country of Zulus and burning their *kraals*, and encamped at the Upoko River; remaining there till the arrival of Brigadier-General Wood's Column with a large convoy of supplies for which it had been sent. The time was usefully employed in reconnoitring, examining the road in advance, making drifts practicable, etc.

A line of telegraph was laid by the half Telegraph Troop (C) Royal Engineers, from Quagga's *kraal* (on the road between Newcastle and Ladysmith), where it joined the colonial line to Doornberg *via* Dundee and Landtmann's Drift, thus placing headquarters in communication with Pietermaritzburg, etc.; flag-signalling being employed to communicate with Doornberg.

On the 16th June the correspondent of *The Times* wrote:

> We are wandering towards Ulundi much as the Children of Israel wandered towards Canaan, without plans, or even definite notions for the future. It would seem not impossible to form some plan of campaign something, at any rate, more definite than the hand-to-mouth manner in which we are now proceeding. Deep science and tactical skill are not necessary to contend with savages; a simple method and plain common-sense suffice, if backed by energy, decision, and determination.

The intelligence now telegraphed that Sir Garnet Wolseley was on his way to Natal to unravel the various tangled skeins of civil and military policy, doubtless acted as the "spur in the head" which expedited Lord Chelmsford's movements.

On the 17th, Brigadier-General Wood arrived with the supplies, and next day the force advanced to the Upoko River, where the road from Rorke's Drift to Ulundi crosses it. Here there was a halt for a day, and a depot formed, called Fort Marshall. Colonel Collingwood was left in charge of the two posts, Forts Newdigate and Marshall; and the whole line of communication in the enemy's country, and such of the garrison as were left in frontier-posts for the purpose of patrolling, were placed under the command of Major-General Marshall.

Fort Marshall was about twenty-five miles from Rorke's Drift, and sixteen from Fort Newdigate; from this post to Koppie Allein (on the Blood River) the distance was twenty-one miles.

Having struck down into this road, which runs into Zululand in an easterly direction, a glance at the map will show how needless was the waste of time and money spent in concentrating stores at Conference Hill—so far removed from the line of communications with Pietermaritzburg.

The combined column reached the Umhlatusi River on the 21st, having traversed difficult and mountainous ground, where in many places the train was obliged to pass by single wagons.

The Zulus took no advantage of the many opportunities for

attack that presented themselves, and the march to Ulundi was practically unopposed. At this halting-place Fort Evelyn was built; and on the 24th the march was resumed.

Cetshwayo's messengers, 'Mfunzi and 'Nkisimane, came up from Pietermaritzburg on the 24th, and next morning were sent to the king with Lord Chelmsford's reply to his message.

A very awkward drift on the Uvulu River was passed by the column, after crossing which a day's halt was made, when a cavalry patrol was sent out to destroy some military *kraals*. Two more *indunas* came in to ask for peace, and were sent back to Ulundi in the evening. On the 27th the force arrived at Entonjaneni, where the arrangements for the final advance on Ulundi were made, tents and all unnecessary baggage left behind, and a strong post formed with the aid of wagons. Four hundred wagons, 6000 oxen, and 800 mules were left entrenched here; the remaining 200 wagons, with ten days' provisions, accompanying the advancing force. This evening two more messengers came in from the king with elephant tusks, some hundred head of oxen, and two trunks, the property of Lord Chelmsford. The messengers were sent back next day.

The Natal Colonist of June 28th says:

> Again we hear that Ketshwayo has sent to Government, asking why Lord Chelmsford continues to advance. He (the king) hopes the General will not persist in advancing, as in that case he will be forced to fight, and what he wants is peace. This, we believe, makes the eleventh message he has sent in to the same effect. The General affects to doubt his *bona fides*. How is this to be established? Can his lordship think of no better guarantee than one which the most vigorous supporters of the war cannot term anything but childish?

This latter question is explained in another issue of the same paper, in which the editor remarks:

> It is argued that the Zulus or the Zulu king cannot be sincere in desiring peace, because when the chance offers our troops are fired upon. If people would but consider for a moment, that until there is a truce or armistice agreed on

we are living in a state of war; that our troops are in the Zulu country, making war upon its inhabitants, missing no opportunity of inflicting damage and injury upon them, burning their *kraals*, destroying their grain, ravaging their gardens, and firing on the natives themselves at every chance, what right, they would ask themselves, have we to expect that the Zulus should refrain from retaliation, however desirous they may be of seeing peace restored, and an end put to all the devastation and horror of prolonged warfare? We do not profess to be otherwise than desirous of peace—peace with honour and security for the future—and yet are we not invading their country, and almost vaunting that we shall dictate its terms only when our invading columns have met at Ulundi, and planted the English flag there?

On the 30th the descent into the valley of the White Umvolosi was commenced, through a country covered with scattered bush and aloes. Two *indunas* were escorted in during the day, one bearing a letter from Cetshwayo to Lord Chelmsford,[2] and the other the sword of the Prince Imperial, which the king sent in immediately on learning the value attached to it.[3]

Sir Garnet Wolseley having been ordered out to Natal as Governor of Natal and the Transvaal, and Her Majesty's High Commissioner for the eastern portion of South Africa landed at Durban on the 28th June. On the 30th Lord Chelmsford sent him the following message:

Five miles from Entonganini; ten miles from Umvolosi River. King's messengers have just left with message from me. I must advance to position on left bank of river. This I do tomorrow, but will stop hostilities, pending negotiations, if communicated demands are complied with by 3rd July, noon. There are *indunas* come with cattle and guns. I have

2. Written for him by a Dutch trader, residing with him.
3. This information he obtained through his messengers 'Mfunzi and 'Nkisimane, who were in Pietermaritzburg in June. The message (sent by Mr. Colenso) being, that the young officer killed at the Styotyozi river was a Prince; that his sword would be desired by his family, and that if Cetshwayo wanted to make peace he had better return it. The result was that, as soon as the king received the message, he sent the sword on to Lord Chelmsford.

consented to receive 1000 captured rifles instead of a regiment laying down its arms. As my supplies will only permit of my remaining here until the 10th July, it is desirable I should be informed by you of the conditions of peace to be demanded. White man with king states he has 20,000 men. King anxious to fight; Princes not so. Where is Crealock's column? Signal.

On the 1st July the Flying Column and General Newdigate's division reached, without opposition, the southern bank of the White Umvolosi, within five or six miles of the royal *kraals* of Ulundi. Defensible *laagers* were at once formed, and the position made secure before night. Large bodies of Zulus were seen in motion at Ulundi. Next day the 2nd Division closed up their *laager* to that of the Flying Column, and a stone redoubt was erected on knoll in rear; so that a small garrison might hold the post, leaving the main force unencumbered to operate as desired. The Zulu army was not seen, and no messengers arrived from the king; but a large herd of white (royal) cattle was observed being driven from the king's *kraal* towards the camp, and shortly afterwards driven back again.

On the 3rd, as the Zulus were firing on watering-parties at the river, and no message had come in, a reconnaissance on the farther side was ordered. At noon, the cattle, sent in with the last messengers from the king, were driven back across the river, and about the same time Colonel Buller crossed lower down with the mounted men of the Flying Column to reconnoitre towards Ulundi. Detaching parties to cover his flank, he advanced rapidly to within about 200 yards of the Ulundi river, and about three-quarters of a mile from Ulundi, when he came upon about 5000 Zulus concealed in the river-bed, who at once opened fire, while large bodies of the enemy, moving down on each flank, endeavoured to cut off his retreat.

Colonel Buller, having effected the purpose for which he had gone forward—feeling the enemy and reconnoitring the ground—retired with a loss of three men killed and four wounded. Many officers distinguished themselves in endeavouring to save the men who were lost, as well as in bringing in dismounted men: Commandant D'Arcy, Lieut.-Colonel Buller, Captain Prior, Lord William Beresford, Lieutenant Hayward, and also Sergeant Kerr are mentioned.

On the 4th, at 6.45 a.m., the force crossed the river, leaving the camp garrisoned by the 1-24th Regiment, a company of Engineers, and casualties (about 900 Europeans, 250 natives, with one Gatling gun).

Lieut.-Colonel Buller, with the light cavalry of the flying column, crossed in advance, and occupied the high ground in front without opposition; the main body following, marched up the broken ground out of the valley, and formed a hollow square, the ammunition-carts, etc., in the centre, and the guns in position ready to come into action without delay. The Flying Column formed the front half, and the 2nd Division the rear half of the square; front, flanks, and rear covered by the cavalry. In this formation the troops advanced to the spot selected by Colonel Buller, which was about 700 yards beyond the Nodwengo *kraal*, and about the same distance from a stream that crossed the road halfway to Ulundi; high ground, commanding the adjacent country, and with little cover beyond long grass, near it.

The guns were posted in the angles and in the centre of each face of the square, and each face had a company of infantry in reserve.

Large numbers of Zulus were now seen coming from the hills on the left and left front, and other masses on the right, partly concealed by the mist from the river, passed the Nodwengo *kraal* to surround the square.

The cavalry on the right and left became engaged at 8.45 a.m., and, slowly retiring as the enemy advanced, passed into the square, which immediately opened fire.

The Zulu advance was made with great determination, but their movements appeared to be without order. Some individuals managed to reach within thirty or forty yards of the rear face, where there was some cover, but the main advance on all sides was checked at some distance by the heavy artillery fire and steady volleys of the infantry. These were so effective that within half an hour the enemy wavered and gave way, when the cavalry dashed out to complete their discomfiture. Passing out by the rear face of the square, Colonel Drury-Lowe (who had been already wounded) led the 17th Lancers in the direction of the Nodwengo *kraal*, dispersing the enemy and killing those that could not reach the shelter of the *kraal* or the bush below; then wheeling to the right, he charged through the enemy, who were endeavouring to reach the mountains beyond.

In this manner the whole of the level ground was cleared. Lieut.-Colonel Buller's command also took up the pursuit, doing much execution until the enemy mounted the slopes of the hills and were beyond their reach. But even then a place of safety was not gained, for some guns were moved out from the square, and got the range of the enemy retreating over the hills. The brunt of this day's work fell on the cavalry. Even in the pursuit the greater part of the Zulus turned and fought for their lives. Overtaken by a Lancer, a Zulu would stop just before the fatal thrust was delivered, and, dodging like lightning, evade the lance, sometimes seizing it and holding on till the Lancer was relieved by a comrade.

The Irregular Horse, Mounted Infantry, and Native Horse (Captain T. Shepstone's Basutu and the Natal Native Horse under Captain Cochrane), thoroughly searched the ground, disposing of the enemy who had taken refuge in *dongas*, bush, and long grass. 600 Zulus are said to have fallen before the cavalry alone 150 of them being credited to the Lancers.

Thus was fought the battle of Ulundi.

It was impossible for the ill-armed enemy to pass the belt of fire that encircled the square, even had they not been shaken by the accurate artillery fire whilst yet at a distance.

The ease with which the attack was repelled may be gathered from the fact that the average number of rounds fired by the infantry actually in the ranks was less than six-and-a-half rounds per man (6.4 rounds).

The troops certainly were very steady, and the firing—generally volley-firing by sections—was as a rule under perfect command.

We have heard of an officer calmly smoking his pipe whilst in command of his company during the engagement.

As soon as the wounded had been attended to, the force advanced to the banks of the stream near Ulundi, whilst the cavalry swept the country beyond. Ulundi was fired at 11.40 a.m., and the adjacent *kraals* shortly afterwards. At 2 p.m., the return march to the camp commenced. Every military *kraal* in the valley that had not previously been destroyed was in flames; and not a sign of the Zulu army was to be perceived.

The British force engaged consisted of 4062 Europeans and 1103 natives, with 12 guns and 2 Gatlings. The loss: killed, 2 officers (Captain Wyatt-Edgell, 17th Lancers, and the Hon. W. Drummond, in charge of the Intelligence Department), 13 non-commissioned officers and men, and 3 natives; wounded, 19 officers, 59 non-commissioned officers and men, and 7 natives.

The Zulu force is estimated variously; some put it at 12,000, some at 20,000. Being scattered over a large extent of country, and some of the regiments engaged having already suffered heavily, it is not easy to arrive at a reliable conclusion. It is probable that the correct number lay between 15,000 and 20,000.

As regards the Zulu loss, Lord Chelmsford says:

> It is impossible to estimate with any correctness the loss of the enemy, owing to the extent of country over which they attacked and retreated; but it could not have been less, I consider, than 1000 killed.[4]

Using the same reasoning on the 6th, Lord Chelmsford says:

> But judging by the reports of those engaged, it cannot be placed at a less number than 1500 killed.

From the statements of prisoners it would seem that the attacking force was about 15,000 strong, 5000 being in reserve. At a meeting of the Zulu Council on the 2nd July, it appears that it was resolved by the King to send in the royal coronation white cattle as a peace-offering; but as they were being driven towards the English camp on the 2nd, they were turned back at Nodwengo by the Umcityu Regiment, who refused to let them pass, saying, as they could not fulfil all the demands,

---

4. Despatch, 4th July.

it was useless to give up the cattle, and therefore they would fight. The king was then at Ulundi; he said that—

> . . . . as the Inkandampemvu (Umcityu) Regiment would not let the cattle go in as a peace-offering, and as we wished to fight, the white army being now at his home, we could fight, but we were to fight the white men in the open, and attack before the Nodwengo and Ulundi *kraals*, where we were on the day of the fight. . . . The army is now thoroughly beaten, and as it was beaten in the open, it will not reassemble and fight again. No force is watching the lower column, and none has been sent there. How could there be, when all were ordered to be here to-day? We mustered here by the king's orders at the beginning of this moon, about ten days ago. We have not been called out before.

The natives belonging to the British force were exceedingly struck at the idea of their being brought into the square, whilst the soldiers formed a *laager* of their bodies round them.

The special correspondent of *The Daily News*, Mr. Archibald Forbes, performed a very gallant act after the battle of Ulundi. Finding that no despatch was being sent off by the General to announce the victory, he determined to take the news himself, and, "taking his life in his hand," set out alone to ride right through the Zulu country. This he did, riding the whole night, having frequently to dismount and actually *feel* his way—the tracks of the wagons on the upward route.

Next day, after a ride of nearly a hundred miles, he reached Landtmann's Drift (in fifteen hours), and was enabled to telegraph to Sir Garnet Wolseley the news of the victory of the 4th.

A few brief remarks on the return march are all that are necessary. The day after the battle of Ulundi (5th July) the whole force retired to Entonjaneni, and remained there till the 9th, when the flying column moved on the road towards the coast to Kwamagwasa, *en route* to meet Sir Garnet Wolseley.

On the 10th the 2nd Division marched from Entonjaneni, and arrived at the Upoko River on the 10th.

Lord Chelmsford accompanied the flying column. We cannot leave Brigadier-General Wood's command without a word of notice. From the beginning to the end of the campaign its work was done in a thoroughly soldierlike manner, leaving little or nothing to be desired. There was a thorough reciprocal confidence between commander and men, and a total absence of those "scares" which were occasionally heard of during the campaign.

Where all did well, it may seem a little invidious to single one out for mention, but we will quote the concluding words of Brigadier-General Wood's despatch of 5th July, referring to Lieut.-Colonel Redvers Buller, not only on account of this officer's merit, but "to point the moral" as to where was the neglect which led primarily to the disaster to the headquarters column in January:

> He has never failed to cover the column with his mounted men, for from ten to twelve miles in front, and on the flanks.
>
> Constitutionally fearless, he is prudent in counsel, and though resolute, is very careful of the lives of his troops in action. He possesses, in my opinion, all the attributes of a perfect leader of light cavalry.

It is stated (*Standard*, August 22nd, 1879) that, on reaching the White Umvolosi, despatches arrived from Sir Garnet Wolseley, requesting Lord Chelmsford to fall back and meet him at Kwamagwasa—a mission station, where it had at one time been proposed that the 1st and 2nd Divisions should effect a junction.

On the 4th, Lord Chelmsford sent a despatch to Sir Garnet Wolseley, in which he said:

> As I have fully accomplished the object for which I advanced, I consider I shall now be best carrying out Sir Garnet Wolseley's instructions by moving at once to Entonjanini, and thence to Kwamagwaza.

Why the blow struck at Ulundi was not followed up it is difficult to say. If Lord Chelmsford's instructions permitted him to advance and engage the enemy, they would be sufficiently elastic to enable him to follow up the victory. The king was known to have a new *kraal* in a strong position at the junction of the White and Black Umvolosi Rivers, within a day's march, of Ulundi; the Zulu army was thoroughly beaten and dispersed, and there was absolutely nothing to prevent an advance for the destruction of this stronghold, the moral effect of which on the native mind would have been very great. There was an ample force, willing hearts, and no lack of supplies. The solution of the problem must be sought in Lord Chelmsford's words: "I have fully accomplished the object for which I advanced." He withdrew at once from the scene of his victory, and resigned his command.

CHAPTER 22

Capture of Cetshwayo

Sir Bartle Frere, whose continued popularity spoke somewhat of colonial approval of the war, had returned to the Cape
in June, and his reception at Cape Town "capped the climax
of an uninterrupted triumph," according to *The Natal Mercury*.
That he thought himself deserving of the honours due to a
conqueror returning home in triumph we may gather from the
fact that he sent no instructions to suppress any demonstrations
of delight at his return, although at that very time the latest and
perhaps the saddest tragedy of all the sad results of his policy had
just been enacted, and Natal, as with one voice, was lamenting
the Prince Imperial's death.

"So be it," says *The Natal Witness* of June 12th, 1879, com-
menting upon this text:

> Sir Bartle Frere's reception capped the climax of an unin-
> terrupted triumph. We are quite ready to believe this, and, as
> we have said, we are glad at last to have so decided an intima-
> tion of what Sir Bartle Frere has intended to do. There are tri-
> umphs of various kinds. There is the triumph which surrounds
> the statesman, who, by gentle persuasion, by cautious reforms,
> by a personal example of uprightness and unselfishness, has
> reduced threatening elements of danger, and evolved peace
> and security out of storm and terror. There is the triumph
> which is his who, impressed with a deep sense of the value of
> human life, lays his head upon his pillow every night in the
> happy confidence that never through his means, either directly
> or indirectly, has a human life been needlessly sacrificed. There

is the triumph of the philanthropist, who, feeling deep in his heart the claims of an aboriginal people to the consideration of a civilised power, has, in his dealings with that people, been careful rather to strain doubtful points in their favour, than to take advantage of their presumed simplicity. There is the triumph of the Christian legislator, who regards the authority entrusted to him as entrusted with a solemn injunction to use that authority in the name of his divine Master, for the purpose of spreading and confirming the kingdom of peace and good will. There is the triumph of the diplomatist, who, in respect of his dealings with state questions, can lay his hand upon his heart, and affirm that he never misled his superiors, ... never wrote a line which he did not believe to be true. All these triumphs we doubt not will be yet achieved by Sir Bartle Frere, if only the fatigue caused by his 'troubles and journeying' does not suggest an early return to Europe.

Would Sir Bartle Frere be supported by the home government? and would Lord Chelmsford be upheld by his military superiors in England? Such were the questions perpetually asked in the colony, to which there seemed no full and sufficient answer. True, both had received messages of sympathy and confidence; but these were sent palpably on the spur of the moment, and long before all the facts of the case had been brought to light; and, on the other hand, Sir Bartle Frere had received a very severe rebuke in the despatches mentioned in Chapter 12. Still the tide of events was permitted to flow on, and many doubted the reality of the condemnation.

From the time of the disaster at Isandhlwana, prophecies were current that Lord Chelmsford would be recalled, and as misfortune pursued our arms the prophecies were renewed. Many were the conjectures as to who would be sent to replace Lord Chelmsford should he be recalled, and a general idea was prevalent that the sprightly Sir Garnet Wolseley and his "brilliant staff" would once more grace the shores of Natal. The despatch announcing his approach reached the colony in the middle of June, and the telegram to Lord Chelmsford announcing his appointment ran as follows:

Her Majesty's Government have determined to send out Sir Garnet Wolseley as Administrator in that part of South-Eastern Africa in the neighbourhood of the seat of war, with plenary powers, both civil and military. Sir Bartle Frere, instructed accordingly by Colonial Office. The appointment of a senior officer is not intended as a censure on yourself, but you will, as in ordinary course of service, submit and subordinate your plans to his control. He leaves this country by next mail.[1]

Sir Garnet Wolseley landed at Durban on the 28th June, and proceeded direct to Pietermaritzburg, where he was the same day sworn in as Governor of Natal. Certainly Sir Garnet did not let the grass grow under his feet. On Sunday, the 29th, he telegraphed to Colonel Walker at Fort Pearson:

Send back Zulu messengers immediately to the king with following message from me: 'If the king wants peace he must send Umnyamana, Umfanawendhela, and Vumandaba to General Crealock's column, where I will depute an officer of rank to hear what the king has to say. I alone have power to make peace. All the other Generals are under my orders.' Explain to the messengers who I am. They are to tell the king, and remind him that I was here as Governor before, and had many communications with him then.[2]

The message from Cetshwayo was delivered by two Zulu messengers at the Lower Tugela, on June 25th, to Mr. Fynney, Administrator and Border Agent.

We are sent by the king straight to you, We were ordered not to go to the troop at the Umlatazi, as other messengers (Sintwangu) will go there. . . . The king asks you to speak to the great white Chief with the upper column, and ask to stay the advance of the troops till he (the king) can hear plainly what he has done, what great sin he has committed. If he ever killed a white man or white woman, or ever took cattle from a white man before the war? Did he ever walk over the words spoken at the Umlambongwenya *kraal* by Somtseu?

1. Sent *via* St. Vincent, 29th May, 1879.
2. P. P. (C. 2454) p. 149.

(Sir T. Shepstone). The king wished us to say if he is to be destroyed he could die happy if he knew first really what wrong he had done. The king begs you will speak to the great white Chief with the upper column to stay a further advance till chosen representatives from both sides can meet and hear really the cause of the war, and what wrong he has done. The king does not ask for favour if it is proved he has been wrong. He wants to hear, and he wishes the troops not to advance till he can hear; for if they do he cannot help fighting, as there will be nothing left but to try and push aside a tree if falling upon him.

This is our message from the king to you, and he ordered us to tell you that it is from himself; even the *indunas* do not know he has sent it.[3]

On the same day (29th) Sir Garnet sent the following order to Captain McLeod:

Make arrangements at once, with Swazis, for massing north of Pongolo River, with view to invading Zululand. Spread abroad news that the invasion will take place immediately, but do not let them cross river without my orders. When they are ready to cross let me know, and I will send you further instructions. Impress urgently upon them that women and children must not be murdered, but promise them all cattle they take. This promise to be made as public as possible. I am now High Commissioner, with full powers to decide all terms of peace. All reports must be sent to me, care of General Clifford, 'Maritzburg.[4]

The object of this message was "to establish a standing menace, and to bring formidable pressure to bear in that quarter upon the Zulus."

The barbarity of the Swazis in warfare, and the keen delight with which they would have found themselves let loose upon their hereditary enemies the Zulus, whose army was either scattered or destroyed, was a well known fact, and many wondered that such a course should be proposed.

---

3. *ibid.* p. 154.
4. *ibid.* p. 150.

Captain McLeod, a hardy soldier and brave man, had been for many months in about as unenviable a position as can well be imagined in an unsettled border district in war time, threatened both by Boers and Zulus. He had been posted at Derby, to guide and control the movements of our ally the Swazi king, who, it was imagined, would be stanch to us or not, according to the fortunes of the Zulu war.

Captain McLeod knew the Swazis well, and how little chance there would be of keeping them under control if once let loose upon the helpless Zulu people; he therefore begged that they might be used only as a last resource.

With the view of still further spreading alarm through the Zulu country, Sir Garnet sent a message to the Amatongas that he might "possibly ascend the Maputa River with a force and use their territory as a base of operations against the Zulus from the north."[5]

On the 30th, after a long conference with General Clifford and Commissary-General Strickland, Sir Garnet Wolseley had an interview with about seventy Natal native chiefs, who had been assembled at his request, and addressed them, through an interpreter, to the effect that the great English Queen had sent him to carry on the war against Cetshwayo, and to thank them for what they had already done. That the chiefs need have no fear but that the Queen would send as many armies as are necessary, if the troops sent were not sufficient.

> They may depend upon it, and the past history of our nation is a guarantee thereof, that when we give a promise we will perform it. Our war is not against the Zulu people, but against Ketshwayo, who has broken all his promises. We have no wish to rob the Zulu people of their property or their land; but tell the chiefs this, that I say this war is going to be finished by us, and finished in a satisfactory manner. The Queen is most anxious that the war in Natal should be finished.

Then (as there was a scarcity of grass for draught-oxen) Sir Gar-

---

5. *ibid.* p. 149.

net requested the chiefs to furnish a certain number (2000) of their young men to carry provisions for the troops; the men to carry their arms whilst so employed, and to be paid and fed by him.

Once more, then, we hear the words: *"Our war is not against the Zulu people!"*

These "carriers" were taken from the Tugela Valley, which had lately suffered from the Zulu raid, and where many of the men had belonged to the native levies raised for the defence of the border; they naturally did not appreciate an employment which removed them from the protection of their families, and which was at variance with their customs[6] and prejudices.

There was not much work for these "carriers" after all; they were assembled at the Lower Tugela, and marched up to Fort Chelmsford, each man with a fifty-pound *mealie*-bag on his head.[7] Their commander, Major Schwabe, left the loads there, and took the men on to Port Durnford, where they were employed as required. Having, after some time, received their pay, the "carriers" quietly walked off to their homes.

The Commander-in-Chief remained but two days in Pieter-maritzburg, returning to Durban on the 1st of July. The same evening he embarked on board H.M.S. *Shah*, intending to land at Port Durnford, and thus reach the scene of action. For once in

---

6. Amongst the wild natives of South Africa it is thought that the carrying of burdens is not a manly task. In a family of travelling Zulus the women and lads perform the duties of carriers, while the man of the party marches ahead, unencumbered except by his weapons, ready if necessary to defend his flock against the attack of man or beast. An officer, travelling in the eastern province some years ago, met and questioned a party proceeding in this fashion. "Why," he asked the leader of the little band, "do you allow these women and girls to carry heavy loads, while you, a strong able-bodied man, have nothing but your assegais and knob-kerries in your hand?" Such questions are not seldom resented when they touch on native customs, and are asked in an overbearing manner. This officer was uniformly kind and courteous to the natives, and the man smilingly replied, "It is our custom, and the women prefer it;" referring his questioner to the women themselves for their opinion. The chief of these latter thereupon replied, with much grace and dignity: "Does the white chief think we would let our man do woman's work? It is our work to carry, and we should not like to see him do it."

7. The appearance of the native carrier on the march was very ludicrous. Picture a stalwart Kafir carrying his sleeping mats, provisions, cooking-pot, drinking-gourd, shield, bundle of assegais and knob-kerries, and perched on top of all, on his head, a fifty-pound mealie-bag; the result was likened to a Christmas-tree.

his life Sir Garnet's good fortune deserted him; the heavy surf on the beach prevented his landing, and the *Shah* brought him back to Durban. Here he received the news of the battle of Ulundi, telegraphed to him by Mr. Archibald Forbes.

No one quite knew what Lord Chelmsford was about, but everyone understood that he would try and end the war before he was superseded; and the general feeling in the colony was certainly one of hope that "poor Lord Chelmsford" might get a chance, win a battle, and have his bonfire in the enemy's city of straw. Some few, indeed, argued that as Lord Chelmsford could not possibly, in the time left him, settle the Zulu question by the sword, it might occur to him at last to pay some attention to the hard-pressed Zulu monarch's repeated messages imploring peace, and propose some conditions possible for Cetshwayo to accept and fulfil. Without further bloodshed an honourable peace might thus have been concluded before Sir Garnet Wolseley could step upon the scene.

We left the 1st Division at the Umlalazi River, close to the landing-place, Port Durnford. There the force remained, General Crealock occupied in receiving the submission of the neighbouring Zulus, who were flocking in from every direction.

But whilst Lord Chelmsford, on his approach to Ulundi, was inquiring, "Where is Crealock?" Crealock was quietly established near the coast, his military activity being displayed in the burning of Empangeni and other *kraals* north of the Umlatuzi River. As the Zulus all round were coming in, and no *impi* was even heard of, the object of this exhibition of force seems a little doubtful. As was remarked by *The Cape Times*:

Why the British soldier was ordered to destroy the shelter, and, with the shelter, the store of grain food of some thousands of poor women and children whose husbands and fathers were making their submission, we can no more understand than we can comprehend the strategy by which a large British force was held back for months at the edge of the enemy's country, while commissariat supplies were accumulating sufficient to support a long campaign, the whole work before them being to march a hundred miles, and with one fight close up the war. If they were beaten they could fall back on the base; but with caution and generalship defeat was out of the question.

However, Major-General Crealock must have the credit of quieting the eastern portion of Zululand before the termination of the war. From his despatches of the 5th July we gather that the "district people are all wanting to come in," that he was "sending back the people to their districts; difficulty of feeding them would be great." His division paraded under arms to receive the "official submission" of "Mabilwana, Manyingo, and other chiefs," who, with some 250 men, double that number of women and children, and their cattle, etc., had come in—these people belonging to the coast district, but were not strictly speaking warriors, or necessarily belonging to the Zulu army; nor could their submission be looked upon as any desertion of their king by the fighting-men of the nation. They were told that the General accepted their submission, and should look to them in future to keep peace in that district. If any Zulus were found in arms, their chief or headman would suffer; but, if they behaved themselves well, he would give them back their cattle and his protection. The men then received passes (or tickets) and were permitted to return to their districts.[8]

Sir Garnet Wolseley crossed the Tugela with his staff and escort on July 6th, and proceeded to the headquarters of the 1st Division, near Port Durnford, which he reached on the 7th. He at once set to work "to reduce the excessive rate of expenditure which has so far been maintained in connection with this war," and "arranged with the Commodore to embark the naval brigade at the earliest opportunity," and also "dispensed with the services of some of the colonial troops." Reinforcements of all

---

8. A splendid elephant's tusk (the Zulu emblem of international goodwill and sincerity) had been sent by Cetshwayo, with one of his messages, to General Crealock; this Sir Garnet Wolseley sent home to the Queen, who thus has received a valuable present from her dusky antagonist.

kinds were stopped, including a fine battalion of marine infantry and strong detachment of marine artillery, just arrived at the Cape in H.M.S. *Jumna*.

On July 10th, Sir Garnet also put on one side "the plan of a Swazi invasion."[9] All the chiefs up to St. Lucia Bay tendered their submission, and sent in their arms.

Sir Garnet Wolseley and Lord Chelmsford met at St. Paul's on the 15th July, the latter arriving with Brigadier-General Wood's flying column. This Sir Garnet inspected on the following day, taking the opportunity of decorating Major Chard, R.E., with the Victoria Cross, awarded him for his gallantry at Rorke's Drift.

Lord Chelmsford left St. Paul's on the 17th, on his way home. His "brilliant victory" had turned the tide of popular favour somewhat in his direction, and he found that (as he said) "nothing succeeds like success."

In Durban he was accorded a reception which must have been highly gratifying to his feelings. One of his last remarks in Natal, in reply to a speech made as he was about to embark, was to the following effect:

> I think I may say confidently that we have now seen
> the beginning of the end of this campaign, and any success
> which has attended my efforts, I feel, is due to the prayers of
> the people, and the kindly ordinations of Divine Providence;
> for I am one of those who believe firmly and implicitly in
> the efficacy of prayer and in the intervention of Providence.

In this comfortable frame of mind Lord Chelmsford passes from the scene.

Sir Garnet Wolseley completed the chain of forts across Zululand, commencing with St. Paul's, an English mission station on the coast road a little north of where it crosses the Umlatusi. Fifteen miles west of this is Kwamagwasa. Twenty miles a little south of west lies Fort Evelyn, on the road from Rorke's Drift to Ulundi. Fort Marshall about twenty miles west-south-west of Fort Evelyn, Fort Newdigate, twelve miles north-west of Fort Evelyn, and a fort on Itelezi Hill completes the chain to the Blood River.

---

9. P. P. (C. 2454) p. 163.

Some of these forts were constructed on the upward march of the 2nd Division and flying column, to keep open their communications. In addition to these, Fort Cambridge was built near where the road from Conference Hill crosses the White Umvolosi; and a little later an entrenched post (Fort George) was thrown up near Enhlongana mission station, thus thoroughly, by these detached posts, commanding the country.

Patrols were pushed out in various directions, by one of which the two guns lost at Isandhlwana were found between Ulundi and Maizekanye. They had not been spiked, but the Zulus had screwed rifle-nipples into the vents, and had also apparently tried to load the guns by ramming home shells, but without cartridges.

The Cavalry Brigade was broken up, and a fresh disposition of the troops made. Sir Garnet visited various posts, interviewing the Zulu chiefs who had surrendered themselves. Some of the most important, however, of those who came in, and were supposed to have submitted and deserted their king, had, in point of fact, no such intention, appearing merely to make their often and vainly repeated attempt at procuring "terms" for Cetshwayo and themselves. It had always been prophesied that the Zulu nation would desert their king. Before the war began, some of those who professed to understand the people best, declared that they would be thankful to throw off the yoke of one whom, it was alleged, they regarded with fear and hatred, and would side with the English as soon as the latter crossed their border.

The fallacy of this idea was discovered to our cost.

It was then asserted that the Zulu army had given a temporary strength to the authority of their king, which would last until we had beaten his troops and proved our superiority, and this assertion was used by those who insisted that no peace must be made, however earnestly desired by the Zulus, until we had beaten them and shown them that we were their masters.

After Ulundi, it was argued that the people would be glad to procure peace by giving up their king, whose unconditional submission, or capture, was announced by us to be the only possible conclusion to the war.

The Zulus had ceased to struggle with their powerful conquerors, and it now only remained to find Cetshwayo, who was said to be north of the Black Umvolosi River, with a very small following. A flying column, under Lieut.-Colon el Baker Russell, was sent out from Fort Newdigate early in August, but his patrols were not successful.

On August 14th, a cavalry force under Major Barrow, with Lord Gifford, started from Ulundi to try and find Cetshwayo, who had hitherto eluded all attempts to capture him. Day after day it was reported that the pursuers were close upon the fugitive: they had come to a *kraal* where he had slept the previous night, they reached another where he had been that very morning, and then they lost "the scent," and for some time could trace him no farther. They tried in vain to persuade his people to betray him, but this "hated tyrant," although beaten and powerless, flying through the land now in the possession of his conquerors, had still such a hold over the loyalty and affection of his people, that they were true to him in his adversity, and refused to give him up or to set his enemies on his track.

Severe measures were taken to procure by force the information which could not otherwise be obtained. Orders were given to one party of the pursuers that at each *kraal* they reached, if the inhabitants refused to speak, so many huts should be burnt, so many principal men and women taken prisoners, and all cattle confiscated. Many *kraals* were thus treated, and so many prisoners collected in this manner, that the number to be taken at each *kraal* had to be reduced from eight to four, then to two, and at last to one of each sex; thus proving how steadfast were the people generally in their loyalty to their king. On approaching some of these *kraals*, the headmen came out and offered the passes or papers promising protection, given them on surrendering their arms; but the unhappy people received another lesson on the text, "When we give a promise we will perform it," and were told that their papers were worthless now; they must tell where the king was, or suffer like the rest. One of the officers concerned in carrying out these orders, exclaimed at the time with natural indignation: "I don't care what may be said of the necessity of catching Cetshwayo; necessary or not, we are committing a crime in what we are doing now! "

These measures proving useless, five prisoners were flogged to make them speak yet they held their peace. An interpreter, who accompanied Major Barrow's party, writes:

> I had been a long time in Zululand. I knew the people and their habits, and although I believed they would be true to their king, I never expected such devotion. Nothing would move them. Neither the loss of their cattle, the fear of death, or the offering of large bribes, would make them false to their king.

For many days this work of trying to persuade or force the people to betray their king was continued, and, at last a woman was frightened into giving a clue, which resulted in taking prisoners three brothers, at whose *kraal* the king had slept the night before. The interpreter says—

> They were questioned but denied in the most solemn way that they knew anything about the king. We threatened to shoot them, but they said: 'If you kill us we shall die innocently.' This was about nine o'clock at night, a beautiful moonlight night, and the picture was rather an effective one. There were all our men sitting round at their fireplaces, our select tribunal facing the three men, who were calm and collected, whilst we, as a sort of inquisition, were trying to force them to divulge their secret. As a last resource we took one man and led him away blindfolded behind a bush, and then a rifle was fired off to make believe that he was shot. We then separated and blindfolded the remaining two, and said to one of them: 'You saw your brother blindfolded and led away; we have shot him. Now we shall shoot you. You had better tell the truth.' After a good deal of coaxing one told us where the king had slept the night before, and which was about fifteen miles away, and also where he had seen him that very morning. . . . it was now eleven o'clock. Lord Gifford gave orders for our party to saddle up, which was smartly done, and we started off with the two brothers as guides. We left the one

brother behind so as to keep on the screw, to make the two believe he had been shot. They took us over as ugly a piece of country as ever horse crossed, and at daybreak we surrounded the *kraal*. But disappointment was again in store for us, for our bird had flown about twelve hours previously.

The direction he had taken being pointed out, the party followed until they got within four or five miles of a *kraal*, where the king had halted for the day. Lord Gifford sent off a note addressed to Captain Maurice, saying he was on the track and hoped for speedy capture; and, finding the *kraal* could not be approached without his being seen, seems to have made up his mind to wait till nightfall. It is perhaps fortunate that this arrangement was not carried out, as, in the darkness and hurry of a night attack, it is possible that we might have had the additional wrong laid upon us of having shot the Zulu king.

Amongst other patrols sent out to look for Cetshwayo was one under Major Marter, King's Dragoon Guards, consisting of one squadron dragoons, ten men mounted infantry and Lonsdale's Horse, and one company Natal Native Contingent, their orders being to get on the king's track and capture him, if possible, and to reconnoitre the Ngome Forest, and report if it could be traversed.

This force started on the 27th August, Major Marter sending two natives on in the direction of the Ngome to impress upon the people that until the king was captured they could not have rest, as troops would be constantly on the move amongst them, and require supplies, etc., and to suggest it would be to their advantage to give him some hint or sign about the king. He had found the natives friendly, but they said frankly that if they knew the king to be close by they would not tell him; he, therefore, remembering the language of symbols was pleasant to the native mind, endeavoured, by indirect means, to obtain the information he sought. Having got over about twenty-four miles of rough country, the little column halted on the summit of the Inenge Mountain, and, starting at daylight next morning, had crossed the Ibuluwane River about ten o'clock, when a Zulu came from the hill in front, sent by a headman to whom the scouts had been, and began to talk on indifferent subjects, not appearing to wish to speak about the king. After some time he casually remarked: "I have heard the wind blow from this side to-day," pointing to the Ngome Forest, "but you should take that road until you come to Nisaka's *kraal*," showing a track leading upwards and along the side of the range.

About half an hour afterwards a native brought a note addressed to Captain Maurice. As this officer was out in another direction on the same service, Major Marter opened and read it. It was from Lord Gifford, who said he was on the track again and hoped for a speedy capture of the king, but gave no information as to where either the king or Lord Gifford were. Sending the man on in Captain Maurice's direction, Major Marter proceeded to Nisaka's *kraal*, some distance up the mountain. After some talk a suggestion of guides was made to Nisaka, who said they had better go to his brother's *kraal* on top of the mountain, and called two men to go as guides. On reaching this *kraal* the guides made signs for the party to halt where trees hid them from being seen from below, and then took Major Marter on to the edge of the precipice, crawling along on hands and knees; they then stopped, and told him to go to a bush a little farther on and look down. He did so, and saw a *kraal* in an open space about 2000 feet below, in a basin, three sides of which were precipitous and covered with dense forest. He considered it would be useless to approach the *kraal* from the open side, as one minute's warning would enable the king to escape to the nearest point of the forest; and therefore decided to venture down the side of the mountain under cover of the forest, feeling that the importance of the capture would warrant the risk.

Having rejoined his men, Major Marter ordered the natives to take off their uniform, and, with their arms and ammunition only, pass down the precipitous mountain to the lower edge of the forest nearest to the *kraal*, and remain concealed till the cavalry were seen coming from the forest on the other side; they were then to rush out towards the open side of the *kraal* and surround it. The cavalry left led horses, pack-animals, and every article which could make a noise or impede their progress, and followed Major Marter, leading their horses down the descent in single file. They left the upper part of the mountain at 1.45 p.m., and, after a scramble over rocks and watercourses, floundering in bogs, and hampered everywhere by trees and gigantic creepers, reached the foot about three o'clock, having lost two horses killed in the descent, and one man having his arm badly hurt. In a little dell they mounted, and at a gallop dashed out—one troop to the right, one to the left, the irregulars straight to the front over boulders, through high grass and every impediment, up to the *kraal*; the natives reaching it at the same moment.

Seeing that the men in the *kraal* were armed with guns as well as *assegais*. Major Marter desired his interpreter to call out that if any resistance were offered he would shoot down every one and burn the *kraal*; and then dismounting, with a few of his men, he entered the enclosure, which was strongly stockaded. A chief—Umkosana—met him, and was asked where the king was; after some delay, seeing it was a hopeless case, he pointed out a hut on the farther side of the enclosure. Major Marter called on the king to come out, but he insisted the officer should go in to him. A threat of setting fire to the hut was then made, when the king asked the rank of the officer, and, after some further parley, came out and stood erect and quite the king, looking at Major Marter, saying: "You would not have taken me, but I never thought troops could come down the mountain through the forest."

Besides the Chief Umkosana, there were with Cetshwayo seven men and a lad, five women and a girl, of his personal attendants.

There were twenty guns in the *kraal*, four of them rifles that had belonged to the 24th Regiment, much ammunition, some belts of the 24th, and many *assegais*, one of which—the king's—was sent by Sir Garnet Wolseley to the Queen.

Taking the most open line of country, the party set out for Ulundi, Major Marter taking personal charge of the king, who was in good health, and showing no signs of over-fatigue.

On the evening of the second day three men and a woman sprang suddenly into the thick bush through which they were passing and tried to escape; but two of the men were shot. They had been repeatedly warned that anyone trying to escape would be shot.

On the morning of the 31st August, Major Marter safely reached the camp at Ulundi with Cetshwayo; who is described by his captor as "a noble specimen of a man, without any bad expression, and the king all over in appearance and manner."

Sir Garnet Wolseley did not receive the fallen king himself, or accord him any of the signs of respect to which he was entitled, and which at least generosity demanded. That this was deeply felt is apparent from the words of an eye-witness, the interpreter attached to Major Barrow's force.

> Cetywayo, who appreciates nicely the courtesies due to rank—as those who knew him tell me—felt this keenly. Sir Garnet Wolseley did not see him at all, and Mr. John Shepstone only had an interview with him to tell him that he would leave under the charge of Major Poole, R.A., for—no one knew where. The instructions to the Major were, on leaving Ulundi, to proceed to Pietermaritzburg *via* Rorke's Drift, but the camp had not been left many miles behind before a messenger to the Major from the General gave Port Durnford as the port of embarkation.
>
> Cetshwayo spent less than three hours amidst the ruins of Ulundi, and when he left them he was not aware of his destination. His hope was that he was going to Pietermaritzburg. . . . This he believed was where he was going until he came to Kwamagwasa, and he said, "This is not the way to the Tugela." He grew moody after this, and used to moan, "It was better to be killed than sent over the sea."

The party reached Port Durnford on the 4th September, and was immediately embarked for Cape Town. There the king met with a fitting reception, and was conveyed to the castle, where he remained under strict surveillance in the custody of Colonel Hassard, C.B., R.E., Commandant at Cape Town.

One peculiarity regarding the treatment of Cetshwayo may be illustrated by the following personal anecdote:

A son and daughter of the Bishop of Natal, on their way to England, called at Cape Town on board a steamer at the time of the king's arrival. They asked permission to see him, feeling that if anything could be a solace to the captive it would be an interview with members of a family which he knew had kindly feelings towards him.[10] This request was refused by Sir Bartle Frere, who regretted that he could not "at present give anyone permission to visit Cetewayo," and said that "all intercourse with him must be regulated by the orders of the General Commanding H. M. Forces in the Field, to whom all applications to communicate with the prisoner should be referred." After this communication, it was rather surprising to find that several of the passengers on board the mail-steamer, leaving the Cape the next day, had not only seen the king, but had found no difficulty in so doing.[11]

---

10. Mr. Colenso was acquainted with, him, having, as already related, paid him a visit in 1877.
11. At the same time many residents in Cape Town obtained, from mere motives of curiosity, that interview which, to those who had desired it for humanity's sake, had been refused, while all who know his language, or are likely to sympathise, are rigidly excluded. Orders were given afterwards that the name of the Bishop of Natal should not be mentioned to Cetshwayo, "because it excited the prisoner."

CHAPTER 23

Conclusion

The fall of Ulundi was looked upon by some as the finishing touch to the Zulu power and the end of the war, while others considered peace ensured only and completely by the capture of the king. Much, however, remained to be done before Natal could be thought of as at peace with her neighbours and herself, and what has been commonly called the "Settlement of Zulu-land," was a task which required the gravest consideration and the most careful handling.

Sir Garnet Wolseley's first act in this direction was to call together as many of the principal Zulu chiefs and officials as could be found, and to address them upon the situation. This meeting took place at Ulundi on the 1st of September, the day after the captive king's departure for Port Durnford. About 200 Zulus, including two of Cetshwayo's brothers, and his prime minister Mnyamana, had responded to the summons; and seating themselves in rows four deep, with the principal chiefs in front, a few paces from the flagstaff at Sir G. Wolseley's tent, waited in perfect silence. When Sir Garnet, with his staff, at last appeared, he addressed the assembled chiefs through Mr. John Shepstone, who accompanied him as interpreter. He informed them that it was six years that very day since Cetshwayo was crowned king of the Zulus, and that he was now carried away never to return. This, he told them, was in consequence of his having broken his coronation promises, and having failed to make and keep such laws amongst his people as the Queen of

England could approve, therefore his kingdom was taken from him; and would now be divided amongst a number of chiefs, who would be expected to rule with justice. In future no life was to be taken without trial, and trivial offences were to be punished by fines; no standing army would be allowed, nor the possession of guns and ammunition by any Zulu; nor would any stores be permitted to be landed on the Zulu coast, in case, under the guise of merchandise, arms should be brought into the country. The young men would be allowed to marry when and whom they pleased, provided they had sufficient for the support of a wife, and could obtain the consent of the girl's parents, and "smelling out" for witchcraft was to be put down. Nevertheless, the Queen had no wish to force our laws and customs upon them. By their own rules of war and conquest, Zululand now belonged to her; but she had already enough land in Africa, and had therefore no intention of depriving the Zulus of theirs. Finally, the missionaries were not to be forced upon them, and the Zulus were even forbidden to encourage their settling amongst them.

To secure the fulfilment of all these commands, Sir G. Wolseley told the chiefs that he intended to leave an English officer as resident, to be the eyes and ears of England, to watch over the people, and to see the laws observed and that the chiefs ruled with justice and equity. With what machinery the officer in question was to perform so wide a task does not appear. Whether his position is to be a real one, requiring several British regiments to support it, or whether it is to be a mere farce, a fine-sounding pretence, remains yet to be proved.

At the conclusion of the General's discourse he produced a document, the purport of which, he said, he had now told them, and which was to be signed by all the chiefs whom he had chosen as rulers of the land, to each of whom a duplicate copy would be given, while he retained a similar one himself.

The first to sign his name was Mr. John Dunn, whose chieftainship was by far the largest; and after him the Zulu chiefs touched the pen while Mr. Shepstone made their crosses for them, in place of the signature which they could not form.

For once in the history of Natal, all classes, from whatever widely differing motives, were united in condemning the arrangement. On September 16th *The Cape Times* says:

> The so-called settlement of Zululand, is regarded with anything but satisfaction in Natal, if we may accept the press of that colony as representative of public opinion. Sir Garnet Wolseley was probably acting under instructions in making peace on a barbarian basis; such a peace, however, has no guarantee for continuance, but on the contrary an inherent weakness, forbidding any hope of permanence. A savage nation is now divided into a number of savage nations, each leaning to the other with all the force, of common blood and common traditions, while to check the impulses of that force there is absolutely nothing beyond the influence of two or three British residents, unsupported by any armed retinue, and clothed with no more than a shadow of authority. And as the embodiment of British civilisation, and as Her Majesty the Queen's own representative in Zululand, is placed Mr. John Dunn.... But whatever John Dunn's merits may be, his appointment as Chief Resident in Zululand is a shock to civilisation. His ways are Zulu ways; his associations, Zulu associations; his very habits of thought imbued with the Zulu character. A white man who for twenty years or more has lived the Zulu life, wedded Zulu wives, and chosen their society in preference to that of such women as a white man should love and honour, is not the man to represent the Queen of England in a nation of savages. The settlement of Zululand means simply the appointment of a dozen Cetywayos, with a white man to look after them, who is a Cetywayo in all but colour. And now Sir Garnet Wolseley skips off in his light and airy fashion to the Transvaal, flattering himself that he has made things pleasant in Zululand. It is a miserable delusion....

The "engagements" into which the Zulu chiefs entered are:

> 1. I will observe and respect whatever boundaries shall be assigned to my territory by the British Government through the Resident of the division in which my territory is situated.

2. I will not permit the existence of the Zulu military system, or the existence of any military system of organisation whatever, in my territory, and I will proclaim and make it a rule that all men shall be allowed to marry when they choose and as they choose, according to the good ancient customs of my people, known and followed in the days preceding the establishment by Chaka of the system known as the military system; and I will allow and encourage all men living within my territory to go and come freely for peaceful purposes, and to work in Natal and the Transvaal and elsewhere for themselves or for hire.

3. I will not import or allow to be imported into my territory by any person, upon any pretext or for any object whatever, any arms or ammunition from any part whatsoever, or any goods or merchandise by the sea-coast of Zululand, without the express sanction of the Resident of the division in which my territory is situated; and I will not encourage or promote, or take part in, or countenance in any way whatever, the importation in any other part of Zululand of arms or ammunition from any part whatever, or goods or merchandise by the sea-coast of Zululand, without such sanction, and I will confiscate and hand over to the Natal Government all arms and ammunition, and goods and merchandise, so imported into my territory, and I will punish by fine or by other sufficient punishment any person guilty of or concerned in any such unsanctioned importation, and any person found possessing arms or ammunition, or goods or merchandise, knowingly obtained thereby.

4. I will not allow the life of any of my people to be taken for any cause, except after sentence passed in a council of the chief men of my territory, and after fair and impartial trial in my presence and after the hearing of witnesses; and I will not tolerate the employment of witch-doctors, or the practice known as smelling-out, or any practices of witchcraft.

5. The surrender of persons fugitive in my territory from justice, when demanded by the government of any British colony, territory, or province, in the interests of justice, shall be readily and promptly made to such government; and the

escape into my territory of persons accused or convicted of offences against British laws shall be prevented by all possible means, and every exertion shall be made to seize and deliver up such persons to British authority.

6. I will not make war upon any chief or chiefs, or people, without the sanction of the British Government, through the Resident of the division in which my territory is situated.

7. The succession to the chieftainship of my territory shall be according to the ancient laws and customs of my people, and the nomination of each successor shall be subject to the approval of the British Government.

8. I will not sell, or in any way alienate, or permit, or countenance any sale or alienation of any part of the land in my territory.

9. I will permit all people residing in my territory to there remain, upon the condition that they recognise my authority as chief, and any persons not wishing to recognise my authority and desiring to quit my territory I will permit to quit and to pass unmolested elsewhere.

10. In all cases of dispute in which British subjects are involved I will appeal to and abide by the decision of the British Resident of the division in which my territory is situated. In all cases when accusations of offence or crime committed in my territory are brought against British subjects, or against my people in relation to British subjects, I will hold no trial and pass no sentence except with the approval of such British Resident.

11. In all matters not included within these terms, conditions, and limitations, and in all cases provided for herein, and in all cases when there may be doubt or uncertainty as to the laws, rules, or stipulations applicable to matters to be dealt with, I will govern, order, or decide in accordance with the ancient laws and usage of my people.

The following letter, addressed to the Right Hon. W. E. Gladstone, and published in *The Guardian* of December 10th, 1879, by the Dean of 'Maritzburg, contains such valuable and important matter that we quote it verbatim:

The Deanery
'Maritzburg
Natal
September 27th, 1879

Sir—Though I have not the honour of being known to you, yet, as the affairs of South Africa must necessarily engage the attention of Parliament when it next meets, I venture to hope you will not consider it an intrusion if I lay before you some of the conclusions I have arrived at after thirty years' residence as a clergyman in Natal. I do so as I know from experience how extremely difficult it is for those who have passed their lives in the midst of a highly organised society, to realise the conditions of a colony, and especially of one which is brought into contact with the undeveloped races of South Africa. The first question that presents itself is, What is the meaning of the apparent antagonism of the native races, at the present time, to the white man? I attribute it immediately to the natives suddenly and unexpectedly finding themselves in the possession of firearms. When the Diamond Fields were first opened out, no restrictions were placed on the gun-trade by the Cape Government, and so soon as this became known the natives flocked there in thousands from all parts of South Africa, hiring themselves out to work, and stipulating to be paid in rifles. Young men everywhere will arm themselves if they can, and especially in a country in which there is abundant room for hunting, and still more so when the young men are savages, and know of no distinction except that which comes from exhibiting prowess in war. I do not myself think they were influenced by any feelings of hatred to the white man, or that there existed any deep-seated conspiracy amongst the chiefs or old men. But the young men suddenly discovered they could obtain firearms, so got them; and having got them, they then desired to use them. Everywhere they were armed, and so everywhere they began to talk of fighting; the leaven had been put in and the whole lump worked. The war which arose is now over, and the Cape Government is engaged in steadily disarming the natives under its rule; its loyal subjects, the Fingoes and the

Basutos, as well as the recently conquered tribes. Sir Garnet Wolseley told the Zulus also to bring in their guns; but they have treated his order with contempt, and he has made no attempt to enforce it; the Zulus themselves, I am afraid, will soon adduce this as evidence that they were not beaten. I may say, also, the Natal Governor always placed restrictions on the natives possessing firearms, and, so far as he could, enforced those restrictions on his own natives returning from the Diamond Fields, and they have proved perfectly loyal. Whilst at the time I deprecated the reckless trade allowed by the Cape Government, still it seems to me rather hard, after having allowed the natives to purchase guns, to set to work to disarm them. The wisest course I consider would be to impose a tax on the possession of firearms generally, granting privileges to members of volunteer corps, etc. In that way, without drawing invidious distinctions between white and coloured, our own young men would be exempted from paying by serving as volunteers; and if the tax were a heavy one the natives would be deterred from keeping guns, and, further, the Government would know exactly to what extent they were armed.

To leave, however, the native races in general, and to confine ourselves to the Zulus. They never went to war with us, but we with them; they have always been excellent neighbours; for thirty years they have never been accused of stealing a sheep, or an ox, or a horse from the Natal side. Natal had no quarrel with them nor Cetywayo with us; it has been our misfortune that it has been found convenient to carry on the war from Natal; but Sir H. Bulwer, our Governor, has been true to the colony in insisting that it was no war of ours. If there was any justification of the war, it must be sought in the interests of Transvaal, and then it can only be accepted as a judgment. The Crown had not a shadow of right to annex the Transvaal. True, they were not governing themselves very well in that State; neither, perhaps, is Germany, but we do not annex Germany. We did take over the Transvaal, however, in direct violation of engagements which had been entered into with the Dutch Boers. Shepstone, in his proclamation, was obliged to say that we must read between the lines of that engagement *i.e.* the promises of the British Government were worth nothing. The simple fact was that the Cape and Transvaal merchants had been overtrading in that republic; it was bankrupt, so many of them were on the brink of insolvency. I cannot say more without mentioning names, but there was no difficulty in seeing what influences were brought to bear on Lord Carnarvon. The Republic was annexed; farms were accepted at a nominal price in payment of debts, and resold again in London, say at sixpence per acre, which amply repaid the merchant, who thus saved himself, whilst the Boers were left without their independence, and poorer than ever. Had we stayed our hand, finding themselves hopelessly bankrupt, in a few months they might probably have sought our assistance, and then we could have annexed them without their having a grievance; as it is they cannot forget it. I am sorry for them, for they are a simple people. Shepstone went up as Governor, and Cetywayo at once asked to have his old disputes with the Boers arranged in former days both he and his father, whenever they had had any difference with the Transvaal, always sent messengers in to the Natal Government to advise with it—and Shepstone, the Secretary for Natal Affairs, according to his wont, always temporised, admitting in a half-and-half way that they were right, but advising patience. When, however, he found himself at the Transvaal he suddenly sided with the Dutch, and Cetywayo became greatly incensed and declared himself betrayed. I believe he would at once have invaded the Transvaal, but from fear of us in Natal. He hesitated, however, and according to the old maxim, he who hesitates does not fight; but before he had quieted down Sir B. Frere interfered with his *ultimatum*, and Cetywayo stood grandly on the defensive. He is a savage, and his ambition was to be a great savage: I do not mean a cruel one, but a powerful, influential savage. He was ambitious, but disliked progress, and such men must fail; so he has fallen, but with dignity. He has never attacked a neighbour, white or black; he has defended his country bravely, and has been guilty of no excesses. It has been our war, not his. Sir B. Frere says most truly that almost everyone he spoke to encouraged him to go to war; but I am afraid he avoided those who, he was told, were against war and when will not Englishmen advise war? No argument was used, except the one that Cetywayo might overrun Natal at any moment; but he had never shown a disposition to do so, and we were stronger than men would allow. Men who do not trust in the arm of God do not see the defences which surround them. The Tugela, the river which separates Natal from Zululand, was a great protection, as in summer-time, even if fordable, the Zulus would not cross it, lest it should rise in their rear; and in the winter, our dry season, they cannot keep the field, as their naked bodies are quite unable to bear exposure to the cold nights. Moreover, though our own army will never acknowledge it, Cetywayo's force did not exceed 30,000 naked savages. Of course we are told they were 60,000 or 80,000 strong; but if you casually inquire of any officer who has been in Zululand whether the *kraals* were thickly dotted over the country, he will tell you artlessly, "No, quite the contrary." I have again and again inquired of traders as to the density of the population relative to Natal. I have inquired of those who have lived at Ulundi, and have seen Cetywayo's regiments mustered, and I am confident that 30,000 is the very outside at which the Zulu force could be put. I may return to this. I mention it now to show why I do not agree with Sir Bartle in his view of our position; and certainly I cannot admit, because a neighbour is powerful, that therefore we are justified in going to war with him.

But, now that we have been at war, on what terms is peace to be arranged? In the Cape Colony the natives—as the Basutos, the Fingoes, and others—live in districts to themselves, not intermingled with the white man. The young men leave their homes, and go into the colony, and work for a time in the towns or on the farms; but their home is in Basutoland, Fingoland, etc. The same holds good in the Transvaal. The natives there are on the border; but Natal is the one exception to this rule; in this colony we live intermingled; and a few years ago we were regarded as living in the crater of a volcano. It was thought that the Natal natives, who outnumber the European settlers eighteenfold, might at any moment overwhelm us, so that Cape politicians and others refused to be connected with this colony. In 1876, however, before the rising of the natives on the frontier, I was bold enough to point out to my fellow-colonists that our supposed weakness was in reality our strength. And so it has proved. During the last two years Natal has been the oasis of South Africa; everywhere else the natives have either been in arms, or shown themselves disaffected, if we except the Fingoes; but the position in which they stand to the Kafir tribes around them compels them to be loyal, so they are scarcely to be taken into account.

Whilst, then, throughout South Africa the natives have been a source of uneasiness, the overwhelming native population of Natal (360,000, against 22,000 whites) has been perfectly true to the Government, and the grounds of their loyalty are now, I think, recognised in Natal. They are these:

1. The natives are not, like Englishmen, self-reliant, but naturally dependent; consequently, they use the machinery of Government much more than we do. An Englishman dislikes appealing to a magistrate, as it implies a want of power to take care of himself or to govern his dependents. Not so the native; he habitually leans upon the magistrate. Thirty years ago in Natal the native leant upon his chief; now he has become familiar with the magistrate, who has become a necessity to him. I argue, therefore, that a people will not plot or even desire to throw off an authority which enters into their daily life.

2. Natives who have resided amongst white men feel the need of their presence. The native races cannot develop themselves—nor, when in some degree developed, can they stand by themselves—as their wills are weak, and intellectually they are lawyers, fond of argument, but without imagination; so they can neither plan nor construct. In their independent state they have no criminal law, no commercial code, no municipal one, no law of tenure of landed property; they possess only a few customs regulating marriage and the division of their cattle amongst the family; but, scattered amongst white men, they are able to expand. The effect is seen in many ways amongst others, in the increase of their families.

3. They are naturally fond of trading. In many ways they may be compared to the Celtic race, as they cannot rise above the tribal organisation; but, unlike the Celt, they are not intellectual; and, unlike him, their natural bent is towards trading. They are good soldiers, but they prefer trading to everything; consequently, on this account, they are unwilling to separate from the white man.

4. The natives never go to war unless they can first send their cattle to the rear; but this they cannot do when distributed amongst the Europeans, and this operates alone as a great check. During the thirty years I have been in Natal we have only had three chiefs give the slightest trouble, and these three have all been on the borders, and so have been able to send their cattle away. I am convinced, therefore, that, if the Government wishes to maintain peace and to develop the native races, it should intermingle them with the Europeans. The Aborigines Society at home will probably object. It is easy to say the white man seeks only to dispossess the native, but whatever the individual motive, the white man is the benefactor by his presence. He may have hunted down the North American Indian and the Aborigines of Australia, but not so in South Africa. Here not only does the magistrate protect him, but the Kafir is a worker, which the North American Indian and the native of Australia is not. The white man wants the Kafir's labour, and to secure it has to be just and kind. A farm-servant in England is by no means so independent as a Kafir out here. Mix up the races therefore, and to some extent at least the problem of governing and improving the native race is solved. After the defeat at Isandhlwana, new-comers like the military thought our natives might rise; but their wives, children, wagons, cattle, etc., were in the colony, so they made common cause with us, and showed themselves zealously loyal. I consider it, therefore, to be most foolish to try and keep the races apart; we must intermingle them. It was Alexander's principle and the Roman rule; the present European families have been founded on this method so we must go on mingling, not separating.

I send you a copy of Sir Garnet Wolseley's conditions of peace, as published in *The Natal Witness*. They are universally condemned here.

1. The chiefs are to be under British Residents, and they must be supported by a force. But who is to pay? It is said the Zulus are not to be taxed, as that would amount to annexation; or, rather, it would test Sir Garnet's arrangements. If he is afraid to tax the Zulus the Residents will be afraid to control them. The test of defeat with Kafirs is the loss of cattle they do not estimate the loss of life; but we have not taken cattle. Indeed, the balance is on their side: they have carried off more than we have.[1] The test of submission is obedience, and they have with one accord disobeyed the order to give up their guns. The test of the Queen's authority in South Africa is the payment of taxes. Even Cetywayo offered to pay a hut-tax; and if Sir Garnet does not impose one, all the young men in Zululand, before a year is over, will point to their cattle, their guns, and their immunity from taxes, and boast that they were not beaten. If the Zulus are to be controlled by British Residents they should pay a hut-tax. Our natives pay a hut-tax of Us. per hut. I have understood that the Cape Government wish it to be uniform throughout South Africa, and to be fixed at £1. We estimate the population at three-and-a-half persons to a hut, and at 14s. it amounts to 4s. per head. Besides that the natives on farms pay rent to the farmer, and the more they adopt our habits the more do they pay through the Customs. The Zulus could readily pay £1 per hut, or, say £36,000 per annum. Cetywayo's Government was an expensive one. His commissariat alone was a heavy drain upon the resources of the people. Savages, as well as civilised persons, understand that they must support their Government; the Zulus, therefore, would recognise the justice of being taxed; and not to tax them is, I consider, to abandon one of the duties of Government. Moreover, it is said we are to be taxed to pay our quota of the recent expenditure. But our natives will hardly understand first fighting the

---

1. We think this statement is hardly correct.

378

Zulus, and then having to pay for it. It will seem to them as if they were the offending party, if they, and not the Zulus, are taxed.

2. The conditions discourage trade. It ought to be encouraged to the utmost. Instead of forbidding importation by sea, a Custom-house should be established at the one port or landing-place.

3. The alienation of land is forbidden, in order to keep out the white man; but he should be encouraged to enter, and so long as the land is held in common by the whole tribe there will be no improvement in agriculture.

Or, to take the conditions in order—2 is impossible; the young men will be quarrelling with one another at weddings and other gatherings, tribal fights will ensue, and the chiefs must have a force at their command. 3 I have touched upon. 4 is nugatory; if a chief wishes to put to death he can give a man a mock trial and have done with it. 6 overlooks that wars often do not begin with the chiefs; the young men bring them about. 8 I have touched upon. The whole implies the active and constant superintendence of the Resident, and that will be resisted: some *kraal* or *kraals* will be disobedient to orders, the chief will be unable or unwilling to enforce obedience, and the Resident must call in other assistance at great expense; and at whose? There is nothing enduring, nothing practical in this settlement, if it deserves to be called such. It is not likely to last, and everyone expects, after a short interval, more bloodshed and more reckless expenditure. The burden cannot be thrown on the Colony, as the Government has not been consulted on the terms of peace. The whole thing is a cruelty to the Zulus, to the colonists, and to the suffering home population, for there will be another £3,000,000 or more to be voted yet; but during the whole time meat was 8d. and bread 4d. per pound. 1s. 6d. *per diem* was consequently ample allowance for the keep of a soldier; of course I am aware there were numerous other sources of expenditure, but it is extreme folly to send an army out to a distant place, with power to draw upon the Treasury at will; it is too great a trial for human nature. As a blind, all sorts of things are said about the colonists; a great deal or even all may be true, but it does not explain half. That, however, is by the way; but I must mention, before concluding, that one of the newly-appointed chiefs is a white man named John Dunn. He left home when about fifteen or sixteen, and has since lived with the Zulus, taking to himself a number of wives. This appointment is looked upon as an outrage to public morals and as an insult to the colonists. I say nothing about the missionaries, as I do not wish that they should lean upon the civil power; the Church must do her proper work in her proper way. I simply write as an Englishman, to one who largely guides the counsels of the nation, to lift up my voice against what has been done, and is being done, in this part of the empire. Trusting you will excuse my thus trespassing upon your time, believe me to remain yours most respectfully,

James Green
Dean of 'Maritzburg

But at all events we had gained one definite result by all the blood and money spent in the Zulu war. The most important and earnestly insisted on immediate cause of our attack upon Zululand was the invasion of our soil, and the violation of our sanctuary, committed by Mehlokazulu and his brother, sons of Sihayo, when they seized and carried off two women who had taken refuge in Natal. We *requested* the Zulu king to deliver up the young men to us for judgment and for punishment, and he begged us to accept a fine in *lieu* of the persons of the offenders. We declined this proposal and repeated our *request*, which suddenly became a *demand* when it appeared in the ultimatum, and as such remained.

It was said at the time that, had the young men been given up even after the troops had crossed the border, hostilities would have been suspended until the rest of the demands could be complied with. But they were not, so we went to war.

And now, at last, the war was over, one of Sihayo's sons had fallen in battle, and Mehlokazulu, the other, was in our hands. Here was what we had fought for, and obtained! What would be done with him? By the military authorities he could only be treated like any other prisoner of war, and released unharmed amongst the other Zulus. He was therefore handed over to the civil authorities at Pietermaritzburg to be tried by them, although he was denied the same advantages of counsel which are accorded by law to other civil prisoners.

This denial was commented upon unfavourably by those who desired justice to be done, but, apparently, Mehlokazulu required no counsel, for he was not tried. He had committed no offence on British soil punishable in a Zulu subject by British law. His own king could have punished him by our request, but we had deposed and transported that king, and there was no law by which we could have inflicted anything beyond a trifling fine for trespass upon the man whom we had compassed heaven and earth, and shed so much of England's noblest blood, to seize. The magistrate declined to commit him for trial, and Mehlokazulu was permitted to return to his home. *The Natal Colonist* of October 27th remarks:

> Doubtless, the legal adviser of the Crown was concerned in the case, and framed the charge which there was the best chance of being substantiated. And this is the result—'there was no evidence to maintain the charge.'. . . . It is a miserable conclusion to a most miserable affair. . . . The charge which, as we have seen, is almost made the chief occasion of the war which has desolated so many homes, and cost millions of money, completely breaks down when brought to the test of legal trial, and the prisoner is, of necessity, set at liberty. We never believed much in the other pretexts for the war put forward by Sir Bartle Frere, but we confess that we always thought the outrage by Sihayo's sons was one to be visited with condign punishment, whether it was one which would justify war or not; and even though we knew it was only a pretext, seeing that it only took place long after war had been determined on, and preparations for it had been begun to be made.

But the ultimatum and its demands are things of the past. Rivers of blood have flowed to enforce these demands, and now they are put on one side as utterly valueless, both by the settlement of Zululand and the release of Sirayo's son.[2]

With this humiliating fact we must close our record of the Zulu War. In doing so, we feel that too many of the circumstances which we have thus recorded reflect no credit on the name of England that name which as English men and women we most desire should be honoured by the world at large; and we realise with pain that, so far as our work may be perused by dwellers upon other shores, so far have we lessened the glory of our motherland in their eyes. But, however much we may regret the necessity, we do not therefore think it a less imperative duty to bring to the light as much as possible whatever wrong and injustice has been committed and concealed by those to whom England has entrusted her power and her fame. That the light of publicity should be thrown upon them is the first step towards their cure, or at least towards the prevention of any further wrong, and it is with the truest loyalty to our Sovereign, and the deepest love and reverence for our country, that we have undertaken the task now completed.

2. The Daily News, 30th October, 1879.

ALSO FROM LEONAUR

A JOURNAL OF THE SECOND SIKH WAR by *Daniel A. Sandford*—The Experiences of an Ensign of the 2nd Bengal European Regiment During the Campaign in the Punjab, India, 1848-49.

LAKE'S CAMPAIGNS IN INDIA by *Hugh Pearse*—The Second Anglo Maratha War, 1803-1807. Often neglected by historians and students alike, Lake's Indian campaign was fought against a resourceful and ruthless enemy-almost always superior in numbers to his own forces.

BRITAIN IN AFGHANISTAN 1: THE FIRST AFGHAN WAR 1839-42 by *Archibald Forbes*—Following over a century of the gradual assumption of sovereignty of the Indian Sub-Continent, the British Empire, in the form of the Honourable East India Company, supported by troops of the new Queen Victoria's army, found itself inevitably at the natural boundaries that surround Afghanistan. There it set in motion a series of disastrous events-the first of which was to march into the country at all.

BRITAIN IN AFGHANISTAN 2: THE SECOND AFGHAN WAR 1878-80 by *Archibald Forbes*—This the history of the Second Afghan War-another episode of British military history typified by savagery, massacre, siege and battles.

UP AMONG THE PANDIES by *Vivian Dering Majendie*—An outstanding account of the campaign for the fall of Lucknow. *This is a vital book of war as fought by the British Army of the mid-nineteenth century, but in truth it is also an essential book of war that will enthral military historians and general readers alike.*

BLOW THE BUGLE, DRAW THE SWORD by *W. H. G. Kingston*—The Wars, Campaigns, Regiments and Soldiers of the British & Indian Armies During the Victorian Era, 1839-1898.

INDIAN MUTINY 150th ANNIVERSARY: A LEONAUR ORIGINAL

MUTINY: 1857 by *James Humphries*—It is now 150 years since the 'Indian Mutiny' burst like an engulfing flame on the British soldiers, their families and the civilians of the Empire in North East India. The Bengal Native army arose in violent rebellion, and the once peaceful countryside became a battleground as Native sepoys and elements of the Indian population massacred their British masters and defeated them in open battle. As the tide turned, a vengeful army of British and loyal Indian troops repressed the insurgency with a savagery that knew no mercy. It was a time of fear and slaughter. James Humphries has drawn together the voices of those dreadful days for this commemorative book.

LEONAUR

ALSO FROM LEONAUR

WAR BEYOND THE DRAGON PAGODA by *J. J. Snodgrass*—A Personal Narrative of the First Anglo-Burmese War 1824 - 1826.

ALL FOR A SHILLING A DAY by *Donald F. Featherstone*—The story of H.M. 16th, the Queen's Lancers During the first Sikh War 1845-1846.

AT THEM WITH THE BAYONET by *Donald F. Featherstone*—The first Anglo-Sikh War 1845-1846.

A LEONAUR ORIGINAL

THE HERO OF ALIWAL by *James Humphries*—The days when young Harry Smith wore the green jacket of the 95th-Wellington's famous riflemen-campaigning in Spain against Napoleon's French with his beautiful young bride Juana have long gone. Now, Sir Harry Smith is in his fifties approaching the end of a long career. His position in the Cape colony ends with an appointment as Deputy Adjutant-General to the army in India. There he joins the staff of Sir Hugh Gough to experience an Indian battlefield in the Gwalior War of 1843 as the power of the Marathas is finally crushed. Smith has little time for his superior's 'bull at a gate' style of battlefield tactics, but independent command is denied him. Little does he realise that the greatest opportunity of his military life is close at hand.

THE GURKHA WAR by *H. T. Prinsep*—The Anglo-Nepalese Conflict in North East India 1814-1816.

SOUND ADVANCE! by *Joseph Anderson*—Experiences of an officer of HM 50th regiment in Australia, Burma & the Gwalior war.

THE CAMPAIGN OF THE INDUS by *Thomas Holdsworth*—Experiences of a British Officer of the 2nd (Queen's Royal) Regiment in the Campaign to Place Shah Shuja on the Throne of Afghanistan 1838 - 1840.

WITH THE MADRAS EUROPEAN REGIMENT IN BURMA by *John Butler*—The Experiences of an Officer of the Honourable East India Company's Army During the First Anglo-Burmese War 1824 - 1826.

BESIEGED IN LUCKNOW by *Martin Richard Gubbins*—The Experiences of the Defender of 'Gubbins Post' before & during the sige of the residency at Lucknow, Indian Mutiny, 1857.

THE STORY OF THE GUIDES by *G.J. Younghusband*—The Exploits of the famous Indian Army Regiment from the northwest frontier 1847 - 1900.

Lightning Source UK Ltd.
Milton Keynes UK
30 December 2009

147987UK00002B/25/P